The
London & North Western Railway

Eight-Coupled Goods Engines

Frontispiece: *An all-out effort by a 'Super D' - No. 49387 passes Topley Pike signal box with a freight from Miller's Dale to Buxton in the early 1950s.*

E. R. Morten

The
London & North Western Railway

Eight-Coupled Goods Engines

Edward Talbot

First Published 2002
© Edward Talbot 2002
ISBN 0-9542787-0-4

Printed by The Amadeus Press, Cleckheaton, West Yorkshire

Published by
Edward Talbot
32 Waterside Court, Gnosall, Stafford, ST20 0AR
et@steam.u-net.com

ACKNOWLEDGEMENTS

In producing this book, I have enjoyed the invaluable help of many friends and fellow enthusiasts. As always, J. P. Richards made available his unique knowledge of the ways of Crewe, as well as providing photographs and drawings, some of which were his own work. Harold Walkley generously agreed to the reprinting of his articles recalling his days as a fitter at Abergavenny and patiently replied to many enquiries on technical matters. Bill Broadbent, who had fortuitously written to me on another subject, discoursed at length on his experiences at Crewe, and particularly on the eight-coupled coal engines and the characteristics of their Joy valve gear. Michael Bentley provided recollections of his early days on the footplate, as well as much information and photographs from his collection. He also read the text and made many valuable comments. C. P. Atkins and the library staff at the National Railway Museum were, as usual, extremely helpful on my visits there, as was Richard Gibbon, curator of engineering.

Valuable help and information, especially about allocations and workings, was also provided by Eddie Bray for Nuneaton, Neil Fraser for Huddersfield, Harold Froggatt for Crewe, and Harry Hall and Alf Manktelow for Willesden and Watford, while Robin Davies, W. L. Harris, Robert Head, Jack Gahan, Murray Houchin Hughes, Yuko Ishibiki, Jim Jarvis, Peter Lang, Andy Lowe, David J. Patrick, J. W. P. Rowledge, Ray Stacey, Peter J. Stead, Clive Taylor and David Tee also gave valuable help and information of various kinds. Mike Williams and Roger Bell made their extensive collections of photographs available, as well as helping with obscure points of information, and others who went to great trouble to provide photographs were David A. Anderson, John Blyth, Roger Carpenter, Peter Groom, F. W. Shuttleworth, Peter Ward and Ron White of Colour Rail.

The photographs and drawings are credited to their sources where known. Those not credited are from the author's collection. Official LNWR pictures are credited as 'LNWR' with the Crewe negative register number added when shown on the print. Many of the negatives are now in the National Railway Museum, York. Photographs credited to R. G. Jarvis are reproduced courtesy of the Midland Railway Trust. The London & North Western Railway Society (membership enquiries: 3 Chieveley Court, Emerson Valley, Milton Keynes, MK4 2DD) through its *Journal* and meetings is a constant source of information and inspiration. To all who have helped in any way I offer my sincere thanks.

Edward Talbot
Stafford
January 2002

CONTENTS

Plate 1: *Still doing what it had been built to do fifty years earlier, 'G2A' No. 49287 sets out along the main line south of Rugby with an up mineral train on 24th July 1958.*

Peter Groom

PREFACE

My earliest recollection of the LNWR 0-8-0s is of misty days at Stafford in the cold winter of 1946. There were always several on the shed, and I can still vividly recall them moving about, from the coaler to the ash plant and then to the turntable, almost invariably engulfed in steam and making noises which no other engine ever seemed to make. At the time, Stanier engines seemed the last thing in modernity and the 0-8-0s very outdated. On the road, however, as when leaving for Crewe with a heavy goods, they invariably seemed to get away well. They hardly ever slipped, unlike more modern engines, and their exhaust beat, though strange, seemed vigorous and purposeful, so that they always seemed surprisingly competent. Only much later did I realise that in 1946 there were still many engines about with features dating back to the Webb era and come to regret not taking more notice of them.

This favourable impression of their abilities was confirmed by my father, who was a driver at Stafford shed and regularly had a 'D', as he invariably called them. He spoke of them with amusement - 'up in the roof for the brake, down in the cellar for the water' - but always with approval and respect. Occasionally, though not often, when asked about his day's work, he would say that he had had 'a rough trip' with such-and-such an engine, but it was never with a 'D'.

Even recently, while preparing this book, I have had the same impression of competence in conversation with men who knew the engines well. They mostly started work on the footplate in the 1940s and early 1950s at former LNWR sheds where traditional methods of handling the engines were passed on from one generation to another, but when the engines were already at least twenty years old and many were much older. They all make the point that although outdated by the more modern engines at that time, they invariably did the job economically and reliably. Their opinions are well summed up in the words of a former Watford driver, Alf Manktelow, who started work as a fireman in the 1950s. 'Many a time I have got on to a 'D' at Bletchley after it had been on the road eight hours or more and the box was full of ash and the pressure gauge reading only 80lb, and with 70 wagons of coal to

Plate 2: *My father with fireman Jim Mitchell, on the footplate of 'Super D' No. 49126 at the south end of Stafford station about 1960.*
Author

Plate 3: *A 'Super D' leaving Northampton with a 60-wagon coal train for London on 9th July 1921. On the extreme right is Nort* *tower, can just be made out the signals controlling the south side of Northampton Castle station. The signal box is Duston Junc* *runs underneath it past the box. It is fully described in Jack Nelson's classic book* LNWR Portrayed. *The distant signal, centre r*

The engine is No. 1108, which was built at Crewe in October 1912. It is well cleaned in the full lined livery and its paintwork *be applied at Crewe in September 1914 at the outbreak of war and was resumed from October 1921, officially for passenger e* *been fitted either during a visit to works or at a shed.*

The train is made up very largely of private owner wagons from Staffordshire and Warwickshire collieries. So far as can be n *if not the second; three Cannock & Leacroft Colliery; one Coggins & Arthur; one West Cannock; another Coggins & Arthur; a F* *Chase; a Bradfords; and then they generally become unidentifiable except for another Cannock Chase, an NSR wagon lettered*

Few who have ever heard a 'Super D' hard at work can fail to recreate in the mind's eye this summer evening scene and to in

This photograph, perhaps the finest ever of a traditional British goods train, was taken by Leslie J. Thompson and is reprodu

4

ʝine shed, the town itself forms the background to the picture and on the extreme left, beyond the train to the right of the church
ɔhich was unusually arranged so that it could control both the main line, which the train is on, and the line to Blisworth, which
ʾed.

ʾ in remarkably good condition in view of the fact that it must have been applied more than eight years earlier. Lining ceased to
ʾh a few goods engines seem to have been done exceptionally. The tender is the 1916 Cooke type in plain black and could have

ɔm the engine backwards, they are: Gornall & Co. of Brighton; two Kingsbury collieries, the first of which is lettered 'Tamworth',
ʾher West Cannock; a Foxfield, Blythe Bridge; an AGD; another West Cannock; an unidentifiable high-sided wagon; a Cannock
ɔith the NSR Staffordshire knot in between, a Holly Bank and, well down the train, GE and LBSC wagons.
ound for many minutes more as the engine accelerates its train up the gradient towards Roade.

ʾ courtesy of W. G. Allen.

take to Wembley yard. But it would still steam and do the job and get along the road almost as well as if it was fresh off the shed.To my mind, they were good engines, even in the 1950s when there were more modern types available'.

When I produced *An Illustrated History of LNWR Engines*, I deliberately finished the story at the end of the LNWR period, as it would have been impossible in one volume to continue until the final withdrawal of all LNWR engines in LMS and BR days, and also incidentally, as one reader wanted, to include full lists of all engines (that would have occupied almost the whole of one volume in itself). Nevertheless, it was obvious that classes built in the final years of the LNWR merited more complete attention as many of them spent far more of their working lives in LMS and BR ownership than in that of the LNWR. The twentieth-century passenger engines have been covered in several books, and so I decided that the eight-coupled goods engines, as the most long-lasting of all LNWR engines and in many ways the most successful, should be dealt with first.

Unfortunately, it has taken much longer to produce the book than I originally expected. There are several reasons for that, not all of which are my responsibility, but one advantage has been that research has kept producing more and more information which it has been possible to include.

I hope the book will give pleasure to all who read it, and be seen as a fitting account of some remarkable engines and also as a modest tribute to the men at all levels who worked on them in the traditions of Crewe.

INTRODUCTION

The London & North Western Railway is not generally thought of as a coal-hauling railway. Its fame rests in the popular mind on other things: on its express passenger trains such as the 'Corridor', with their splendid carriages and shining black engines; on its through services to Scotland, Ireland and even America; on Euston station, with its Doric Arch and Great Hall; on Crewe Works, 'the greatest locomotive works in the world'; on the Menai Bridge, and on its fine hotels and steamers. These things are often described by contemporary writers who knew it well and admired it, and were well publicised by the company, but little attention was paid to such mundane things as trains of coal.

Nevertheless, since it served most of the major coalfields in the country, South Wales, the West and East Midlands, Lancashire, West Yorkshire and Cumberland, as well as most of the major industrial areas and conurbations, it not only had a considerable coal traffic but other mineral traffic too, such as coke, ironstone and limestone. For the same reasons, it also had considerable general goods traffic. When it ceased to exist as an independent company in 1922, it owned over 500 eight-coupled engines designed specifically for coal and heavy goods traffic, some twenty per cent of its capital stock. No other pre-Grouping company had so many engines of this type.

As industrial development proceeded throughout the nineteenth century, so people were drawn into the cities and towns to work in the expanding industries. The population itself increased, thanks to improvements in public health, and since coal was the staple fuel, so the demand for it steadily increased too, and production rose accordingly. Thus the tonnage of coal and other minerals carried by all the major railway companies gradually rose (see *Appendix 1*).

On the LNWR much of the mineral traffic was local, between the coalfields and consumers nearby, both industrial and domestic, but a significant proportion required haulage over long distances. From the Locomotive Department point of view, the most difficult long-distance goods work was over Shap on the Lancaster and Carlisle section, but there was also significant mineral traffic northwards from South Wales and across the Pennines. In the South Wales district in particular, with its steep gradients and heavy coal traffic, short-distance mineral work needed reliable motive power; and in the industrial Midlands and Lancashire there was heavy freight traffic too, both long-distance and local. The largest single flow of coal traffic, however, was between the Midlands and London, a distance of more than one hundred miles. Such was the quantity and continuity of traffic on this route that it was akin to a pipeline. A continuous flow of loaded trains headed south and a continuous flow of empty wagons returned northwards.

Thus the main line south of Rugby was the busiest section of the whole of the LNWR. It had been effectively four-track all the way to London from 1882 when the Northampton loop was opened, the section between Bletchley and Roade being widened to four tracks in the previous year. As the population of London increased during the late nineteenth century, so the demand for coal increased also and with it the need to run more trains over this section. To run more coal trains would require more engines, more wagons and more men, would increase total train miles and line occupation, and thereby make operating more difficult. In short, it would put up costs generally. The obvious solution was to haul more wagons per train, and to do that more powerful engines were required, as the largest engine then available was a small 0-6-0 of a design which was then essentially some thirty years old.

This 0-6-0, Webb's '17in Coal Engine', was produced

in what had already become the time-honoured way of Crewe. An existing design was modified only as much as was necessary to meet the new requirement, so as to keep as many parts as possible standard to both. This had been the practice since Joseph Locke first laid down that engines should be of standard design as far as possible. Thus the Trevithick double-framed engines of the 1840s were built as 2-2-2 passenger and 2-4-0 goods engines. Over the years improvements such as straight frames, larger fireboxes and direct action were introduced, and a tank engine version of the 2-4-0 was built, but the basic design remained the same.

No distinction was made at that time between goods and mineral traffic and the 'Crewe Goods' was used for both. On the Southern Division the small engines built by Edward Bury for the London & Birmingham Railway began to be replaced under his successor, James Edward McConnell, by six-coupled engines in the early 1850s, and the famous 'Wolverton Goods' was introduced in 1854.

The 0-6-0 type was introduced on the Northern Division in 1858 when John Ramsbottom built the first of the famous 'DX' class, which was in fact a major break with Locke's desire for standardisation. However, the 'DX' was built in such large numbers, especially after 1862, when all locomotive work was concentrated under Ramsbottom's superintendence at Crewe, that it very soon became the standard LNWR engine itself and was arguably one of the most successful British steam engines ever. Between 1858 and 1872 no less than 943 were built (86 of them for the Lancashire & Yorkshire Railway). Of the 1,976 engines owned by the LNWR at the end of September 1872, 835 were 'DX' class, more than 40 per cent of the total stock, the next largest class being the 'Newton' 2-4-0s, which numbered 86.

Again, though they were intended for goods traffic, the 'DX' 0-6-0s were used indiscriminately on goods and mineral work and no doubt displaced the 'Crewe Goods' from main-line duties. They were soon found to be very versatile engines, with a surprising turn of speed, and in practice they were used more as what later became known as 'mixed-traffic' engines, being equally at home on most passenger trains. If a train was too heavy for one 'DX', then two were used.

Twelve years after the introduction of the 'DX', the need arose for a purpose-built shunting engine, as the older non-standard types used on such duties were being withdrawn. So Ramsbottom simply took the 'DX', reduced the size of the driving wheels from 5ft to 4ft 3in and fitted a saddle tank, so producing the 'Special Tanks'.

When F. W. Webb took over in 1871, mineral traffic must have been sufficiently heavy to justify an engine designed specifically for it, as he very quickly produced the '17in Coal Engine' 0-6-0. This was not, in fact, a new design as such but was essentially a 'DX' with the 4ft 3in wheels. Alternatively, it could be regarded as a 'Special Tank' with a tender instead of a saddle tank. One advance was that fourteen years after the introduction of the 'DX' it was possible to make the boiler of steel and so raise the boiler pressure from 120lb to 140lb.

The '17in Coal Engine', with its cast-iron H-section wheels, Webb chimney and cab, and black paint with numberplates, actually looked quite different from a Ramsbottom engine. Essentially, however, it was still a 'DX', but its smaller wheels and higher pressure gave it greater tractive power, and so it was better suited to hauling heavy loads at low speed. Introduced in February 1873, the class eventually totalled 500. In 1881 an 0-6-2 tank version was introduced. It was intended for local mineral and goods work but was widely used also on local passenger trains and on shunting. In all, 300 were built, making a total of 800 essentially identical engines. If the 'DX' and 'Special Tank' totals are also added, the number of closely similar engines rises to over 1,900.

By the early 1890s this '17in Coal Engine' was still the most powerful engine available for main-line mineral work. In 1887 a new timetable had been ordered to be drawn up for the Rugby-Willesden section. It was worked out on the basis of 45 loaded wagons of coal travelling at an average speed of 15mph. But traffic was still growing and unless more trains were to be run, increasing total train miles, more wagons had to be hauled per train. While the 0-6-0 was still perfectly adequate for short-distance work in the major conurbations and coalfields, and for pick-up goods work on main lines, it was clear now that something better was needed for long-distance main-line work. The solution was the eight-coupled coal engine, and once the type had been introduced, no more six-coupled engines were built by the LNWR for this work.

Plate 4: *An 'A' class three-cylinder compound passing Mirfield on the Lancashire & Yorkshire Railway with a westbound goods about 1904.*

D. J. Patrick collection

Chapter One
F. W. WEBB - THE COMPOUND ERA

The first question which had to be settled was whether the new engine should be simple or compound. Mr Webb had built his first compound engine some ten years before and was a firm believer in compounding for economy and for greater power. Nevertheless, perhaps because all his previous compounds had been passenger engines, except for one experimental goods tank engine, and compound goods engines were little known on any railway, he decided to build both simple and compound engines of equal power for comparative trials. This was in fact the first time he had put his belief in the superiority of compounding to the test in this way.

No. 2524

The design of the simple 0-8-0 was evolved in the already time-honoured manner of Crewe. Existing standard components were used as far as possible and the only new parts were those essential for the new type. The aim was to produce a more powerful version of the '17in Coal Engine' and so the new engine had the same H-section cast-iron wheels, nominally 4ft 3in in diameter but actually 4ft 5½ in with new tyres, the same axles and the same 7in by 9in axle boxes, the axles being spaced at 5ft 9in centres in the frames. The Crewe standard cylinders, however, were no longer the 17in by 24in cylinders of the 0-6-0, first introduced on the 'DX' class in 1858. They had been replaced by those of the '18in Goods' in 1885, which used Joy valve gear, and for the 0-8-0 they were enlarged to 19½in diameter, the largest cylinders produced at Crewe up to that time. The steam chests were placed above, rather than between, the cylinders, both because of their size and to suit Joy valve gear, and the valve travel was 5in, at a time when 3½in to 4½in was more common. As in the '18in Goods', there was a central frame with a 5½in bearing in equilibrium to take up the bending stress due to the coupling and connecting rods. With the 9in bearings, this gave a total bearing surface for the crank shaft of 23½in. Previously Webb coupling rods had always been plain straight-sided rods of light section but the 0-8-0 had rods no less then 4½in deep. They were all 5ft 9in long and were designed so as to be interchangeable. The leading and trailing axles had ½in side play, to help the engine to negotiate curves, though the total wheelbase was no greater than some other engines which did not have sideplay. Equalising links connected the first three pairs of springs but were not provided between the two rear-most axles. The intermediate axle had a tranverse spring mounted above it and the the trailing wheels a transverse spring mounted below, as in the 'Crewe Goods' 2-4-0.

The boiler was the experimental type that had been introduced on the 'Greater Britain' class some fourteen months previously. It had a combustion chamber, 2ft 7in long, part way along the barrel and sets of tubes on either side of it. Presumably, the idea was that the combustion chamber would allow the combustion of gases to be completed. At the bottom of the chamber was an ash chute, which opened to release the ash when a valve on the footplate was operated. This ash chute was, of course, essential, as the chamber was bound to serve as an ash-trap and there was no other way of clearing it out. There was also another ash chute under the smokebox in the traditional way. The boiler pressure is uncertain. A contemporary account of the engine when new gives 160lb, as does F. C. Hambleton's description and account of the comparative trials, but an official drawing of the engine in original form, dated 1892, gives 175lb. Possibly the pressure was originally 160lb but was raised later to 175lb.

In addition to its unconventional boiler, No. 2524 had one other unusual feature, small but important. The brake rigging was designed to economise on parts by using a single rod from the cylinder under the cab. Unfortunately, the pivots necessary in the single-rod design absorbed a considerable proportion of the available brake power. The drawback seems to have been quickly appreciated as subsequent eight-coupled engines had the normal arrangement of parallel rods.

Otherwise, the engine had all the standard Crewe fittings and all the usual features of the day. For the sake of standardisation with the '17in Coal Engine', the same splashers were used, but as the boiler was pitched higher, 7ft 10½in, and the cab floor and footplate were raised accordingly, 4ft 5in above the rails, there was a space of 9½in between the splashers and the treads of the tyres. This feature was perpetuated in all the 0-8-0s. Had the footplate been pitched 4in or so higher still, no splashers at all would have been needed, but clearly Mr Webb, despite his concern for economy, was sufficiently concerned with appearance to provide them. Indeed, the splashers over the rear wheels, which were hidden behind the cab side-sheets, were much less deep than those over the other wheels. The chimney was 2ft 10in high, the same as on the 'Teutonics'. No. 2524 was the first goods engine to have a steel bufferbeam and the first to have metal brake blocks.

The tender was essentially the same as that used on *Greater Britain* with the same deeper frames to bring it up to the level of the footplate and the same 1800-gallon tank. It was soon replaced by a 2000-gallon tender on the same frames and was almost certainly rebuilt with a 2000-gallon tank itself, as 1800-gallon tenders of this type do not feature in any later photographs. Both types of tender still had wooden frames, wooden rear bufferbeams and wooden brake blocks.

Plate 5: *Official view of the first LNWR 0-8-0 No. 2524, taken on 3rd November 1892. Details such as the ash chute, mud plug under the third ring of the boiler and the rods from the steam brake cylinder under the footplate are clearly shown. The blower valve is on the left-hand side of the smokebox.*

LNWR B33

One difference in No. 2524 was that although there was a sandbox on the leading splasher, as on the '17in Coal Engines', no rear sanding was provided on the engine, and instead sandboxes were fitted on either side at the front of the tender. Rear sanding was, of course, important on a goods engine to improve the braking capacity of the tender, when controlling a heavy train, and for running in reverse. It was particularly useful in bad weather for shunting or reversing a train into a siding, perhaps to clear the main line for a passenger train. It seems strange, however, for Crewe to put a sandbox on the tender, as it meant that the tender was no longer 'common user', though perhaps this was not so important, as large numbers of such tenders were needed. This arrangement continued on all the Webb-built 0-8-0s and was only abolished by Mr Whale. He replaced it with a rear sandbox on the engine, probably soon after he introduced the 'D' class in 1906. The tender sandbox was then abolished, though it still survived for some years on many tenders built previously.

The first LNWR 0-8-0 emerged from Crewe Works in October 1892 numbered 2524, and the last of the '17in Coal Engines', No. 2109, was completed in the same month. Although in a sense No. 2524 was a prototype, it laid down certain standards which were to survive throughout all the various classes of eight-coupled engines to be built by the LNWR. In particular, all the eight-coupled engines basically had the same frames, the same wheels, the same axles and the same axle-boxes, which were modified only so far as was necessary to accommodate different arrangements of cylinders, different boilers and so forth. It was thanks to this basic frame design, common to all classes, that the successive rebuildings were able to be carried out so easily and economically, and eventually led some forty years later to what was in effect one class, the 'Super Ds', derived from all the earlier classes. The 'Super Ds' had their origin, however unlikely it might seem, in No. 2524, the first Crewe-built 0-8-0.

Class 'A'

Eleven months after the completion of No. 2524, the first three-cylinder compound 0-8-0 was completed. Its

Plate 6 (left): *The original tender of No. 2524 was one of very few, perhaps only two, which had the standard 1800-gallon tank mounted on deeper side frames, designed to raise the tanks to match the higher footplates of this engine and the 2-2-2-2 compounds. These tanks were almost flush with the side frames. As no photographs are known showing them in service, they were probably soon replaced by 2000-gallon tanks, the sides of which overhung the frames slightly. This tender has a sandbox behind the footstep, to assist with braking and for running in reverse; it would be especially useful when shunting in bad weather or when reversing a train into a siding off a main line to allow another train to pass.* LNWR B34

Plate 7 (far left): *Front end of No. 2524.* LNWR B33

Plate 8 (left): *Footplate view of No. 2524. The large lever on the floor below the fire-hole door controls the blow-off cock.* LNWR B33

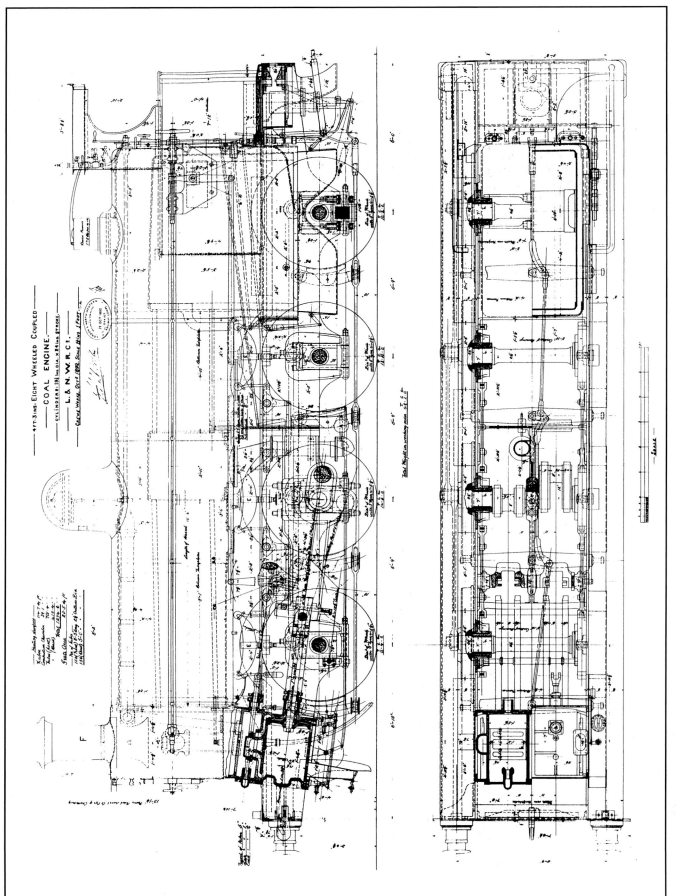

Figure 1: *General arrangement drawings of No. 2524. Features of particular interest are the boiler design with combustion chamber; the centre frame supporting the weighbar shaft and the centre of the crank axle; the smaller splasher over the rear wheel; and the design of brake rigging, which economised on parts but wasted a sizeable proportion of the available brake power in pushing or pulling against pivots. It was soon replaced by the arrangement shown in Figure 4, the drawing of the class 'A', which used more parts, parallel rods and so forth, but delivered more brake power to the brake blocks.*

LNWR

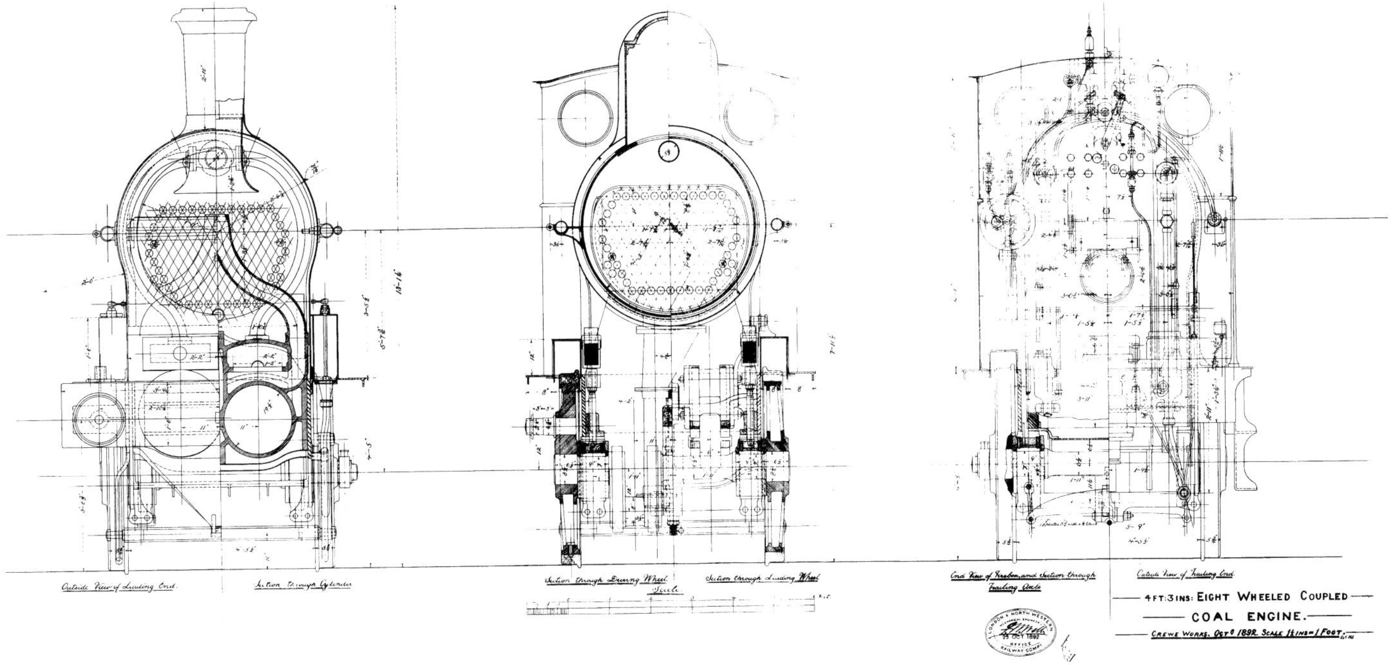

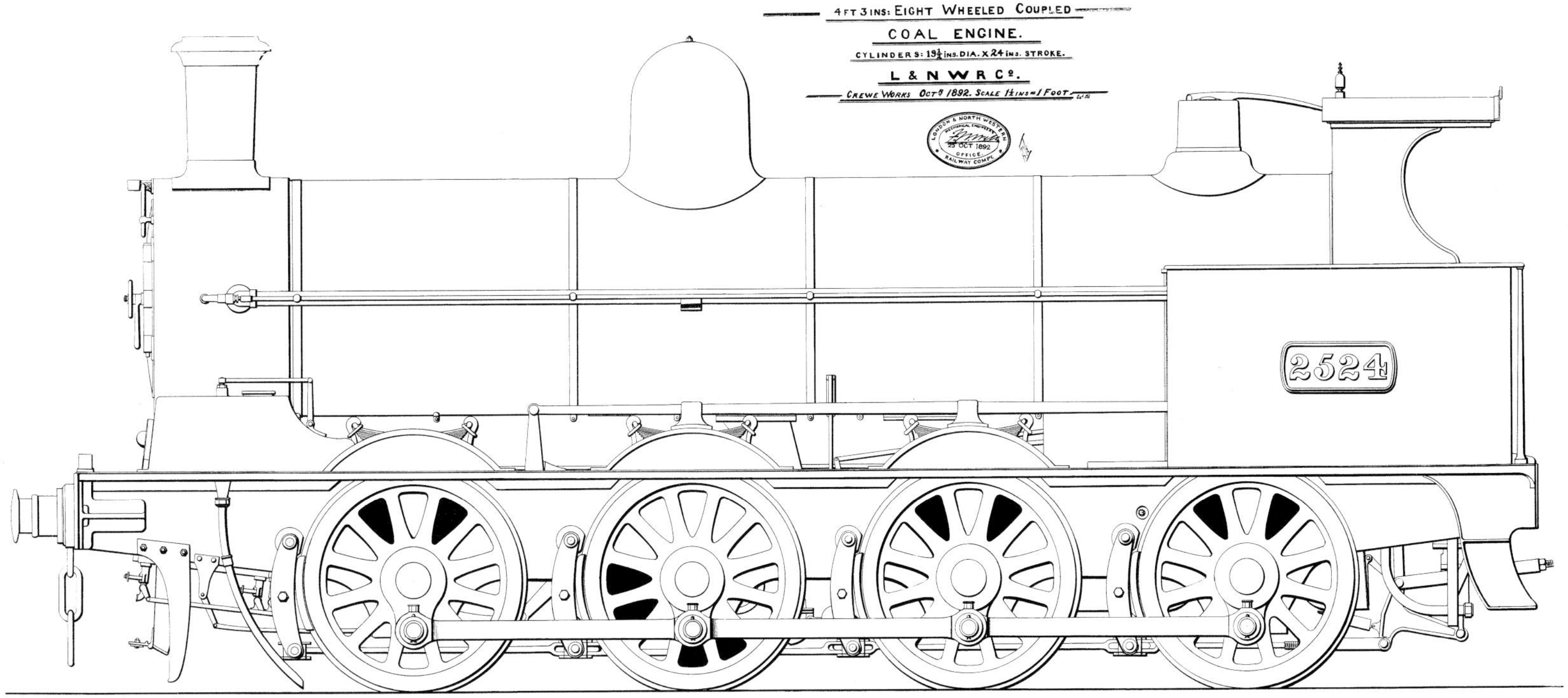

4 FT. 3 INS. EIGHT WHEELED COUPLED
COAL ENGINE.
Crewe Works Oct 1 1882. Scale 1 Inch / Foot 1/12

4 FT. 3 INS. EIGHT WHEELED COUPLED
COAL ENGINE.
CYLINDERS 18¼ INS. DIA. X 24 INS. STROKE.
L & N W R Cº.
Crewe Works Oct 1 1882. Scale 1 Inch / Foot 1/12

Figure 2: *Cross-sectional drawings of No. 2524.*   LNWR A254, courtesy NRM

Figure 3: *Offical drawing of No. 2524.*   LNWR A252

13

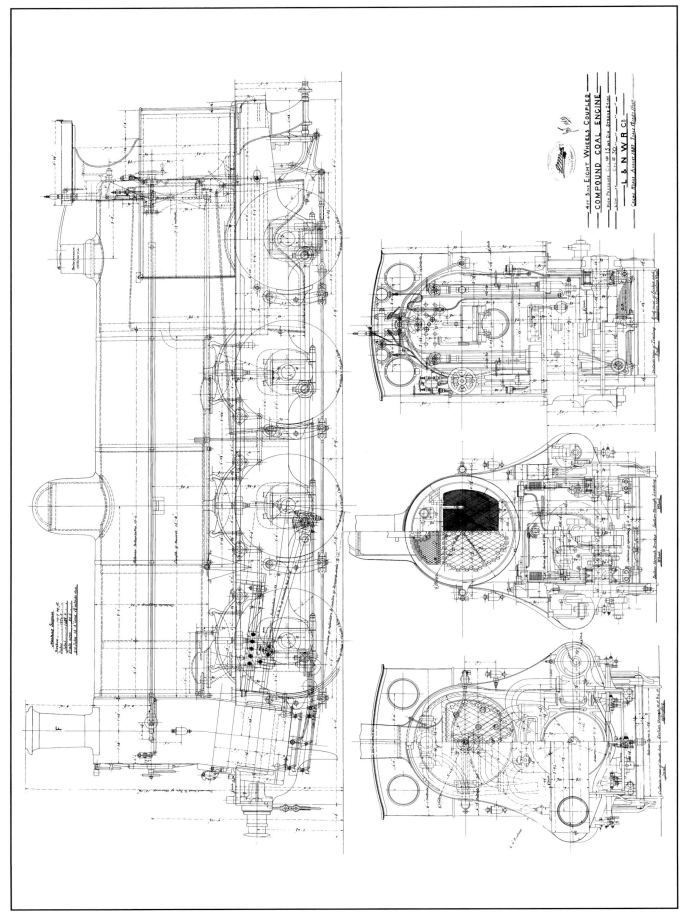

Figure 4: *Official drawings of class 'A' compound No. 2525.*   LNWR A287, courtesy NRM

14

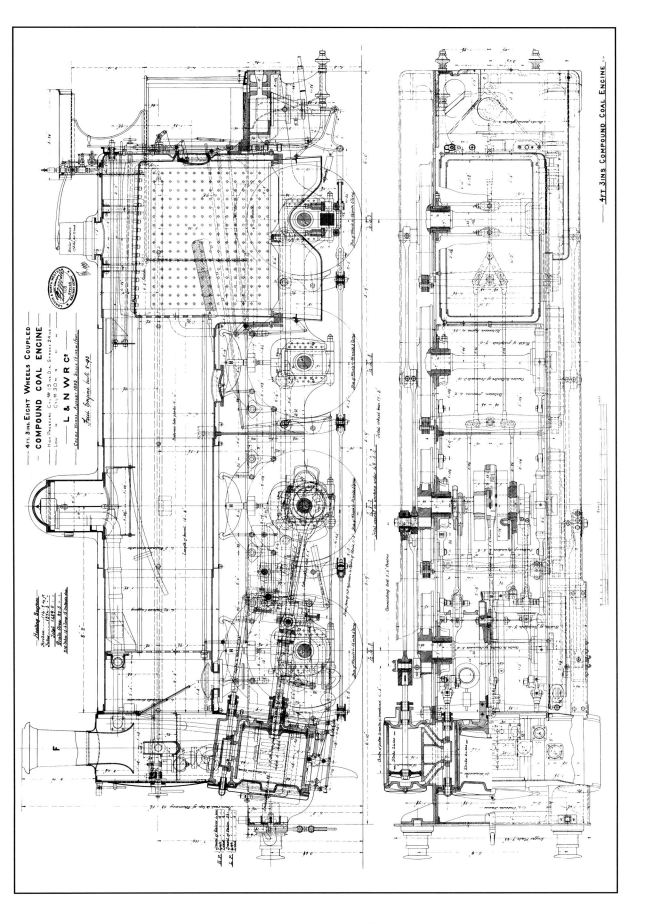

Figure 5: *Official drawings of class 'A' compound No. 2525. The arrangement of the brake rodding has been altered from that used at first on No. 2524.*
LNWR A288

Plate 9: *No. 2524 passing Coleham Shed, Shrewsbury, with a loco coal train, probably from Abergavenny to Crewe. The date is quite soon after completion, 1893-4 (coal rails began to be fitted on tenders from mid-1895), but the original tender tank has already been replaced. This can be seen by the slightly increased over-hang over the frames.*
R. W. Pilcher, D. J. Patrick collection

design was essentially the same as No. 2524, except that it had two high-pressure cylinders outside, operated by Stephenson valve gear, and one large low-pressure cylinder inside, which had a slip eccentric and so was always in full gear. All three cylinders were in line and were inclined at an angle of 8½ to 1 so as to drive on to the second axle, and so all had connecting rods the same length, 5ft 9in, as on 2524. All three sets of motion had rocking shafts, the high-pressure to clear the leading axle and the low-pressure to reach the slide valve above the cylinder. The low-pressure crank was balanced by extending the webs backwards, in the same fashion as the 'elephant's ear' on the three-cylinder compound passenger engines.

Unlike previous Webb compounds, all wheels were coupled. Hitherto, Mr Webb had emphasised the importance of divided drive in his compounds, with high and low-pressure cylinders driving different uncoupled axles. The reasoning behind this was that if the supply of steam to the different cylinders was not in proportion to their volume, slight slipping would take place and easily rectify the situation. This supposed advantage was now set aside, most probably because of the difficulty of arranging for divided drive of four axles, but coupling the axles had two other advantages. Firstly, in an engine intended for slow heavy pulling, it gave a significant improvement in adhesion, and secondly the valves of the inside cylinder, which were always in full gear, were now always in the optimum position in relation to the outside cylinders.

Any disadvantage of coupling was partly overcome by the fitting of a bypass valve. This enabled the exhaust from the high-pressure cylinders to escape directly up the blastpipe rather than pass to the low-pressure cylinder and was operated by the driver when he thought the latter might become choked. At first the valve was operated by a complicated linkage passing through the boiler. Since the valves of the low-pressure cylinder were always in the optimum position, there

was no need for the engine to have the low-pressure relief valve which was fitted behind the chimney on the compound passenger engines.

By the time the compound 0-8-0 was being built, two advances had been made from No. 2524 that were applied to it from the outset. Firstly, the boiler with the intermediate combustion chamber had been abandoned and so a conventional boiler was used. It had 210 1¾in tubes, which since the front tube-plate was recessed 2ft 5in into the barrel, were only 13ft 6in in length. This recess served two purposes. It reduced the weight on the front of the engine and it accommodated an ash chute, or hopper, with a weighted door, passing behind and to the right of the inside cylinder. The boiler pressure was the same as on the 'Greater Britains', 175lb psi, and the ashpan had dampers back and front, a novelty on an LNWR tender engine, as were the closed dials on the pressure gauges. The other main difference was that a larger tender holding 2000 gallons of water was fitted. An unusual feature was the way the sides of the smokebox curved downwards and outwards over the high-pressure cylinders resembling the 'Problems' and giving the class a distinctive style and appearance.

The first three-cylinder compound was numbered 50 and emerged from Crewe Works in September 1893. It was renumbered 2525 in July 1894. As a result of experience with the class in service, two minor changes were made. Firstly, beginning with No. 2528, the fourth of the class built in November 1894, flangeless wheels were used on the third axle so as to enable the engine to negotiate sharp curves more easily. The first three engines were then converted to conform and this became a standard feature of all LNWR eight-coupled engines for the rest of the company's existence. Secondly, after a time the linkage through the boiler to operate the bypass valve was replaced by the system used on the three-cylinder compound passenger engines, where the valve was operated by the driver in the cab pushing or pulling the hand wheel connected to

Plate 10: *The first 'A' class three-cylinder compound 0-8-0 No. 50 as built, photographed at Crewe Works on 26th September 1893. Except for differences associated with being a compound, it is basically the same as No. 2524 in layout and detail. The blower valve is on the left-hand side of the smokebox and the large pipe behind the handrail conveys oil pipes from the lubricator in the cab to the inside cylinder. Just visible above the running plate, immediately in front of the cab side-sheet, is the bracket supporting the rear end of the boiler. Brackets were fixed either side of the firebox and rested on the top of the frames but were not fastened to them. They allowed the boiler to expand to the rear as it heated up, its front end being fixed to the cylinders.* LNWR

the left-hand boiler handrail. The official view of No. 1867 after completion, taken on 21st September 1899 shows this modifications

Comparative Trials

In order to establish which engine was more economical, comparative trials were held between Crewe and Stafford on 1st April 1894. Everything was done to achieve a fair comparison. Two trains were made up of about 690 tons each and ran side by side at the same speed, the line being specially cleared for the purpose. Four trips were made in all, and after the second trip the engines changed trains, the whole idea being to make sure that both engines did the same amount of work. Coal was supplied in weighed bags, water consumption was measured accurately, and efforts made to ensure that both engines had the same amount of fire and water in the boiler at the end of the tests.

Dynamometer car readings were taken and the results showed that the compound used 23.38 per cent less coal and 24.5 per cent less water than the simple engine, developed 656hp compared with 608.6hp, and achieved a drawbar pull of 11.5 tons as opposed to 10.75 tons. Its coal consumption was 46.48lb per mile. Unfortunately, no attempt seems to have been made to quantify the performance of the different boilers, with their different pressures (if that of No. 2524 was 160lb) and very different designs, and so it is impossible to say how much the results were affected by this factor. In

any event, with other things being equal, theory indicates that a 175lb engine would use 3 per cent less fuel than a 160lb one. It may be that the boiler of No. 2524 was unable to produce sufficient steam, as the engine's cylinders were replaced after the trials by new ones of reduced diameter, 18½in by 24in. If so, the boiler design may have been the problem rather than the size of the cylinders. However that may be, Mr Webb decided that henceforward the three-cylinder compound would be the standard heavy goods engine, though No. 2524 continued in service unaltered as a simple engine.

Some modern commentators have asserted that Webb was 'obsessed' by compounding and have implied that these trials were arranged to give the results he wanted, namely to prove that the compound was superior in efficiency and power output. Of course, the two engines were not strictly comparable, as No. 2524 had a different boiler design as well as possibly a lower pressure. But it is highly improbable that a man such as F. W. Webb, whose strict Victorian morality is attested by numerous anecdotes, and an engineer of outstanding ability, secure in his position as head of the locomotive department, should set out to falsify test results, consciously or unconsciously.

It is possible that being already convinced of the superiority of compounding he neglected to ensure the two engines were as identical as possible. However, the same result was obtained by George Hughes of the Lancashire & Yorkshire Railway in careful trials of two

Plate 11: *Another view of No. 50 on the same occasion. Just noticeable is the slightly wider footplating as far back as the slide-bar support. One coupling rod links the first three axles, and another one, fitting outside it, the rear two. The tender is the standard 2000-gallon type. Again, there is a sandbox on the front of the tender and no rear sandbox on the engine. On the far right is the side door leading into the back of the paint shop, while behind the engine is the white screen used by the official photographer to avoid the need to paint out the background on the glass negative later.*

LNWR

Plate 12: *Cab view of an 'A' class 0-8-0 in the paint shop.*
R. P. Richards

of his eight-coupled engines, one compound and one simple, some years later. Again, the compound was found to be superior, and no one has suggested that Hughes was 'obsessed' by compounding. In general, compounds are found to be superior in economy and power output. The question engineers face is whether these advantages are worth the additional mechanical complications. Webb's view was that they were.

The boilers with combustion chambers on the 'Greater Britains' and No. 2524 seem to have been replaced quite quickly with boilers of conventional design. This is not surprising, in view of the difficulty of dealing with any leaking tube ends inside the combustion chamber. Indeed, the surprising thing is that the experiment lasted long enough for the boiler to be tried on No. 2524 at all.

With a conventional boiler the usual method of dealing with a defective tube at a shed was to drive it out from the firebox end. Two men would get into the firebox. One would hold the 'dolly' against the end of the tube and the other would hit it with a 28lb hammer until it could be removed through the smokebox. Swinging a hammer in the confined space of a firebox was a far from easy operation in any case but it would have been impossible in the combustion chamber, even if two men could have got into it. It would have been no easier to change a tube in the works, and indeed to build the boiler in the first place must have presented major difficulties: somehow the tube ends would have to be expanded by men working in the combustion chamber.

All this would have been bad enough, even if the combustion chamber had been effective, but it seems certain that its effect was minimal at best. Flame would not pass far into the tubes from the firebox, because of the same principle that operates in the miner's safety lamp, and certainly would not reach the combustion chamber. If some of the gases leaving the firebox were still unburnt, having been cooled by passage through the tubes, they would have to be re-ignited in the com-

bustion chamber and, unless they were already mixed with the requisite amount of air, they would need more air before they could be burnt completely.

Despite all this, it is clear that this boiler constituted no great handicap to the engine, since its performance on test was not inferior to engines with conventional boilers. At first, this might seem something of a mystery. In locomotive boilers, however, steam is mostly generated around the firebox and the tubes adjacent to it. As the gases pass through the tubes they are cooled, and when they reach the front end of the tubes in long boilers, such as those of the 'A' class and 2-2-2-2 compounds, their temperature has dropped so much that they do little more than warm the feedwater. So, despite an apparently significant difference, the performance of both types of boiler was effectively the same. The combustion chamber and the tubes beyond it were ineffective so far as steam-raising was concerned. But the conventional boiler was equally ineffective in the same area. Both boilers had the same steam-raising capacity, since they were identical in all important dimensions, in the firebox and tubes adjacent to it.

This characteristic of long boilers was confirmed in later work under Beames at Crewe, when the large boiler for the 'Claughtons' was being developed. It seems certain too that Webb was already aware of it, and that the intermediate combustion chamber was an attempt to raise the temperature of the gases passing through the front-end tubes. When it failed, he reverted to the 'Teutonic' boiler in his later compound passenger engines, the 'Jubilees', and when more power was needed in their successor, the 'Alfred the Great' class, the boiler was increased in diameter but not in length.

Plate 13: *Front end view of No. 50.* LNWR B45

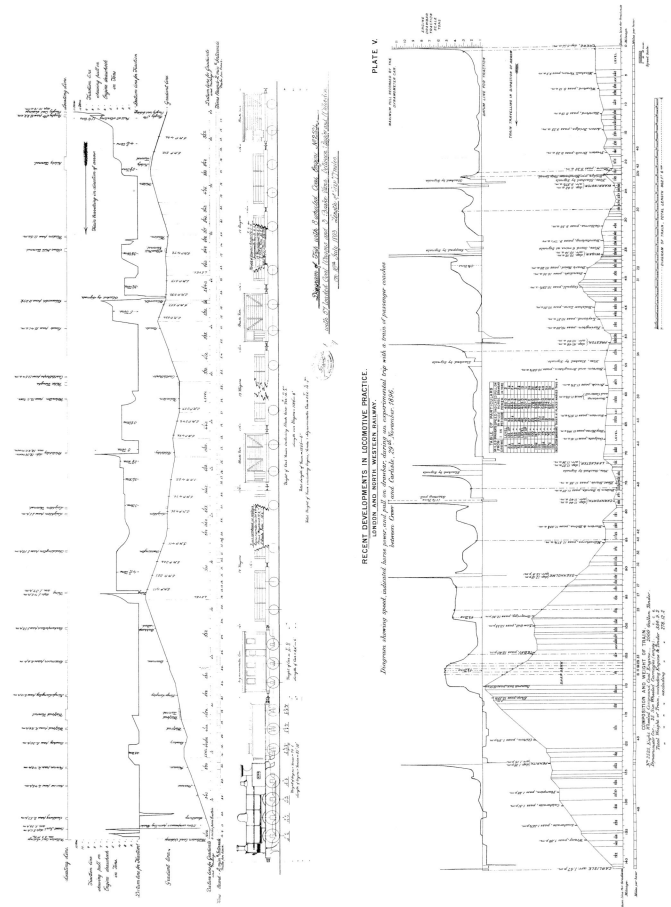

Figure 6: *Official diagram showing details of the performance of No. 2524 during a test trip from Rugby to Willesden on 16th July 1893.*

Figure 7: *Official diagram showing details of the performance of 'A' class No. 2525 when hauling a test train of 25 six-wheel coaches from Crewe to Carlisle on 29th November 1896. LNWR A330, courtesy NRM*

When the original boiler on No. 2524 was replaced is uncertain, as is the form of the replacement boiler. Possibly it was a 'Greater Britain' boiler, as it may have been easier to modify, the 'A' class boiler having a different arrangement for the ash chute. If so, it would have had greater heating surface. It seems certain too that the replacement boiler had a pressure of 175lb.

Other Trials

In addition to the trials held to compare them directly, both engines were tested on other occasions also. On 16th July 1893, before the comparative tests between Crewe and Stafford, No 2524 hauled a test train from Rugby to Willesden. It consisted of 57 loaded coal wagons, 3 brake vans and the six-wheeled dynamometer car, the total weight excluding engine and tender being 778 tons. The maximum tractive effort of just over 11 tons was exerted in starting from Rugby. Up the 1 in 330 gradient to Tring 411ihp was developed, the pull on the drawbar being $4^7/_{16}$ tons at a speed of 12mph. The highest ihp was 557 up the gradient of 1 in 326 from Blisworth towards Roade; the speed was 13mph and the pull on the drawbar 5 tons. The maximum speed on the whole journey was 25mph.

Late in 1896 two trial runs were made with No. 2525.

The first, on 29th November, was from Crewe to Carlisle, and the load was 25 empty six-wheel coaches, which with the dynamometer car weighed 278 tons. A maximum pull of $11^1/_2$ tons was exerted in starting away from a signal check north of Carnforth, and a maximum of 704ihp was recorded in climbing the 1 in 75 to Shap at 19mph, the drawbar pull being $5^1/_8$ tons. The maximum of 781ihp was developed at 27mph on an up gradient of 1 in 120.

A few days later, on 1st December, the same engine worked from Edgeley to Heaton Lodge over Standedge, a distance of $29^1/_2$ miles. The train consisted of 45 loaded goods wagons, a brake van and the dynamometer car, weighing some 369 tons. A drawbar pull of $11^1/_2$ tons was recorded in starting up a gradient of 1 in 66 and 745ihp was developed up 1 in 125 climbing to Standedge at 21mph, with a drawbar pull of $5^1/_{16}$ tons. The highest pull on the drawbar while running was $7^3/_4$ tons and the highest speed on the whole journey 27mph.

The 'A' Class in Service

Between 1894 and 1900 a total of 110 further 'A' class 0-8-0s was built. The last eighty, beginning with No. 1801 in 1897, had piston valves and the last of the

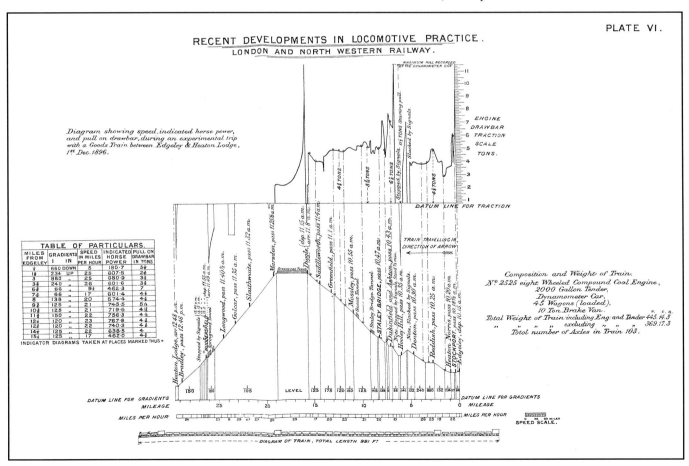

Figure 8: *Official diagram showing the performance of 'A' class No. 2525 on a test trip between Edgeley and Heaton Lodge on 1st December 1896.*

Plate 14: *An unidentified 'A' class at work on the main line. It must be one of the early engines, as the tender has no coal rails, and in view of its spotless conditon may well be new. Probably it is on an Abergavenny - Crewe loco coal train. Many photographs of coal and mixed goods trains at this period show cattle wagons immediately behind the engine. It seems that they were probably picked up at a wayside station, rather than from the originating point, so as to provide a quick transit.*
D. J. Patrick collection

Plate 15: *No. 50 passing Shrewsbury when still in 'as built' condition - there are no coal rails on the tender and flangeless driving wheels have not yet been fitted on the third axle (even at this distance, the flange can be seen clearly). Though it is probably on an Abergavenny - Crewe loco coal train, the route was also used by coal trains to Birkenhead for bunkering ships. This traffic is believed to be the reason for the construction of the branch from Whitchurch to Tattenhall Junction, to enable coal trains to avoid the gradients over the Great Western line via Wrexham and bring them into Chester the right way round to take the Birkenhead line.*
R. W. Pilcher

Plate 16: *No. 2551 now with the bypass valve fitting on the side of the smokebox.* M. Williams collection

Plate 17: *Class 'A' No. 2545 in immaculate condition, possibly new, with a down goods at Crewe in 1896-7. The warehouse behind the engine was demolished to make room for the approach tracks to the new down island platform which was put in as part of the rebuilding of Crewe station in the early 1900s. The photograph was probably taken from the south end of what was then the main down platform.*
R. Bell collection

Plate 18: *Class 'A' No. 2534 climbing Shap with a down mixed goods train on 18th July 1899. In fact, it seems to have stopped so as to pose for the official photographer, who may well have been transported to the spot on the footplate. Whatever, all cred- it to him for manhandling his weighty equipment, producing 12in by 10in glass plates to this remote spot and obtaining such a masterpiece. At this period LNWR wagons were not fitted with tarpaulin bars, which accounts for the irregular shapes of the sheeted loads. As was common at the time, the leading wagon has brakes on one side only, the far side. The flush-sided vans about half-way down the train are not LNWR vehicles - Earlestown did not produce such wagons until about 1908. Near the back of the train is a pantechnicon, which is probably mounted on an implement wagon with drop floor.* LNWR C633

Plate 19: *An unidentified 'A' class heads an up coal train round the curve near Weedon in the late 1890s. The Grand Union Canal is out of the picture on the right.* D. J. Patrick collection

Plate 20: *Class 'A' No. 1801 arriving with a down goods in the sidings at Carlisle Upperby in 1898. The low viewpoint well illustrates how much space there was between the driving wheels and the splashers. Head-code boards, as in the top lamp bracket, were in use on the Northern Divison at this period, and similar boards appear in many photographs, south of Crewe, for instance, and in North Wales. Perhaps they were in use all over the system, but their significance is uncertain.*

Dr Tice F. Budden

Plate 21: *Class 'A' No. 2545 sometime in the late 1890s. It is possibly still quite new, as it is in immaculate condition. The tops of the splashers, the boiler stay and the reach rod are all polished to perfection, so that in all probability the insides of the frames are as clean as the rest of the engine. No wonder then that the driver and fireman pose proudly on the footplate, well aware that they are in charge of the last word in goods engines.*

D. J. Patrick collection

Plate 22: *Class 'A' No. 1822 at an unidentified location. A beautiful picture of the LNWR at the turn of the centtry.* J. M. Bentley collection

Plate 23: *Class 'A' No. 1824 at Carnforth, sometime after 1902 (centre lamp sockets came into use on 1st January 1903). The lubricators on the cylinder ends are different from earlier pictures, being cylindrical in shape, and the relief valves on the steamchest of the centre cylinder have been removed and blanked off. The engine has a plain three-link coupling, instead of the screw coupling in earlier pictures, so in view of the shunter's pole on the bufferbeam and the sun-hatted shunters on the shunters' truck, it is probably in regular use for shunting. For some reason there are two lamp sockets on the right-hand end of the bufferbeam.*

A. G. Ellis collection

class, No. 1880 had a Belpaire firebox with circular grate and watertube firebars; presumably, this was a short-lived experiment as nothing more is known about it. No. 50 was the only one fitted with a vacuum ejector.

In service the class earned the reputation of being excellent engines. Many of them were allocated to South Wales and worked in that district and between Abergavenny and Crewe, presumably hauling trains of Welsh coal, and others worked between Crewe and Carlisle, where their eight-coupled wheels must have been a great advance in hauling general goods trains over Shap. They also worked from Crewe to Leeds, and occasionally even appeared at Buxton, when one had been borrowed by Stockport. At some stage they acquired the nickname 'Johnny Dougans' among the men, after one of the shed foremen at Crewe, who announced, the story goes, that when viewed from the front the engines reminded him 'of his missus'!

From time to time they put up remarkable feats of haulage. In 1900 No. 1815 started a train of 120 wagons, including three 10-ton brake vans, up the 1 in 177 from Basford Wood and reached Whitmore in 43min

start to stop. Then on 10th February 1901 No. 2543 hauled 81 wagons from Crewe to Edge Hill. No doubt, these feats were achieved under specially arranged conditions, as trains of these lengths could not normally be accommodated in sidings, but nevertheless they show the engines as being competent haulers of heavy loads at slow speeds, which is what they were intended to do. Up to 28th February 1899 the first 81 engines covered 3,628,727 miles and later, when the whole class was completed, the average mileage was 30,731 miles per year at a coal consumption of 48lb a mile.

The first 'A' class were converted from compound to simple quite soon after Mr Whale took over in the middle of 1903. This might seem surprising, since they were still quite new engines, none being more than ten years old, and though smaller than the 'B' class, which continued to be built until August 1904, they were less complicated. However, the reason for their rebuilding is explained in a minute of 12th April 1904, which states: 'Some of the cylinders require renewing and as there are no castings on hand, it is proposed to convert them to non-compound engines with 19½in cylinders. This

28

will be cheaper than altering them to four-cylinder compound engines and it will not be necessary to provide an additional pair of leading wheels.' This latter is a reference to Mr Whale's concern about the weight of the front of the 'B' class. Within less than ten years, all the 'A' class were converted to two-cylinder simple 0-8-0s of class 'C', class 'C1' or class 'D'.

Class 'B'

In the years around the turn of the century there was a considerable and rapid increase in the loads of express passenger trains, which resulted in the introduction of the 'Jubilee' and 'Alfred the Great' class four-cylinder compound 4-4-0s, and eventually caused a crisis in the Locomotive Department. It seems highly probable that a similar situation arose with goods traffic also but that it attracted less public attention. Certainly, Mr Webb saw fit in 1901 to introduce a much more powerful eight-coupled coal engine, later designated class 'B'. It had two high-pressure cylinders outside, of the same size as those of class 'A', 15in by 24in, and two low-pressure cylinders inside, 20½in by 24in, all driving on the second axle as on class 'A' and using the same connecting rods. In fact, this gave a smaller overall cylinder capacity than the class 'A' but the boiler, which followed the same arrangement as the 'A' class, with the front tubeplate recessed to reduce weight at the front end and to accommodate an ash chute, was 5in larger in diameter and had increased pressure, 200lb psi. It was the largest boiler used on the LNWR up to that

time, so that its capacity to produce steam was greater and the engine overall was more powerful.

The low-pressure cylinders were the same as on the 'Jubilees' and 'Alfreds', in which the front piece of the frames carrying the cylinders was bolted inside the main frames. The purpose of this was to allow enough space for the bogie to move without fouling the frames, and the same arrangement was followed on the 'B' class, though of course they had no bogie.

Apart from obvious differences caused by the changes in the boiler and cylinders, the basic design and general appearance were the same as the 'A' class. At first the 'B' class had the same arrangement of sandboxes, one on the leading splasher and one on the tender, but soon after Mr Whale took over in 1903, a second sandbox was fitted on the driving splasher, worked by rodding from the leading one. Like the 'A' class, the first 'B' class had a boiler stay of steel plate, which can be seen in photographs between the second and third splashers. This was changed to a steel casting, triangular in shape, when seen end on, probably from the third batch introduced in March 1902. All developments of the 'B' class, the 'E', 'F', 'G', 'G1' and 'G2' classes, had the same arrangement of sandboxes on the two leading splashers, while developments of the 'A' class, the 'C', 'C1' and 'D' classes, had only one larger one on the leading splasher.

The early batches of 'B' class were fitted with 2000-gallon tenders but some of the later batches had 2500-gallon tenders, as introduced in 1902 on the last thirty

Plate 24: *Two unidentified class 'B' 0-8-0s double-head a train of coal empties through Harrow about 1905. Probably as early as this, certainly by the 1920s, southbound coal trains generally took sixty wagons, northbound empties eighty. There were therefore fewer northbound trains than southbound, and so to return engines to the north and reduce line occupation double-heading of northbound empties was regular practice.*
D. J. Patrick collection

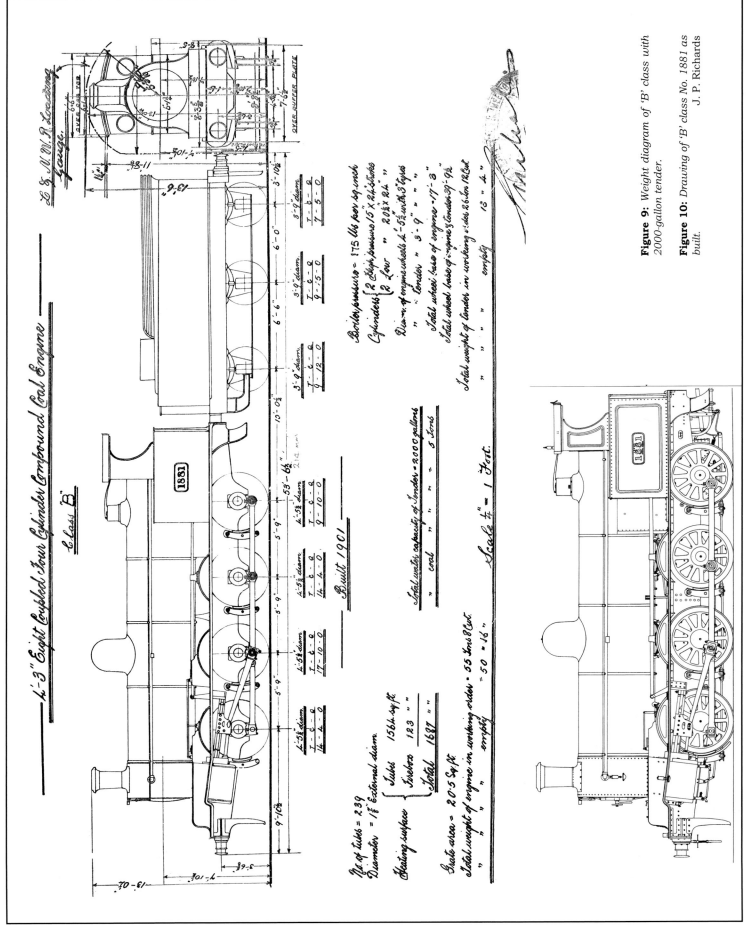

— 4'-3" Eight Coupled Four Cylinder Compound Coal Engine —

Class 'B'

1881

Built 1901

Boiler pressure = 175 lbs per sq.inch
Cylinders { 2 High pressure 15" x 24" stroke
          { 2 Low   " 20½ x 24 "
Diam. of engine wheels 4'-5½" with 3 tyres
         " tender = 3'-9 "
         Total wheel base of engine = 17'-3"
         Total wheel base of engine & tender 39'-9½
Total weight of tender in working order 26 tons 12 cwt.
         " " " " empty   13 " 4 "

No. of tubes = 239
Diameter = 1⅞" external diam.
Heating surface { Tubes   1564 sq.ft.
                { Firebox 123 " "
                  Total   1687 " "
Grate area = 20·5 sq.ft
Total weight of engine in working order = 55 tons 8 cwt.
         " " " " empty 50 " 16 "
                  = empty 13 " 4 " Fart.

Scale ¼ = 1 Foot.

Figure 9: _Weight diagram of 'B' class with 2000-gallon tender._

Figure 10: _Drawing of 'B' class No. 1881 as built._

30

'Alfred the Great' class 4-4-0s and used on the 'Bill Bailey' 4-6-0s.

These four-cylinder compounds of class 'B' seem to have been faster than class 'A', probably because of the higher boiler pressure, and in 1903 the first of the class, No. 1881, was fitted for working vacuum-braked trains and tried on Leeds-Manchester passenger trains. However, it seems the experiment did not last long.

Some of the first engines of class 'B' were sent to work coal traffic between Northampton and Willesden, the usual load being 54 loaded coal wagons and one brake van. The average load for such a train, including engine and tender, was 820 tons, and the speed 22mph. The route included a continuous 5½-mile climb at 1 in 200.

The suggestion that increased goods traffic was creating problems as well as passenger traffic is based on the fact that in October 1902, Robert Turnbull, superintendent of the line, and George Whale, running superintendent, made a report to a meeting of the company's officers on the position with eight-coupled compound coal engines. Why the report was called for is unknown but it seems likely that they were required to explain why there were insufficient of the engines available.

Their reply was that 'a certain proportion' of them were under repair in the works, causing smaller engines to be used for the trains they were diagrammed for. The situation would be remedied 'by sending more of them to the larger sheds to meet all emergencies when they became available'. They stated that in addition to the 111 three-cylinder engines in service in March 1901, a further 52 four-cylinder engines had been turned out of the shops up to the end of September 1902, making 163 eight-coupled engines in all. Some of the 'B' class had been put to work between Colwick and London, and to and from Carlisle, 'where the gradients are heavy'. The three-cylinder engines released at Colwick, Carlisle, Preston and other places were then put to work mineral traffic between: Rugby and London; Nuneaton and Stafford; Nuneaton and Peterborough; Birmingham and Peterborough; Bescot and Crewe; and Carnforth and Shrewsbury. Other four-cylinder engines had been put to work minerals and other heavy traffic between Buxton and Liverpool; Buxton and Greenfield; Carnforth and Manchester; Nuneaton and London; Oxford, Tring and Cambridge; and Springs Branch and Garston. 'The engines are doing good service effecting a very considerable saving on train miles weekly', presumably by hauling greater loads.

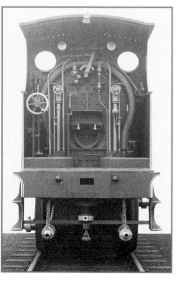

Plate 25 (above): *The first of the 'B' class, No. 1881, photographed on 20th September 1901. Although the appearance has been changed by the larger boiler and the 'piano' covers over the rocking arms actuating the inside cylinders, the layout is basically the same as that of the three-cylinder compounds and No. 2524. One detail difference is the steel-plate boiler stay visible between the driving and intermediate splashers. The tender is the standard 2000-gallon type.*
LNWR B79

Plate 26 (far left): *Front end of No. 1881. The covers over the rocking arms extend almost the full width of the engine. There are two clips securing the bottom of the smokebox door.* LNWR C721

Plate 27 (left): *Cab view of No. 1881.* LNWR C722

Plate 28: *Four 'B' class apparently coupled together. The leading engine has two of the inspection covers giving access to the front ends of the inside cylinders raised. It is quite likely that both this and the following picture were taken during a trial run of engines just ex works, as they all seem to be in absolutely mint condition. So the location is perhaps Whitmore or one of the places used for trial trips from Crewe.*
D. J. Patrick collection

Plate 29: *Class 'B' No. 2342, with shed plate '29', Carlisle, probably on the same occasion. The boiler stay is now a casting, triangular in shape when viewed end on.*
A. G. Ellis collection

The numbering of the compound coal engines was unusual in that twenty of the 'B' class were numbered 1881-1900, following on from the 'A' class 1801-80. Consecutive numbers such as these were very unusual in the Crewe system and the reason for these was related to the operation of the duplicate list, which at one time had used the numbers 1801-2000. When that series had been filled, a new duplicate list had been opened from 3001 upwards. About 1892 it was decided to make no further additions to the 1801 list and in 1897 the surviving engines in it were renumbered in the 3001 list. Thus 200 consecutive numbers became available simultaneously for new engines, the first hundred being taken by 0-8-0s and the next 75 by 'Jubilee' and 'Alfred the Great' 4-4-0s.

By the retirement of Mr Webb in May 1903 the LNWR had over 250 0-8-0 heavy goods engines of classes 'A' and 'B'. Most other major British companies at that time were still building 0-6-0s and the first Great Western 2-8-0, for example, did not appear until 1904. For an engineer whose 'small engine' policy is sometimes criticised, this is a remarkable record. The 'B' class continued to be built for more than a year after Mr Webb's retirement. In all 170 were built, making a total of 282 eight-coupled goods engines in service by the end of 1904.

The 'B' class were commonly known as 'Swammies' by LNWR enginemen but the origin of this nickname is now uncertain. A possible explanation is that it was derived from the fact that their front ends were always 'swamped' in steam leaking from the joints around the cylinders. Whatever the origin, an old Stafford engineman used to tell the story of how, soon after he started as a cleaner just after the Great War, a driver took him on one side and said, 'You see that cloud of steam over there? Well, somewhere inside that cloud of steam is a "Swammy"'! Another commonly used nickname, 'piano fronts' or simply 'pianos', was obviously derived from the appearance of the cover over the rocking arms of the inside cylinders, which was shaped like the lid of a piano.

The clouds of steam, of course, were caused by leaks from the piston-rod gland packing and valve-spindle gland packing. In the slide-valve design with Joy valve gear the gland where the rod pushes the valve is under steam at boiler pressure all the time, and so leaks of steam in the 'B' class were costly in coal. In later piston-valve designs, however, the gland is only under pressure from exhaust steam, and so any leaks hardly matter.

Plate 30: *An unidentified 'B' class on the up slow line at Bushey troughs. The train consists mainly of loaded coal wagons but at the front are a couple of cattle wagons. The engine is probably new, as the date must be early, probably 1903, since there are pools of water lying about between the running lines. Timbers were laid soon after this date to protect the ballast from water sprayed up by engines using the troughs.*

D. J. Patrick collection

Plate 31: *Another 'B' class with a mixed goods on the down slow line at the south end of Bushey troughs a year or two later.*

R. Bell collection

Disaster at Buxton

A 'B' class was involved in one of the most spectacular accidents ever to occur to any British engine. The boiler of No. 134 blew up as the engine was starting away from the yard at Buxton early in the morning of 11th November 1921. Both the driver and fireman, W. Holmes and W. Fletcher from Oldham shed, who had worked into Buxton the previous day and lodged in Fairfield, were killed, but several eyewitnesses survived to describe what happened.

The engine had come off the shed and arrived in the yard at 12.25am to work the 12.45am train to Oldham. It was a very cold night and it was freezing 'very hard'. The guard, G. Hannah, also of Oldham, had gone to speak to the driver, as was usual before departure, to hand him his 'ticket' stating the load and so on. As the train had been made up to 40 wagons and the limit for the 'B' class was 35, he arranged for five to be taken off. When that was done and the engine was back on its train, the guard looked for the 'right away' signal from the head shunter, passed it to the driver and began to walk back to his van. He had just got as far as the tender when the explosion occurred, and he was thrown 'some distance on the ground and covered with water and ashes'. After picking himself up, he could see nothing but steam and smoke and could find no trace of the driver or fireman. Their bodies were later found some 500 yards away in a plantation. The engine had made about four beats and there was nothing unusual about them. He had not seen the pressure gauge but the firehole door was open, as the fireman had just finished 'feeding'. He would expect the engine to start away with a full head of steam but it had not been blowing off.

The head shunter said he gave the green light for 'right away' and the driver whistled in response but it was five minutes later when the engine started. He was 37 yards away and saw the smokebox door fly open and fire come out before he was thrown under a wagon. The engine had not been blowing off, which was unusual, as 'they have to have a full head of steam to get out of the siding.' This was a reference to the fact that at Buxton there was a steep climb out of the yard itself and it was the practice for engines before departure to be 'hotted up', in the parlance of the local enginemen, that is, for a good fire to be built up, the boiler well filled and steam to be blowing off, so as to be able to lift the train out of the sidings up the 1 in 60 gradient so that the bank engine could come up behind.

Enormous force was released by the explosion. The frames of the engine at the firebox end were doubled back and the rails beneath it bent and twisted, the boiler disintegrated and was left a mass of twisted tubes, one of the axles, 10in thick, was broken and a wheel forced off, and the tender, weighing 38 tons, was forced backwards, still coupled to the dragbox of the engine, and derailed, as were several wagons behind it. From the nature of the damage, it seems clear that the crown of the firebox, already subjected to far greater pressure than that for which it had been designed, finally gave way when the load on it was increased by the water in the boiler surging backwards as the engine started. This is consistent with the head shunter's account, the inrush of water and steam into the firebox driving fire and flames down the tubes with such force as to blow off the smokebox door.

The official enquiry under Major G. L. Hall, Royal Engineers, heard evidence from many sources, as well as eyewitnesses, previous drivers of the engine, fitters

Plate 32: *An unidentified 'B' class works at a steady 20-25mph through the rural landscape near Kenton with a coal train for London about 1905. Track, verges and hedgerows are in perfect order as is the train - this was surely the golden age of railways in Great Britain. Again, immediately behind the engine is a cattle wagon which has probably been attached at a station en route for rapid transit to London.*
H. Gordon Tidey/D. J. Patrick collection

Plate 33: *Class 'B' No. 1041 at Wigan Springs Branch shed with a group of men, probably cleaners, and their foreman on the right. In the background is Stanley Corn Mills. Crewe paint shop ceased lining out in September 1914, so the date must be during the Great War or just after. The cleaners have worked well. The covers on the ends of the outside cylinders were often well polished on these engines.*

Tom Taylor collection.

Plate 34: *Class 'B' No. 2575 with an up goods in the MSJA platform at Manchester London Road on a typically murky Manchester day. It is easy now to forget what conditons were like in Manchester, and indeed all the industrial cities of Britain, when thousands of chimneys filled the air with smoke from coal fires. But this evocative picture of a dirty engine on a dirty day is an effective reminder of the realities of the coal-burning era, when dense fogs lasted for days on end and were sometimes so thick that passengers fell from platforms. The date could be any time up to about 1920. No. 2575 is still lined beneath the dirt but at least the numberplate has been cleaned. The smokebox door now has four clips, while on the front of the tender is a stoneware bottle, probably containing the fireman's cold tea.*
W. H. Whitworth

and other shed staff, H. P. M. Beames, chief mechanical engineer, and staff from Crewe Works, and staff from Messrs Beardmore's, Parkhead Works, Glasgow. No. 134 was one of eighteen engines sent to Beardmore's for general repair in October 1920, because of a backlog of work at Crewe resulting from the Great War. There seems to have been good co-operation between Beardmore's and Crewe at that time, as in addition to repairs, the company was building a large batch of 'Prince of Wales' 4-6-0s. The repair of No. 134 took 39 weeks and was completed in July 1921. On 4th August it was allocated to Longsight, which sent it to Stockport shed, both Stockport and Buxton being sub-sheds of Longsight under the LNWR shed organisation. There seems to have been a variety of problems with the engine and it did not return to actual service until 23rd August.

A month later, on 23rd September, came the first sign of impending disaster. Driver Allen of Warrington shed reported, 'Steam gauge goes all round', but it was not realised that the gauge was accurate and the safety valves faulty. The pressure gauge was again reported on 22nd October, once at Stockport and again at Farnley Junction, but as before the real cause of the problem went unrealised. Next the engine was out of service from 28th October to 8th November with injector trouble. This was a common problem on 'B' class because of the high working pressure but in the case of No. 134 must have been accentuated by the fact that the pressure regularly exceeded 200lb psi. The pressure gauge was reported for the last time on 10th November, the day before the explosion, by driver Winstanley of Sutton Oak shed, who had brought the engine up to Buxton. He had seen the gauge reading 300lb psi (its maximum) when at Dove Holes and reported the fact to Mr Oldfield, the Buxton shed foreman, adding that something more was amiss and that if the engine was not sorted out, it would blow up. The safety valves were still not suspected, even though no one at the enquiry recalled them lifting in October, and so again the pressure gauge was changed. This required the steam to be blown out of the boiler (only after this accident did LNWR engines have a cock fitted to the pipe leading to the pressure gauge to enable the gauge to be changed when in steam). The fire was re-lit and the engine prepared by driver G. H. Moss, who noting the pressure gauge had been changed, handed No. 134 over to driver Holmes with a pressure of 120lb psi.

The overhaul at Beardmore's had been carefully supervised both by the company's works foreman and staff from Crewe. Although the general quality of work had been good, however, the safety valves had been incorrectly repaired, with insufficient clearances between the fixed and moving parts when cold, and so there was even less chance the valves would lift off their seats when hot and after expansion had taken place.

The safety valves of the other engines repaired by Beardmore's were then examined at Crewe Works. Beames himself gave evidence that the safety valves from No. 437 gave no sign of blowing off at 210lb psi.

'We therefore took the valves to pieces and found that both the wing halves were fast in the seatings. They were so fast that I could not remove either of them without the aid of a screw pin we put into one of the tap holes. We only got the valve out of the casing by hammering outside the case. Both wing halves were in that state.'

As for the other engines, the valves of No. 18 of Bescot shed blew off at 200lb psi exactly. No. 1225 of Abergavenny reached 210lb before the lever was lifted manually to release the valve, No. 1017 reached 210lb without blowing off and No. 647 of Crewe South, whose valves were sent to the works, would not blow off at all. The rest of the Beardmore engines all blew off between 195 and 205lb psi. So it seems that enough of the Beardmore-repaired engines had faulty safety valves to make an explosion almost inevitable in suitable circumstances.

It is precisely to guard against those very circumstances, of course, that boilers are fitted with pressure gauges. On No. 134 the gauge had been reported defective on four occasions, the last being the previous day. On the three previous occasions the gauge had been assumed to be at fault (referring to this explosion, J. M. Dunn has stated that LNWR gauges always got 'light') and on the fourth occasion it was replaced. However, despite the driver's strong warning on the last occasion of the possibility of an explosion, nothing was done to check the safety valves nor was the gauge tested against the valves. After the accident, it was tested at Crewe and found to be correct. In fact, it was standard practice for pressure gauges to be tested at Crewe before despatch to the sheds and for fitters simply to replace them and not check them in any way.

No doubt in the five minutes' wait before the departure of No. 134, the blower was hard on, and the crucial questions, about which it is only possible to speculate, are what pressure was reached and what reading was shown on the gauge. It seems certain that the gauge would have shown its maximum of 300lb, and equally certain that the driver and fireman both noticed it and assumed it to be incorrect. Neither could conceive the possibility that the gauge was correct and the safety valves at fault, testimony perhaps to the reliability of Ramsbottom safety valves as maintained at Crewe over many years, but of course a tragic and fatal error.

On these engines, as on the compound 4-4-0s, which also had 200lb psi boilers, it was a common complaint that the injectors would not work 'when high in steam', so perhaps it was understandable that this caused the drivers of No. 134 no apprehension, and perhaps in any case the very cold temperatures on the night of the accident counteracted the effect of the high pressure on the injectors to some extent. However, it is surprising that no driver had noticed that No. 134 or any of the other engines with faulty valves was more lively than usual, though perhaps that was one of the factors behind driver Winstanley's warning.

The investigation was very thorough. A boiler of similar age to that of No. 134 was hydraulically tested at

Plate 35: *Class 'B' No. 1432. The date could be any time up to the 1920s. Despite plenty of background 'information' the location has not been identified.*
D. J. Patrick collection

Plate 36: *Technically a poor picture but with much of interest. 'B' class No. 842 outside the one-road shed at Windermere, being prepared to work on up goods, perhaps to Wigan. The fireman breaks off from oiling and watches the photographer from between the frames.*
A. B. Macleod

Plate 37: *Class 'B' No. 1436, about 1920, fitted with Cooke buffers. The engine is still lined but its 2500-gallon tender is in plain black.* LGRP

Plate 38: *Two years after the grouping No. 1881, the first of the 'B' class, was repainted in full LNWR livery and sent to the Stockton & Darlington centenary celebrations, presumably as a representative of the Webb compound type. It is seen here at Crewe South shed after its return. It still has its 2000-gallon tender but now, like many 'B' class at this period, has Cooke buffers and an oil box on the hand rail, introduced by Beames. It was renumbered LMS 8900 in December 1926 and scrapped in 1928.*
R. Bell collection

Crewe. At a pressure of 600lb psi, three times the working pressure, the roofing bars were bent and the crown plate came down slightly, but only one roofing bolt was broken, proof of the boiler's sound design and excellent workmanship. What pressure was reached when the boiler of No. 134 exploded can only be guessed but it must have been extremely high.

In summing up, Major Hall stated: 'My general conclusion in this very serious case is that so many factors, some of them not necessarily constituting an element of danger in themselves, contributed to the result that no responsiblity can fairly, in the circumstances, be assigned to any individual.'

The Last Webb Compounds

The first conversions from class 'B' were to class 'E' and class 'F' 2-8-0s, and only a few of the class were so treated. A more extensive conversion was that to class 'G', which first took place in 1909 and continued until 1917, a total of 32 engines being altered. From then onwards conversion was direct to class 'G1' and 38 had been converted by the time of the Grouping in 1923, when 53 of the 'B' class passed into the ownership of the LMS. Of these 43 were converted to class 'G1' up to the end of May 1927, making a total of 91 'B' class converted directly to class 'G', but the remaining 10 were then scrapped and all had gone by the end of 1928. The last two, LMS Nos. 8919 and 8938, were withdrawn on 31st December 1928 and were the last Webb compounds of any type in service. They were offered for sale but as no buyers appeared, they were cut up on 5th February 1929.

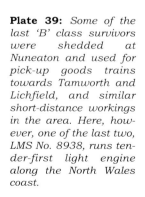

Plate 39: *Some of the last 'B' class survivors were shedded at Nuneaton and used for pick-up goods trains towards Tamworth and Lichfield, and similar short-distance workings in the area. Here, however, one of the last two, LMS No. 8938, runs tender-first light engine along the North Wales coast.*

Plate 40: *For some reason the official photograph of the first 'E' class, No. 1886, was not taken in the usual place by the paint shop in Crewe Works but near Crewe South shed, on 15th October 1904. Parts from withdrawn three-cylinder compounds were ordered to be re-used in the radial truck but the cast-iron wheels at least must have been new, as the compounds had spoked wheels. To the right, beyond the engine, is the Tranship Shed.* LNWR A450

Plate 41: *Class 'E' No. 1017 takes water from Castlethorpe troughs with down coal empties on 16th August 1916. It has probably been through Crewe Works recently as the engine is plain black, Cooke buffers are fitted and the boiler stay seems to have gone, but the tender is lined.*

Leslie J. Thompson

Plate 42: *Class 'E' No. 1585 at Wigan Springs Branch, its lined paintwork in good condition, though the date appears to be about 1920. The tender is a Webb 2000-gallon type.*
W. H. Whitworth

Chapter Two
GEORGE WHALE - COMPOUND TO SIMPLE

In May 1903 F. W. Webb retired owing to illness and was succeeded by George Whale. For more than a year - up to August 1904, to be precise - Crewe Works continued to build 'B' class compounds and if Mr Whale had been particularly averse to the design he could certainly have cancelled some of the later orders. When they were completed, however, no more new eight-coupled engines were built while he was in charge at Crewe, but much work was done in modifying the compound coal engines, mainly in converting them to simple.

Class 'E'
The first alteration occurred very soon after he took over and before all the 'B' class had been completed. One of the earlier engines, No. 1886, was fitted with a leading radial truck in August 1904, making it into a 2-8-0. The purpose of this alteration was to reduce the overhanging weight at the front end of the engine by taking some of the weight off the leading coupled axle, so as to reduce the stress on bridges and to avoid the need for strengthening them.

Other engines were then converted in the same way and all were put to work on mineral trains between Colwick and Willesden alongside unconverted engines. In July 1905, after the work of five engines had been observed for some months, a report was made that the modification had proved satisfactory and that further conversions should be made. The axleboxes and axles from the three-cylinder compound passenger engines then being withdrawn were to be utilised for the conversions. In all, twenty-six 'B' class were converted in this way to 2-8-0s, the converted engines being designated class 'E'.

Plate 43: *Class 'E' No. 18 at an unidentified shed about 1920. It has lost its boiler stay and now has Cooke buffers.*
A. G. Ellis collection

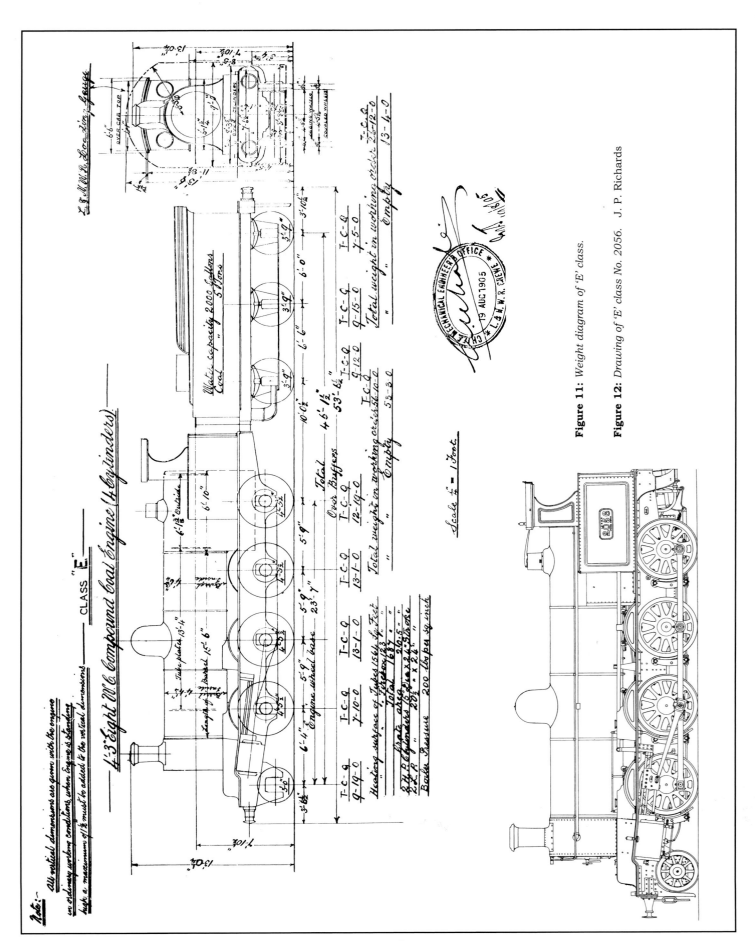

Figure 11: *Weight diagram of 'E' class.*

Figure 12: *Drawing of 'E' class No. 2056. J. P. Richards*

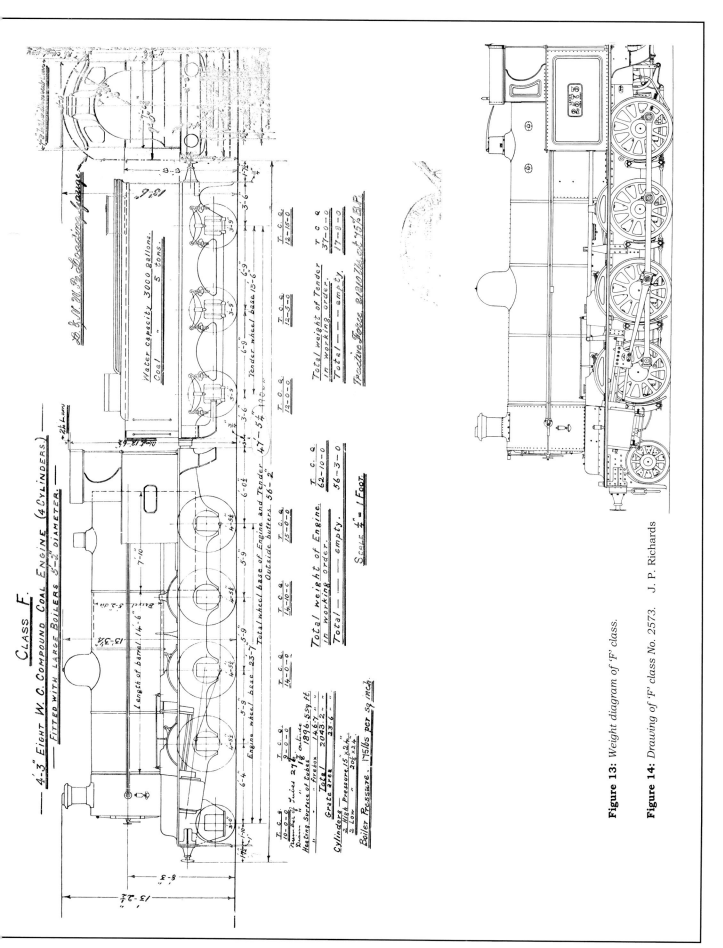

Figure 13: *Weight diagram of 'F' class.*

Figure 14: *Drawing of 'F' class No. 2573.*   J. P. Richards

43

Plate 46: *An interesting contrast in numbering styles - class 'E' No. 9608 and class 'F' No. 9614 at Wigan in early LMS days. LMS engines with the number on the tender usually had 'LMS' in a panel on the cab side but the cab side of No. 9608 seems to be plain black. Both have lost their boiler stays and No. 9608 has also acquired an oil box on the handrail. Both were with-drawn at the end of 1928.*
W. H. Whitworth

Plate 47: *No. 1273 in plain black livery and with Cooke buffers but otherwise little altered, at Hillhouse shed, Huddersfield, probably about 1920. The tender is a Webb 2500-gallon type*

P. F. Cooke

Plate 48: *The first of the 'F' class No. 1273 after completion on 16th May 1906. It has short-taper Whale buffers, a cast boiler stay and a Whale 3000-gallon tender, which was probably replaced after the photograph by a Webb 2500-gallon type, as in later photographs of this engine.* LNWR B113

Class 'F'

The conversion of 'B' class into 'E' class involved really only a very minor alteration but in May 1906 there took place the first major alteration of a 'B' class 0-8-0. No. 1273 was fitted with a leading truck in the same way as an 'E' class, becoming a 2-8-0, but in addition the boiler was replaced by a large Whale boiler, very similar to that used on the 'Precursors' and 'Experiments', in a clear attempt to produce a more powerful engine. Because of the large boiler, it also had two other differences from the 'E' class. Firstly, it had the Whale style of cab instead of the Webb type, and secondly, whereas

the 'E' class retained the 'B' class boiler, with recessed front tube plate accommodating an ash chute, the 'F' class had the ash blower, a standard fitting on all Whale and subsequent LNWR engines.

The class was designated 'F' in the 1911 scheme but only twelve engines were ever converted, ten from 'B' class and two from 'E' class. It seems, unfortunately, that no comparative trials were ever held between the 'B' class and 'F' class, to assess the effect of the large boiler. Probably, it was decided that the large boilers were better employed on 'D' class anyway, and that such trials would serve no practical purpose.

Plate 49: *Class 'F' No. 899, probably about 1920, in lined LNWR livery and with a Whale 3000-gallon tender. The short-taper buffers are mounted on wooden pads; Cooke buffers, which were longer, rendered the wooden pads unnecessary.*
W. H. Whitworth

Plate 50: *Class 'F' No. 647 at Bletchley shed about 1924. It has lost its boiler stay and now has Cooke buffers and an oil box on the handrail.* LGRP

Plate 51: *Class 'F' LMS 'No. 9614 at Wigan in late 1928. It has lost its boiler stay but has not acquired an oil box. The 2500-gallon tender is well shown. This photograph was taken on the same occasion as plate 34.* W. H. Whitworth

Class 'C'

In November 1904 the first conversion took place of an 'A' class compound to simple operation. The result was an engine identical in all major respects to the original 2524 of 1892. The front section of frame carrying the cylinders was cut off, and a new section of frame carrying two 19½in by 24in inside cylinders fitted in its place. No other changes were made, the original boiler being retained, and also, it is believed, the original boiler pressure, 175lb psi. In the 1911 scheme the conversion was designated class 'C'.

In all, fifteen 'A' class were converted in this way. The reason why such a small number was so treated is uncertain but possibly they were found to be under-boilered, because the later 'C1' class was given smaller cylinders with the same boiler, as was No. 2524 some twenty years earlier, and the 'D' class had the same cylinders with large boiler. Nevertheless, the 'C' class must have been reasonably successful as they were used on main-line work well into the 1920s.

All the conversions to 'C' class passed into the ownership of the LMS. In 1924, when through workings began between Toton and Willesden, LMS No. 8953 of Willesden shed was often used on these trains. Five of the class were converted to class 'G1' and the rest were scrapped unaltered, the last survivor being withdrawn in April 1932.

Plate 52: *Class 'C' No. 2529 poses at the north end of Crewe sorting sidings with a mixed goods train on 8th May 1905, only a few weeks after convversion. It has a 2500-gallon tender. The train is on the down independent line, which will take it through the tunnel under the north junction, either to the main line to the north or to the Manchester line. On the right is the spur to the Shrewsbury line and beyond it, out of the picture further to the right, is the Tranship Shed. On the left is the coal stack at the south end of Crewe South shed.*
LNWR A456

Plate 53: *Class 'C' No. 2538 at Willesden on 21st August 1920. The engine has survived the war still with full lining but the 2500-gallon tender is in plain black.* M. Williams collection

Plate 54: *Class 'C' 'No. 1823 taking water in a yard somewhere while working a mixed goods train. The fireman seems to have put the 'bag' in and is now on the coal attending to something. The tender is a 2500-gallon type and is lined, so has probably come from a 'B' class, while the date could be any time after about 1910.*

Plate 55: *A class 'C' or 'C1' at Balham Intermediate on the London Brighton & South Coast Railway with a mixed goods from Norwood Junction to Willesden. It carries 'target' board No. 63 in the right-hand lamp socket to identify the working.*

Class 'D'

The 'C' class had been produced by changing only the cylinders of the 'A' class compounds and retaining the original boiler but it was soon decided, possibly because it was felt that the 'C' class was under-boilered, to change the boiler also. So in further conversions the large Whale boiler as used on the 'F' class was combined with new 19½in by 24in cylinders as in the 'C' class. This produced a much more powerful engine, the 'D' class, the first engine to be so treated being No. 1866 in March 1906. Conversions continued steadily until March 1909, when 63 'D' class were in service, including the original No. 2524, which was converted in December 1906.

The 'D' class was by far the most successful goods engine the LNWR had had up to that time. Mr Whale reported that they could haul five more wagons from Colwick to Willesden with little more coal consumption and at much reduced maintenance. LNWR enginemen gave them the nickname 'Bulldogs', but they were also commonly referred to as 'Ds' from the 1905 scheme, in which all the two-cylinder simple 0-8-0s were classified 'D', and they were classified 'D' also in the 1911 scheme. All the class remained in original condition throughout the rest of the LNWR period. They were converted to class 'G1' by the LMS between July 1923 and November 1937.

Plate 56: *The first of the 'D' class No. 1866 after conversion at Crewe on 12th March 1906. It has short-taper Whale buffers but still has no rear sandbox. As there was no sandbox on the Whale tenders often fitted to these engines, they had to rely on the one sandbox on the front of the engine.*
LNWR B108

Plate 57: *Class 'D' No. 1848 at Buxton about 1910. It has a chimney with plain top and no capuchon, as was common on many Whale engines at the time, such as 'Experiments'.*
Roger Bell collection

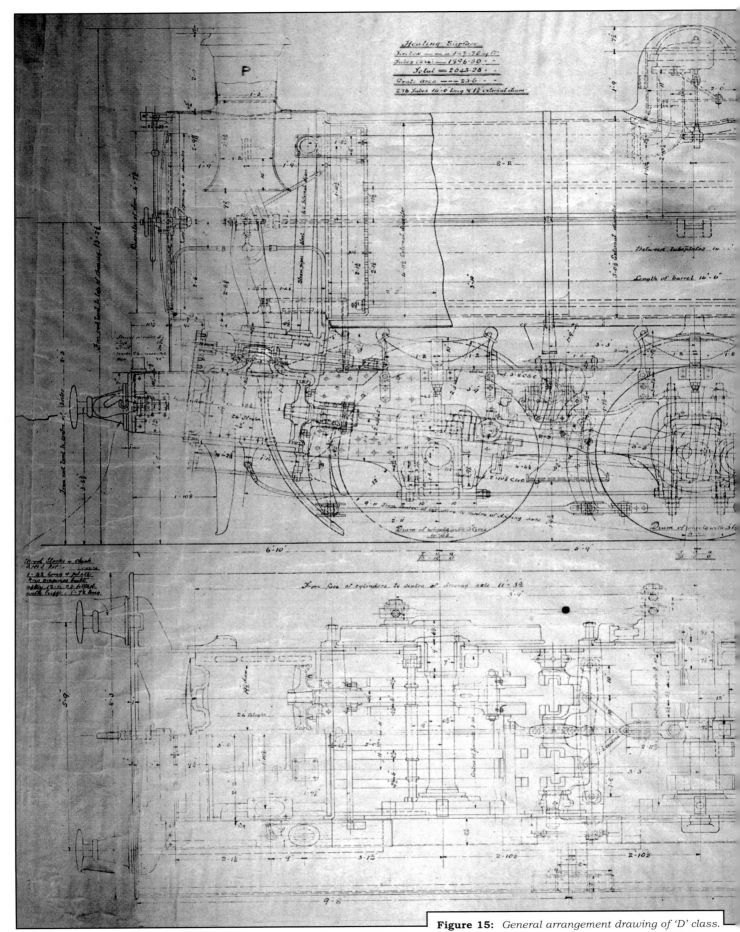

Figure 15: *General arrangement drawing of 'D' class.*

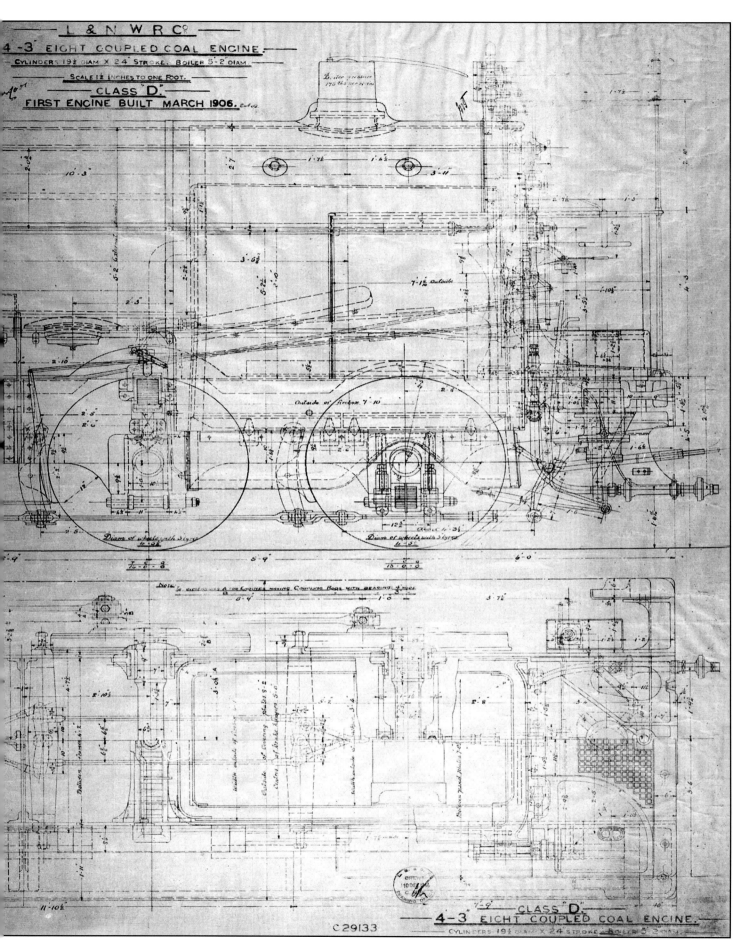

L & N W R Co

4 -3' EIGHT COUPLED COAL ENGINE.

CYLINDERS 19½ DIAM X 24 STROKE. BOILER 5-2 DIAM

SCALE 1½ INCHES TO ONE FOOT.

CLASS "D"

FIRST ENGINE BUILT MARCH 1906.

C 29133

CLASS "D"

4-3' EIGHT COUPLED COAL ENGINE.

CYLINDERS 19½ DIAM X 24 STROKE. BOILER 5-2 DIAM

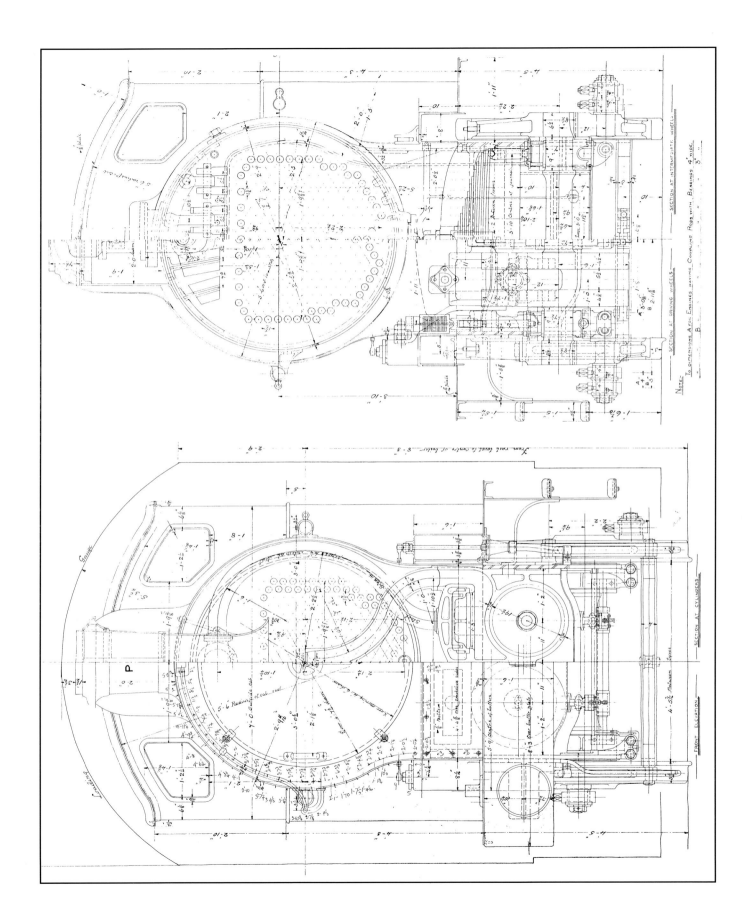

54

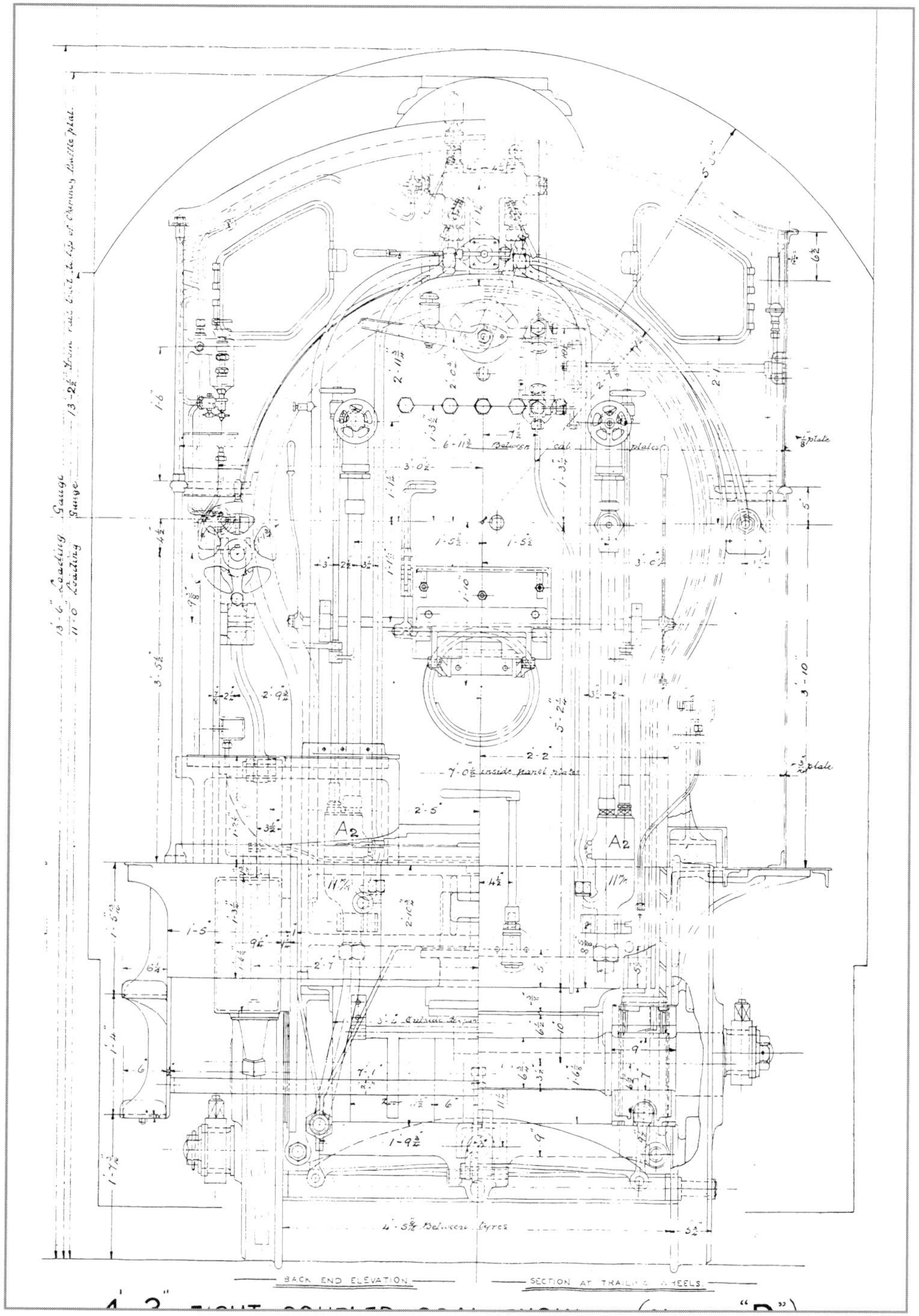

Figure 16: *Cross section drawings of 'D' class.*

Plate 58: *Cab view of 'D' class No. 1866.   LNWR B111*

Plate 59: *The most successful conversions from class 'A' were the 'Bulldogs', officially class 'D'. Here, the first of the class, No. 1866, is still virtually new, with the crew specially posed and with good coal well stacked on the tender. As the photograph was found recently in the East Midlands, it seems very likely to have been taken to record the first run of the class up the main line to London and that the location is Netherfield & Colwick, where the first 'D' class were sent to replace 'B' class on coal trains over the joint line via Northampton to London.*

Peter Lang collection

Plate 60: *Class 'D' No. 1827 at Rugby shed about 1910 in 'as built' condition.*

H. Sheddon

Plate 61 (above): *Class 'D' No. 1839 also at Rugby on the same occasion as the previous picture.* H. Sheddon

Plate 62 (right): *Class 'D' No. 1878 at Hillhouse about 1926. Its steel-plate boiler stay has been removed, and it has oil boxes on the handrail, Cooke buffers and a 2500-gallon tender.* P. F. Cooke

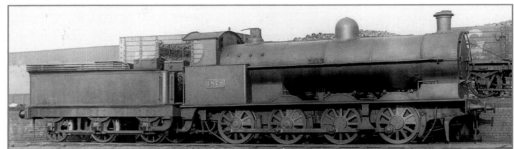

Plate 63: *A 'D', LMS No. 9039, in typical LMS condition, probably in the early 1930s. Its LNWR shed plate - '6', Bescot - is on the smokebox door in LMS style but its 'A' class origins are revealed by the rods, with flush leading crank pin and rear section fitting outside the front one. The tender is the final Cooke type introduced in 1916.*

Class 'C1'

Conversions to 'D' class eventually produced a surplus of spare 'A' class boilers in good condition and it was therefore decided to make use of them by converting the rest of the 'A' class with the original boiler but compensating for its small size by fitting smaller cylinders, 18½in by 24in. They were classified 'C1' in the 1911 scheme and were built between March 1909 and September 1912.

The original 'A' class boiler, of course, had a recessed front tubeplate and an ash chute in the base of it. No official information exists as to whether this arrangement was perpetuated in classes 'C' and 'C1', but it seems definite that it was not, as photographs in which the chute would have been visible do not show it, and so both these classes must have had the ash blower fitted in the base of the smokebox.

Perhaps it was intended originally that the 'C1' class would eventually get larger boilers but they were all withdrawn by the LMS between 1928 and 1932. Presumably, it was felt that the LMS had enough eight-coupled goods engines and that the cost of new cylinders and boilers to convert them to 'G1' class could not be justified.

Plate 64 (above): *Class 'C1' No. 2550 after completion at Crewe Works on 3rd January 1910. It has Whale short-taper buffers and a rear sandbox under the cab. The tender was the 2500-gallon type.* LNWR

Plate 65 (far left): *Front end view of No. 2550. By comparison with the original No. 2524 of 1892, the most obvious difference is that there is no ash chute, an ash-blower in the base of the smokebox being fitted instead.* LNWR

Plate 66 (left): *Cab view of No. 2550. It is interesting to compare these two views with those of No. 2524. One difference is that seats are now provided for the crew but in general, it is still a typical Webb footplate. The large lever below the firehole door controls the 'blow-off cock', which was fixed to the lower part of the firebox and was used to let water out of the boiler, either to empty it or to lower the level if it was too full, a dangerous operation if the lever stuck.* LNWR

Plate 67: *An up coal train leaving Rugby behind class 'C1' No. 1841 about 1920. The engine has a 2000-gallon tender.*

H. L. Salmon

Plate 68: *Through workings by LNWR engines between Toton and Willesden are believed to have started only in LMS days, probably in 1924. Here, class 'C1' No. 1875, its 2500-gallon tender well piled with coal, passes Leicester Midland quite soon afterwards.*

Plate 69: *The early LMS period produced all manner of variations and combinations of both livery and technical details. Here, class 'C1' No. 9001 has lost its numberplate and had its LMS number stencilled in its place. The steel plate boiler stay has been removed and Cooke buffers have been fitted. But though dirty, the 2500-gallon tender still has LNWR lining. The location is Crewe South; in the background is the carriage shed on the up side of the main line.*

Plate 70 (right): *'C1' No. 8995 with boiler stay removed, oil box on the handrail and 2000-gallon tender with LNWR lining and LMS numbers.*
W. H. Whitworth

Plate 71 (below): *Eventually a more standardised LMS appearance became established, as exemplified here in No. 8978 at Watford shed about 1930. One concession to Crewe tradition remains: it has no smokebox numberplate.*
R. Bell collection

Plate 72: *Not a 'C1' class, but for comparison a 'C' class, LMS No. 8961, probably at Crewe South in the late 1920s. As it was LNWR practice to change tenders whenever necessary, the LMS policy of putting the engine number on the tender often caused confusion. Here, however, the number on the tender is the same as that on the smokebox door.* W. H. Whitworth

Plate 73: *'C' class No. 8982 also probably in the late 1920s but in the later numbering style which the LMS eventually settled on. Apart from cosmetic differences as seen here, there was no external difference between classes 'C' and 'C1'.*

Class 'G'

After the success of the large-boilered 'D' class, Mr Whale then turned his attention to converting the four-cylinder compound 'B' class to simple 0-8-0s. Whereas the 'D' class had needed new cylinders as well as new boilers, the 'B' class conversions retained the old low-pressure cylinders, the outside high-pressure cylinders were removed, and the same large boiler as used in the 'D' class was fitted. Since the inside cylinder was 1in larger in diameter than the 'D' class, however, the boiler pressure of the 'G' class was reduced to 160lb psi compared to the 175lb of the 'D' class.

Conversion to 'G' class took place slowly, only thir-teen being converted by the end of 1909, twelve in 1910 and only seven more by 1917. So it may well be that the reason for conversion was as with the 'A' class original-ly, the need to replace some major component, such as the boilers or outside cylinders, and none were avail-able from stock. From 1917, of course, 'B' class began to be converted directly to 'G1' class.

Shortly before he retired, Mr Whale ordered sixty new 'G' class to be built. They were the first new eight-cou-pled engines to be built at Crewe since the last 'B' class was completed in 1904 and were put into traffic after C. J. Bowen Cooke took over in 1910. The new engines could easily be distinguished from the conversions,

Plate 74: *'Piano G' No. 1893, probably about 1920, with Cooke buffers and a 2500-gallon tender. It has lost its cast boiler stay.*
W. H. Whitworth

Plate 75: *LMS 'Piano G' No. 9146 about 1930, with no means of identification other than its front numberplate. It has a Cooke tender of the final type, an oil box on the handrail, Cooke buffers, a screw coupling and, most unusually, is fitted with vacu-um brakes. It has lost its cast boiler stay.*
Roger Carpenter collection

Plate 76 (above): *'Piano G' LMS No. 9069 probably in the early 1930s, with a 3000-gallon Cooke tender of the third type. The LNWR safety valves have been replaced by pop valves.*
W. H. Whitworth

Plate 77 (right): *LMS 'Piano G', No. 9090 in final LMS condition, probably in the early 1930s. It has much the same fittings as No. 9069, including pop safety valves, vacuum brake and three-piece rods, as introduced on the new 'G' class. It also has an LNWR shed plate - '9', Walsall - in the LMS position on the smoke-box door.* W. A. Camwell

Plate 78 (below): *Another view of No. 9090 at the same period.*
W. L. Good

64

since they had the same style of flat covers over the steam chests as the 'D' class, whereas the conversions retained the distinctive 'piano front' covers of the 'B' class. Originally, this shape had been determined by the need to cover the rocking arms connecting the valves of the high- and low-pressure cylinders, but in the simple engines there were no rocking levers and therefore there was nothing for the covers to cover! Of course, the covers earned the class the nickname 'piano front Gs' or 'piano Gs' or even simply 'pianos'.

The new 'G' class was built with the arrangement of sandboxes which was to be standard on all the 'Super Ds' (classes 'G1', 'G2' and 'G2A'), one on each of the leading splashers and one under the cab on either side. There was thus no need for a sandbox on the tender. The arrangement of coupling rods on the new 'Gs', three rods with the centre one fitting outside the two outer ones, was also followed on subsequent classes until jointed rods were introduced on the 'G2s'. All the new 'Gs' were turned out with new 3000-gallon Whale tenders. This was necessary as they were steam-braked and all the Whale tenders built previously were for passenger engines and so were vacuum-braked.

Plate 79: *New 'G' class No. 2653 on completion in January 1910. The arrangement of sandboxes, two on the leading splashers and one underneath the cab, became standard for all subsequent LNWR eight-coupled engines, while three-piece rods, the centre rod fitting outside the other two, were standard until the 'G2s', which had jointed rods. The new 'G' class generally had Whale tenders.*
LNWR B131

Plate 80: *New 'G' class No. 1403 at Wigan about 1912.*   A. G. Ellis collection

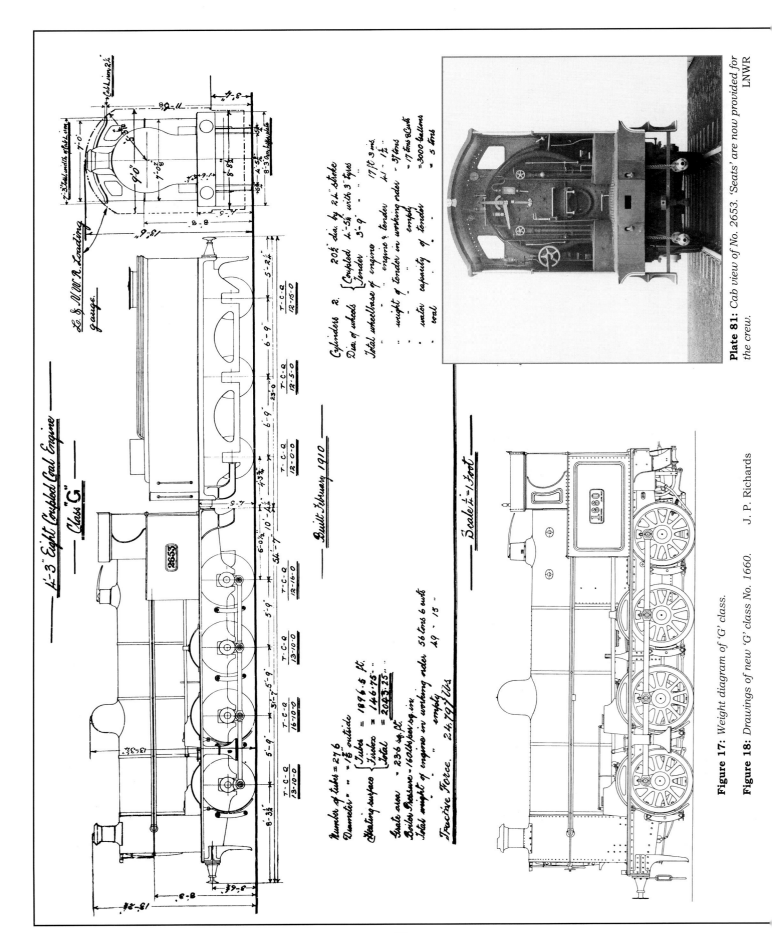

4'-3" Eight Coupled Coal Engine

Class "G"

L. & N.W.R. Loading gauge.

2653

Built February 1910

Number of tubes = 276
Diameter " = 1⅞" outside

Heating surface { Tubes = 1896.5 ft.
Firebox = 146.75 "
Total = 2043.25 "

Grate area = 23.6 sq. ft.
Boiler Pressure = 160 lbs/sq. in.
Total weight of engine in working order 56 tons 6 cwt.
empty 49 - 15 "

Tractive Force. 24,797 lbs

Cylinders 2. 20½" dia. by 24" stroke
Dia. of wheels { Coupled 4-5⅝ with 3 tyres
Tender 3-9
Total wheelbase of engine 17/0.3 ins.
" " engine & tender 41 " 1½
" weight of tender in working order = 37 tons
" " empty = 17 tons 8 cwt
" water capacity of tender = 3000 gallons
" coal = 5 tons

Scale ¼ = foot

1860

Figure 17: Weight diagram of 'G' class.

Figure 18: Drawings of new 'G' class No. 1660.   J. P. Richards

Plate 81: Cab view of No. 2653. 'Seats' are now provided for the crew.   LNWR

Plate 82: *New 'G' class No. 1606 shunting at Guide Bridge on the Great Central Railway about 1912. It now has steps on the smokebox front, to enable the top lamp socket to be reached with safety.*

Plate 83: *New 'G' class No. 9136 in early LMS condition probably in the mid 1920s. It has lost its cast boiler stay and has been fitted with vacuum brakes but still displays its early LMS power code on the cab side, '4'.*

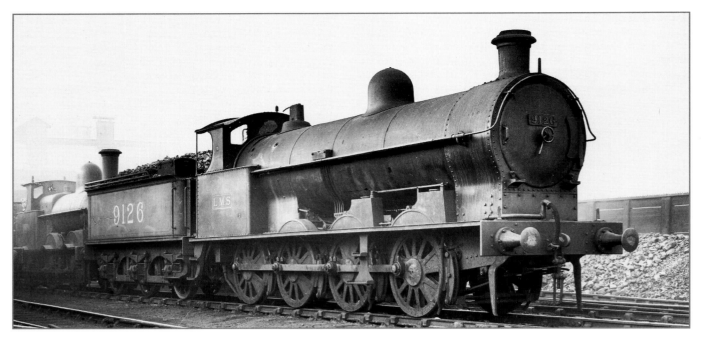

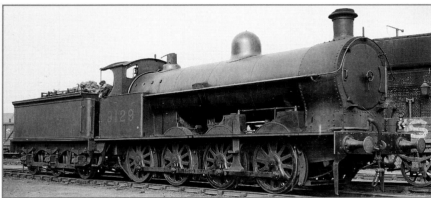

Plate 84 (above): *New 'G' LMS No. 9126 in the late 1920s. It has lost its cast boiler stay and has an oil box on the handrail and vacuum brakes. Originally in LMS power code '4', the class was soon upgraded and '5' is now displayed on the cab side.*

Plate 85 (left): *New 'G' No. 9129 at Willesden on 17th September 1932.*
R. Bell collection.

Plate 86 (below): *A new 'G' in a far from new state, No. 9127 in Crewe Works on 16th August 1936 with an LMS cast shed plate '10D', Plodder Lane. Only three 'Gs' survived in 1936 and all were converted to superheating by the end of 1937.*

Experimental Loading of Coal Trains

Early in 1910 tests were held to find the most economical size of coal wagon. Details were worked out of the number of wagons of various capacities required to carry 500 tons of coal, and of the relative train lengths and weights, empty and loaded, as follows:

500 tons of Coal
Carried in, 9, 10, 15, 20 & 30 ton wagons

Capacity Tons	Number of Wagons	Train Length (feet)	Train Weight (Tons) Unloaded	Loaded
9	62	1146	356	856
10	50	924	287	787
15	33	739	234	734
20	25	624	206	706
30	17	709	292	792

Four trips were run with the 10.10am from Nuneaton via Northampton to Sudbury Reception Sidings, a distance of 92 miles. On each trip the train was made up exclusively of wagons of one capacity only, 8-ton, 10-ton, 15-ton and 20-ton, but it conveyed the same quantity of coal, so that the number of wagons varied accordingly. The same engine was used on each trip, 'Piano G' class No. 1274 of Colwick, shed '7', recently converted from class 'B', and it was manned by the same Nuneaton men, driver, fireman and 'brakesman', and supplied with the same coal, 'sharp' from Colorton.

Details of the tests are given in *Table 1* below. The coal consumption figure makes no allowance for 'lighting up', the length of the train is from front engine buffer to rear van buffer, and in calculating total delays only dead stops were counted, except in the case of the 10-ton train which was allowed two minutes each for slacks at Bletchley and Wolverton.

The report concluded that the trials had shown the superiority of the larger wagon. With the 8-ton and 10-ton wagons, the types in most general use, the coal consumption was 48.6 per cent and 43.2 per cent greater respectively than with the 20-ton wagons, and the evaporation of water 60 per cent and 47 per cent greater. In addition, the length of the respective trains was 73 per cent and 62 per cent greater. All these were disadvantages, as the greater coal and water consumption produced greater working expenses, and the longer trains needed more time 'getting through the blocks', reducing the number of trains that could be worked in a given time, and they also needed longer sidings to back into where necessary.

The average speed for the three trains was 18.5mph from Nuneaton to Rugby No. 5 and 19mph from Rugby No. 1 to Roade Junction, but thereafter speeds varied considerably owing to signal and other checks. With the 20-ton train speed never exceeded 30mph, whereas with the 10-ton and 15-ton trains a speed of 34mph was attained and 30mph was maintained for considerable periods. The reason for this was that the 20-ton wagons, being light in total weight and fitted with oil axle boxes throughout, could be accelerated quickly, but the driver could not risk running at too high a speed, because the oil axleboxes had a lower coefficient of friction than the grease boxes, and so had a lower retardation effect; as there were 'no continuous brakes on any North Western coal trains', he had to rely entirely on his engine brakes and the brakesman's van brakes for pulling up his train.

The 15-ton train had 30 wagons with oil boxes out of 34, but the train had stood all night in a sharp frost, which had solidified the oil, and so the coefficient of friction was higher, until the heat generated by running had liquefied the oil again.

In each of the four trains all the wagons were full, in the sense that they could not hold any more coal. However, while the loading figures showed that the 10-ton and 15-ton wagons were loaded to only 85 and 87 per cent of their registered capacities, the 8-ton and 20-ton wagons were loaded to 94 and 96 per cent of their capacities respectively. Even then the tare of the average 20-ton wagon was 42 per cent of the average load, whereas for the 8-ton wagon it was 68 per cent. So in this respect too it was more economical to carry coal in the larger wagon.

In hauling the 20-ton wagon train the coal consumed by the engine was only about 67 per cent of that required for the 8-ton wagon train. Thus the engine was much more efficient hauling the 20-ton wagon train. But the figures for water consumption in relation to coal hauled show that the boiler was more efficient when hauling the 15-ton train and least efficient with the 20-ton train. This may have been merely one of those inconsistencies which

Table 1

Date: 1910	4th Jan			11th Jan			13th Jan			6th Jan		
Capacity of wagons	8 tons			10 tons			15 tons			20 tons		
No. of wagons	58			52			34			23		
Type of axle box	grease			grease			30 oil/4 grease			oil		
Average load of wagons	7	11	0	8	11	1	13	1	2	19	4	0
Average tare of wagon	5	5	0	5	5	3	7	6	2	8	2	2
Total weight of coal hauled	442	13	0	445	4	0	444	12	0	441	16	0
Total tare	314	12	0	274	19	3	249	4	1	186	19	1
Dynamometer car	34	14	0	34	14	0	34	14	0	34	14	0
Break van	20	8	0	20	8	0	19	18	0	19	13	0
Total weight hauled	812	6	0	775	5	3	748	8	1	683	2	1
Weight of coal burnt by engine	2	15	0	2	13	3	2	3	3	1	17	0
Coal consumption lb per mile	67.6			64.6			52.4			45.0		
Gallons of water evaporated	5061			4635			4042			3155		
Lb of water per lb of coal	8.20			7.80			8.30			7.61		
Lb of coal per ton mile	.082			.083			.07			.065		
Lb of coal per ton hauled per mile	.151			.145			.118			.101		
Total time on journey	*			7h 25m			6h 8m			5h 27m		
Total delays	*			1h 40m			1h 15m			50m		
Average speed deducting delays	*			16mph			18.8mph			20mph		
Weather conditions	*			dull/damp			bright/clear			dull/damp		

All weights are tons, hundredweights and quarters
*no details available

Plate 87: 'Piano G' class No. 1274 posed on the up slow line somewhere south of Tring with a Nuneaton-Willesden test train consisting of 52 10-ton wagons on 11th January 1910. The driver is near the front of the engine, the fireman on the footplate, four officials from the dynamometer car are by the cab, and another, with bowler hat, is looking out of the dynamometer car. Possibly the latter is the author of the report on the trials. The engine was converted from class 'B' in the previous September.   LNWR A533

occur in test data from time to time. The results for coal consumption in relation to coal hauled show that the engine was slightly more efficient when hauling the load in 8-ton wagons than in 10-ton wagons but this may be explained by the fact that the time on the journey was about 1½ hours longer with the 10-ton train.

The drawbar pull varied directly with the load; on passing Middleton, where very nearly the heaviest work of the trip was being done, the horsepower developed at the engine drawbar was 482 for the 20-ton train, 580 for the 15-ton train and 682 for the 10-ton train. With the 15-ton train stops were made at Stoke Hammond and Leighton due to a hot axle on a privately owned wagon with grease axleboxes.

A final comment was that the engine always seemed to get away well and there was very little slipping. Despite the findings of the report, and the suitability of the London coal traffic for larger wagons, little seems to have been done to adopt them. Probably other factors, such as the conditions in collieries and in customers' sidings, and a reluctance to invest more capital militated against them.

War Service

During the Great War twenty-six of the new 'G' class were loaned to the Government and sent to France for service with the Railway Operating Division. They were prepared at Crewe Works and a memo from H. P. M. Beames to the shops lists some of them by number and then states: 'The work for the above engines must have preference to any other work to enable us to despatch the engines to their destination as early as possible.' Some accounts say that they were given Webb tenders of the final 2500-gallon type, like the '17in Coal Engine' 0-6-0s sent to France, but that is not so, and they in fact retained their steel-framed Whale tenders. This is proved both by photographs and by records of the tender numbers. They were shipped to France from Portsmouth between March and April 1917 and worked mainly in the Calais-Hazebrouk area on supply trains for the Western Front. They were returned to England by the Calais-Richborough train ferry between April and August 1919. While in France, the letters 'ROD' and their LNWR numbers were painted on the tender sides in large insignia. Possibly some had to be renum-

Plate 88: *Three 'G' class, the nearest No. 1591, in a workshop somewhere in northern France, possibly at St Etienne, during the Great War.*

Table 2

Engine	Tender	Route	Date sent	Date returned	Allocation August 1921
1354	261	Bushbury	4.3.17	14.6.19	Shrewsbury (30)
1540	48	and	4.3.17	17.5.19	Widnes (35W)
1609	695	Portsmouth	4.3.17	23.7.19	Swansea (33)
1699	686	"	4.3.17	20.8.19	Rugby (8)
1578	759	Leamington	10.3.17	9.7.19	Ashford Works
2032	1376	and	10.3.17	17.4.19	Buxton (16B)
2654	705	Portsmouth	10.3.17	14.6.19	Abergavenny (31)
2660	786	"	10.3.17	17.4.19	Buxton (16B)
1629	795	"	14.3.17	15.8.19	Ashford Works
1637	47	"	14.3.17	17.5.19	Widnes (35W)
1776	602	"	14.3.17	15.8.19	Swansea (33)
2658	844	"	14.3.17	12.5.19	Bescot (6)
1570	1479	"	4.4.17	20.8.19	Speke Junction (35)
1735	1535	"	4.4.17	13.5.19	Widnes (35W)
1700	661	"	7.5.17	19.6.19	Ashford Works
1774	237	"	7.5.17	12.5.19	Ashford Works
1462	790	"	15.5.17	17.7.19	Springs Branch (25)
2014	192	"	15.5.17	21.7.19	Swansea (33)
2656	952	"	1.5.17	23.7.19	Abergavenny (31)
1385	902	"	1.5.17	9.6.19	Shrewsbury (30)
1690	832	"	1.5.17	9.6.19	Stockport (16S)
1727	1076	"	1.5.17	23.7.19	Widnes (35W)
1322	1051	"	1.5.17	9.7.19	Edge Hill (26)
1591	68	"	1.5.17	17.7.19	Ashford Works
1634	783	"	1.5.17	17.7.19	Edge Hill (26)
1639	121	"	6.6.17	21.7.19	Edge Hill (26)

bered to avoid clashing with the numbers of other 'ROD' engines such as Robinson 2-8-0s.

Details of the 'G' class sent to France are given in *Table 2*. No. 1639 was sent in May 1919 but was returned to Crewe for repairs and eventually went in June. No. 2655 was also sent to France but returned to Crewe for repairs and then remained in England on the LNWR. No. 1634 was returned to Crewe for repair in May 1918, returning to France in June, and No. 1700 returned for repairs in January 1919, returning to France in February. The reason why some engines were at Ashford Works is uncertain but possibly they were sent there for repair because Crewe Works was unable to cope with the backlog of repair work after the war.

Class 'G' to class 'G1'

Except for the first of the new 'G' class, No. 2653, which became the first of the 'G1' class in January 1912, all of the 'G' class remained in original condition throughout LNWR days and were converted to class 'G1' by the LMS between May 1924 and the end of 1937.

Plate 89: *A compound and a simple join forces to take a train of coal empties out of London to the Midlands.*
D. J. Patrick collection

Chapter Three
C. J. BOWEN COOKE and H. P. M. BEAMES
- THE SUPERHEATER ERA

When C. J. Bowen Cooke took over from George Whale in 1910, sixty new 'G' class were already on order from Crewe Works and so he had no need to concern himself immediately with heavy goods engines. His first priority was the trial of superheating on the 'George the Fifth' and 'Queen Mary' class 4-4-0s. When its advantages had been proved and more 'George the Fifths' ordered, he turned his attention to applying superheating to the 0-8-0s.

Class 'G1'

In the same way that the 'George the Fifths' were a superheated version of the 'Precursors', so were the new 0-8-0s a superheated version of the 'G' class. In fact, they were identical except for the alterations connected with superheating: the boiler with Schmidt superheater, piston-valve cylinders instead of slide-

valve, superheater damper, mechanical lubricator and so on. In appearance, they differed mainly because the smokebox was extended to accommodate the superheater header, again as in the 'Georges'.

A batch of thirty was ordered immediately and the first was completed in February 1912. In the previous month the first of the new 'G' class, No. 2653, had been taken into Crewe Works and fitted with a boiler having a Schmidt superheater. Since the thirty 'G1s' were already being built, this conversion could hardly have been experimental but was perhaps simply to check in some way that the concept was well founded before all the new 'G1s' were built.

The boiler for this conversion seems to have been the first of the thirty boilers for the 'G1' class. This supposition is based on the fact that the last of the thirty 'G1s' was delayed 'awaiting equipment', which probably

Plate 90: *Class 'G' No. 2653 after conversion to superheating and becoming the first class 'G1' superheated 0-8-0.*

Plate 91: *Official photograph of No. 1384, strictly the second 'G1' to be built, on completion in February 1912. The tender is the second Bowen Cooke type, introduced on* Prince of Wales.
LNWR

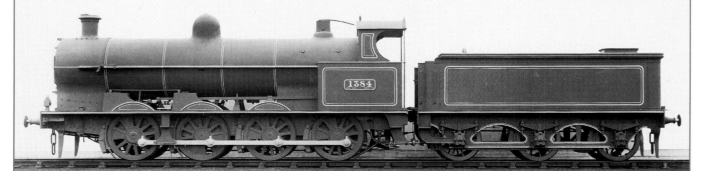

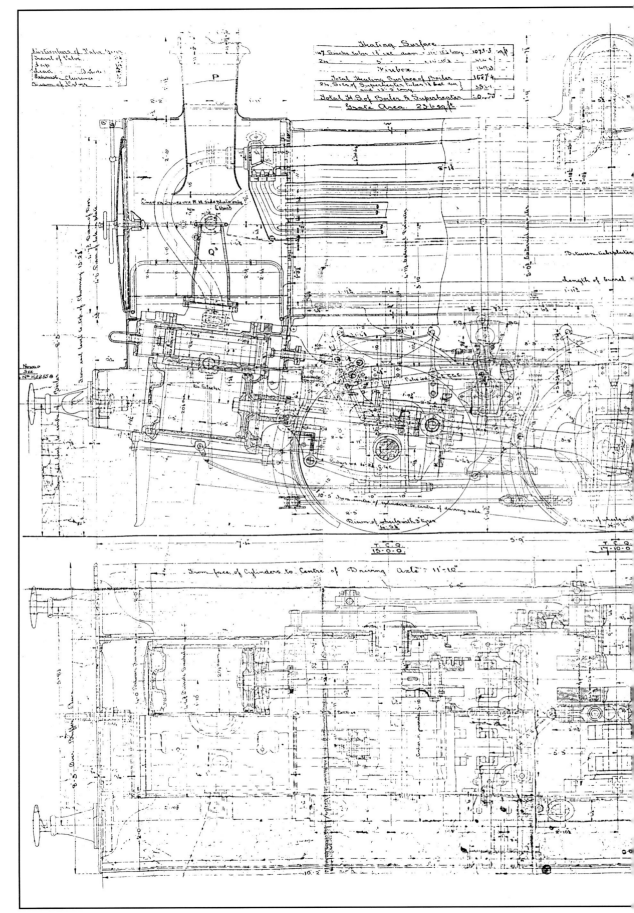

Figure 19: *General arrangement drawing of class 'G1'.*

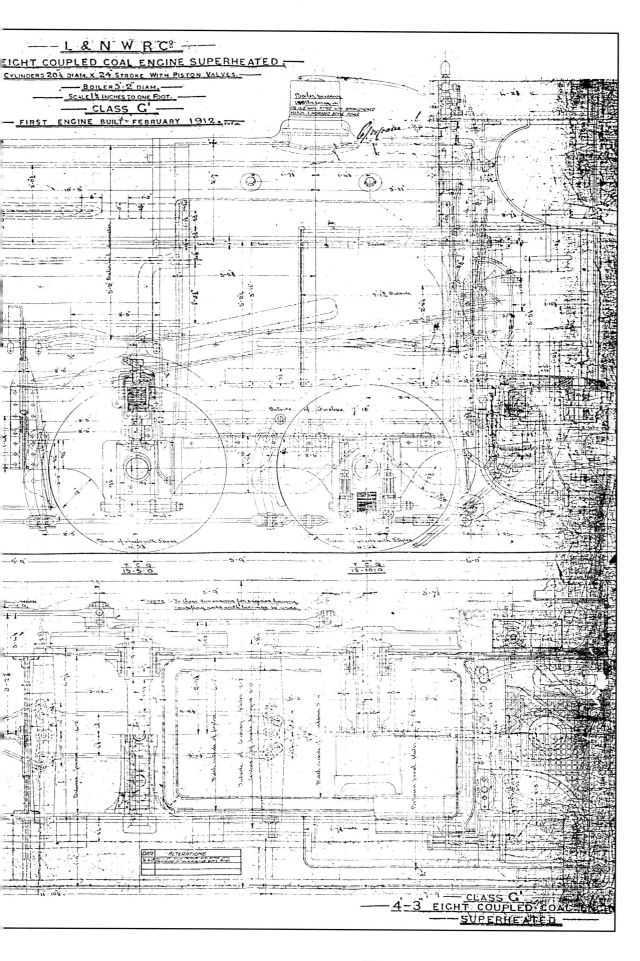

L & N W R Cº

EIGHT COUPLED COAL ENGINE SUPERHEATED.

CYLINDERS 20½ DIAM. X 24 STROKE WITH PISTON VALVES.

BOILER 5′.2″ DIAM.

SCALE 1½ INCHES TO ONE FOOT.

CLASS G′

FIRST ENGINE BUILT FEBRUARY 1912.

CLASS G′
4′-3″ EIGHT COUPLED COAL ENGINE
SUPERHEATED

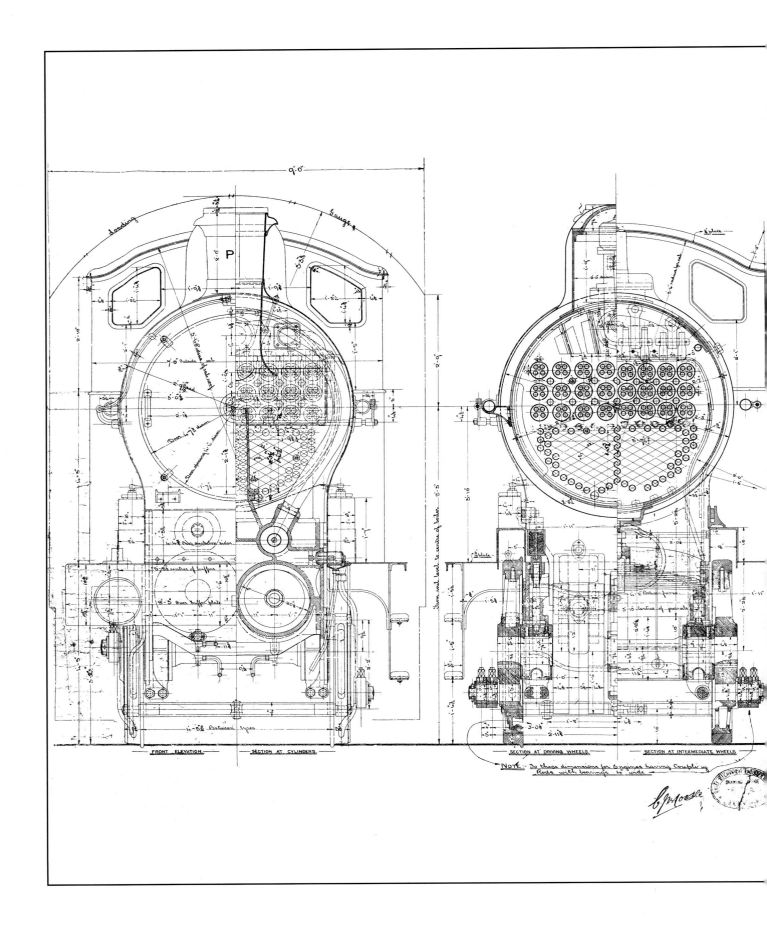

FRONT ELEVATION   SECTION AT CYLINDERS   SECTION AT DRIVING WHEELS   SECTION AT INTERMEDIATE WHEELS

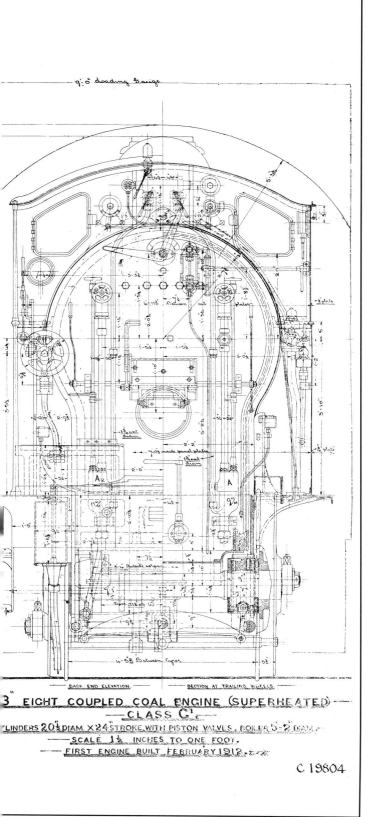

9'-0 loading gauge.

BACK END ELEVATION.   SECTION AT TRAILING WHEELS.

3" EIGHT COUPLED COAL ENGINE (SUPERHEATED)
CLASS G1.
CYLINDERS 20½ DIAM. X 24 STROKE, WITH PISTON VALVES, BOILER 5-2 DIAM.
SCALE 1½ INCHES TO ONE FOOT.
FIRST ENGINE BUILT FEBRUARY 1912.

C 19804

Figure 20: *Cross-sectional drawings of class 'G1'.*

Plate 92: *Cab view of No. 1384.*

Plate 93: *Class 'G1' No. 1192 in plain wartime black but with a lined Whale tender, heading north past Hatch End with a train of coal empties about 1920. The leading wagon is lettered 'East Cannock'.*

F. R. Hebron

Plate 94: *'G1' class No. 2246, built in September 1913, with the new style of Cooke tender introduced on the production 'Claughtons' earlier that year. It is standing on the up slow line at Stockport, probably waiting for the road into Edgeley yard, and is in typical pre-war condition except that the cylinder lubricator between the splashers seems to have some unusually complicated pipework.*

meant that no boiler was immediately available for it, because the first boiler of the thirty had gone on No. 2653. Whatever the truth of this, No. 2653 was put into traffic in January 1912. Unlike the production batch, it retained its original slide-valve cylinders, as happened later in the case of some engines of earlier eight-coupled classes when converted to superheating.

The new 0-8-0 enjoyed the same instant success as the 'Georges'. Further orders were placed and by the outbreak of the Great War one hundred new 'G1s' had been built. In 1915 two more orders were placed, E269 and E270, each for ten engines, but because much of the capacity of the works was diverted to war production, they were not completed. The orders were then placed with Beyer Peacock of Manchester and drawings and even some parts were sent there from Crewe (ten 'Prince of Wales' class were built by the North British Locomotive Company at the same period). For some reason, however, quite possibly again the pressure of war work, Beyer Peacock did not complete them and the order was eventually cancelled. In late 1917 the orders were reissued at Crewe and the engines were finally built. They had motion numbers 5277 to 5296, which were presumably the numbers allotted to the original orders.

When first built the 'G1s' had three-link couplings

and steam brakes for the engine only, but the 1914 and subsequent batches were built with vacuum brakes and screw couplings, to enable them to work passenger trains if necessary. Earlier engines were then similarly equipped, but over some years, and when this was done, the engine brakes were converted from steam to vacuum, following the practice with passenger engines which had started in 1913.

In the early years, they were generally coupled to Cooke tenders of whichever type was being built at the time: the type with the single coal-rail introduced on *George the Fifth*; the double-rail type introduced on *Prince of Wales*; or the flared coping type introduced on the production 'Claughtons'. Except for these distinguishing features, all these three 'types' were, in fact, identical and all could be fitted to the 'G1s', as could the larger Cooke tender with square-end frames that came later. The one restricting factor was that an engine with steam brakes had to have a tender with linkage for coupling to the engine brake rigging, and similarly with vacuum-braked engines. So the 'G1s' could be matched with any type of Whale or Cooke tender, and generally were, though some even had wooden-framed Webb tenders at times.

In general, the 'G1' class remained unaltered in appearance throughout LNWR days but one minor modification took place in 1918 when the last thirty were being built to orders E281-3. On 8th June H. P. M. Beames issued a memo to all foremen that in future 'all 4ft 3in superheater goods engines' would be turned out without smokebox damper gear and that any work in hand need not be completed except in those cases in which a 'very slight amount' would finish the engine. Then on 12th October he issued a further memo to the effect that thereafter no more engines, either new or converted, would be fitted with superheater damper gear. Presumably, it had been found to be unnecessary.

By the end of 1918 the total of 'G1s' built new had reached 170. No more new engines of the class were ever built but already the first conversions had been made from other classes, class 'B' No. 500 being converted in June 1917 and class 'E' Nos. 1884 and 1885 in August. Conversion to class 'G1' then continued steadily, firstly directly from the surviving Webb compounds. By the end of 1922 the total number of class 'G1' was 235. Conversion continued unchanged into LMS days, classes 'C', 'D' and 'G' being dealt with until eventually the total number of engines either built or converted to class 'G1' reached 449. All these were never in service at the same time, as by the time all the conversions had been made, five others had already been converted to class 'G2A'.

'Super D'

Since the 'G1' class was the first LNWR superheated class of 0-8-0 and was nothing more than a 'G' class with superheater and associated modifications, it may seem surprising that the nickname 'Super D', meaning 'Superheated D' class, was applied to it by LNWR enginemen, rather than 'Super G' or something similar. The precise derivation of the term is obscure but it seems to have had its origin in the classification scheme which was drawn up for goods engines about 1905:

5ft 4-cylinder compound 4-6-0 classified:	4-cylinder 'A'
4ft 3in 4-cylinder compound 0-8-0 classified:	4-cylinder 'B'
4ft 3in Coal Engine 0-6-0 classified:	Coal Engine 'C'
4ft 3in 2-cylinder simple 0-8-0 classified:	Coal Engine 'D'

The origins of this scheme are now unclear though it may have been devised by the Traffic Department. Also unclear is how the three-cylinder compound 0-8-0s were classified but possibly they were included in class

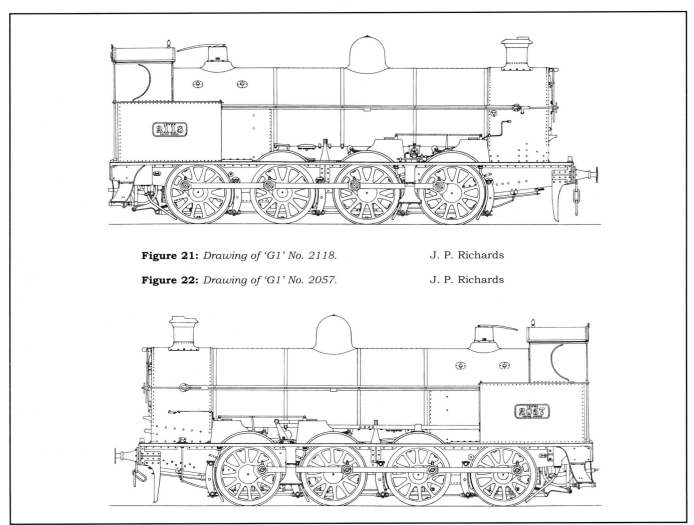

Figure 21: *Drawing of 'G1' No. 2118.*　　　　J. P. Richards

Figure 22: *Drawing of 'G1' No. 2057.*　　　　J. P. Richards

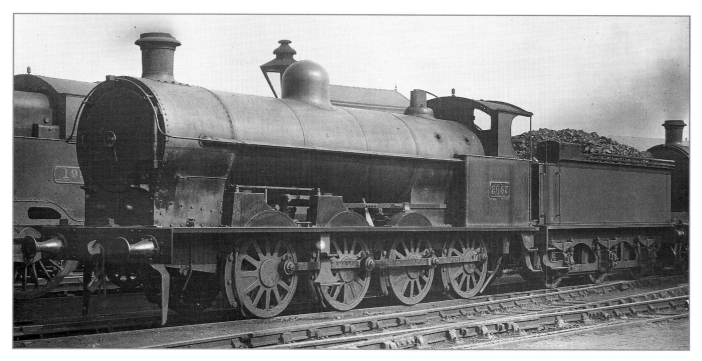

Plate 95: *Class 'G1' No. 2057, shortly after its conversion from class 'B' in December 1921, coupled to a Whale tender. It has direct action (the reversing rod is higher to the left of the driving splasher than to the right of it) but still retains the cast boiler stay. It has lost its compound wheels and rods and instead has new wheels with flush axle ends and three-piece rods.*

Plate 96: *'G1' class No. 644, which was converted from class 'B' in January 1924, coupled to a Cooke tender. It too has three-piece side rods but only the first two axles have flush ends. There is a Ramsbottom lubricator between the leading splashers and an oil box on the handrail.*

'B'. However that may be, the classification 'D' at this time referred to the two-cylinder simple 0-8-0s which became class 'C' in the 1911 scheme, and when the large-boilered version appeared in 1906 (class 'D' in the 1911 scheme) that too seems to have been referred to as 'D'. In other words, the term 'D' was not derived from the class designated 'D' in the 1911 scheme but from the 1905 scheme in which any simple 0-8-0 was described as a 'D'.

Thus the term 'D' referring to any simple 0-8-0 was already well established when the different varieties came later (the 'C1' in 1909 and the 'G' in 1910). There was no real need for enginemen to distinguish between these different classes and so they simply continued to refer to them all as 'D' class, even after the 1911 scheme had classified them as 'C', 'C1', 'D' and 'G'. In any case, the latter scheme seems to have been introduced by the Locomotive Department to identify the various classes on official drawings and documents in the works but was not in daily use by enginemen or even by the men in the shops at Crewe, who invariably referred to them all as 'four foot threes', after the diameter of the driving wheels.

At some stage these 'D' classes were further subdivided, according to the following note by C. Williams:

'D' classes		Engine No.
'D'	18½ cylinders	1835
'D1'	19½ cylinders	1872
'D2'	20½ cylinders	1774, 2251, 1900
'D3'	20½ cylinders	2374

The building dates of these engines were as follows: No. 1835 was converted from class 'A' to class 'C1' in August 1912; No. 1872 from class 'A' to 'D' in February 1907; No. 1774 was a new 'G' built in August 1910; No. 2251 was converted from 'B' to 'G' in June 1908; No. 1900 from 'B' to 'G' in November 1906; and No. 2374 was built new as a 'G1' in November 1912. So it is possible that this scheme was drawn up in late 1912, but there is in fact no information as to when it was devised, by which department and for what purpose, and indeed whether it was ever used.

In any case, none of these classification systems seems to have been used by the Traffic Department in its *Appendix to the Working Timetable*. An edition early in 1916, for example, introduced a new power classification scheme, using descriptions of the classes to

Plate 97: *Class 'G1' No. 2655. The date is probably about 1917, as it has the power classification number - (1) - painted on the frames just behind the lifeguard, a system introduced about 1916 (see inset right). It seems to have been into Crewe Works recently for repair - the paintwork has been touched up but the wheels have been painted completely. The tender is the second Cooke type with 'double bar' or 'double bead' top.*
A. G. Ellis collection

identify them (see *Appendix Four*). Engines were grouped according to haulage capacity and allocated to one of six power classes, the most powerful being numbered 1 and the least 6. The number was painted on the frames of the engine over the lifeguard. Maximum loads were then laid down for each power class over the various sections of line.

The descriptions of certain classes in this system are puzzling. For instance, class 1 comprised '20½in D or superheater goods'. The former presumably refers to 'G' class in the 1911 scheme, since the 'D' class proper had 18½in cylinders. The system also refers to '19½in large boiler', which presumably means class 'D', though the latter had 18½in cylinders, to '19½in small boiler', presumably class 'C', and to '18½in small boiler', class 'C1'. In the April 1916 *Appendix* the 0-8-2 tanks were added to class 1

Despite all these difficulties, the term 'D' is clearly used here to denote what was class 'G' in the 1911 scheme. It thus seems that the term was already well established among LNWR enginemen when the first superheated engines came into use and so they simply became known as 'D Superheater' or 'Superheated D' class. This was naturally shortened in everyday speech to 'Super D', a name which was in common use throughout the whole period the engines were in service. Even in BR days enginemen not only used the term regularly but commonly shortened it still further and referred to any of the superheated 0-8-0s as a 'D'.

The 'G1' Class in Service

The finest hour of the 'G1' class was not in BR or even LMS days but probably soon after they were introduced, working the 'Jellicoe Specials' during the Great War. These were 40-wagon trains of coal from South Wales to Grangemouth for the Fleet at Scapa Flow. They were hauled from Abergavenny to Chester by the Great Western, mainly by '2800' class when sufficient of them were available, then over Shap to Carlisle by the LNWR and finally by the Caledonian Railway. This traffic continued every day throughout the war from 1914 to 1919. For much of the time fifteen trains per day were scheduled and run, and often as many as four extras. It seems that only about half of these went north over Shap and the rest went by other routes but probably most of the empties returned over Shap. The demands which this traffic, in addition to all the other wartime traffic, put on the Locomotive Department were of course considerable. For many trains no 'Super Ds' were available and they were hauled by earlier eight-coupled engines, by '19in Goods' 4-6-0s and even by double-headed combinations of older Webb engines. But eventually a number of 0-8-0s were specially kept for this work at Chester and Carlisle and carried a letter 'A' on the cabside, denoting they were reserved for Admiralty traffic, Nos. 1107 and 1435 being two of them. They were the ideal engine for working such trains over the northern hills and no doubt there were many stirring occasions for the eyes and ears of the enthusiasts of the day.

A 'G1' on Test

It was not until after the end of the Great War that a 'G1' worked north of Carlisle. The occasion was a test run at the request of the Caledonian Railway, which was interested in comparing its performance against that of an 'ROD' 2-8-0. At the time, the government was trying hard to sell its unwanted 'RODs' to the railway companies and the Caledonian had recently obtained 50 of them on loan. The reason for the trials was clearly

Plate 98: *'G1' No. 1121 at Carlisle Upperby shed probably quite soon after completion in February 1918. A number of 'G1s' in good condition were reserved for use on the Admiralty coal traffic between South Wales and Grangemouth and carried an 'A' on the cabside to indicate that they were not to be used for other traffic. Vacuum brake is fitted.*

Plate 99: *An unidentified 'G1' taking water on the up slow at Castlethorpe troughs about 1919. The engine is plain black but the tender is still lined. Except for the four wagons at the front and one or two vans at the end, the train consists mainly of loaded coal wagons.*

Leslie J. Thompson

to help the Caledonian to evaluate its design. The story goes that William Pickersgill, the Caledonian locomotive superintendent, had sought Crewe's opinion of the 'ROD' and that this led to the LNWR lending the 'G1' so that the Caledonian could discredit the 2-8-0.

However that may be, there was certainly a proposal at the time that the Caledonian should use eight-coupled engines generally for main-line work, most probably 'RODs'. In fact, it already had eight 0-8-0s of the '600' class, introduced by McIntosh in 1901. They were roughly comparable to an LNWR 'D' class, with boilers about the same size, but higher tractive effort. They had been built to haul 30-ton wagons of coal fitted with Westinghouse brakes but their use seems to have been confined to coal trains in Fife. Pickersgill's response to the proposal was that it was pointless to use eight-coupled engines unless sidings were lengthened to take longer trains, and when the civil engineer reported the cost of acquiring land for that purpose, the proposal was dropped.

About a year later, incidentally, the Caledonian's neighbour, the North British Railway, was also interested in introducing eight-coupled goods engines, to reduce operating costs by working larger trains than its 0-6-0s were capable of. In January 1921 Great Western '2800' class 2-8-0 No. 2804 was tried on Glenfarg Bank and in August 1921 North Eastern Railway 'T3' class 0-8-0 No. 903 was tried also. Neither on the Caledonian nor on the North British, however, did any change in locomotive policy occur as a result of the trials, perhaps because the Grouping took place shortly afterwards.

The main purpose of the comparative trials of the 'ROD' and 'G1' seems to have been to measure the maximum effort each engine was capable of making in pulling heavy loads up adverse gradients. Unlike most trials, no attempt was made to achieve economical working, and indeed no measurements at all seem to have been taken of coal and water consumption. The engines were set to work loads of almost 900 tons up gradients of 1 in 143 and steeper on the Caledonian main line south of Motherwell. By comparison, in 1915,

when train loads were raised to the maximum so as to take the greatly increased traffic of wartime, the load limit on the LNWR main line from Stafford to Tring, a far easier route than the Caledonian main line, was 675 tons, and even from Tring to Willesden, largely downhill, only 825 tons was allowed.

After stopping and restarting the train twice to measure starting pull, both engines were then driven all-out up the gradients towards Law Junction until they were 'brought to a stand', in other words, 'stalled'. Few, if any, other trials in British locomotive history have required an engine to be worked at maximum effort until it stalled. Details of the experimental trips were contained in a report, stamped 'Chief Mechanical Engineer's Dept, L&NWR, Crewe' and dated 29th January 1920, and are reproduced in *Tables 3* and *4*.

The test run of the LNWR 0-8-0 took place between Motherwell and Carlisle over Beattock Summit on Sunday 18th January 1920. 'G1' class No. 2421 worked a train of almost 893 tons, including the LNWR dynamometer car, and was in the charge of driver J. McKail and fireman N. Bell of Upperby shed, Carlisle, and of a Caledonian driver as pilotman. Caledonian officers present were W. Drummond, chief locomotive inspector, J. Menzies, chief mechanical inspector, Messrs Moodie and Hunt from St Rollox Works drawing office, and a traffic inspector. From Crewe Works came the works manager, W. Dick, and the senior locomotive draughtsman, T. E. Sackfield, while also present was Robert Turnbull, superintendent of the line, and Mr Ford.

The train started from Mossend, 1½ miles north of Motherwell, just before 11.30am, and shortly after passing through Motherwell and on to the main line from Glasgow, it was stopped and re-started twice for test purposes, firstly on a gradient of 1 in 143 and secondly on 1 in 116. On the second re-start at the south end of Motherwell a maximum drawbar pull of 16½ tons was recorded. From here the line runs perfectly straight for four miles of rising gradients of 1 in 116, 1 in 137 and 1 in 102. Accelerating its train up these gradients, the

Plate 100 (right): *The only one known photograph of a 'G1' working as an 0-6-2, presumably as an experiment to enable it to negotiate sharp curves or steep humps. Presumably too, the flangeless intermediate wheels have been replaced with a flanged pair. The effect must have been to reduce haulage capacity by roughly 25 per cent, to the level of a '17in Coal Engine'. The experiment seems to have been short-lived as nothing is known of it.*

Plate 101 (below): *While most 'G1s' may have spent their time trundling along main lines on long goods train or working in yards, some occasionally visited more salubrious surroundings. Here, No. 2343 sits in Euston station, probably on empty stock working, on 30th July 1921.*
                                                D. J. Patrick collection

engine took 23¾ minutes to pass Wishaw South, a distance of only 2½ miles, by which time it was travelling at 8½ mph. As more of the train came on to the 1 in 102 speed dropped and 19½ minutes later the engine stalled some 300 yards beyond the end of the straight section, on a curve of about 32 chains radius.

The sight and sound of the engine working up to this point must have presented a spectacle that was impressive in the extreme. In full forward gear and with full regulator, its huge train strung out behind it, it was travelling at less than walking pace, each exhaust beat not only being loud but well spaced from the next, and this continued for almost 20 minutes, until finally the pressure of steam inside one of the cylinders was insufficient to move the piston to the end of its stroke. Once

the engine had stalled, the steam in the cylinder would condense and the temperature fall, so that there was no chance of restarting unaided.

When the engine stalled, a maximum drawbar pull of 16½ tons was recorded again. This high figure was probably due to the weight of the train as it pulled back on the engine. The other pulls of 16½ tons were recorded on starting, when the effect of hauling on a loose-coupled train was probably similar. At this point the official report notes that the LNWR engine had travelled 120 yards further up the incline than the GCR engine 'before being brought to rest'. A banking engine then helped the train through Garriongill Junction as far as the south end of Law Junction, where it came off.

Dynamometer recording started again from Law

Table 3

Experimental Trips hauling Mixed Goods Trains between Glasgow (Mossend) and Carlisle (Kingmoor)

First Trip GCR 'MM' 2-8-0 Locomotive No. 2078 on 9th November 1919

Second Trip LNWR 'G1' class 0-8-0 Locomotive No. 2421 on 18th January 1920

Recorded miles from GCR	Recorded miles from LNWR	Station	Passing Time GCR (Start)	Passing Time LNWR (Start)	Speed in mph GCR	Speed in mph LNWR	Drawbar pull in tons GCR	Drawbar pull in tons LNWR	Gradient	Remarks
		Mossend	10.46am	11.28 1/2am			10 1/16 max	12 max	1 in 2016 down	Weather similar for both trips, bad rail and little down wind.
1 3/4	1 3/4	Motherwell	10.54 1/2	11.35 1/2	11	8	4 3/4	3 7/8	1 in 143 up	
1 7/8	1 7/8	Motherwell (south end stop)	10.55 1/2	11.36 1/4					1 in 143 up	) Restarting test No. 1
1 7/8	1 7/8	Motherwell (south end start)	10.55 3/4	+			11 max	13 1/2 max	1 in 143 up	)
2 full	2 full	Motherwell (south end stop)	10.59 3/4	11.40 1/2	+				1 in 116 up	) Restarting test No. 2
2 full	2 full	Motherwell (south end start)	+	11.44			13 3/4 max	6 1/2 max	1 in 116 up	)
2 1/2	2 1/2	Dalzell Steel Works Box	11.10 1/2	11.54 3/4	5	7	10 7/8	10 7/8	1 in 116 up	
2 1/2	2 1/2	Flemington	11.12 1/2	11.57	5	8	11 1/4	10 1/4	1 in 137 up	
2	2	Shieldmuir Box	11.19 1/4		5 1/2		11 1/8		1 in 137 up	
3 5/8		Wishaw South	11.28 1/2	12.7 pm	5	8 1/2	11 5/8	10 1/4	1 in 102 up	
4 3/4	4 3/4	Law Junction North (stop)	11.51 1/2	12.27			15 max	16 max	1 in 102 up	GCR engine brought to a stand just past 85 1/4 milepost. Train divided and engine took 19 wagons to Law Junction with dynamometer car not registering, afterwards returning for remainder of train. This was taken to Law Junction with dynamometer car registering (time away 12.31pm). LNWR engine brought to a stand 130 yards beyond 85 1/4 milepost. Train assisted to Law Junction (south end) by bank engine in rear, with dynamometer car not registering.
							12*	11 1/2*	1 in 102 up	
6	6 full	Law Junction North (start)	12.31pm				14 3/4 max		1 in 102 up	
6 1/2		Law Junction Box	12.38 1/4		7		9 1/8		1 in 113 up	
7 1/8		Law Junction (stop)	12.44						1 in 99 up	
7 1/8	6 full	Law Junction (start)	12.54 1/2	1.2 1/4			14 3/4 max	16 1/2 max	GCR 1 in 99 up / LNWR 1 in 140 up	GCR train as at start, 19 wagons having been reattached. LNWR start from south end of station after dropping bank engine, dynamometer car recommenced registering.
7 7/8	6 3/4	Hallcraig Box	1.4 1/2	1.11 1/4	8	9	10 tons	9 1/8	1 in 140, then 1 in 261 up	
9 1/4	8 3/4	Carluke	1.13 1/2	1.18 1/4	6	7	11 5/8	10 1/2	1 in 98 up	Opposite engine.
10	8 7/8	South of Carluke		1.29 1/4	2	2	13	11 1/8	1 in 98 up	Max running pull at 81 1/4 milepost.
10 1/8	9 1/4	Braidwood Box	1.33 3/4	1.34 3/4	8	9	10 3/4	10 3/4	1 in 130 up	
10 1/2	9 3/8	Braidwood station	1.34 1/2	1.34 3/4	8	9	10 1/2	9 3/4	1 in 130 up	GCR raining slightly.
12 1/4	11 5/8	Craigenhill Box	1.50	1.47 3/4	12	12	9	7 1/4	1 in 190 up	
13 3/4		Cleghorn Terra Cotta Box	1.53 1/4		27		3 7/8		level	
14 1/2	13 3/4	Cleghorn	1.55 3/4	1.54 1/4	29	25	Nil	Nil	1 in 204 down	
16 1/8	15 1/4	Carstairs Sand Quarry Box	1.59 1/4	1.58 3/4	21	17	Nil	Nil	1 in 336 down	
17 1/4		Carstairs No. 1 Box	2.2 3/4		8		Nil		1 in 207 down	
17 1/2 full		Carstairs Station North End (stop)	2.6						1 in 207 down	GCR 10 wagons detached and train pushed back about 340 yards for photographical purposes - restart at time shown but actually 340 yards behind stopping place.
	16 5/8	Carstairs Station South End (stop)		2.5 1/4					1 in 207 down	LNWR 10 wagons detached, restart at 3.14pm from same point.
17 1/8 full		North of Carstairs Station	3.24				6 1/8 full		1 in 207 down	
17 3/4		Carstairs Station North End	3.26 1/4		12		2 7/8 full		1 in 207 down	GCR same place as first stop.
	16 5/8	Carstairs Station South End (start)		3.14 1/4				2 3/4	1 in 207 down	LNWR same as stopping place.

18¼ bare	-	Strawfrank Box	3.28¼	-	13	-	Nil	-	1 in 165 down	
21⅜	20⅛	Leggatfoot Box	3.43¼	3.32¼	12	18	7⅝	4	level	
22⅞	21⅝	Thankerton	3.46½	3.35½	34	31	3¾	2¾	1 in 100 up	
24¼	-	Signal slack	3.50½	-	13	-	Nil	-	1 in 1020 up	
24½	23¼	Symington (stop)	3.52¾	3.40¼	-	23	-	4	1 in 1020 up	GCR stop to pick up pilot for single-line working.
	23¼	Symington (start)	+	(pass)			Max 10			
28¼	27	Lamington	4.3	3.47½	17	41	Nil	2	1 in 340 down	
31	29¾	Wandelmill	4.14¼	3.52½	6	28½	Max 8¾	4¼	1 in 332 up	GCR dead slow to drop pilot. Max. pull after dropping pilot 8¾ tons.
33⅝	32⅜	Abington	4.23	3.58¼	22	25½	5⅝	4⅜	1 in 392 up	
36⅛	34⅞	Crawford	4.29½	4.4½	21½	22 full	5¼	4½	1 in 392 up	
38⅜	37½	Elvanfoot	4.38¾	4.13½	27	27½ full	4¾	5	1 in 1070 down	
41½	40¼	Summit (milepost 49⅞)	4.52	4.23¾	10	7¾	10⅛	8⅝	Top of 1 in 99 up immediately prior to shutting off steam.	
41¾	40½	Summit (stop)	4.53	4.25½	-	-	-	-	1 in 835 down	
41¾	40½	Summit (start)	5.18¾	5.3	-	-	Max 12	8⅝	1 in 835 down	
51⅝	50⅜	Beattock Station (stop)	5.56	5.41¾	-	-	-	-	1 in 260 down	Stop to examine boxes.
51¾	50½	Beattock Station (start)	6.4¾	6.2	-	-	Max 4½	Max 4½	1 in 260 down	LNWR 1 wagon detached due to hot box.
57	55⅝	Wamphray	6.15¾	6.12	38	33½	1¼	1⅛	1 in 330 up	
59¾	58⅜	Dinwoodie	6.20¾	6.17½	38	37	1⅝	1⅜	1 in 326 down	
62⅜	61⅜	Nethercleugh	6.25½	6.23	34	30 full	1½	2⅛	1 in 528 up	
65⅝	64¼	Lockerbie	6.32	6.29½	25½	25	3⅝	3	1 in 528 up	
68⅞	-	Castlemill Box	6.41¼	-	13½	-	4⅞	-	1 in 200 up	
71⅜	70	Ecclefechan	6.47¾	6.43¾	35	36	1½	Nil	1 in 203 down	
74¾	73⅜	Kirtlebridge	6.54¾	6.49½	1½	29	Max 9	Nil	1 in 493 up	GCR signal slack. Max pull just past station.
78½	77 full	Kirkpatrick	7.6	6.58½	32	28	Nil	Nil	1 in 200 down	
82⅞	81½	Gretna	7.16¼	7.8¼	34	33½	1	Nil	1 in 193 down	
85¼	84⅛	Floriston Station	7.22¼	7.17½ (stop)	3	-	8⅞	-	1 in 616 up	LNWR stopped to examine hot box; was then shunted to let express pass. Dynamometer car not registering. Start from same point on main line.
85⅝	-	Floriston Yard Siding (stop)	7.26½	-	-	-	-	-	1 in 616 up	GCR shunted into siding to let express pass. Back clear of the siding a distance of 550 yards without registering.
85⅝	-	Floriston on main line (start)	7.45½	-	-	-	Max 10	-	1 in 616 up	
-	84⅛	Floriston Station (start)		7.52¼	-	-	-	Max 12⅜	1 in 616 up	
87¾	86⅛	Rockcliffe	7.54	8.0¾	25½	21	4⅝	3⅛	1 in 978 up	
90	88½ (bare)	Kingmoor Sidings (Carlisle) arrive	8.2¼	8.9						

\+ Immediate restart
* Average or useful pull
Note: some of the fractional mileages in the columns on the left may be incorrect, as many are barely legible on the original.

Table 4

Comparison of Experimental Trips between Glasgow (Mossend) and Carlisle (Kingmoor)
First Trip GCR 'MM' 2-8-0 Locomotive No. 2078 hauling mixed Goods Train on 9th November 1919
Second Trip LNWR 'G1' class 0-8-0 Locomotive No. 2421 hauling mixed Goods Train on 18th January 1920

Detail of Comparison	*GCR 2-8-0 Locomotive*	*LNWR 0-8-0 'G1' Locomotive*
Cylinder diameter	21 inches	20 ½ inches
Cylinder stroke	26 inches	24 inches
Driving wheels diameter	4 feet 8 inches	4 feet 5½ inches (with new tyres)
Total heating surface	1756 square feet	2046 square feet
Boiler pressure	180lb per square inch	160lb per square inch
Weight on coupled wheels	67 tons 3 cwt 0 qr	60 tons 5 cwt 0 qr
Total weight of engine and tender in working order	123 tons 15 cwt 0 qr	99 tons 10 cwt 0 qr
Coal capacity of tender	7 tons	6 tons
Water capacity of tender	4000 gallons	3000 gallons
Maximum tractive force at 85% boiler pressure	31,325lb	26,347lb
Weight of train behind tender (Mossend to Carstairs)	884 tons 12 cwt 0qr	892 tons 16 cwt 3 qr
" " " " " (Carstairs to Beattock)	751 tons 0 cwt 0 qr	765 tons 0 cwt 2 qr
" " " " " (Beattock to Kingmoor)	751 tons 0 cwt 0 qr	750 tons 0 cwt 0 qr
Running time (Mossend to Law Jct)	1 hr 5¼min	55¼min
" " (Law Jct to Craigenhill Box)	55 ½ min	45 ½ min
" " (Craigenhill Box to Carstairs)	16 min	17 ½ min
" " Carstairs to Summit)	1 hr 32 min	1 hr 11¼min
Miles from Carlisle when brought to rest	85 miles 430yd *	85 miles 310yd *
Maximum drawbar pull when brought to rest	15 tons	Beyond limit of recording apparatus (16½ tons)
Maximum running pull during journey	13 tons (south of Carluke)	11½ tons (south of Carluke)
Driver	William Smith (CR)	J. McKall (LNWR Carlisle)
Fireman	Alexander McGregor (CR)	W. Bell (LNWR Carlisle)

* The mileposts are numbered from Carlisle to Glasgow. These trips were taken travelling towards Carlisle, therefore, the LNWR engine climbed 120 yards higher up incline than the GCR engine before being brought to a stand.

The final deductions are:

First part of trial from Motherwell to Law Junction
LNWR engine lifted 892 tons to vertical height of 213 feet at an average speed of 5.3 miles per hour.   Average dhp 267 due to gravity only
GCR engine lifted 884 tons to vertical height of 213 feet at an average speed of 4.5 miles per hour.   Average dhp 325 due to gravity only

Second part of trial from Law Junction to Craigenhill Box
LNWR engine lifted 892 tons to vertical height of 200 feet at an average speed of 7.4 miles per hour.   Average dhp 266 due to gravity only
GCR engine lifted 884 tons to vertical height of 200 feet at an average speed of 6.1 miles per hour.   Average dhp 216 due to gravity only

No account of coal consumption was taken.

Junction up a gradient of 1 in 140, where again a pull of 16½ tons was recorded. On the 1 in 98 gradient south of Carluke a pull of over 11 tons was recorded at 2½mph, speed eventually dropping to 2mph. Up the following 1 in 130 the train accelerated to 9½mph and eventually passed Craigenhill Box 45½ minutes after leaving Law Junction, a distance of 5⅝ miles. At Carstairs the train stopped again, to leave ten wagons, reducing the load to 765 tons. After that a speed of 41mph was recorded on the falling gradient of 1 in 340 through Lamington. The train stopped at the top of Beattock Bank and again at the bottom to detach a wagon with a hot box, reducing the load once more to 750 tons. At Floriston it was shunted out of the way of an express and in restarting from there, a pull of over 12 tons was recorded. Final arrival at Kingmoor Sidings at was at 8.9pm. The report concludes laconically, 'No account of coal consumption was taken', but it would be interesting to know how much of the nominal 6 tons of coal was left in the tender of No. 2421 after such a trip lasting more than 8½ hours.

The report contains no conclusion as to the relevant merits of the two designs, other than the statement that the LNWR engine travelled 120 yards further up the incline before 'being brought to a stand'. Nor has any record survived of the influence of the tests on the deliberations of the Caledonian authorities. Certainly, the 'G1' had the edge, in the sense that it was some 20 per cent lighter overall than the 'ROD' and much cheaper to build, but in actual performance there was little real difference between them. Perhaps then that is the interesting feature: that although the two engines came from completely different traditions of design, their capacity for useful work was very similar.

'Strengthened Motion'

The 'G1' class originally had an indirect-action form of Joy valve gear similar to that fitted on the 'Prince of Wales' class. This was found to suffer from excessive wear and to counteract this a modified form with direct action was produced for the 'Princes' in 1920. When this had been shown to have overcome the problem, some 'G1' class were similarly altered. The valve travel was reduced slightly to about 4½in by the change. This in turn made the gear slightly less efficient, as the valve no longer moved more quickly during opening and closing of the ports, which is the key feature of the efficiency of the Joy gear. The travel could only have been

Plate 102: *'G1' No. 1285 rolls round the curve at Colwyn Bay with an up goods about 1920. The train seems to consist mostly of open wagons carrying stone, probably from the quarry at Penmaenmawr.* D. J. Patrick collection

Plate 103: *'G1' No. 2237 at an unidentified shed about 1920. The engine is plain black but the tender seems to be lined.* D. J. Patrick collection

Plate 104: *No. 885 was built new as a 'G1' in May 1916 and is seen here at Hillhouse shed, Huddersfield, about 1925, having been fitted with a Belpaire boiler. The short handrail on the cab sidesheet appears only on Belpaire-fitted engines. The cab roof has already been cut back to suit the LMS loading gauge and fitted with a rain strip. The latter has the circular loop, to suit a carriage-heating relief valve, which would be fitted near the front corner. In fact, pictures showing these relief valves in position are extremely rare.*

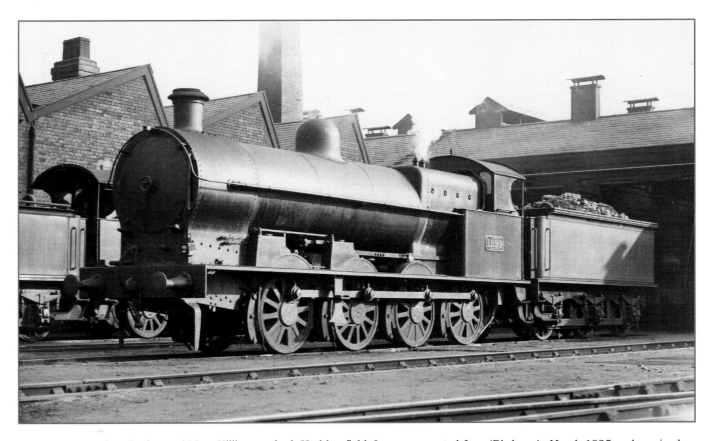

Plate 105: *Class 'G1' No. 1299 at Hillhouse shed, Huddersfield. It was converted from 'B' class in March 1925 and received its LMS number in April 1927.*

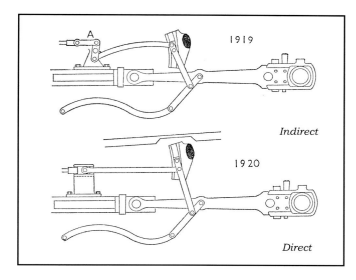

Figure 23: *Direct and indirect forms of Joy valve gear.*
Courtesy W. B. Broadbent

increased by making the Joy yoke more inclined and that would have increased the pressure on the guides and all the pins too, including the jack link in the connecting rod. (The jack link is also known as the 'prop'

link or, in workshop jargon, the 'connecting' link.) Clearly this was undesirable, as the purpose of the alteration was to reduce the wear on the pins. The 4-6-2 tanks had direct motion from new and so were designed appropriately, as were the 'G2s' later. Engines of the 'G1' class with this modification were then said to have 'strengthened motion' but the term more properly applied to the 'G2' class.

By the end of 1922 the total number of 'G1' class in service was 235 and conversions continued uninterrupted right into the LMS period, the last conversions being from classes 'D' and 'G' in 1937. The total number of 'G1' class eventually reached 449, although this number was never in service at the same time, as some engines had already been converted by then to class 'G2A'.

Class 'G2'

For more than two years after completion of the last new 'G1' class in December 1918, no more new eight-coupled goods engines were built at Crewe. The works was busy with 'Claughtons' and 'Princes'. Then in June 1921, under Capt H. P. M. Beames as chief mechanical engineer, the first of the 'G2' class appeared. Basically, it was a straightforward development of the 'G1' class and outwardly it was identical, there being no obvious

Plate 106: *The last 'G2', No. 13, at Crewe Works when first built, awaiting final completion. There are firebricks on the running plate to be laid in the base of the smokebox. Beneath the boiler handrail is the ejector pipe. The drain pipe from it runs vertically down the frame plate about a foot behind the front bufferbeam. Behind the ejector pipe is the blower valve. When the fireman turned the blower full on, another quarter turn operated the ashblower in the base of the smokebox, stirring up the ashes to be ejected through the chimney by the draught from the blower. The engine has the cast boiler stay, which was cut away when the second brake cylinder was fitted. It went into service in October 1922.* M. Williams collection

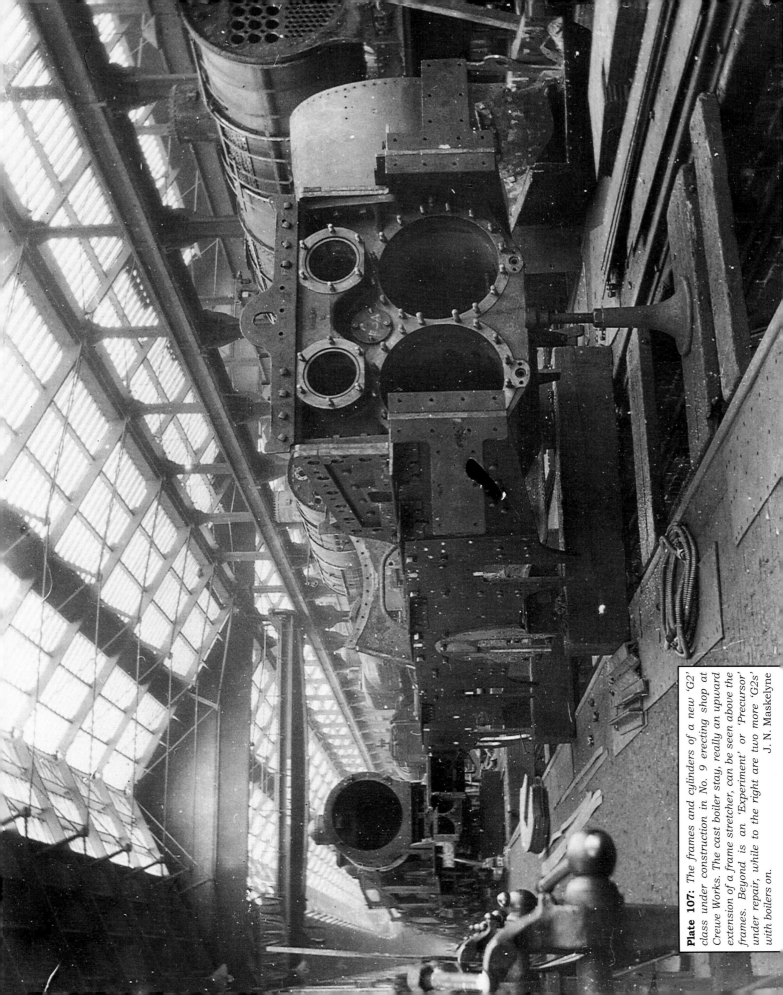

Plate 107: *The frames and cylinders of a new 'G2' class under construction in No. 9 erecting shop at Crewe Works. The cast boiler stay, really an upward extension of a frame stretcher, can be seen above the frames. Beyond is an 'Experiment' or 'Precursor' under repair, while to the right are two more 'G2s' with boilers on.* J. N. Maskelyne

Plate 108: *Class 'G2' No. 570 soon after completion in 1922. It has a Ramsbottom lubricator between the leading splashers. Externally, the 'G2' was virtually indistinguishable from the 'G1'. The only difference was in the wheels and rods. The wheels had slightly thicker bosses, with flush axle ends, and so the spokes were not vertical but were canted in slightly to the rim. The balance weights were arranged basically in the same way except for those on the intermediate wheels, where some had a 'block' weight originally, as here, opposite the crank pin, and others had a curved weight inside the rim. Pin-jointed rods were introduced on the class.*

means for an observer to distinguish one from the other. Only an expert would notice that the axles were larger in diameter, by at least an inch, that the wheels were slightly different, and that the firebox support on the running plate was larger. These small features were the only outward signs of significant internal differences, as the frames and motion had been thoroughly redesigned to give greater strength, the valve gear was of the direct action type from new, and the boiler pressure was increased to 175lb psi, compared to the 160lb of the 'G1'. The term 'strengthened motion' as applied to the 'G2' thus had a significantly different meaning from what was referred to in the modified 'G1'. In fact, the only thing the two had in common was direct action.

In the 'G2', as the axles were larger in diameter, the axleboxes were larger accordingly, and the horn brackets were larger and of slightly different shape. The big ends were larger, and the gudgeon pins were the same length but about an inch larger in diameter, with thin-wall bushes (about $\frac{1}{2}$in thick), whereas the later 'G2A' had thick-wall bushes. The piston rods were $\frac{1}{2}$in larger in diameter and the gland packing, though basically the same material, was in narrow segments compared with the wide segments of the 'G2A'.

The 'G2' class was unique among all the LNWR eight-coupled goods engines in that it was never rebuilt from or to any other class. In all, sixty were built. At the time production at Crewe Works was still disrupted by the aftermath of the Great War and the actual dates when the engines were put into traffic were much later than those shown on their numberplates, which had been made to show the expected dates. One consequence of this was that the number of the 'B' class No. 134, which exploded at Buxton on 11th November 1921, was re-used on a 'G2' which carried the building date October 1921, though actually it was built in April 1922.

Unfortunately, details of tender orders in general have not survived and so it is not known whether these engines had new tenders or were supplied with whatever suitable tenders were available when they were completed. However, details of the tender numbers of the last two batches of 'G2s', built to orders E301 and E302, have survived, but again it is not known whether the tenders were new or not. As all the tenders are known to have been of the final type of Cooke tender except for No. 1725, which was one of the earlier types, it may well be that the engines to order E301 had new tenders and those to order E302 had secondhand tenders as available. But it may equally well be that engines of both batches had new or secondhand tenders at random. Details of these numbers are as follows:

Plate 109: *'G2' No. 403 at Crewe South shed, probably when first built and just off the works. The rods are burnished as is the handrail on the cab. The tender, the final Cooke type, seems to be new also.*   W. H. Whitworth

Plate 110: *Class 'G2' No. 396 still in original condition except for Ross pop safety valves, which were introduced in 1924. The curved balance weight on the intermediate wheel is well shown.*

Plate 111: *Class 'G2' No. 2371 about 1925. It has been fitted with a Belpaire boiler, the cab roof has been cut back and there is a handrail on the cab side-sheet - always fitted with Belpaire fireboxes; but it still has LNWR lamp sockets. The tender is the final Cooke type, which seems to have been fitted to the 'G2s' when new, but in this case is lined and so must have come from a passenger engine, probably a 'Prince'.*
A. G. Ellis collection

Order E301		Order E302	
Engine	Tender	Engine	Tender
344	114	758	1802
872	1466	1012	1805
2182	1704	2414	1836
895	327	2429	1421
994	878	2517	890
36	959	231	1725
2381	1912	308	1832
2383	1793	403	1483
2386	365	2178	505
2399	447	13	1881

The last of the class, No. 13, went into service in October 1922.

Belpaire Boilers

In 1924 Beames produced a range of boilers with Belpaire fireboxes to suit many classes of LNWR engines, among them the superheated 0-8-0s. One factor behind the adoption of the Belpaire firebox seems to have been the boiler explosion of 'B' class No. 134 at Buxton. While there was no doubt that the cause of the explosion had been faulty safety valves, and that the design of the boiler was in no way responsible, it seems that Beames decided on the Belpaire firebox for three main reasons: it could be stayed to give greater strength; it gave greater heating surface area within the same dimensions; and it provided more space above the inner firebox.

The first boiler built with a Belpaire firebox was No.

4315 in July 1924. It was fitted to 'G1' class No. 931, later to become LMS No. 9252. Belpaire boilers were so arranged as to be easily interchangeable with round-top boilers, only modifications to the cab spectacle plates being needed. Although Crewe then built only Belpaire boilers as replacements, round-top boilers continued in service for many years. Boilers were removed from engines entering the works for major overhaul, were repaired separately and fitted to the next suitable engines being repaired. Thus an engine entering the works with a round-top boiler could emerge with another round-top or a Belpaire, according to what was available, and similarly an engine entering with a Belpaire boiler could emerge with another Belpaire or with a round-top.

As often seemed to happen in steam locomotive engineering, apparent improvements in the time-honoured ways of doing things had unexpected consequences, not all of them good. T. M. Herbert, who was later to become head of the LMS research department, investigated the renewal of firebox stays on round-top and Belpaire boilers at Springs Branch shed and in January 1930 reported that round-top boilers on 'Super Ds' required one stay to be changed for every 644 miles run, compared to one every 244 miles for engines with Belpaire boilers. Similar figures were obtained for other classes in the study. He suggested modifications, but no further information seems to be available.

Plate 112: A 'G1' hard at work in early LMS days. It is approaching Great Barr with down coal empties that are no doubt destined for Bescot yard. No. 9320 is still in pure LNWR condition, even having lamp sockets, instead of lamp irons, and an 'unvandalised' cab roof. The only LMS features are the front numberplate, 'LMS' where the cabside numberplate used to be, and the number on the tender, which is the first Cooke type. In the background are the up signals for Perry Barr North Junction: if the home signal is 'off' with the distant on the separate post to the left is 'off', the road is set for Aston.

Chapter Four
LMS AND BR - THE 'SUPER D' ERA

After its merger with the Lancashire & Yorkshire Railway in 1922, the LNWR ceased to exist as an independent company. George Hughes of the LYR, as the senior chief mechanical engineer, became head of the locomotive department, in preference to H. P. M. Beames, and a year later, when the combined company was itself absorbed into the much larger LMS group, Hughes again obtained the same position on the LMS with Beames as his deputy. Since the LNWR-LYR company was so short-lived, it made little difference who was appointed chief mechanical engineer, but so far as the LMS was concerned, it was an important appointment. The new company, with its vast and diverse locomotive stock and numerous workshops, needed someone to establish standard practices and a consistent progressive policy, as well as to develop more powerful engines.

After a creditable start, however, Hughes resigned abruptly less than three years later. He seems to have been thwarted in his plans for larger engines by E. C. Trench, chief civil engineer, and J. E. Anderson, chief of motive power. The latter favoured the Midland small-engine policy, while Trench also disapproved of heavier engines. As Hughes' deputy, Beames might have been expected to take over, but the outcome of the struggle for power was that Henry Fowler of the Midland was appointed. Thus, any chance of Beames obtaining the senior post had now gone and henceforth, with one or

two notable exceptions, Crewe practice ceased to have any major influence on locomotive design on the LMS.

The LMS Renumbering

In 1923 the LMS introduced a renumbering scheme to bring all the engines it had acquired into one unified system. The scheme was basically that used previously by the Midland Railway (Midland Railway engines were unchanged). Passenger tender engines, passenger tank engines, goods tank engines and goods tender engines were numbered by classes in that order.

There were three basic principles to the renumbering. Firstly, instead of the LNWR system, in which the numbers of engines were scattered at random throughout the capital list, each class was numbered together in a block. Secondly, classes were grouped according to wheel arrangement. Thus, in the case of the eight-coupled engines, the 0-8-0s were numbered before the 2-8-0s. Within each wheel arrangement, the oldest class had the lowest numbers and the newest the highest. Thus, the 'B' class survivors started at 8900, the other classes followed in order of age and the newest 0-8-0s, the 'G2s', were the last at 9395-9454. Then came the 'E' class, as the older of the two compound 2-8-0 classes, the 'F' class and finally the 'MMs'.

Thirdly, engines were to be numbered within each class in ascending order as built, the oldest first and the newest last. So, in the case of the 'G' class, for

Plate 113: *Class 'G1' No. 8934 was converted from class 'B' in October 1923 and so was among the very first LNWR engines to be given an LMS number. This photograph at Hillhouse shed shows it soon afterwards. Except for the large LMS numerals on the tender and 'LMS' in the first style on the cab side, the engine is still in pure LNWR condition. Beames' Belpaire boilers and supplementary oil boxes on handrails were introduced later, and there is no LMS power class on the cab side and no front numberplate.*
R. K. Blencowe collection

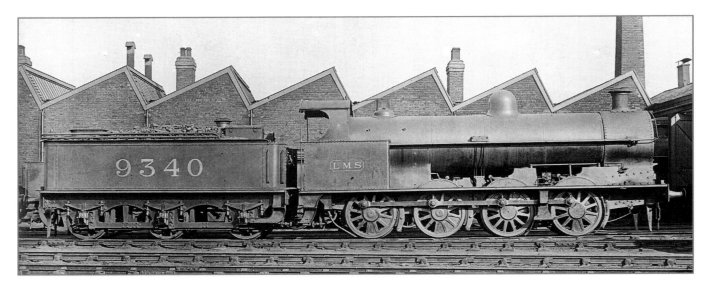

Plate 114: *Class 'G1' No. 9340 was converted in February 1926 and is seen here also at Hillhouse. Compared with No. 8934, it has a supplementary oil box on the handrail, 'LMS' in a panel on the cab side and power class '5' just above it but otherwise is still in LNWR condition, even with its lamp sockets not yet replaced by lamp irons.*

example, those which were converted from 'B' class before the new 'G' class was built, came first, then came the new 'G' class in a block, and finally came those converted after the new 'G' class was built. Similarly, in the case of the 'G1' class, the engines built new were numbered in one block, 9155-9334, but were preceded by 9154, the first 'G', which was converted to 'G1' before the new engines were built. Next came the rebuilds from other classes to 'G1', 9335-9394. This block included all engines rebuilt up to the end of January 1923. Subsequent rebuilds, however, were not then renumbered into a block with the 'G1s' but retained whatever number they had been given under the scheme in their previous classes.

The method by which the individual numbers were allocated within each class seems to have been to take all the engines built in a given month, put their LNWR numbers into numerical order and then allot new LMS numbers to them consecutively. Of course, when the LNWR numbers had been put into numerical order, they were no longer in the order as built. So, contrary to the intention of the scheme, in many cases LNWR engines were not renumbered in order as built and in fact most LNWR engines did not receive the numbers they should have had. In addition, many other errors were made in renumbering. For the practical purposes of the LMS, of course, this did not matter at all, but LNWR partisans were scathing that the LMS could not even apply its own numbering scheme correctly and had succeeded in giving the correct numbers to only about 20 per cent of the LNWR stock.

The only later renumbering affecting eight-coupled engines was in July 1930 when the surviving 'E' and 'F' class engines were renumbered 8892-8899 to allow further Fowler '7F' 0-8-0s to be numbered in the 96XX series. The basic scheme for the eight-coupled engines was as follows:

Class	Numbers
Ex 'E'/'F'	8892-8899
'B'	8900-8952
'C'	8953-8967
'C1'	8968-9001
'D'	9002-9064
'G Piano'	9065-9076
'G New'	9077-9144
'G Piano'	9145-9153
'G1' ex 'G'	9154
'G1' new	9155-9334
'G1' rebuilds	9335-9394
'G2'	9395-9454
'E'	9600-9610
'F'	9611-9615
'MM'	9616-9645
0-8-2 Tank	7870-7899
0-8-4 Tank	7930-7959

The LMS Power Classification System

In 1923 the LMS also introduced a power classification for all its locomotive stock, which again was based on the former Midland Railway system. The least powerful engines were classified '0', the most powerful '7'. Most LNWR engines were given low ratings, by comparison with Midland engines, a 'G1' for instance being in class '4' along with the Derby class '4' 0-6-0. Early in 1925 the system was revised to reflect more accurately the true capability of each class, and from April 1928 the letters 'P' or 'F' were added after the number to indicate passenger or freight. The system as it applied to the eight-coupled engines was as follows:

Class	1923	1925	Class	1923	1925
'B'	3	3	'G'	4	5
'C'	4	4	'G1'	4	6
'C1'	4	3	'G2'	5	7
'D'	4	5	'MM'	5	7
'E'	3	3	0-8-2 tank	5	6
'F'	3	3	0-8-4 tank	5	7

Comparative Trials

In September 1925 the LMS held some tests with coal trains over the Midland Division between Toton and

Brent. The engines involved were 'G2' No. 574 and two Midland 0-6-0s, '4F' No. 3866 and '3F' No. 3756. Both the 'G2' and '4F' were superheated, the '3F' being saturated. Runs were made with the 'G2' and '4F' working singly, and with the '4F' and '3F' double-headed, both with loaded trains to Brent and with empty wagons back to Toton. The Horwich dynamometer car was used, the object of the tests being: 'to ascertain the comparative coal, water and oil consumption and engine performance'.

The main findings of the tests, as taken *verbatim* from the official report, were as follows:

——— Table 5 ———

Engine Performance - 1

Engine	Load behind tender tons	Max drawbar horse-power & corresponding speed hp	mph	Average drawbar horse-power hp	Max. drawbar tractive effort & corresponding speed tons	mph	Average drawbar tractive effort tons	Speed in mph max.	average
			Toton - Brent Loaded Mineral Train						
574	753.75	682	30.0	332.6	6.14	13.9	3.461	35.0	17.43
3866	768.8	621	27.5	363.1	7.03	11.9	3.727	36.8	17.22
3866) 3756)	1335.9	896	13.2	611.4	11.85	12.0	6.586	40.0	16.74
			Brent - Toton Empty Mineral Train						
574	416.5	648	32.0	345.7	5.45	15.0	2.558	40.5	22.45
3866	404.19	628.6	21.0	368.1	5.718	15.0	2.852	39.0	21.2
3866) 3756)	676.31	932	19.7	587.4	8.52	18.5	4.325	40.0	22.25

Engine Performance - 2

The following table gives particulars of the work of the engines when hauling the loaded trains up the average gradients of 1 in 200 between Harringworth and Weldon North (section A) and Bedford and Leagrave (section B).

Details of the working and performance are given as an average over each section. Engine No. 574 has 4.5 revolutions from mid to full forward gear and the position of the reverser is given as revolutions from mid gear. No. 3756 has 7 notches and No. 3866 12 notches from mid to full forward gear, and the position of the reverser in the case of these engines refers to the notch used. All engines steamed well.

Engine	Load behind tender - tons	Section	Boiler pressure lb psi	Rev. gear	Regulator	Water in glass	Speed mph	Drawbar horse-power	Drawbar tractive effort - tons
574	753.75	A	171	1.5	.5	.8	13.72	451	5.5
574	753.75	B	175	1.5	.5	.9	14.42	424.7	4.93
3866	768.8	A	170	5.5	.6	1.0	12.2	419	5.75
3866	768.8	B	170	6.0	.7	.9	15.88	487.35	5.235
3866) 3756)	1335.91	A	175 165	6.0 4.0	.3 .6	.9 .9	10.92	698.9	10.71
3866) 3756)	1335.91	B	175 170	4.0 3.0	.3 .5	1.0 1.0	14.3	749.8	8.78

The average booked speed between Bedford and Leagrave is approximately 15.5 mph and it would appear that the present booked speed on the 1 in 200 gradient between Bedford and Leagrave in normal weather requires an average drawbar horse-power of about 480 tons (5.2 tons pull) for a single loaded mineral train, and about 820 tons (8.9 tons pull) for a double-headed train.

Table 6

Coal Consumption

The following table gives the consumption of coal excluding shed duties, the average actual speed of the train, and the air temperatures at the start of each trip.

Engine	Load behind tender - tons	Average actual speed mph	Coal used tons	lb per mile	Lb per ton-mile exc. eng	inc. eng	Lb per dbhp hour	Lb per sq ft grate per hour (excluding stops)	Air temp	Hp mins per ton-mile
Toton - Brent Loaded Mineral Train										
574	753.17	17.48	3.51	61.7	.0818	.0726	4.16	45.6	68	1.18
3866	768.8	17.22	3.37	68.2	.0886	.0802	4.25	55.8	62	1.25
3866) 3756)	1335.9	16.74	7.075	124.6	.0984	.0833	4.41	49.5	58	1.27
Brent - Toton Empty Mineral Train										
574	416.5	22.45	2.45	43.5	.1046	.0851	3.33	41.5	65	1.88
3866	404.19	21.2	2.755	48.7	.1204	.1003	3.23	48.9	56	2.24
3866) 3756)	676.31	22.25	5.19	91.7	.1353	.1094	3.84	48.23	54.5	2.11

Comparing engine No. 574 with No. 3866, No. 574 had the following percentage increase or decrease in coal consumption:

	Loaded Mineral Increase	Decrease	Empty Mineral Increase	Decrease
Lb per ton-mile excluding engine	-	7.67	-	13.1
Lb per ton mile including engine	-	9.48	-	15.1
Lb per drawbar horsepower hour	-	2.1	3.1	-
Lb per sq ft grate per hour excluding stops	-	18.3	-	15.1

In the case of the Midland Divison engines, the small ejector was used throughout each run to maintain the vacuum on the engine and dynamometer car. In the case of No. 574, the vacuum was maintained by the pump.

NOTE: In comparing the coal consumption figures, it should be borne in mind that the Western 'A' engine No. 574 is a class 5 engine and the train loads it hauled were well within its capacity.

Water Consumption

The following table gives particulars of the water consumption. All water was taken at the booked stops.

Engine	Load behind tender tons	Water total galls	Galls per train mile	Lb per ton-mile exc. eng.	inc eng.	Lb per dbhp	Lb per lb of coal
Toton - Brent Loaded Mineral Train							
574	753.17	5355	42.1	.5576	.4947	28.33*	6.82
3866	768.8	5400	42.4	.5515	.4988	26.42	6.22
3866) 3756)	1335.9	11300	88.96	.6657	.5947	31.4	7.13
Brent - Toton Empty Mineral Train							
574	416.5	4345	34.3	.8239	.6691	26.25	7.88
3866	404.19	4980	39.15	.9695	.8075	26.0	8.06
3866) 3756)	676.31	9500	74.8	1.106	.8946	31.38	8.16

* There was some leakage from a tender feed union on this trip, and as the time of the trip, including stop, was 7.3 hours, this figure has no doubt been affected.

From the above figures, the water consumption of engines Nos. 574 and 3866 would appear to be almost identical for equal amounts of work done.

The report concluded that timekeeping was well within the capacity of all the engines and that the main deviations from booked time were due to signal checks. It pointed out that in comparing the coal consumption figures, 'it should be borne in mind that No. 574 is a class 5 engine and that the train loads were well within its capacity.' Quite possibly, they were too light for optimum performance, whereas those of No. 3866 may have been too heavy. There was little difference in water consumption but the 'G2' used considerably more oil. As regards the motion, this can be partly explained by the fact that it had smaller wheels, and more of them, than the '4F', needing more revolutions to cover the same distance, but its greater consumption of oil in the superheater can be only partly explained by its greater size. Either the lubrication system was less efficient or was not set up correctly, or perhaps a combination of the two.

Early Years

The lack of direction, incompetence and indecision in early LMS locomotive policy eventually led to the largest railway company in the country being forced, as a desparate last-minute measure, to order the 'Royal Scots' from an outside locomotive builder. The apparent success of those engines and the publicity surrounding them tended to mask the failure of leadership which produced them. The same failings of management were even less noticeable in freight locomotive policy but they were no less real. It was only when Stanier took over, almost ten years after the LMS was formed, that locomotive affairs were given any proper direction.

For this sad state of affairs Hughes was in no way responsible. To his credit, he quickly recognised the need for a new heavy freight engine. In November 1923 he proposed that 100 2-8-0s should be included in the 1924 locomotive buildng programme at a cost of £500,000 and told the locomotive committee that he was 'endeavouring to design an engine that could run over all sections of line of the amalgamated companies'. In April 1924, however, he reported that it had not proved possible to produce a suitable design and that

Plate 116: *In the mid-1920s the LMS started a system of reserving engines in good condition for the hardest duties, not only passenger engines, such as 'Claughtons' and 'Princes', but also certain 'G2s'. They carried an 'S' on the cab sidesheet, denoting 'Special'. Here, one of them, No. 9422, stands at Willesden on 23rd April 1927.*   F. M. Gates/R. Bell collection

100 '4F' 0-6-0s would be built instead, 70 at Crewe and 30 at Horwich. In view of later events and of what was ordered, it seems likely that the Midland faction thwarted Hughes' intention.

Later in the same year the suggestion was made by a member of the locomotive committee that the company should consider buying some of the 300 'ROD' 2-8-0s which the government wished to dispose of. The general manager's reply was that there were already 30 of the type in service on the Western Division where they were restricted from working on certain main lines. They were also restricted from working over the whole of the Midland Division on acount of excessive axle loads and insufficient loading gauge clearance, and they were not permitted in sidings underneath which were iron or timber bridges. Moreover, they had steel fireboxes, which would eventually have to be replaced by copper, and their driving wheels were too small for the speed required for main-line mineral traffic. Having successfully scotched that suggestion, he went on to say that 70 of the planned '4F' 0-6-0s would be built at Crewe and 30 at St Rollox, not at Horwich as previously stated.

In July 1924, when the next locomotive building programme was under discussion, Hughes reported that the design of a new engine was being considered to enable the Toton - Brent trains to be hauled by one engine instead of two, but certain bridges needed strengthening. Nothing more was mentioned of this plan, however, and only nine months later Hughes resigned. What political machinations induced him to make that decision are uncertain, but it is clear that the Midland faction had achieved control, as the new chief mechanical engineer was Sir Henry Fowler. Achieving power is one thing, using it wisely another, and those in authority were to prove over the following eight years that they were quite incapable of producing engines that met the requirements of the company. In short, they had no idea what to do.

Just as they tried to overcome their inability to produce an express passenger engine by buying one from an outside builder, so they solved the problem of the Toton - Brent trains, in a fashion, by buying a Beyer-Garratt. That would have been a good decision - the concept was well proved - had they not insisted on Midlandising it. Not even that solution, however, was tried for a general heavy goods engine. The notes of C. Williams show that the provisional 1927 locomotive building programme for 'A' Division, the former LNWR lines, included, along with five each of the proposed large 4-6-2 and 2-8-2 designs, 100 'G2s' with Stephenson motion. No doubt, the latter modification was an attempt to Midlandise the 'G2' by doing away with Joy gear, an effective and well tried feature of the design. As regards the large 4-6-2, incidentally, Sir Henry Fowler told the locomotive committee that the engine he had designed was suitable for the Euston - Glasgow Central main line but was too high for certain bridges near St. Enoch. This seems a minor problem, but the design is not mentioned again in the minutes.

Again, in a building programme for the five years 1928-32 400 'G2s' are shown. Perhaps all these proposals for 'G2s' were influenced by the performance of the 'G2' in the 1925 tests and if these engines had been built, it would certainly have been much better for the LMS than what actually happened. The 'G2s' were described by E. S. Cox, no great admirer of Crewe practice, as:

'by far the best Crewe design of modern times. Although made up of ingredients common to other types, they were combined in a more harmonious manner, and the generally low load factor of freight working abated many of the bad habits which higher duties called forth from their stable mates. On test they rather mystified the Derby brigade by producing marginally lower coal figures than for the Derby class '4F' 0-6-0s. Justice was restored, however, by their addiction to hot boxes, and an overall repair cost some 50 per cent above the home product. The boiler could not be faulted, having already been re-arranged in Belpaire form under Hughes' direction.'

It may be, incidentally, that Cox's reference to the 'addiction to hot boxes' of the 'G2s' is exaggerated by his anti-Crewe bias. Certainly, an LMS fitter at Abergavenny from 1946 to 1952 cannot recall one instance of a hot box on a 'G2' and of the other 0-8-0s the most affected were the 'G2As' numbered in the 89XX series. The role played by Hughes in the design of the Crewe Belpaire boilers is also uncertain.

However that may be, nothing in fact came of these proposals to build more 'G2s', and eventually Derby decided to develop its own eight-coupled design. To this end, as E. A. Langridge has recounted, trials were held between a 'G2' and a Somerset & Dorset 2-8-0, a Midland design dating from about 1911. The engines hauled coal trains on alternate days from Toton to London over the Midland main line via Syston, Melton Mowbray, Kettering and Bedford to Brent. When the 'G2' was found to be superior, the 2-8-0 was taken into Derby Works for the valves to be cleaned and adjusted. The trials were resumed, but once again the 'G2' was found to be better. Derby drawing office was then told to design an 0-8-0 based on the 'G2' but with a chassis having Midland wheels, axles, axle-boxes, spring gear and so forth (as on the engine found to be inferior - hardly a sensible method of producing a better engine!).

The result was the class 'G3' or Fowler '7F' 0-8-0, commonly known as 'Austin Sevens', of which 175 were built, all at Crewe in 1929-32. Of these, 50 were allocated to Division 'A' to bring the virtues of Midlandisation to the old North Western lines in place of the LNWR 0-8-0s, 34 to the Midland Division to take over the harder turns not covered by the Garratts, and 91 to the Central Division (former LYR lines). Despite their vices, which concerned the fitters, the management and the accountants, they were quite popular with LNWR enginemen, as they were powerful and free-steaming. Firemen gave them the nickname 'arse-warmers' (!), since they had very short footplates, as indeed did LNWR 0-8-0s.

The fact that the 'G3s' were a failure, because they had small standard Midland axleboxes unsuited to such powerful engines, soon became clear to the LMS authorities. Twenty more were on order when Stanier

Plate 117: *Another 'Special' 'G2', No. 9425, at Rugby on 14th May 1928.*　　　　　　W. Leslie Good

Plate 118: *No official picture seems to have been taken of the first 'G2' No. 485 on completion but one was taken of LMS No. 9447 on 11th December 1928, perhaps to show the paint scheme adopted then and used to the end of the LMS (no 'SuperDs' ever appeared in the LMS 1946 scheme). Photographic paint seems to have been applied everywhere - except for the hook and coupling which seem to have either been burnished or painted glossy black. As well as a Beames oil box on the handrail and the paint scheme, the engine has several LMS features typical of the period: lamp irons instead of LNWR sockets, front numberplate, cab roof altered to LMS loading gauge and power classification code '7'.*　　LNWR B176

Plate 119: *Class 'G1' No. 9137, which was converted from class 'G' in October 1927, taking water on the up main line in Penrith station probably in the late 1920s. It has the detail alterations of early LMS days, an oil box on the handrail, lamp irons and a front numberplate, and its tender has come from an 'MM' 2-8-0.* J. J. Cunningham

Plate 120: *A 'G1' climbing out of Buxton on the Ashbourne line with a train of Territorial Army troops travelling to their summer camp in 1930.* E. R. Morten

Plate 121: *Class 'G1' No. 9213 in the top yard at Buxton in July 1930. In 1926 the LNWR shed at Buxton was transferred to the Midland division and an order was sent to Derby for 50 or 60 cast Midland-type '20' shed plates, as seen here. In 1935, when new all-line shed codes were introduced by the LMS, the situation was reversed and Buxton shed reverted to the Western Division under Longsight as shed '9D'.*
E. R. Morten

Plate 122: *Class 'G1' No. 8908 at Bescot, its home shed ('6', on the smokebox door), still with its number on the cab side in smaller numerals than standard, on 13th August 1933. Its cab roof is still unmodified, and it has three-piece side rods, steam brakes only - vacuum brake is still not fitted - and a Whale tender; but it has pop safety valves, an oil box on the handrail and a front numberplate.*
F. M. Gates/R. Bell collection

Plate 123: *'G1' No. 9042 at the same place on the same occasion. It has pin-jointed side rods and makes an interesting comparison generally with No. 8908.* F. M. Gates/R. Bell collection

Plate 124: *Class 'G1' No. 9061 in ex works condition about 1931. The small brackets apparently holding the down pipes in position on the shed wall actually held the ends of bolts which passed through the wall to the brackets supporting the cross beams holding the shed roof. They are depicted clearly in Jack Nelson's classic LNWR Portrayed.*

W. H. Whitworth/M. Williams collection

Plate 125: *Class 'G1' No. 8966 in typical workaday condition in the early 1930s. The 'LMS' on the tender is almost illegible.*

Plate 126: *Class 'G1' No. 9047 in 1934.*

Plate 127: *Class 'G1' No. 9089 at Crewe in 1935. It has LMS buffers both front and rear.* Photomatic

Plate 128: *An up goods train south of Lancaster headed by 'G1' class No. 9365 about 1932. No doubt, after taking the shot, the photographer would lower his camera and enjoy the excellent view of the fascinating variety of wagons and loads as they passed under the bridge.*
H. Gordon Tidey

Plate 129: *Class 'G1' No. 9128 at Watford in 1934.*

R. G. Jarvis

Plate 130: *Super-power on the up slow line at Whitmore about 1933, as 'G1' No. 9272 double-heads an unidentified '19in Goods', which is taking water.*

Plate 131: *Class 'G2' No 9452 starting the climb to Whitmore on the up slow line with a long mixed goods train on 9th May 1936 - it has just left Basford Hall and is passing Chorlton, a mile or so further south.*
E. R. Morten

Plate 132: *Class 'G1' No. 9388 at Stoke on 30th April 1933 with first type of Cooke tender.*
W. L. Good

Plate 133: *Class 'G1' No. 8897 at Crewe South shed on 3rd March 1934, with direct action and LMS buffers.*
A. G. Ellis collection

Plate 134: *In March 1934 the LMS renumbered certain pre-grouping engines by adding 20,000 to their numbers to allow all standard classes to be numbered below 10,000. Some ex-LNWR engines were renumbered in error at Crewe Works but the mistake was soon corrected. Here, 'G1' No. 29014 seems to have been receiving attention from the cleaners, who have perhaps gone for a break before tackling the tender tank. The location is the south end of Crewe South shed; the carriage shed on the up side of the main line is in the background.*
A. G. Ellis collection

Plate 135: *Also renumbered in error was 'G2' No. 29442.* B. J. Miller collection

Plate 136: *Class 'G2' No. 9445 of shed '5', Northampton, at Willesden shed on 15th May 1934. This type of smokebox door, secured by eight lugs instead of a central hand-wheel and carrying the top lamp-iron, was used mainly on 'Claughtons', but also appeared on some 'Prince of Wales' 4-6-0s as well as 'Super Ds' at this period.* H. F. Wheeler/R. Carpenter collection

Plate 137: *Class 'G2' No. 9453 at Crewe South on 19th April 1936. It seems to have been recently repainted during a visit to works but the wheels are already getting dirty.* L. Hanson

Plate 138: *Class 'G2' No. 9449 at Northampton on 20th January 1934, with Cooke 'double bar' tender.* L. Hanson

Plate 139: *Class 'G2' No. 9444 of shed '2C' (Warwick) on Rugby shed about 1938, matched with a Whale tender.*

W. A. Camwell

Plate 140: *A down freight on the slow line at Castlethorpe in the late 1930s. It is about to run on to the troughs. The train consists firstly of coal empties, then a rake of vans and then more coal empties. The engine is 'G2' No. 9415, its Cooke tender still well stacked with coal some 50 miles after leaving London.*

H. Gordon Tidey

Plate 141: *A down goods on the fast line at Castlethorpe troughs in the late 1930s. It is apparently double-headed by a 'Super D' and a 'George the Fifth' 4-4-0 but on closer inspection the 'George' seems 'dead', with no coal in the tender, and so is probably on its way to Crewe.* H. Gordon Tidey/R. Bell collection

Plate 142: *Class 'G1' No. 9312 approaching Crewe with an up empty stock train on 3rd March 1938.* E. R. Morten

Plate 143: *Class 'G1' No. 9295 on an up mixed goods probably in the late 1930s. It has just topped the climb to Shap and has started the descent towards Tebay.*

H. Gordon Tidey

Plate 144: *An up goods starting the descent from Whitmore on the up slow line on 31st July 1937. The engine is thought to be 'G1' No. 9198.*

E. R. Morten

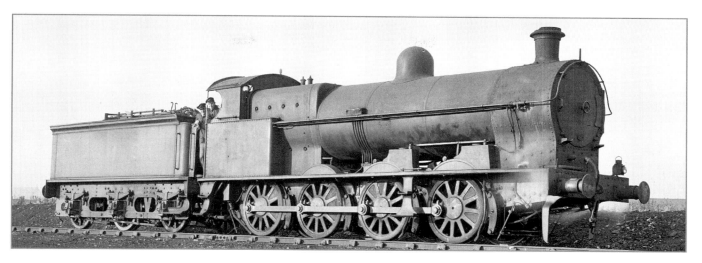

Plate 145: *An interesting study in detail differences. Class 'G1' No. 9102 at Wigan (L&Y) on 3rd October 1936.* R. G. Jarvis

Plate 146: *Class 'G1' No. 9384 in Bletchley yards on 29th May 1937. Both engines have desanding gear.* J. M. Jarvis

Plate 147: *Class 'G1' No. 9204 about 1938.* C. L. Hodgetts

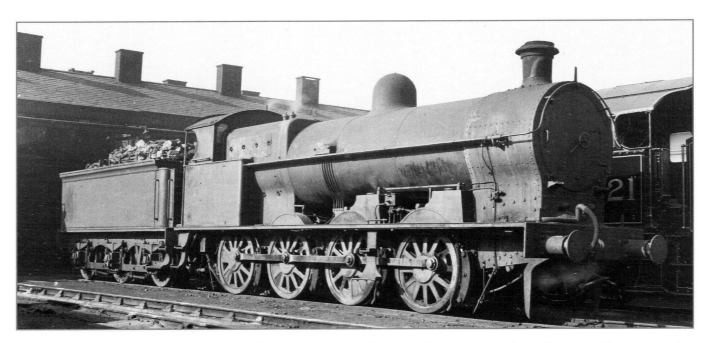

Plate 148: *In a book such as this an unreal impression may be given that all engines were clean all the time. Photographs of clean engines are more attractive and show detail better, and photographers prefer clean engines to dirty ones. Of course, the majority of engines were far from clean - a steam engine is a difficult thing to keep clean anyway, and was especially so in winter in areas where the atmosphere was polluted from coal-burning; there was also less concern about goods than passenger engines. So the majority of 'Super Ds' spent most of their time in a state that was far from clean, though most were respectable and few were really filthy. Here, to redress the balance, is a less than spotless 'G1', at Crewe South on 30th May 1937. The number, from the notes of the photographer, is 9331. There is a large patch on the side of the firebox but the tender is well piled with coal and doubtless, despite its exterior, the engine will soon be hard at work on its next turn. By contrast, on the right is a gleaming 'Royal Scot', No. 6121, ex works in LMS red livery.* J. A. Whaley/Colour-Rail

Plates 150-1: *Also photographed at Crewe South on the same day as No. 9331 was 'G1' No. 9077 (above), still with the early style of pop safety valves, and No. 9205 (below). Compared with another photograph taken on 10th September 1933, probably the last previous occasion when it was ex works, No. 9205 is still in the same condition except for having LMS instead of Cooke buffers.*

J. A. Whaley/Colour-Rail collection

Plate 152: *Class 'G1' No. 9369 with Whale tender about 1936. It was once numbered 29369 in error. The '2' seems to have been painted out but is just visible.*

C. L. Turner

Plate 149 (opposite): *Class 'G1' No. 9301 of Bescot shed, '3A'. The engine still has an LMS numberplate on the smokebox door and Ramsbottom safety valves, but the date must be at least 1935, when LMS shed codes and cast shed plates were introduced. The location is Crewe South shed.*

W. A. Camwell

Plate 153: *Class 'G1' No. 9098 at the east end of Chester station about 1938.* C. L. Hodgetts

arrived, but only fifteen of them were built. The reason given for the cancellation of five engines was that they would be produced as a new 2-8-0 design in the 1933 programme. In the event, the Stanier '8F' was not actually produced until 1935. So another period of delay followed. Eventually, the 'G3s' were concentrated on the old Lancashire & Yorkshire lines, perhaps because the work was more of a short-distance nature, and in BR days they were scrapped earlier and became extinct before the engines they had been built to replace.

Class 'G2A'

While all this was going on, Crewe was happily continuing in its time-honoured manner, with the conversion of earlier LNWR eight-coupled engines to class 'G1'. Then in 1935 the decision was taken to upgrade class 'G1' to 'G2' standards by fitting a 175lb boiler, 'strengthened motion and improved brake power'. In fact, many 'G1s' already had one or both of these latter improvements anyway, and many of the altered engines lacked one of them, so in reality the only significant change was the boiler.

The engines so altered are generally referred to as class 'G2A' but that term does not appear in the minutes of the LMS locomotive committee at all. Although there are many references to the 'former LNWR 0-8-0s' as late as the mid 1940s, they are always described as class 'G1' and 'G2'. Some Crewe Works drawings show class 'G2A', so perhaps it was a term used by the works to differentiate the converted engines from the other two classes. Whatever the explanation might be, there

is nothing about the alteration in the minutes and how it came about is unclear.

Perhaps, when no satisfactory new design had been produced to replace the LNWR 0-8-0s, and none was seen to be imminent, it was decided to produce a modest upgrading by fitting 'G1s' with 175lb boilers. So perhaps again, the key to the conversion lies in the boiler building programmes (see *Appendix Six*). It is clear from the minutes that the LMS spent a lot of money on new boilers. In the 1920s new 'G1' boilers were built, obviously for conversions from non-superheated classes as well as for replacements. In the 1930s new boilers are shown as 'G1'/'G2' and 20 were built in 1931-2, 115 in 1933-4 and 150 up to the end of 1940. Possibly many if not all of these later boilers were built to take 175lb and were fitted with safety valves set at 160lb or 175lb according to which engine they were to be used on. Some 'G2As' actually reverted to 'G1', presumably because when they needed a boiler change only an older 160lb boiler was available. All this, of course, is purely speculation but at least it seems to fit the evidence.

Whatever the truth might be, the development of the 'G2A' class was entirely in the best North Western traditions of Crewe. If the Grouping had not occurred and if the LNWR had continued on its own independent course, the 'G2A' class might well have been produced anyway. Yet in fact it was a purely LMS development, sanctioned by LMS management presumably, as a consequence of the failure to produce a reliable heavy freight engine, and carried out when Stanier himself

Plate 154: *Climbing from Carlisle to Shap, class 'G1' No. 9196 passes Wreay with an up goods in 1939.* E. E. Smith

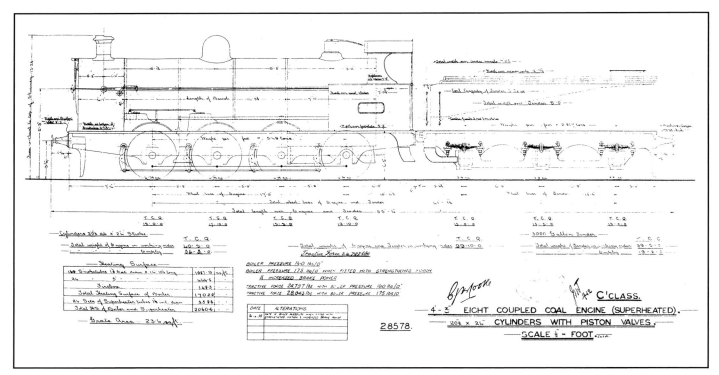

Figure 24: *Weight diagram of a 'G1' altered to show details of a 'G2A'.*

Plate 155: *Class 'G2A No. 9094 at Stoke in 1948. It has a cast Stanier chimney and smokebox door handles instead of the LNWR wheel, two features which seem to have been introduced simultaneously about 1944. Presumably, Stanier-style chimneys were preferred rather than new ones in the old LNWR style, and the use of handles was preferred as they enabled wheel spanners to be dispensed with.*

A. G. Ellis collection

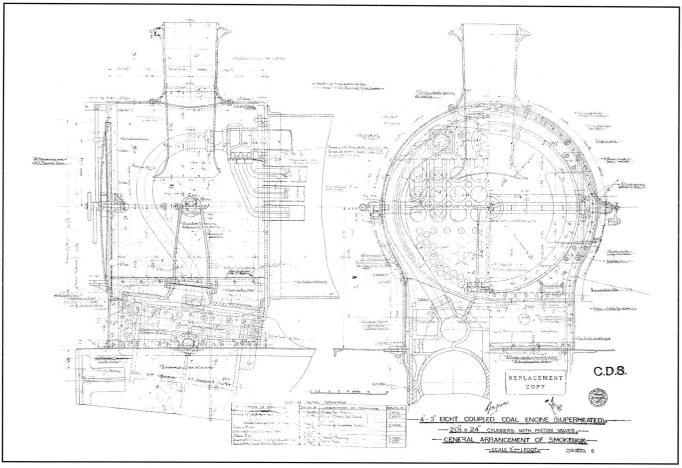

Figure 25: *Drawings of the smokebox of a 'Super D', originally produced in LNWR days (signed by Bowen Cooke and initialled by J. N. Jackson) and altered to show subsequent changes. A Stanier cast chimney is shown but not door handles in place of the wheel, though the drawings are believed to be dated 1946.*

was chief mechanical engineer. In effect, the 'Super Ds' became an unofficial LMS standard class, and on that basis it is even possible to argue that they were Stanier engines, though doubtless the great man would not have been particularly happy with the thought!

Historians of the LMS often like to write about Stanier's 'scrap-and-build' policy (and, incidentally, like to contrast it with the LNER's policy of perpetuating pre-grouping classes). By this they mean that Stanier produced new modern designs in large numbers, and scrapped the pre-grouping engines that previously did the same job. This is partly true of the former LNWR passenger classes, although they had in fact reigned on the main line as long as most classes, steam, diesel and electric, before or since. The engines displaced by the 'Scots' from the hardest turns in 1927, were finally swept away by 'Baby Scots', 'Jubilees' and 'Black Fives', and by the 'Scots' that themselves had been pushed aside by Stanier 'Pacifics'. But what is usually overlooked is that the same process did not take place with heavy goods engines.

When the Stanier '8F' 2-8-0 was eventually produced

in 1935, far too few were built to have any effect on the continued reign of the 'Super Ds'. Only 126 had been completed for the whole of the LMS by 1940 and in any case many of them went to the Midland Division, where apart from the Garratts, themselves handicapped by the same Midland axleboxes as the Fowler '7Fs', much of the heavy coal traffic was still being handled by '4F' 0-6-0s, Derby's 'Big Goods'. On the Western Division the 'Super Ds' continued to reign unchallenged throughout both the 1930s and the Second World War.

The '8Fs' were modern engines and came to be accepted for that reason, though some critics claim they needed a larger superheater, as they had a tendency to be heavy on coal and water. Of course, during the Second World War, they were built in very large numbers, as were their austerity derivatives, the War Department 2-8-0s, and it was only when all these engines became available after the war, in numbers far greater than the LMS could ever have anticipated in the late 1930s, that the 'Super Ds' finally lost their place as the leading heavy freight engine on the lines of the old London & North Western Railway.

Plate 156: *Class 'G1' No. 9222 leaves Shugborough tunnel with an up goods on 16th April 1949. It was never converted to 'G2A' but was scrapped in 1951.*
E. S. Russell

Plate 157 : *Class 'G2A' No. 49323 outside Watford shed on 14th April 1949. The large numerals on the cab side are the style first favoured by Crewe for British Railways' numbers. In some cases they were applied in a dark shade, almost orange, as used by the LMS, but in others the late LMS 'straw' was used.*

H. C. Casserley

The first five conversions to class 'G2A' took place in 1935. At the end of 1937 the LMS had 509 'Super Ds', made up of 444 'G1s', 60 'G2s' and 5 'G2As'. In 1938 more conversions to class 'G2A' were made, by the end of 1939 117 had been so treated, and further conversions were continued throughout the war years. After the war, with the flood of more modern engines that suddenly became available, there was no longer any need to upgrade 'Super Ds'. The last conversions to 'G2A' were made in 1947 and in the same year the unconverted engines began to be scrapped.

British Railways

At the end of 1947, 502 'Super Ds' passed from the LMS into the ownership of British Railways, one of the largest pre-Grouping classes to do so. They were made up of 123 'G1s', 60 'G2s' and 319 'G2As', and they were renumbered, as were all LMS engines, by the addition of 40,000 to their LMS numbers.

No major changes resulted from the new order. The 'Super Ds' still continued to be based at former LNWR sheds, mainly on the Western Division but also on the Central Division of the former LMS, part of which now became the London Midland Region. Although they had been displaced from the hardest duties by Stanier '8F' 2-8-0s, which had become available after the war, there was still plenty of work for them to do. The war-surplus 'WD' 2-8-0s did not affect the 'Super Ds' directly, since they were concentrated by the LMR on the Central

Division, where they mainly displaced the Fowler '7F' 0-8-0s, but their availability in large numbers enabled the Stanier '8Fs' to be concentrated on the Western and Midland Divisions, and so had an indirect effect on the 'Super Ds'.

Thus, no wholesale scrapping of the 'Super Ds' took place at this stage. Nevertheless, the construction of replacement boilers for the class had ceased in 1944, and now, when it was considered too expensive to repair an engine, it was scrapped. So the class was steadily reduced by withdrawals.

The 'G1s' were naturally withdrawn more quickly than the other two classes, and the last survivor, BR No. 49140, originally built as a class 'G' in September 1910, was taken out of service in 1955. In the late 1950s, the BR standard class '9F' 2-10-0 became widely available, first displacing the Garratts on the Midland Division and then the Stanier '8F' from the hardest duties, and as BR freight traffic was itself declining under heavy road competition, there was much less work available for the 'Super Ds' and the class began to be withdrawn more quickly. Nonetheless, the last survivors remained in service to within four years of the end of steam on British Railways. The last four, two 'G2A' class, both originally class 'B', Nos. 48895 and 49361, and two 'G2' class, Nos. 49407 and 49430, were all withdrawn together in December 1964. Thus the line of development which had started with No. 2524 in 1892 came to an end. The 'Super Ds' were extinct.

Plate 158: *No. 49121 still had the early style of numerals in September 1951, when seen here in Abergavenny shed yard. It has had its rear sandbox filler moved to the cab sidesheet.*

Plate 159: *'G2A' No. 49035 at Swansea Paxton Street on 23rd April 1955. Though generally in typical BR condition, it still bears evidence of its Webb compound origins - in the cut-away boss of the leading wheel.* L. King

Plate 160: *Class 'G2A' No. 49230 at Crewe on 12th March 1949, fitted with a snow plough.*
M. Williams collection

Plate 161: *When the 0-8-4 tanks were scrapped, they were replaced as snow-plough engines at Buxton by 'Super Ds', which were fitted with tender cabs for the purpose, with rear footsteps and handrail. Here, 'G2A' No. 49348 stands in the shed yard on 12th March 1955, having been on snow-plough duty. Buxton, of course, was notorious for heavy snow. A note by J. M. Dunn on the back of the print says: 'Buxton was the only LNW shed where the breakdown train was officially supplied with whiskey!'*
F. W. Shuttleworth

Plate 162: *Another 'G2', No. 49408 at Wigan Springs Branch on 4th April 1953. The tender has the final type of 'back cab' and the rear sand filler has been moved to the cab side.*   A. G. Ellis collection

Plate 163: *'G2A' No. 49387 passing Higher Buxton on the Ashbourne line on 28th September 1951. It already has the standard numerals, though less than four years after nationalisation, and has a good coating of grime, but all the same is clearly going well.*
E. R. Morten

Plate 164: *After withdrawal in October 1955, 'G1' class No. 49140 was used for a time as a shunter in Crewe Works, where it is seen here in August 1956. Clearly, it has borrowed an ex works tender and to prevent buffer-lock has been fitted with oval buffers, presumably from a 2-6-4 tank rather than a 'Princess Coronation'!*

Plate 165: *Another scene in Crewe Works in the late 1950s. 'G2' No. 49414 has been given the Crewe treatment and no doubt will soon be hard at it, back on the main line again, once a few more fittings have been replaced and a few more dabs of black paint applied.*

L. King

Plate 166: 'Super Ds' were famous for leaks and wheezes at the front end, which of course became more visible on a winter's day, and here No. 49239 shows this propensity at Sutton Oak shed on 27th February 1955. Like a lot of engines in the 492XX series, largely those built new as class 'G1' in 1912-18, it still has indirect action. Assorted fire-irons are lying around, and there are two braziers, to prevent water pipes freezing up and perhaps incidentally to provide some warmth for men working in the area.

F. W. Shuttleworth

Plate 167: *'G2A' No. 49230 at Chester on 6th September 1955. The tender has the final type of 'back cab' but the rear sand filler must still be in the usual position in the cab.*   A. G. Ellis collection

Plate 169 (opposite top): *'G2A' No. 49230 banking a Rowsley-Buxton train near Litton on 27th August 1955.*   E. R. Morten

Plate 170 (opposite bottom): *'G2' No. 49426 at Patricroft shed In August 1958. It is allocated to '26F', Lees. The tender is the first Cooke type.*   Peter Groom

Plate 168: *A typical 'G2A' of the mid-1950s, No. 49088 has a Cooke tender of the third type.*   R. Bell collection

Plate 171: *'G2A' No. 49344 in Willesden shed yard on 11th January 1959. It still has indirect action (on engines with direct action the reach rod is higher to the left of the sandbox than to the right).* Peter Groom

Plate 172: *'G2A' No. 49078 in Willesden shed yard on 18th June 1960, an interesting comparison in its details with No. 49344 above. The position of the reach rod with direct action (higher to the left of the sandbox than to the right) is clearly shown.* Peter Groom

Plate 173: *Another typical 'Super D', No. 49114 at Peterborough Spital shed on 13th October 1957.*   L. King

On 17th May 1961 David A. Anderson was at Oxford when no fewer than four 'Super Ds' arrived from Bletchley. The seven photographs which he took of them repay careful study of such details as lubricators, sandboxes, desanding gear, electrification flashes, tenders and so forth; and make the conclusion seem perfectly reasonable that no two 'Super Ds' were identical at this time, and for a long time before! This diversity does not extend to the BR crest and perhaps surprisingly at this late date, all four engines have the first type.

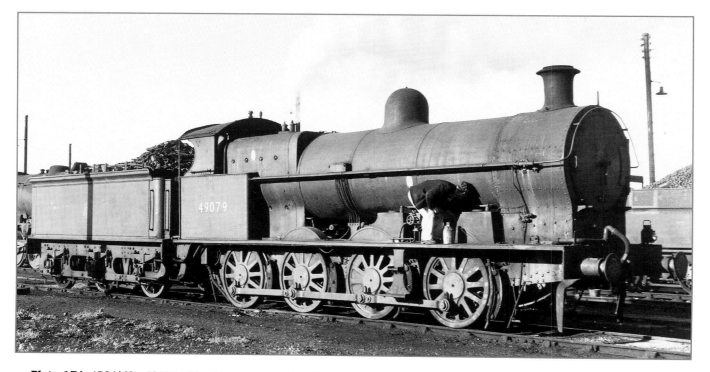

Plate 174: *'G2A' No. 49079. The driver seems to be oiling the motion.*   David A. Anderson

Plate 175: *'G2' No. 49439 taking water. The different angle of the rear sandpipe for steam sanding (part of 'improved rear sanding'), compared with gravity sanding, can be seen clearly in this picture and that of No. 49403. The tender is the final Cooke type with cab and associated modifications. Its number seems to be 1715.*

David A. Anderson

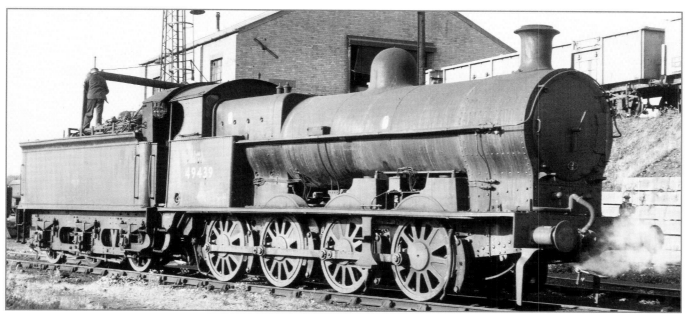

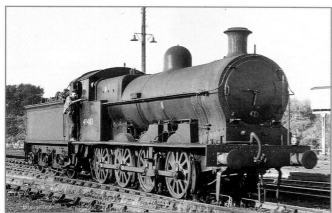

Plate 176: *Another view of 'G2' No. 49439 taking water. This engine has two pipes coming down from the oilbox on the handrail instead of the more usual four and so must have two Wakefield fountain-type lubricators in the cab. A view of the cab of this engine appears in plate 218.* David A. Anderson

Plate 177: *'G2' No. 49403. The concentration of the fireman as he makes his way along the outside of the cab shows the imporrtance of the short handrail fitted on the Belpaire engines.* David A. Anderson

Plate 178: *A general view of No. 49403. It also has only two pipes coming from the oilbox on the handrail; and so must also have two Wakelfield fountain-type lubricators in the cab.* David A. Anderson

Plate 179-80: *Two views of No. 49314. Of particular interest is the tender, which was once fitted to a 'Claughton'. The small sidesheet behind the handrail on the front of the tender is virtually a straight extension of the tank side, to match the door on the 'Claughton' cab. On non-'Claughton' tenders, the front of the tank curves inwards before this sidesheet is attached. Its 'Claughton' origins also explain why there is a disused steam-heating pipe on the rear.* David A. Anderson

Plate 181: *'G2A' No. 49094 waiting to back under the coaling plant at Stafford about 1961. It has just been through Crewe Works and had a full repaint, complete with electrification flashes but without its BR crest being renewed, and is now on the way to its home shed, Bletchley, '1E' at this time.* Author

Plate 182: *No. 49216 in store at Bescot on 29th September 1962. It was withdrawn a few weeks later, no doubt still with indirect action as seen here.* Peter Groom

Plate 183: *'Super D' No. 49125 on the turntable at Bescot about 1961. The old Bescot station is in the background.*

J. B. Bucknall

Plate 184: *No. 48895 inside Bushbury shed on 29th September 1962.*

Peter Groom

Plate 185: *Of the last four surviving 'Super Ds' two had originally been 'B' class compounds and two were 'G2s'. Here 'G2A' No. 48895, one of the last two former 'B' class, originally built in May 1904, waits by the water column at Bescot on 15th August 1964. The last four survivors were all withdrawn four months later in December 1964.* Peter Groom

Plate 186: *Here, on the same day, one of the last two 'G2s' No. 49430 stands on the turntable at Bescot. The yellow stripe on the cab side indicates that the engine was not allowed to work 'under the wires' south of Crewe.* Peter Groom

Plate 187: *Class 'B' 0-8-0s under construction in No. 8 erecting shop, Crewe Works, on 5th August 1903. Many interesting details can be seen of components normally hidden from view in completed engines, such as the boiler stay and the way the cylinders were bolted to the frames. The slots in the footplating where the splashers would be fitted are visible on several engines, and in the right foreground is the top of an LNWR chimney. In the right foreground are bogie frames, presumably for 'Bill Bailey' 4-6-0s.*

LNWR A460

Chapter Five
TECHNICAL ASPECTS

Originally No. 2524 and the 'A' class three-cylinder compound 0-8-0s had straight frames of 1in plate set 4ft 2in apart, the firebox being 3ft 11in wide. When the 'A' class engines were converted to two-cylinder simple 0-8-0s of classes 'C' and 'D', the outside high-pressure cylinders were removed and the front part of the frames holding the low-pressure cylinder was cut off. A new front section of frames holding the new cylinders was then added at the front. The distance across the new cylinders was 4ft 2in and the cylinders were either 19½in or 18½in in diameter according to the class. The joint was just ahead of the leading axlebox and a piece of steel plate was bolted across the joint to give adequate strength. Thus when converted these classes still had continuous in-line frames.

In the case of the 'B' class, however, the front piece of frames holding the low-pressure cylinders was in effect a separate unit and was bolted inside the main frames. The reason for this was that the low-pressure cylinders on these engines were the same as on the 'Jubilee' and 'Alfred the Great' class 4-4-0s, in which the front portion of frames was narrowed so as to allow adequate side-play for the bogie. The distance across the cylinders was 4ft. Thus when the 'B' class engines were converted to simple, to 'G' or 'G1' class, there was no need to alter the frames. The outside cylinders were removed, and in the 'G' class the old low-pressure cylinders were retained with high-pressure steam. In the 'G1' class they were usually replaced by new piston-valve cylinders but some fourteen engines were converted retaining their original slide-valve cylinders with direct Joy motion. Thirteen of them were later altered to piston valves, but one, No. 641 LMS No. 9151, was unique in retaining slide valves until scrapped on 15th August 1952. At least four 'B' class (including Nos. 410 and 2118) are known to have been so treated at Rugby.

The list below shows the original class and numbers of engines converted to superheating while retaining slide valves, the date of conversion (SV) and the date of fitting piston valve cylinders (PV), and finally the LMS number:

Class	No.	SV	PV	LMS	Class	No.	SV	PV	LMS
'B'	410	11.18	10.25	9331	'B'	1448	12.17	6.25	9273
'B'	500	6.17	2.25	9265	'E'	1885	8.17	7.25	9267
'G'	641	3.27		9151	'E'	1889	6.20	12.27	9345
'B'	904	5.19	4.24	9337	'B'	2118	4.18	4.25	9292
'B'	1043	6.18	4.24	9304	'B'	2568	12.19	11.25	9342
'B'	1066	12.17	5.22	9272	'E'	2574	1.20	6.22	9343
'B'	1094	10.18	8.28	9324	'G'	2673	1.12	11.27	9154

The same arrangement of frames (the front portion holding the cylinders fitting inside the main portion) is believed to have been used in the new 'G' class of 1910, which probably had the 'Jubilee' low-pressure cylinders bored out to 20½in, and it was certainly used in the 'G1' and 'G2' classes. Thus, the old 'B' class low-pressure cylinders were the same width, 4ft, as the new 'G1' piston-valve cylinders. The 'C' and 'D' class cylinders and smokebox were 2in wider at the base and so when they were converted to 'G1' class the front portion of the frames had to be cut off and replaced with a new section fitting inside the old main frames in the same fashion as the 'B' class and new 'G1' class.

Like all LNWR engines with two inside cylinders and Joy valve gear, the 0-8-0s had a central frame, a steel casting bolted between the cylinders and extending as far as the frame stretcher to the rear of the driving axle. Its purpose was to support the driving axle at its mid point and to add strength to the frames in this crucial area. At some stage in LMS days it was decided as a matter of routine to cease fitting the brasses in the bearing supporting the axle, though the centre bearing casting remained in position. Presumably, the reasoning behind this decision was that the bearing served no essential purpose and so maintenance costs would be reduced if it were not fitted. The date when this began is not known for certain but is thought to have been quite early, perhaps before 1925, but it may have been associated with the introduction of 'The Belts' in Crewe Works and the drive to speed up overhauls. Later, from about 1945 onwards, the centre frame itself was removed from most engines, probably all, as they went through works.

No doubt, this made things easier for the men who had to work between the frames, as they no longer had to manoeuvre round it, and no doubt too, these alterations were made for the same reason, to reduce maintenance costs. E. A. Langridge has criticised the centre bearing on the grounds that its effect could not be measured. There seems little doubt, however, that the removal of both the bearings and the frame had an adverse effect on the life of the main frames themselves. Certainly, after the removal of the centre frame, cracks began to appear around the driving horns on the 'G2As', though not on the 'G2s', which were relatively crack-free. This was probably because their frames were thicker and had less of a curved cut-out on the lower edges.

The frames of all the 0-8-0s were built with a cross-member between the second and third axles, which supported the rear of the centre bearing casting and was extended upwards to form a stay secured to the boiler. In No. 2524, the 'A' class and the first twenty 'B' class up to No. 1900 built in December 1901, the stay was made from 1in steel plate; it had angles riveted to the sides, top and front to fix it to the frames, boiler and centre bearing casting respectively. A circular opening was cut in it, presumably to give access to the boiler mud hole. Originally, No. 2524 and at least the first five

Three views of No. 9186 about 1936.
G. H. Platt, M. Williams collection

Plate 188: *The left-side front end. The reach rod is higher in front of the driving splasher than to the rear of it - it curves up behind it, indicating that the engine has direct action. On the side of the smokebox are the oil pipes to the valves of the left cylinder; they run along the back of the smokebox to the lubricator on the other side. Lower down, partly hidden by the running plate, is the anti-vacuum valve.*

Plate 189: *The right-side front end. LMS buffers are already fitted but not desanding gear. The drain pipe from the ejector pipe runs down the side of the smokebox, through the running plate and down the frame. In front of the ejector pipe, rather shadowy on the side of the smokebox, is the blower valve. The rod curving up beneath the frames operates the cylinder drain cocks. Between the splashers is a Wakefield cylinder lubricator. It feeds the two pipes on the side of the smokebox which carry oil to the valves. Below the pipes, at the base of the smokebox, is the anti-vacuum valve. Two similar pipes lead across the back of the smokebox to feed the valves of the left cylinder. The thick pipe curving into the left-hand side of the lubricator is the heater pipe which reduces the viscosity of the oil. Three separate coupling rods are fitted, the centre one outside the outer two. These were known to the men as 'Whale' rods, as they were used on the new 'G' class of 1910, though they were actually introduced by Mr Webb on No. 2524. On these three-piece rods, of course, the bushes on the driving and intermediate wheels were narrow, as two bushes had to fit on one pin.*

Plate 190: *Further back on the right-hand side. There is a man-hole or mud plug under the boiler. In his book written in 1893 Bowen Cooke mentions that a piece of zinc was fitted inside this man-hole to act chemically on the water and deter the formation of scale on the boiler plates and tubes. The rod coming out of the firebox casing operates the front dampers. It has a counterweight just in front of it. The other rod, just visible in front of the intermediate splasher, operates the cylinder drain cocks. Just to the right of the brake hanger for the intermediate wheels is the crank-shaft bearing for the leading brake cylinder. Inside the brake stretcher of the rear wheels can be seen the compensating or equalising lever. The rear sandpipe has been bent up close to the wheel and the end cut off parallel to the rail to prevent water driving up into it. To the left are telescopic feed pipes between engine and tender.*

Plate 191: *The Wakefield cylinder lubricator on another 'Super D' about 1929, showing clearly the heater pipe, and also the rod linking the sanders on this side of the engine and its pivot on the splasher for the crankshaft across the engine to the sanders on the left side. The lubricator was driven by a crankshaft off the right crosshead; it could not be fitted on the left because of the reversing arm, and even here it made it difficult for the men to oil the motion.* R. S. Carpenter collection

Plate 192: *View of the right-hand side of the smokebox of an unidentified 'Super D'. The large pipe entering the smokebox is the exhaust from the vacuum ejector and ran alongside the boiler from the cab. The small pipe running vertically down from it is the drain pipe, which carried away any condensation. The handrail outside the ejector pipe carried steam to the blower, the connection to which can be seen just ahead of the ejector pipe. The other two small pipes supplied oil to the valves of the right cylinder.*
J. P. Richards, M. Williams collection

Plate 193 (below): *Another view of the same engine from the same viewpoint but looking further towards the rear. The ejector exhaust pipe and handrail, with supplementary oil box, are well shown, as is detail lower down such as the linkage between the two sandboxes and the bracket on the side of the firebox supporting the rear of the boiler.*
J. P. Richards, M. Williams collection

of the 'A' class did not have this opening but they were soon modified accordingly, so it was clearly an after-thought necessitated by the need to allow access.

In the third batch of 'B' class, beginning with No. 813 built in March 1902, the plate stay was replaced by a one-piece casting which incorporated all the angle fixings that had previously been riveted, as well as stiffening ribs along the bottom, around the opening, which was now oval, and along both sides. In photographs, the side ribs appear triangular in section and so cast stays can easily be distinguished from plate. The cast stays were then used on all the 0-8-0s built subsequently, including the 'G2s'.

It may seem difficult now to understand what the thinking was behind this stay. A boiler is an immensely rigid structure, unlikely to sag or buckle, and so in no need of support. The stay, however, made the frames more rigid, resisting any forces bending them upwards, and that was its function. Though it may seem doubtful that frames would need such strengthening, those of the preserved 9395 are now 'banana-shaped'. An obvious disadvantage is that when the engine was in steam, the boiler and frames would expand rearwards by different amounts, thus bending the stay between the top of the frames and the underside of the boiler.

Whatever the reason, at some time between January 1922 and August 1925 the stays of both types began to be cut off level with the top of the frames, thus no longer being secured to the boiler. This can be seen in

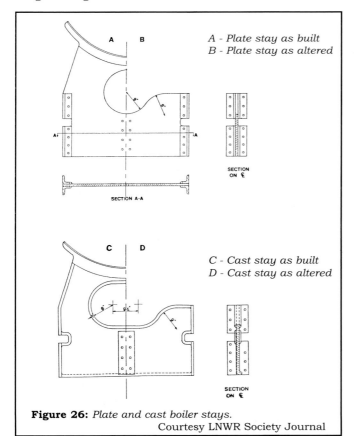

Figure 26: *Plate and cast boiler stays.*
Courtesy LNWR Society Journal

A - Plate stay as built
B - Plate stay as altered

SECTION ON ₵

SECTION A-A

C - Cast stay as built
D - Cast stay as altered

SECTION ON ₵

photographs, as the lower edge of the oval access hole with its flange or stiffening rib remains, whereas the part which has been cut has no such rib. In some cases, however, new frame stretchers were fitted, with strengthening rib all the way along the top.

The change was probably made to allow greater access to fitters working between the frames. It is sometimes said to be associated with the fitting of the second brake cylinder, giving 'increased brake power', and that may well be so; but in practice it seems to have been carried out as a matter of routine, on all engines of all classes entering the works, irrespective of whether they were also fitted with the extra brake cylinder at the same time. It may also have been made at the same time as the removal of the centre bearing, to make the engines generally easier to work on.

The axleboxes on the early eight-coupled engines, No. 2524 and the 'A' class and 'B' class, were the standard Webb 7in by 9in boxes as introduced on the '17in Coal Engines' in place of Ramsbottom's 7in by 7in axleboxes on the 'DX' class, and the cast-iron wheels were basically the same also. When Webb began to scrap the '17in Coal Engines', their wheels were often re-used on eight-coupled engines, on 'B' class, for example, and can be identified in photographs by their different arrangement of balance weights, and axles and axleboxes were also probably re-used, when in good condition. The same wheels were still in use on the 'G1' class some twenty years after Webb retired, and remained in use on 'G2As' well into BR days, and the same axleboxes were used on all these engines too, except that the crank axles were enlarged to $7\frac{1}{2}$in from No. 2524, to 8in in class 'G' and to $8\frac{1}{2}$in in class 'G1' and all later rebuilds. In the 'G2' class and the 0-8-4 tanks the wheels were slightly redesigned, with different balance weights and with the spokes slightly canted inwards to the rim and the axles were thicker by about 1in, it is believed, and so the axleboxes themselves were larger.

LNWR axlebox brasses were given letters to identify them. The 'G1s' and 'G2As' had 'W' brasses on the leading, intermediate and trailing boxes, and 'H' on the driving boxes, while the 'G2s' had 'R' and 'Q' brasses respectively. The Webb 'Coal Tank' had 'X' brasses, incidentally, and though the continued use of axleboxes designed by Webb in the 1870s may seem archaic and their re-use false economy, it was well justified by events. The 'Super Ds' continued in service with their 'old' axleboxes longer than the Fowler '7F' 0-8-0s built to replace them in the 1920s, which had the notorious Midland axleboxes.

The frames of all the earliest classes were re-used in the rebuilding to 'G1' class. During the 1940s, and probably at other periods too, the section of the frames around the crank axle was cut away when worn and a new piece welded in. Some of these frames must then have dated from the 1890s. All the 0-8-0s had 1in frames, except the 'G2s', which possibly had $1\frac{1}{8}$in frames, as in the 4-6-2 tanks and 'Claughtons' (though the preserved No. 9395 has 1in frames), and the same thicker frames were then also used in the 0-8-4 tanks.

Three views of the front end of 'G1' No. 8922 at Warwick Milverton in 1929.

Plate 194 (above): *General view showing smokebox and running plate. Except for the LMS numberplate, the engine is very much in LNWR condition with smokebox door wheel and Cooke buffers. The plate at the side of the base of the smokebox covers the anti-vacuum valve, which allowed air into the cylinder when steam was shut off and so prevented any pumping action that might draw smokebox gases and ash into the cylinder.* J. P. Richards, M. Williams collection

Plate 195 (left): *View looking along the left-hand side and showing the flat leading big end, retained from the original compound and designed to allow the connecting rod to pass. There are two coupling rods, the leading one fitting on the first three axles, and the rear one fitting outside it, as on the compounds. The position of the reach rod signifies that the engine has been converted to direct action.* J. P. Richards, M. Williams collection

Plate 196 (right): *Close-up of the bufferbeam and of an LNWR screw coupling, showing the flattened portion or 'gedge' of the first link, which allowed the coupling to be worked into the slot behind the hook. No desanding apparatus is yet fitted and the bufferbeam has not had the additional strengthening which was applied later.* J. P. Richards, M. Williams collection

Plate 197: *View for comparison, some thirty year later than No. 8922, of 'G2A' No. 49287 shunting at Aylesbury on 30th April 1958,. It has one-piece side rods, the standard later arrangement, but still retains indirect action - the reach rod is lower at the front end because with indirect action the weighshaft is lower. The brake gear, leading sand-pipe and desanding pipe are all well shown.*

M. Williams collection

Several books give the weight of all the 'Super Ds' as 60 tons but in fact the 'G2s' were heavier than 'G1s' and 'G2As'. Weights, of course, varied, depending how much had been machined off tyres and whether the boiler had been changed from Belpaire to round top. When engines were returned to their sheds after overhaul, the works sent the weight chart with the individual weights on each axle and the 'G2s' generally weighed some 64-66 tons, whereas the other classes weighed about 60 tons. In some places this meant that they were banned, while earlier classes were allowed. In South Wales the 'G2s' and 0-8-4 tanks were allowed over Pensarn Viaduct but not over Cefn Coed Viaduct into Merthyr, though the 'G1s' and 'G2As' were allowed there. When the Western Region took over in 1950, this restriction was removed. The 'G2s' were also banned by the GWR between Hereford and Worcester via Ledbury, a route often used by Abergavenny for excursion trains for shopkeepers to Cadbury's at Bournville. However, although the 'G2s' were officially banned from the Ashbourne - Uttoxeter line too, they worked over it regularly and in practice no distinction was made between them and other 'Super Ds'. Incidentally, as well as the weight chart, the works also sent a list showing cylinder diameters, bearing sizes and the like, so that the shed could order parts such as valve and piston rings before the engine was stopped for repair.

Another factor which enabled these extensive rebuildings to be carried out easily is that the basic dimensions of both the frames and boilers of all the different classes, Webb, Whale and Bowen Cooke, were the same. Once the large Whale boiler had been introduced on the 'F' and 'D' class, all subsequent boilers were the same size but varied to suit the different classes in pressure (in some cases a matter of fitting suitable safety valves), in whether saturated or superheated, and in the type of firebox, round-top or Belpaire. So the 'C', 'C1' and 'D' classes all had 175lb psi pressure, the 'G' class 160lb, the 0-8-2 tanks 170lb, the 'G1' class 160lb but superheated, the 'G2' 175lb superheated and so on. So 175lb psi pressure was already common in 1906, and Crewe had in fact built 200lb psi boilers in 1897.

On the other hand, the use of the same basic frame dimensions for engines of different weights had a fundamental disadvantage. Ideally, all the coupled axles of an engine should carry the same weight so as to equalise tyre wear on all wheels. Whale was concerned about the weight at the front of the 'B' class but the 'D', 'G', 'G1' and 'G2' classes were all equally as bad. Only the 'C' and 'C1' classes had reasonably equal weight on each axle. Most other British 0-8-0s had the last two axles closer to each other and to the crank axle, which gives a much better weight per axle. The GWR 2-8-0 was unusual in that the rear two axles carried more weight than the front two, and the same pattern was followed by the Stanier '8F' 2-8-0, whose weight distribution was 8 tons 10cwt, 15 tons, 15 tons, 16 tons and 16 tons. The GWR 2-8-0 had its springs connected by equalising levers between the first and second wheels and the third and fourth, but this was abandoned in later examples.

On No. 2524 and the 'A' and 'B' class compounds, equalising levers were fitted between the first, second and third wheels, which had plain springs mounted on brackets above the axle in the orthodox manner. The large boiler adopted by Whale, with its larger firebox,

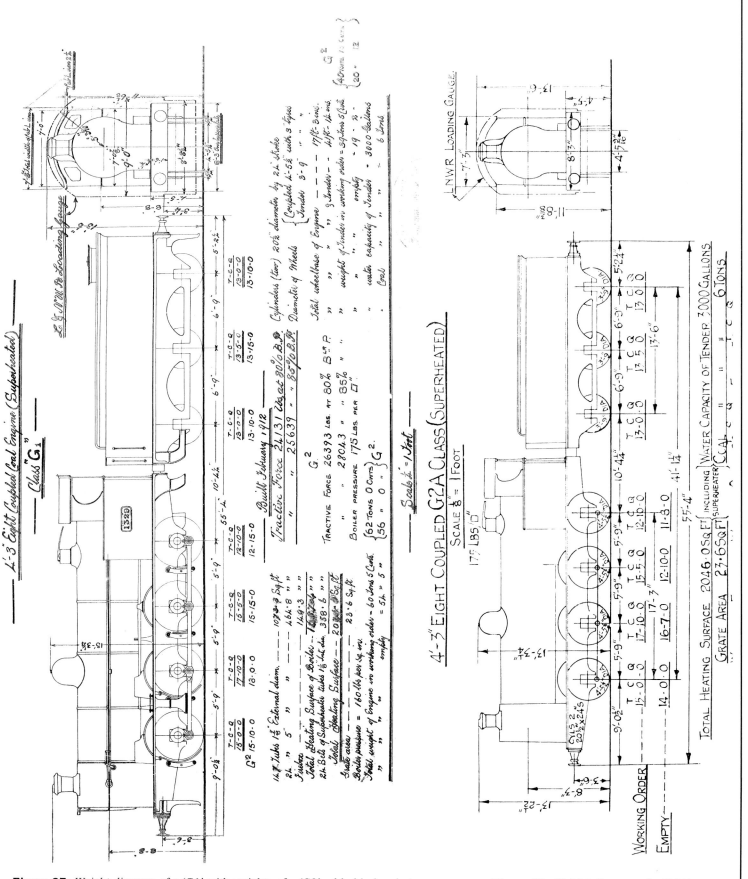

Figure 27: *Weight diagram of a 'G1' with weights of a 'G2' added in brackets.*

Figure 28: *Weight diagram of a 'G2A'.*

precluded the use of this type of spring on the intermediate axle, and so it was abandoned, along with the equalising levers. Instead, the intermediate axle on Whale and Cooke 0-8-0s had one spring mounted transversely 'upside down'. It was the same type of spring as that used on the radial truck of the 'Coal Tanks', a typical piece of Crewe economy.

This spring, incidentally, was extremely difficult to remove for replacement. The axle had to be lowered on the wheel drop and the spring lifted by means of ropes round the boiler before being swung out over the running plate. On the trailing axle, this type of spring could not be used because of the firebox and therefore a transverse spring was fitted below the axle. This spring was attached to the underside of the axleboxes and had a dry bearing in the centre. When it was being changed (which again was extremely difficult), some fitters used to put grease in the 'dry' bearing, as the drivers complained that it creaked on a rough road.

In the 'G2' class Beames retained the same overall dimensions but redesigned the frames and motion generally to give greater strength and better durability. In addition to thicker plate for the frames, thicker axles and larger axleboxes, the horn brackets were naturally larger too and of slightly different shape, the curved cut-outs in the lower edge of the frames were less pronounced and the big ends were larger. The gudgeon pins were the same length but larger in diameter, by about 1in, and had thin-wall bushes, about $\frac{1}{2}$in thick, whereas the 'G2As' had thick-wall bushes. The piston rods were $\frac{1}{2}$in larger in diameter and used narrow packing instead of the wide segment packing of other 'Super Ds'. The motion plate, known as the 'spectacle plate' from its resemblance to a pair of spectacles, was thicker and heavier, and had double brackets for the bolts of the slide bars, instead of the single brackets of the 'G1s'. All these improvements, plus the Belpaire boiler, meant that the 'G2s' weighed about 6 tons more than the 60 tons of the 'G1s'. The same redesigned features were later used in the 0-8-4 tanks.

The 'Super D' Beat
The successive rebuilding of the 0-8-0s perhaps holds the key to one of the minor mysteries of LNWR engines, namely the uneven exhaust beat of the 'Super Ds'. This phenomenon was at its greatest in these engines but was also noticeable from time to time in other Joy valve gear engines and was a significant part of the attraction of North Western engines for enthusiasts of the day. Don Rowlands described the exhaust beat of the 'Super Ds' superbly in an evocative article in the November

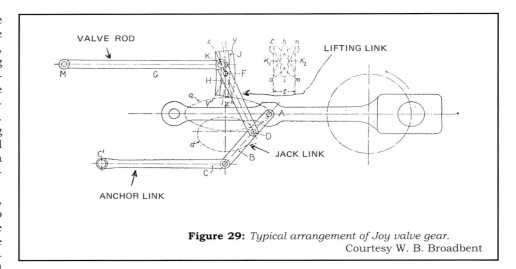

Figure 29: *Typical arrangement of Joy valve gear.*
Courtesy W. B. Broadbent

1988 issue of *Railway World*.

An explanation of the reasons for the uneven exhaust is given on page 149 of *North Western Steam* by Tuplin:

'The alternation of two heavy beats and two light ones in engines with Joy valve gear may be explained by the lowering of the frame in relation to the driving axle by deflection of the springs under the weight of water used to fill the boiler after the operation of setting the valves. Difference in strength between the two heavier beats is a result of imperfections in setting the valves.

'The difference between superheater engines and "wet steam" engines in irregularity of exhaust beats may be explained by the stronger response of the larger valves (piston-valves) of the former to any shift of the valve spindles. Unevenness of beat is probably far less important than it sounds and Crewe Works seemed quite indifferent to it'.

Tuplin is correct in stating that the unevenness was caused by movement of the frame in relation to the driving axle but not that this was caused by the weight of water in the boiler. This factor was allowed for by the drawing office in designing the valve gear, and furthermore, when valve setting was checked at the sheds after valve and piston examination or renewal of worn motion parts, the final check was invariably done with the boiler full. In fact, there was very little variation whether the boiler was full or empty. Equal readings could be obtained for each end of the stroke and, with the reversing wheel two turns back, the normal position for running, the exhaust still had the famous two-heavy two-light beat. Even then, no surge was felt in passenger trains worked by the 0-8-0s as, for example, in the Abergavenny area.

Incidentally, whereas on some railways such as the LNER valves were set at the sheds as a matter of routine, Crewe practice was to set valves in the works only. If the valve gear had to be dismantled during shed repairs, it was simply taken off and put back on in the reverse order. Exceptionally, if valve-setting had to be done at a shed, someone from the valve-setting gang in the Works would go out to do it.

This is confirmed by W. B. Broadbent, who was an engineering apprentice at Crewe Works from January 1942 to March 1945 ('engineering apprentices' were the more democratic successors to the 'premium apprentices', whose fathers had to pay a fee or 'premium' to the chief mechanical engineer of the day). He worked on the valve-setting gang in No. 10 erecting shop for the last three months or so of this period and at the time carried out his own investigation into the phenomenon of the uneven beat. He very kindly wrote the following explanation:

'William Joy's valve gear produces some of the most ideal valve events of any gear, and its application to LNWR locomotives was an important ingredient if not the most significant reason for their remarkable performance. It requires no eccentrics, with their large area of rotational friction surface, and has only the same number of part-rotational fulcrums as Walschaerts' gear (unless a rocker arm is used). Properly designed and set out, it gives adequate valve travel for superheated engines, snappy action with the lap and lead travel, and staccato cut-off from a good long dwell for exhaust and admission.

'The crucial factor in design and construction is the correct positioning of all the various components. The cylinders, steamchests, piston rods and valve spindles must be accurately positioned, both longitudinally and transversely, in relation to the driving-axle centre lines, and the vertical and horizontal centre lines of the weigh-shaft trunnions must also be accurately positioned in relation to the same centre lines. The mechanical forces imposed on the connecting rods would not cause deflection to such an extent as to alter the movement of the valves.

'Certainly Tuplin is right in making the general statement that the uneven beat is caused by the lowering of the frames in relation to the driving axle. Here is the nub of the whole thing: as the frames move vertically in relation to the driving axle (and jack link fulcrum pin in the connecting rod) so does the weighbar shaft move with it. And as the weighbar shaft moves in this way, so do the slipper blocks, in their curved guides fixed to the weighbar, move relatively up or down. In mid gear, when the weighbar shaft guides' tangent is at right angles to the valve rods and valve spindles, there is no movement of the valves except for the angularity deriving from the lifting link swinging fore and aft with the stroke of the piston from end to end of the cylinders. This provides the necessary angularity at the top fulcrum pin of the lifting link coupled to the end of the valve rod to give the required lap and lead travel.

'However, if the reversing screw favours "forward" or "reverse" position, so the weighbar component is swung about its trunnions and as the slipper blocks rise and fall in their curved guides, the fore and aft motion at the fulcrum pin through the slipper blocks from the lifting link is transmitted to the valve spindle through the valve rod which connects its lifting link fulcrum to the valve spindle crosshead.

'Now, if the weighbar shaft trunnions are centred incorrectly in the vertical plane relative to the driving axle centre line, at its running height in the frames, the fore and aft motion transmitted will be unequal when the big end is at the top or bottom position in its circle of rotation.

'Thus the position of the weighbar shaft is the essence of the whole thing. If the geometry of the gear is correctly designed and all the components are correctly made and assembled, the gear will provide equal port openings for steam admission to the front and rear of the cylinders. It will not do so, however, if the weighbar shaft trunnions are not correctly positioned in the vertical plane.

'Ideally this adjustment should always be made when setting valves on a Joy gear engine but in my experience was never done at Crewe. This is not surprising really in view of the considerable weight of the weighbar component, its position between the frames under the boiler and the limited accessibility of the substantial fitted bolts securing the trunnions to the frames, and also the need to dismantle most of the rest of both valve gears, if the position of the trunnions is to be altered. Moreover, all fitted bolt holes for such parts were very accurately marked out on the frames and jig-drilled in the first place, so if the drawing was right, assembly was right.

'It so happened that during the time I was on the valve-setting job, Terry O'Neill, the works No. 3 who was in charge of apprentices, decided that one of my contemporaries, John Dowling by name, and I should do an exercise to improve the lame beat of the good old "Super Ds", as we used to call any and all of the LNWR 0-8-0s. John was given three months in the Deviation mill shop to make a 1½in scale model of the gear, direct and indirect versions, while I persevered, against every human objection and impediment, to set up the

valves on all "Super Ds" that came through my hands in 10 shop with more than ½in variance front and back port openings in full gear, correcting the positions of the weighbar shaft trunnions. I think I managed to get two correctly set, and I can remember hearing at least one of them, having retained their numbers in my pocket book, thumping up from the through goods lines under Crewe North junction with full trains on with an exhaust beat as sweet and even as a nut.

'John's work confirmed the correctness of the original design geometry, although I think there was some suggestion of a small correction to the lifting link dimensions for the direct-drive version. He recalls that the textbook he read before making his model stated that the weighbar shaft centres were "central to achieving correct valve events", and he was told that at Horwich the LYR tanks fitted with Joy gear had a bracket on the main frames, to support the weighbar shaft trunnion blocks, such that its height could be varied by means of flat shims between the brackets and the trunnion blocks. John designed and made his model in this manner and found that even incorrectly dimensioned rods in the valve gear could be tolerated by use of the adjustable weighbar shaft centres.

'In his report he therefore proposed that a similar arrangement should be fitted to all the 500 or so "Super Ds". These findings delighted Terry O'Neill, but his enthusiasm was soon dampened, as he received a sharp rap over the knuckles from Roland Bond, the works manager, for diverting this miniscule portion of apprentice time to the "Super Ds", and resulted in an edict that as all LNWR locomotives would be scrapped as soon as hostilities ceased, no money was to be spent on any modifications or improvements to them. Many were still running twenty years later!

'Terry O'Neill's defence was that there was a substantial coal-saving to be made if all the "Super Ds" had a regular beat, and coal was after all a precious raw material for the war effort. Bond's reply was that this was false economy and his sermon was taken up by Mr Bird, the 10 shop foreman, and by Leach, our valve-section leading hand. I was able to set the valves correctly on the two engines I tackled only because I was fitter-in-charge on nights at the time and so was far removed from any administrative memoranda and was able to talk one or two of the lads on A and B belts into doing some extra work of an unusual nature. Altering the centres of the weighbar shaft trunnions was out of the question. These were bushed castings, cold-riveted to the main frames, so the rivets would have had to be pneumatically chipped off and driven out, and then new holes centred and drilled, and the new cold-fitted rivets hammered over, all of which would have been far too much to do in a twelve-hour night shift. So I achieved the same effect by having the lifting links removed and "jumped" (made shorter) in the forge to reduce the centre-to-centre dimension between the jack link and die block journals, thus bringing the die blocks lower in the weighbar slides (and so satisfying John Dowling's conclusion about the dimensioning of valve gear rods and weighbar shaft-driving axle centres).

'On tank engines, of course, the problem of variations in engine weight causing the weighbar shaft to be in the wrong position was more serious because of the fluctuating weight of water in the tanks. Unfortunately, when I was at Crewe all the 4-6-2 tanks had been scrapped, and I remember grieving over the condemned body of the last "Precursor Tank", so there was no opportunity of first-hand experience of setting valves on those engines, which with 1700 gallon side tanks could vary in weight by 7½ tons on a daily working basis. However, I asked Alf Groves, the leading hand of the valve-setting gang, how they used to allow for that. "Set 'em as if the tanks are half full", was the reply. And that was the basis on which the valve-gear components were dimensioned. So they were seldom adrift by a vertical variance caused by a 3-ton differential in weight on the suspension.

'So, if the gear was designed correctly, and workshop construction and assembly was pretty good, the question remains as to what caused the uneven beat on the "Super Ds", or rather how the weighbar shaft came to be in the wrong place, and the answer seems to be in the weight of the engine. In their final form the "Super Ds" were the direct descendants of various old classes. The "C" class weighed 48 tons, the "D" class and "G" class 56 tons, the "G1" 60 tons and "G2" class 66 tons. When these earlier classes were upgraded to "Super Ds", no new frames, or indeed cylinders in some cases, were needed and so no attention was given to the increase in weight, and being tender engines no 'mean' position was assumed of weighbar trunnions to account for deflection due to weight variation. So most "Super Ds" left Crewe Works with a driving wheel to weighbar centre-line dimension designed for a lighter locomotive, in some cases up to

20 per cent lighter. The uneven exhaust was really a significant trademark only of the 0-8-0s. The other Whale and Cooke engines, indeed all other Joy-gear engines, ran more or less from start to finish as originally designed and built - sweet as a nut!

'In practice, of course, the uneven beat was only really evident in valve gear settings of 50 per cent to full forward or reverse, so it was really only when starting or slogging up stiff gradients that it became noticeable. Nothing was done about it in the Beames era of restoring and retaining as much as possible of existing LNWR stock, constrained by the eagle-eyed accountants sent by Fowler and his merry men from Nelson Street in Derby. Under the Stanier scrap-and-build policy, most of the serviceable LNWR freight and local passenger engines survived. Indeed conversions to class "G2A" began and continued, under Bond as works manager and under Fairburn, until after the war, though both laid down that nothing should be spent on LNWR stock other than to repair what could not justifiably be scrapped.

'So, in the 1940s there were still a lot of "Super Ds" about, but Crewe Works was much too busy, especially during the war, to establish a regular practice of adjusting the height of weighbars as an added time-consuming routine at the say-so of a valve setter perched on the bufferbeam. And above all, the Stanier 2-8-0s were proliferating, and just after the war all the wartime ones returned from War Department service. So who on earth was going to bother about the "CHUFF CHUFF pff pff" of forty-year-old locomotives - except maybe Terry O'Neill, John Dowling and Bill Broadbent!'

Mileages

The total mileage covered by the eight-coupled coal engines throughout their life varied considerably. Naturally, the highest mileages were achieved by the oldest engines, or rather by those which lasted the longest, namely, those of the original 'A' class converted to class 'G1' and later to 'G2A' which survived to the early 1960s. The highest recorded mileages were 1,371,390 by No. 49027, built as an 'A' in November 1894 and broken up as a 'G2A' sixty-five years later in November 1959, and 1,370,289 by No. 48953, built in August 1896 and broken up in October 1962, while the first of the 'A' class itself, originally No. 50, achieved over 1,300,000 as 'G2A' No. 49008. Every 'A' class converted to 'G2A' and surviving to the late 1950s seems likely to have completed well over one million miles, as do many former 'B' class also.

Lower total mileages were covered by engines built later. Many 'G' class built in 1910 and scrapped in the late 1950s as 'G2As' covered about one million miles, and some early 'G1s' built in 1912 ran well over 950,000, though mostly the average was around 900,000, while 'G2s' averaged about 830,000. These are rough generalisations and there are many examples of mileages greater and lower. For example, No. 9249 built in July 1914 ran 963,073 miles, while No. 9302 built in May 1918 ran 662,719, both originally 'G1s' and later 'G2As'. One 'G2', No. 9413, ran 902,006 miles.

The most complete figures for annual mileages are those for the first of the 'G2s', No 9395, though there is no way of knowing how typical they are. It may be that they are on the low side, but without similar data for a number of other engines, it is impossible to confirm that impression. The following table shows the relevant information available. After 1938 no figures are recorded for coal consumption and visits to main works for heavy overhauls are not precisely recorded.

Year	Mileage	Coal Issued		Weekdays out of Service				Allocation
		tons	lb/m	wks	rp	nr	total	
1927	26,754	804				33	33	Bescot
1928	22,338	659		Yes	65	6	71	Rugby 27.4.28
								Willesden 20.8.28
								Bescot 31.10.28
1929	25,410	910	80.22		42	14	56	
1930	18,084	591	73.21	Yes	63	33	91	
1931	22,728	889	87.62		46	9	55	
1932	21,687	855	88.31		58	11	69	Willesden 4.5.32
1933	24,669	779	71	Yes	59	15	74	
1934	29,936	991	74.15		26	19	45	
1935	27,992	850	68		59	8	67	Rugby 13.7.35
1936	22,075	568	58		76	11	87	
1937	18,637	598	72	Yes`	90	19	109	
1938	24,933	789	71		55	1	56	Northampton 11.6.38
1939	25,608			Yes*	50	4	54	Willesden 16.9.39
1940	20,299				49	-	49	Abergavenny 21.9.40
1941	17,790				37	5	42	Edge Hill 26.10.40
1942	20,436			Yes*	87	6	93	Rugby 2.5.42
1943	19,172			Yes*	52	4	56	Northampton 4.9.43
1944	21,584				45	4	49	
1945	20,447				28	7	35	
1946	17,876			Yes*	73	2	75	
1947	18,902				39	9	48	
1948	17,823			Yes*	75	5	80	Nuneaton 7.7.48
1949	21,008				58	3	61	
1950	18,635			Yes*	74	3	77	Speke Jct. 26.8.50
1951	18,699				43	4	47	
1952	16,503			Yes*	60	2	62	
1953	21,304				37	4	41	
1954	18,956			Yes*	68	6	74	
1955	17,807				64	18	82	
1956	14,401				44	11	55	
1957	12,073			Yes*	85	5	90	Buxton 20.4.57
1958	13,512				25	21	75+	
1959	Nil							

* in works but heavy or light repair not stated
+ includes 29 days 'unserviceable'

Abbreviations:
wks - visit to main works for overhaul
rp - days out of service under repair
nr - days not required

For comparison, in 1935 'G1' No. 9031 of Shrewsbury shed ran 34,681 miles, cost £153 in shed repairs, was issued with 953 tons of coal, burnt 62lb per mile and was out of service for 33 days (27 for repairs and 6 when not required). Its average annual mileage for 1927-36 was about 28,000. A more typical coal consumption was 70-80lb per mile. Another 'G1', No. 9051, averaged 15,000 miles a years when shedded at Bescot, Crewe South and Coventry in 1927-9, 24,000 at Swansea and Mold Junction in 1930-1, 25,000 at Mold Junction in 1932-5 and 23,542 at Buxton in 1936.

A notable feature of the mileage statistics is an overall reduction, irrespective of class, and for both passenger and freight engines, in the average annual mileage from 1937 to 1950 of about 25 per cent. This is shown in the following table, based on official London Midland Region statistics, which gives the average annual mileages run by the LNWR eight-coupled classes and by certain other classes for comparison. In the first column under each year is the number of engines in the class at that time. The reduction was the subject of an official investigation in 1951 but no conclusion seems to have been reached as to the cause of the difference. Possibly, there was an actual reduction in traf-

Plate 198: *The driver's side of the footplate. Behind the reversing wheel is the small lever locking it in position and to the right of it is the lever operating the cylinder cocks - there is a similar lever on the fireman's side. Next to that, is the pipe leading from the injector beneath the footplate to the clack valve on the back of the firebox. On the top of the pipe is the wheel which regulated the flow. When it was shut off, the clack could be shut off or removed, by screwing in or unscrewing the brass nut. The handle lower down the rod is for 'fine-tuning' the water supply. To the right of it is the plate acting as a heat shield to protect the driver's legs when comfortably seated (!) or, more likely, leaning over the cab side, and to the right of that is the handle for the LMS firehole door. In the centre, on the floor is the oil pot for the trailing axle. The two pipes inside the side-sheet link the duplex vacuum pipe to the vacuum gauge, the pipe on the left going to the train pipe, the one on the right to the reservoir. Two of the pipes across the firebox come from a Detroit sight-feed cylinder lubricator and carry oil to the valves of the left cylinder. The third pipe, following the bend of the firebox more closely, carries steam from the front end, when the regulator is opened, to the automatic blowdown valve situated near the Detroit lubricator. The piece of string is to secure the knob of the reversing wheel, to stop it moving with the vibration of the engine. Clearly, the driver thinks it more effective than the locking handle, which presumably would shake out of position.* Peter Ward

Plate 199: *The rear of the engine, showing the sandbox, footsteps and rare detail of the 'Claughton' tender front. In rainy weather water spraying up off the rear wheels could be driven up the sand pipe into the box and so clog the supply with wet sand. Then the fitting where the pipe joined the box had to be taken off and the blockage cleared - with care, and a container underneath, as the dry sand would suddenly run through.* Peter Ward

Plate 200: *View looking forward on the right-hand side beneath the boiler over the intermediate splasher. In the foreground is the modified frame stretcher, which originally was extended upwards to meet the boiler. The upper part must have been simply burnt off, as only the curved centre part is still flanged. In the lower left corner is the top of the brake cylinder. The rod near the camera on the right operates the cylinder cocks. Beyond it, extreme right, is the bracket holding the oil pipes from the box on the handrail feeding the driving and intermediate axleboxes. The pipes to the left driving axlebox are on the left. The left big end is at top back angle (the right one must be at bottom forward). It is secured by two cotters, that nearest the camera being fitted first, followed by the locking or 'gib' cotter in front of it.* Peter Ward

Plate 201: *View from the same angle but closer in, showing the weighbar shaft, top right, and beneath it the bolt holes where the centre bearing was once bolted to the motion stretcher plate.* Peter Ward

152

Plate 203 (above): *The same position but looking down at the slide bars with the valve rod in the top left-hand corner and the top of the motion stretcher plate, or 'spectacle' plate, on the left. Two bolts, one each side, fasten each slide bar to it. The top of the slide bar, with the cotter locking it to the piston rod, is in the centre, with oil pots on each slide bar. The oil pipe feeding the leading axlebox comes from an oil pot inside the main frame to the rear of the leading splasher. The tall oil pot on the left still has its original spring cap, which was supposed to be depressed by the end of the long oil feeder to allow oil to flow inside. These caps often stuck and would then be broken off by the men and a cork inserted instead. This has been done to the two other pots but they do not have corks. Inside the frame plate is the horn plate, the pillar above it leading to the spring, which can be adjusted by using a spanner on the lock nut on the pillar.*
Peter Ward

Plate 202 (above): *Close-up of the direct-action valve rod. The bracket is held by four bolts, two either side, whereas the indirect action bracket had four or six bolts either side.* Peter Ward

Plate 204 (right): *View in roughly the same direction as Plate 201 opposite but from below, with the big ends at the top of the picture and the motion stretcher plate at the bottom.* Peter Ward

Plate 205: *View looking up under the cylinders and showing the cylinder drain cocks, both front and rear, the rods operating them, and the crank-shaft connecting them to the curving rod linked to the lever on the fireman's side of the footplate.*

Peter Ward

fic or at least in traffic miles.

Class	No.	1937	No.	1950	No.	1954	No.	1961
'8F' 2-8-0	96	27,253	315	24,423	623	24,047		
'WD' 2-8-0					263	20,655		
'7F' 0-8-0	175	24,859	77	18,372	41	18,784	1	11,050
'G2' 0-8-0	60	26,901	56	19,760	56	19,261	26	14,774
'G2A' 0-8-0					185	19,095	62	14,416
'G1' 0-8-0	444	25,179	25	19,237	1	9,520		
'4F' 0-6-0	742	29,268	684	21,823				
0-8-4 tank	30	20,805	1	17,268				
0-8-2 tank	18	21,233	3	20,811				

The same general pattern of reduced mileages over this period can be discerned in the annual mileages recorded on the *Engine History Cards*, though they vary greatly, not only from shed to shed but also between individual engines at the same shed (thus, the details for Nos. 9031 and 9051 given above may well not be typical). Some sheds obviously had more long-distance turns than others, and engines at sheds where generally lower mileages were run were not necessarily worked less hard and may well have been worked harder. Slogging with heavy loads at slow speeds around industrial Lancashire, West Yorkshire and the West Midlands may have been harder work than clocking up the miles with light trains along the North Wales coast or the Welsh borders.

Some sheds, notably Shrewsbury, Abergavenny and Swansea, seem to have had engines running high mileages more often than others. In the 1940s, for example, Abergavenny engines ran up good mileages as the shed had turns to Liverpool, Carlisle, Rugby, Springs Branch, Stalybridge and Longsight (the men worked only to Crewe, Chester and Stafford, taking rest in the railway hostels). One of Abergavenny's venerable old 'Ds', No. 8899, regularly did the 12 noon to Newport docks and back every day, then ran to Salop and back at night, returning in time to do the same turn to

Newport again the following day, a total of about 190 miles a day.

A good illustration of the differences from shed to shed is the following comparison of annual mileages run by No. 49113 of Abergavenny and No. 49115 of Stafford - the latter seems to have had a much easier life:

No.	1951	1952	1953	1954	1955	1956
49113	28,204	29,503	30,960	28,605	20,713	16,008
49115	16,111	13,361	16,730	19,136	15,081	

Another example is No. 8901 which throughout the 1940s at Rugby ran roughly 21,500 miles a year but after transfer to Shrewsbury ran 25,899 in 1949. No. 9051 averaged 15,000 miles a year when shedded at Bescot, Crewe South and Coventry in 1927-9, 24,000 at Swansea and Mold Junction in 1930-1, 25,000 at Mold Junction in 1933-5 and 23,504 at Buxton in 1936. In 1952 at Abergavenny it ran 35,081 miles. On the other hand, No. 49174 of the same shed averaged roughly 17,000 miles from 1951 to 1957, because most of its work was done at Tredegar, which was a low-mileage depot but one where engines were worked hard. Another example of a high mileage is that of No. 49158 of Crewe South, which ran 29,710 miles as late as 1959. Most engines, however, had one or two years when they ran less than 10,000 miles, because they were stopped for repairs or were awaiting shopping for a long time.

Some typical figures are given for three engines in the table below. Though two of them are 'G2s', the figures would be much the same for 'G2As'. No. 8895 was transferred to Coventry on 12th November 1938; to Rugby on 3rd May 1947; to Shrewsbury on 8th March 1947; to Crewe South on 23rd October 1948; and to Bescot on 28th May 1949. No. 9441 went to Willesden on 10th October 1936; to Northampton on 19th

154

November 1938; to Swansea on 30th November 1940; to Rugby on 3rd July 1943; and to Coventry on 14th January 1950. No. 9451 went to Preston on 6th July 1935; to Nuneaton on 7th August 1948; and to Speke Junction on 2nd December 1950:

No.	1937	1938	1939	1940	1941	1942	1943
8895	23,275	28,344	19,994	20,661	17,388	23,354	28,705
9441	24,881	25,474	24,504	20,173	31,513	32,456	21,877
9451	31,543	26,142	24,512	26,504	16,110	23,791	24,115

No.	1944	1945	1946	1947	1948	1949	1950
8895	22,092	25,637	21,831	21,668	24,350	24,427	
9441	20,644	21,085	22,947	16,639	22,314	22,017	18,935
9451	22,100	22,245	22,104	22,963	20,667	19,178	15,498

Yet another example is No. 9442 which went to Willesden on 10th October 1936; to Northampton on 19th November 1938; to Preston on 4th November 1939; to Rugby on 10th July 1948; and to Coventry on 7th January 1950. Its lowest annual mileages were 20,097 in 1947 and 20,990 in 1939, and its highest were 28,837 in 1938 and 27,161 in 1943.

Three 'G2s', all at Northampton in 1937-9, achieved the following mileages there and at other sheds later:

No.	1937	1938	1939	1940	1941	1942	1943
9445	28,727	25,519	19,319	22,913	29,581	25,786	22,612
9446	23,853	21,432	22,905	26,134	25,260	21,819	18,087
9447	23,790	27,059	21,483	16,059	22,946	20,237	20,320

No.	1944	1945
9445	24,765	16,708
9446	23,963	20,029
9447	20,008	22,141

No. 9445 went to Northampton on 13th July 1932; to Swansea on 30th November 1940; to Crewe South on 19th June 1943; and to Abergavenny on 5th April 1947. No. 9446 went to Northampton on 7th December 1932; to Rugby on 2nd October 1943; and to Coventry on 25th February 1950. No. 9447 went to Northampton on 7th December 1932; to Rugby on 2nd October 1943; to Speke Junction on 7th July 1945; and to Mold Junction on 15th December 1945.

Brakes

Originally, all eight-coupled coal engines had a steam brake cylinder under the cab to apply the brakes on the engine wheels and, by means of a pull rod, the brakes on the tender also. The arrangement economised on brake cylinders, but it had the disadvantage that when the driver braked, the wagons pushing up against the tender, especially on a falling gradient, reduced the distance between engine and tender, and so reduced the effectiveness of the brake. The same kind of effect resulted from wear in the rods.

The 1914 batches of 'G1s' were built with vacuum brakes and screw couplings to enable them to work passenger trains. Their tenders had their own separate brake cylinders obviating the need for pull rods, and the 'G2s' were built new with the same arrangements.

These brakes, both steam and vacuum, were woefully inadequate. E. S. Cox has stated that how the LNWR worked unfitted freight trains at all is 'something of a mystery'. He describes some braking tests on the LYR

section after the Grouping with unfitted trains of equal load descending a gradient of 1 in 100 at 20mph. A Horwich 0-8-0 with vacuum brake stopped its train in 1,520 yards. A 'G2' also with vacuum brake accelerated to 22½mph after 3,860 yards despite full brake application, and the train had to be brought to a halt by another engine inserted in the train as a safeguard. 'G1' No. 1585 with steam brake performed even worse. Again despite full brake application, it had accelerated to 25mph after 3,055 yards, and when the driver blew the whistle, engine brake power was reduced, due to the common manifold supplying both being of insufficient capacity.

Almost certainly as a result of these tests, the decision was taken to provide greater brake power by fitting a second brake cylinder in front of the firebox. If, when this was done, the boiler stay was still in position, it was cut away to allow access to the brake cylinder. The cylinder under the cab then applied the brakes on the rear two axles only and the other one those on the leading two axles. As there was a third cylinder on the tender, there were thus three brake cylinders on an engine. This arrangement was termed 'increased brake power' in official documents and records such as the Engine History Cards.

The modification started in mid 1924 and was applied to all engines which had been built new with vacuum brakes. At the same time engines which had steam brakes began to be converted to vacuum brakes, most being fitted with the 'increased brake power' of two cylinders from the outset. The majority of engines were dealt with in the next ten years or so but the process was long drawn out, particularly of conversion from steam brakes. Some engines were only converted twenty years or so after the brake trials and some even then received only a single vacuum cylinder. Other engines still had steam brakes when they were scrapped in 1949-50, and one, No. 49164, appears to have still had them when scrapped as a 'G2A' in 1962.

One or two engines were fitted with the second brake cylinder at the sheds, using a kit of parts that was sent from Crewe. One of these was No. 9046 or 9051 at Abergavenny. To do the job, the intermediate wheels had to be lowered on the wheel drop, to allow the fitters to drill the main frames using a John Bull and a hand ratchet, a long job. Presumably, it was not thought worthwhile to send the engine to Crewe but the modification was essential to enable the engine to be used on the branch from Abergavenny Junction to Merthyr with its 1 in 38 gradients.

Originally all LNWR vacuum-braked engines had a crosshead pump to maintain the vacuum when running. This device, driven off the crosshead of the right-hand cylinder, had been used since the vacuum brake was first adopted in the late 19th century, the rights to it having been obtained from the GWR in exchange for the rights to water troughs. These pumps continued to be fitted until about 1936, when they began to be removed as engines passed through works. The problem with them, in the 0-8-0s particularly, was that the

Three views of the right side of 'G2A' No. 49093 at Yarnton on 3rd April 1960.

Plate 206: *The high viewpoint shows details from an unusual angle, many of them normally hidden between the frames: the auxiliary oil feed on the ejector pipe and the pipes leading down from it to the bearings; the arrangement of rods operating the sanders, with the pivot on the leading sandbox for the crankshaft from the left-hand side of the engine; the clips securing the ends of the springs on their brackets; and, just inside the frame plate behind the end of the leading splasher, the oil pot for the leading axlebox. There is no mechanical lubricator in the usual place between the leading splashers, so a hydrostatic or displacement type of lubricator must be fitted in the cab. Sometimes in wet weather water used to get into the sandboxes. This happened because the bolt fastening the sandbox to the splasher had worked loose and perhaps the bolt hole had become enlarged slightly. When the fitting had been made tight, the fitter had to reach up under the splasher to fasten the bolt once more.*

Plate 208: *The firebox and cab, showing standard LMS safety valves; LNWR whistle; cab roof cut back with rain strip to compensate (unsuccessfully) for the removal of the flare (the circular piece near the front is to accommodate the steam heater relief valve when fitted); and the vacuum ejector pipe round the cab front (the ejector itself is in the cab on the fireman's side. The fitting in the pipe on the driver's side contains a non-return valve). The window is partially open - the windows on the Belpaire engines did not open fully.*
I. Vaughan, M. Williams collection

Plate 209 (right): *One of a pair of coupled wheels for a 'Super D'. It is not a driving pair, as there is no crank axle, and it is not an intermediate pair, as it is flanged. So it must either be a leading or trailing pair.*
I. Vaughan, M. Williams collection

Plate 207 (opposite): *Another view from the same position but looking a little further back. On the running plate at the side of the smokebox is the bracket by which the firebox is supported on the frames. This bracket, of course, allows the boiler to move to the rear as it expands with heat, the front end being fixed at the cylinders. The intermediate splasher is of the original type, whereas the driving splasher on the right is a replacement made up from sheet. Under the barrel in front of the firebox is the counterweight for the leading dampers and in the same vicinity can just be made out the transverse spring of the intermediate axle, with the adjuster for it, a lock nut and set bolt, on top. In front of that is the second brake cylinder which was fitted to give the engine 'improved brake power', and then the frame stretcher, which has simply had its upper portion cut off. This must be so, because the centre part, originally the lower part of the oval inspection hole, is still flanged, whereas the sides have no flange.*
I. Vaughan, M. Williams collection

157

space to accommodate the pump was very restricted compared to engines with larger wheels. When the engine had been in service for a time and side play developed in the front axle and axleboxes, the connections of the vacuum pump began to rub against the axle box and eventually the studs were smashed off. It was then very difficult to clean them up, redrill and fit new studs in the sheds, and it was pointless in any case unless the side play in the axleboxes was dealt with at the same time.

Another problem with vacuum pumps which occurred with all engines was that the left-hand axlebox was liable to overheating. This was because the left-hand cylinder did more than its share of work in hauling the train since part of the power of the right-hand cylinder was absorbed in driving the pump.

In LNWR days, of course, the vacuum ejector was used only when the engine was stationary. When running, the vacuum was maintained by the crosshead pump. When the pumps were removed, sole reliance was placed on the ejector for maintaining the vacuum, both when running and when stationary.

The pumps were expensive to maintain, but so far as enginemen were concerned, their removal had an undesirable consequence. The use of the ejector when running consumed more steam (not much more, in fact, as the aperture in the ejector when in the 'running' position was small). It also affected steaming on some engines. The exhaust from the ejector was carried along the side of the boiler and into the side of the smokebox. Many engines had a pipe to carry it to the base of the petticoat and so up the chimney. But in others it just exhausted into the side of the smokebox where it affected the smokebox vacuum.

So, as often happened, enginemen used their wits and experience to find a way of overcoming the problem of this extra consumption of coal and water, and the possibility of poor steaming. From the earliest days of the vacuum brake, some means had been provided of releasing the brake when the engine was not in steam. For instance, an engine might have arrived on a shed, the brake applied and the fire allowed to go out. Before it could be moved, perhaps for repair or boiler washout, it was necessary to release the brake. On LNWR 0-8-0s the Budenberg vacuum gauge on the driver's side in the cab had a small fitting intended for this purpose and known by the enginemen from its shape as the 'mushroom' or 'rose'. When this fitting was partly unscrewed - it was not necessary to take it out completely, as it was on quite a long thread - it uncovered a small aperture which allowed air into the reservoir side of the brake cylinder. This destroyed the vacuum and allowed the brake piston to slowly drop by gravity to the base of the cylinder.

The driver's vacuum brake control was duplicated by another control on the fireman's side, the two being linked by a rod so that the brake could be operated from either side of the footplate. From the driver's side, in terms of a clock face, its handle had four positions: at 'twenty to' the brake was off and the ejector working;

at 'twenty five to' the brake was off and in the running position, with the ejector not working and the vacuum pump creating the vacuum; at 'twenty five past' the brake was on; and at 'twenty past' the brake was in the emergency position, the reservoir side vacuum being created to strengthen the brake. So when the pumps were removed, drivers would put the brake in the 'on' position (the third of the above positions), and then unscrew the 'mushroom'. In this way the brake was released and the ejector was prevented from working.

Drivers would do this whenever possible, especially when working hard on an up gradient, but also when running generally, as it helped steaming and saved coal and water. It was even done before starting away on an up gradient. The train would be held on the tender hand brake, which was released when the regulator was opened to take the load of the train and prevent it running backwards, and the aim of saving coal and water was achieved. Whenever drivers judged it necessary - when they needed to stop or to slow the train on a down gradient - they screwed the 'mushroom' back in and moved the brake handle to the 'off' position. This brought the vacuum brake into operation again and then the brake would be applied in the normal manner. In emergency they could just push the lever over to the fourth position, which would quickly create the vacuum in the reservoir side, but not in the train pipe, and apply the brake.

Of course, there would be a delay compared to running with the ejector continually working, so this practice was not officially approved, and drivers could be in serious trouble if they were caught doing it (especially if they actually took the 'mushroom' out and lost it!). But in reality, many inspectors and others in authority must have been well aware that it was a widespread practice. Several photographs by J. M. Dunn, who held senior positions in South Wales and Nuneaton before becoming shed master at Bangor, show engines running with the brake 'out' in this way, so he must have known it was done. Presumably, being practical enginemen themselves, they turned a blind eye to it, as they knew there were good reasons for it and that it was safe enough when drivers knew what they were doing.

Occasionally, brake power was lost because the 'IR' (india rubber) neck ring washer, perhaps better described as a 'bush', on the brake cylinder became worn. The bush consisted of a rubber sleeve with two flanges and a brass ring round the outside to ensure it kept its shape. At some sheds such as Abergavenny, the fitters used to polish the brass of the spindle to avoid damage to the bush. But the spindle on the piston might be rough or damaged, perhaps because the brakes were not adjusted properly, or ash might be drawn into the cylinder, as sometimes happened with the cylinder in front of the firebox, and then the bush might be damaged. The result was that the brakes began dragging, but in any case it was a simple operation to replace the bush. Nevertheless, from late 1934 the brake-cylinder spindles began to be 'totally enclosed' with 'miniature sacks', as they were described

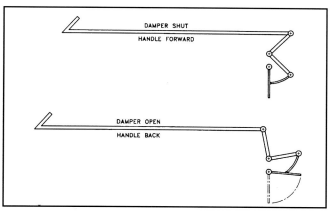

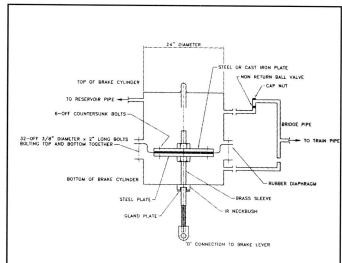

Figure 30: *Details of typical front damper arrangement on LNWR eight-coupled tender and tank engines.*

Figure 31 (right): *Exploded view of 24in vacuum brake cylinder fitted to eight-coupled classes.*

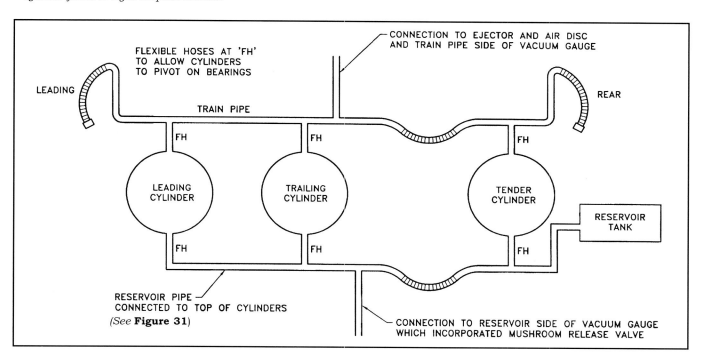

Figure 32: *Layout of vacuum brake pipes on 0-8-0s with 'increased brake power'.*

Figure 33: *Typical layout of cylinder drain cock controls on LNWR eight-coupled tender and tank engines.*

All drawings on this page were prepared by Andy Lowe from sketches supplied by Harold Walkley.

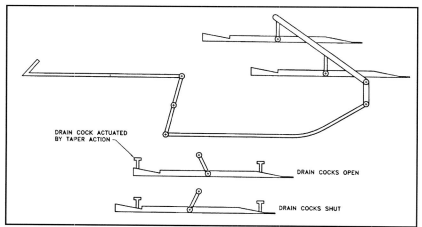

Plate 210: *A 'Super D' at work in South Wales about 1930. Possibly it is between Brynmawr and Abersychain. If so, it is a Tredegar engine, as Abergavenny men always worked chimney-first up to Brynmawr and reversed there on to the Blaenavon line, which entailed a climb of about two miles to Waenavon station, the highest on the LMS. Perhaps more likely, it is near Garndiffaith on the way to Blaenavon High Level, as the type of staff shown here was used on that section. The fittings generally are all in LNWR condition, and the untidy clutter of pipes, lubricators and so on of later years is absent. The position of the brake control at 'twenty five past' shows that the driver is running with the brake 'out'.* J. M. Dunn, LNWRS collection

officially, to protect them from the effect of ash. Until the late 1950s, the vacuum brake equipment was well maintained, but as standards of maintenance declined, so drivers put less trust in the vacuum brake and more in the 'secret weapon' or 'friend in the corner', who had served them well since the earliest days of the steam railway engine, the reverser.

Lubricators

In LNWR days the axleboxes of the 0-8-0s were lubricated by oil pots inside the frames. They were filled by the drivers when oiling round and topped up during a trip as necessary when the opportunity arose. Cylinders were lubricated by displacement lubricators until superheating was introduced on the 'G1s', which required mechanical lubricators. Several kinds of proprietary mechanical lubricators were used by the company and seem to have been fitted indiscriminately on any superheated engine irrespective of class. Thus, lubricators by Wakefield, Trusty and Bosch were in use on 'G1s' as well as those of Crewe's own design. In 1918, 'owing to the impossibility of purchasing' Bosch lubricators, it was decided to manufacture them at Crewe.

Beames must have considered the method of lubri-

cating axleboxes inadequate, because in 1924 he began to fit 'supplementary oil feeders' on the handrails of many LNWR classes, oil boxes with pipes running down to feed the axleboxes. In the case of the 0-8-0s there were five feeds: to driving horn, driving bearing, driving bearing, driving horn and intermediate; the leading axlebox had an oilpot behind the leading splasher and the trailing axlebox had one on the footplate. The leading axlebox horn faces were lubricated by oil splashing from the motion but the intermediate and trailing horn faces were only lubricated by what oil the driver supplied when oiling round. It was not surprising therefore that the sliding surfaces of these boxes, having no regular oil supply, soon became worn.

Detroit sight-feed cylinder lubricators were also fitted on some 'Super Ds', usually on the driver's side but also sometimes on the fireman's side. They needed to be treated with great care when any adjustment was made as there was a danger of scalding with hot steam, water and oil. Detroit lubricators were also fitted on some 0-8-4 tanks on the driver's side in the cab, which incidentally made his view forward even more restricted, but originally these engines had Wakefield hydrostatic lubricators.

In 1937 Stanier recommended that Wakefield foun-

Plate 211: *The rear sandbox and footsteps of a 'Super D' about 1936. Behind the sandpipe is the pipe for the desanding gear. The water feed pipes between engine and tender are the telescopic type. Later they were replaced by the flexible type, which had only one problem. If the fireman had to blow an injector back to clear a blockage, it might burst the water hose. With luck, ice blocking the pipe could be cleared by repeatedly blowing back for a short time. The treads of the steps could be changed when worn as they were secured by a $\frac{1}{2}$in countersunk bolt underneath. Sometimes fitters used a file to cut more grooves. It is surprising how quickly leather boots can wear steel tread! Just in front of the sandbox is the oval slot in the frame which gave access to the washout plug and the tab holding the right-hand injector to the firebox.*
M. Williams collection

Plate 212: *View of a different engine in 1930, showing the solid water-feed pipes and the front of the tender, which is either a Whale type or an early Cooke type. It has brake blocks in front of the wheels.*
M. Williams collection

tain-type axlebox lubricators be fitted in the cabs of 89 engines ('3F' 0-6-0 tanks, '4F' 0-6-0 and '4P' 4-4-0 compounds) as 'this type of lubricator with an indication visible to the enginemen is a cheap form of obtaining a controlled supply of oil to the axleboxes'. As a result, later in the same year the fitting of fountain-type lubricators was authorised for 25 LNWR 0-8-0s 'in place of oil box lubrication'. They were found to be satisfactory in reducing hot axleboxes and in mid 1940 a further 50 were authorised to be fitted, and then another 25. An order dated 11th November 1943 provided for a 'further 75' engines to be so fitted, the work to be carried out on 25 of them 'at the first available opportunity'. Only engines with Belpaire fireboxes and without carriage-warming apparatus were to be so treated. This meant that by the end of 1943 a total of 175 engines was either fitted with or authorised to be fitted with these lubricators.

Engines fitted with Wakefield fountain-type lubricators actually had two such lubricators, one for either side of the engine. Each lubricator had five feeds, two supplying the driving axlebox, and one each the leading, intermediate and trailing boxes. Only two of the five feeds from the oilbox on the handrail were then still needed and so only two pipes were retained to supply the driving axlebox horn faces.

In service these Wakefield fountain-type lubricators were considered by many men to be an abject failure in that they were virtually impossible to regulate. When the driver threw the operating lever over, they poured a large amount of oil down the pipes and it was difficult to regulate them to just drip occasionally. The fitters had sets of needles of different sizes but never succeeded in getting the oil to feed correctly, and so drivers had to take a gallon of oil with them for topping up,

In the 1940s, in addition to the Wakefield fountain-type lubricator for the axleboxes, cylinder lubricators by Silvertown, Dreadnought and Davies & Metcalf were common on 'Super Ds', along with the 'Ramsbottom' type, as the LNWR's own lubricator was known. This type was notorious for leaking oil all over the place but could be relied upon also to supply it where it was needed.

Water Gauges

LNWR water gauges had separate try cocks at top and bottom, operated by plungers or 'buttons', as enginemen called them. In certain circumstances these gauges could give a false reading, as of course did many other kinds of water gauges. In LMS days, some gauges were replaced by Midland-type gauges, at first with unlinked handles, but later with linked handles, which overcame the problem of false readings. On the other hand, it was no longer possible to blow water back through the gauge to clean the inside of the glass. So when a glass became too dirty to see through, the water gauge had to be dismantled to clean or replace it. Standard LMS frames and protectors began to be fitted from late 1932 and allowed blowing through by just opening the drain cock.

Automatic Blowdown Valves

In the mid-1930s, especially in 1935-8, continuous blowdown apparatus was fitted to all engines. The purpose of this was to remove scum from the boiler as the engine was running and so reduce the frequency of washing out and increase the period of availability for traffic. The scum was blown down continuously from a pipe on the fireman's side on to the ends of the sleepers. It was controlled by a handle on the fireman's side, commonly known as the 'scum cock'. This cock was invariably turned off by the men, because they did not like the idea of wasting water, but later the cocks were wired up by the works to prevent them being turned off, and they were then operated automatically. A pipe from one of the main steam pipes in the smokebox or from a tapping off the side of the superheater header - both methods were used - brought steam to the base of the blowdown valve when the regulator was opened. This came under the piston in the valve and lifted a steel ball off its seat, allowing sludge to pass out through the large pipe. When the regulator was closed, the higher pressure in the ball chamber pushed the piston back down again.

At first, the sludge was carried through the tender to cool it before being discharged on to the track but after complaints from the civil engineer in the early 1950s the apparatus was modified again so that the blowdown no longer dribbled on to the sleepers but discharged into the ashpan, as was done initially on tank engines. It was then found that a mixture of boiler sludge and firebox ash was running out on to the track causing more problems.

Some drivers carried a small hobnail in their pocket and if they could see the water in the boiler was clear, they would disconnect the operating pipe nut, place the nail in the end and replace the pipe. This prevented the valve from working. At the end of the shift, of course, they would remove the nail.

The whole purpose of the blowdown valve was to reduce the time taken on boiler wash-out and there seems to have been a constant drive to this end. As late as 1947 it was decided that two additional wash-out plugs be fitted in the door plates of the boilers of 455 'G1' and 'G2' engines 'to facilitate the cleaning of the side water space'.

Sanding Gear

LNWR engines generally were fitted with gravity sanding, sometimes called 'trickle sanding' or even 'hand sanding'. When the driver pulled the sanding lever, sand flowed from the sandboxes on to the rails, which worked well except in high winds. As track ciruiting began to be used widely on the LMS, concern arose that sand on the rails might interfere with the circuits and result in 'false clear' indications. So in 1933 it was decided that to prevent any possibility that track circuiting might fail to give 'the security for which it was provided' desanders would be fitted to all engines with gravity sanding (steam-sanding was thought less likely to interfere with track circuits). The equipment consisted of pipes delivering hot water to the rails ahead of the leading sandpipes and behind the trailing ones. The latter operated when the engine was working forwards and the leading ones when it was working tender-first, both coming into operation in conjunction with the sanders. The valve controlling the desanders was located behind the coal slacking pipe low down on the fireman's side.

In practice, the enginemen found that the desanders could be very useful on greasy rails both to wash the rails and to apply water to help the sand to stick. A spanner wedged into the leading desander valve under the fireman's seat caused the leading desander to wash the rails as the leading sanders were being pulled. This technique was used at Abergavenny and at Buxton and probably at other sheds also. One Buxton job on which it was used was a working to Oldham, on which the engine ran round at Diggle and then went tender-first through Lydgate tunnel in which the rails were invariably greasy and difficult. The trailing washer pipes were as effective as the sanders. By the early 1950s, however, desanders had fallen into disrepair.

Minor Modifications

Many minor modifications were made to the 'Super Ds', during the LMS period especially, and a constant process of making detail improvements occurred. Most of them were made as engines passed through the works for overhaul and so often it was many years until all engines had been treated.

Originally, for example, telescopic connections were fitted between engine and tender supplying water to the injectors. They were replaced by flexible hoses, which were a boon, especially in yards where there were sharp bends, as the telescopic type had a tendency to part in such circumstances. The only drawback to the flexible type was that when the fireman tried to blow back an injector to clear a blockage the pressure sometimes burst the hose. If it was done carefully, however, this operation could be successful. It could even thaw ice blocking the hose, if a little steam was blown back, allowed to do its work, and then the process repeated until the hose was clear.

From May 1930 the LNWR ashblowers fitted in the base of the smokebox to eject ash up the chimney began to be removed to avoid 'damage to coaching stock and to fields and woods adjacent to the line'. At the same time ex-LNWR engines began to be fitted with copper instead of steel ejector steam pipes, and with standard type cone unions. It was not until the late 1930s that all engines were dealt with. At the end of 1931 it was decided that because of considerable trouble being caused by weak trailing springs on the 'G1' class, a stronger type of spring and spring links would be fitted to all engines as they passed through the works. In mid 1932 an improved method of fitting the main steampipes to the smokebox tubeplates was adopted, and at the same time Stanier reported that the blow-off cocks on the firebox doorplates were of 'very little use' and recommended their removal, the opening into the firebox water space to be covered by a blank flange. This was only completed by the end of 1944, 1,356 engines of the 2,400 former LNWR engines authorised to be modified in 1932 having by then been treated, the remaining 1,044 having been scrapped. Other modifications were the substitution of copper ends in place of steel for the smoke tubes, the fitting of light shields to the sliding firedoors, which in some cases had replaced the LNWR flap type, and in some cases Midland type smokebox door rings were fitted.

In mid 1937 Stanier recommended the removal of the steam locking gear on the reversing shaft of 65 0-8-0s, presumably all those so fitted, 'from the use of which no advantage had been obtained'. All 0-8-0s of course had a catch to hold the reverser in position but it was unreliable because vibration caused it to move, and so drivers often tied the reverser in place with a piece of string, as indeed they did the regulator.

Then in mid 1942 Stanier reported that the bufferbeams of the former LNWR 0-8-0s often broke through the drawhook hole and recommended that they be strengthened. The trouble arose when engines were used to haul heavy trains tender-first, out of a yard or up a steep gradient, or when holding a train back against the brakes, as then the strain on the front bufferbeam was much greater. The original design had

Plate 214: *No. 48898 off the road near Fenny Bentley in February 1962 after hitting a large old tree that had been blown down on to the track during a storm - a jack and packing are at hand for re-railing. The lifeguard is bent, the leading sandpipe broken off and the desanding gear damaged. The oil pipes round the firebox come from a Wakefield fountain lubricator in the cab - there must be similar pipes on the other side. The loops in the pipes are air vents, to prevent air locks in the pipes which supply the axle-boxes. Below these pipes is the rod operating the front damper. The pipes from the oil box on the ejector pipe only supply the horn faces of the driving axlebox. Below these pipes is the rod operating the front damper. Between the leading splashers is a 'Ramsbottom' lubricator (so called because it was the standard LNWR type), which was notorious for leaking oil but reliable in supplying it to the cylinders. Two splashers are originals, with beading, but the driving one is a replacement. After re-railing, the engine ran for a month or two without incident. Then a fitter discovered that one of the leading wheels was cracked, no doubt as a result of hitting the tree, and the engine was then withdrawn.* Michael Bentley

Plate 215: *An unidentified 'Super D' hump-shunting at Norton Junction near Pelsall in August 1951. It still has an LNWR flap-type firehole door. A Detroit sight-feed lubricator is fitted high up on the fireman's side of the firebox. Presumably, it was placed there, blocking the view through the window, only because it would have been even more inconvenient if it had blocked the view on the driver's side. But many a fireman had 'Detroit' stamped on his forehead when the engine lurched while he was standing on the pedestal.*

F. W. Shuttleworth

a short cast trough fitted underneath the bufferbeam either side of the coupling drawbar and this was replaced by a much longer trough filling most of the space between the buffers. There was no problem when engines were working forwards, as both the engine drag box and the tender bufferbeam were much stronger.

The piston valves were originally fitted with single wide rings but about 1932 four rings per head began to be fitted. Later on, about 1945, tests were run between Abergavenny and Crewe with an engine fitted with six narrow rings per head, and there was found to be a saving of 5cwt of coal and about 500 gallons of water on a single trip. So six rings were then adopted as standard.

In late 1947, an experiment was carried out with No. 9243, an Abergavenny engine, which had a brass plate on the driver's footstep stating that it had experimental piston valves. The drivers all complained that it was sluggish and when the valves and pistons were examined, it was found that the piston valves had solid heads and no connecting tubes, as on Stanier engines. Obviously, there was so much back pressure caused by the tubeless valves that the exhaust steam could not be cleared properly. Instead of the engine going to Crewe to have the valves changed, the replacement valves were sent in a box to be fitted at the shed.

By contrast, at about the same period No. 9388 was a favourite at Abergavenny, as the drivers said it was five wagons stronger than the others. The engine had been transferred from another shed which had not sent on all the necessary documentation but when the routine valve and piston examination was carried out the reason for the extra power became clear. The cylinder diameter was 21$^7/_8$in, which must have been due to the wartime relaxation of limits of wear, as nothing larger than 20$^1/_8$in was normally allowed. At the next visit to Crewe, the cylinders were lined up, much to the disappointment of the enginemen.

About 1944 it was decided that the 0-8-4 tanks would be withdrawn when their boilers required replacing and in September 1945 it was reported that to cover the work they were doing at Edge Hill and sheds in South Wales thirty class '7F' 0-8-0 freight engines (that is, class 'G2' and 'G2A') would be fitted with back cabs and improved sanding gear at the rear. The improvement consisted of fitting steam sanding and moving the filler pipe from the cab floor, where water often got into it, to the cab side. Eight of the 30 engines were also fitted with carriage warming apparatus at both engine and tender ends (though not an LMS change, some 'Super Ds' had carriage-warming apparatus for a time at an earlier period, the relief valve being visible in the front right-hand corner of the cab roof, for use on banana specials from Garston Docks, as well as on certain passenger turns. The valve was shorter than the old Webb type, and does not seem to have been retained for long on many engines. It is difficult to find photographs showing it but it can be seen more easily in photographs of 0-8-4 tanks). These alterations were to enable the 0-8-0s to work passenger trains and to give the crew the protection of 'back cabs' when running tender

first. Tenders with cabs had steps fitted at the rear, to give access to the water filler, previously reached over the coal. Probably, these steps were fitted at the same time as the cabs but they were certainly fitted in 1951.

Engines dealt with in this way were: Nos. 49113, 49121, 49148, 49168, 49276, 49316 and 49403 at Abergavenny; 48921, 49064, 49161, 49174 and 49409 at Tredegar; 49358 at Swansea; 48898, 49224, 49419, 49429 and 49449 at Edge Hill; and 49220 at Crewe South, from where it probably went to Edge Hill soon afterwards. At the same time Buxton also received some 'Super Ds' with back cabs to replace the 0-8-4 tanks, which had previously been used there for snow-plough duty.

In LMS days, of course, the eight-coupled engines were a natural choice for snow clearing. A note exists that six of them were fitted with snow ploughs at Crewe Works between 30th January and 3rd February 1940: Nos. 8899, 8934, 9030, 9188, 9263 and 9363. It seems, however, that the LNWR did not bother to equip engines specifically for this purpose but relied on the fact that it ran plenty of trains to keep the line clear.

About 1949 a further dozen or so 'Super Ds' were fitted with back cabs, steps on the tender and 'improved trailing sanding gear', which seems to have been the same as on the engines modified to replace the 0-8-4 tanks. Where they were intended to be used is not known but clearly the purpose of the alterations was to make the engines more suitable for tender-first working. Some engines so fitted were: Nos. 48953, 49395, 49400, 49401, 49406, 49435, 49451 and 49454.

External Appearance

The first changes in the traditional LNWR appearance of the eight-coupled coal engines took place in 1924, when Belpaire boilers first came into use as replacements on the superheated engines, and pop safety valves, which from early 1925 were manufactured at Crewe for the whole of the LMS, began to appear on many classes. Both were Crewe innovations partly resulting from the Buxton explosion rather than being a result of the Grouping. Round-top boilers continued to be overhauled and used as replacements but they gradually became less and less common and were no longer in use from about the early 1950s. Similarly pop safety valves were often replaced later by Ramsbottom valves, the change being recorded on the *History Cards* under 'improvements'. Presumably, this occurred when Ramsbottom valves were in good enough condition to be repaired and returned to service. Eventually, of course, probably by about 1940, Ramsbottom valves were no longer to be seen on 0-8-0s.

The most obvious change was the application of LMS livery, with the removal of LNWR numberplates in favour of LMS painted numbers, and the fitting of LMS smokebox-door numberplates, though the latter were soon left off all LNWR engines. A physical change due to the Grouping was the cutting back of the sides of the cab roof to meet the Midland loading gauge. This resulted in complaints from the men that rain water now dripped down their necks when looking out of the cab. Not all engines were altered immediately, especially the older non-superheated types, and some retained the LNWR roof for many years.

A short handrail was first fitted on the cab side-sheets of many engines at this period and seems to be always associated with the fitting of a Belpaire boiler. The cab windows could not be fully opened on the Belpaire engines for cleaning, unlike the windows on those with round-top fireboxes, and so it was essential to clean them from outside. A handrail would enable this to be done more safely, though in general it would enable men to reach the running plate with less risk of slipping and falling off. Another modification was the fitting of oil boxes on the boiler handrails, known officially as 'auxiliary oil feed', to supply oil via pipes leading down to the bearings. Standard LNWR lamp sockets were soon replaced by lamp irons for the sake of standardisation with other companies' engines.

Among later changes, the LNWR Cooke buffers of the 'Super Ds' began to be replaced with parallel-sided buffers. This took place from February 1933 when Stanier reported that to overcome trouble with the buffers of former LNWR engines, new buffers had been ordered from George Turton, Platt & Company Ltd of Sheffield and would be fitted at a rate of 100 engines a year, shunting engines to be dealt with first. Probably from the early war years, the LNWR smokebox door wheel was replaced with two handles, perhaps for no other reason than to do away with the need for a smokebox-door wheel spanner, and from 1944 the LNWR chimney was replaced with the cast Stanier chimney (a large quantity of which was still stored in the works when the last steam engine to be overhauled at Crewe, No. 70013 *Oliver Cromwell*, was turned out on 2nd February 1967, more than twenty years later!).

Finally, all components, both major and minor, were likely to be changed when an engine entered Crewe Works for repair. When an engine arrived in the stripping bay to be dismantled, all parts were stamped with

Plate 216 : *Front end of an unidentified 'Super D' in the 1950s. with Stanier chimney, LMS buffers and two handles on the smokebox door (the door wheel was still in use on some engines up to about 1945). A less obvious difference is the 'strengthened buffer plate', which can be identified by the different pattern of rivets.*

M. Williams collection

Plate 217: *The front end of an 0-8-0 partly dismantled in a running shed to take out the left-hand piston; unusually, the vacuum pipe has been left on. The right-hand cylinder drain cock is still in position but the left-hand one is on the running plate. They were operated by the driver pulling a handle in the cab, and closed by pressing a pedal with his foot. The date is probably late 1930s, in view of the Stanier engine behind and the LMS buffer on the floor.*

M. Williams collection

its number and moved to the appropriate shops for renovation. A small army of progress chasers made sure that these parts, once repaired, found their way to the appropriate place in the erecting shop, as the principle was that they should go back on the same engine so far as possible. One exception almost certainly was the boiler, which would be replaced either by a new spare boiler or by a repaired one from an engine which had entered the works earlier. Other parts would also be replaced, if they could not be repaired or if their repair was not completed in time. In general, most parts found their way back to the engine they had arrived on but the only component which should necessarily have been the same as when the engine arrived in the works was the main frame. In reality, that too was rarely the 'same' as when it arrived. Cracks were welded up, badly cracked sections were cut out and new sections welded in, whole frame plates were replaced at times, and quite possibly the main frames themselves were changed occasionally to save time in returning an engine to traffic. No frames remained 'original' in the literal sense. When the engine was complete, it would be coupled to a suitable tender, almost certainly not the one it had arrived with, tested and despatched to its home shed. One exception to this was that engines with back cabs usually retained the same tender.

A good example of what might happen is LMS No. 8932. When at Abergaveny in 1950-2, it had standard side rods and motion. It must then have been into the works and been fitted with the frames, cylinders, wheels and motion from another 'Super D', because at Buxton about 1957 it had three-piece side rods and an unusual type of motion bracket described as 'gun carriage' style, in which the piston rod was guided by wheels. This was an extreme example, as the 'gun carriage' motion bracket has not been mentioned by any other source and its origins have not been explained. Possibly, it came from an old 'B' class or was experimental, as No. 8932 was often used for trials of this kind - when at Abergavenny, it was the engine fitted with solid piston valves.

In the BR period, and probably even in LMS days, the various combinations of fittings, such as side-rods, wheels, lubricators, oil pipes and electrification flashes in a variety of positions, not to mention different styles of tender, with or without 'back cabs', were enormous. In fact, there were so many small differences of all kinds that it is doubtful if any two engines of all the 500 or so in service in the 1940s were identical.

Plate 218: *Cab of No. 49439 after withdrawal. It has two Wakefield fountain-type lubricators. Next to the one on the fireman's side is the automatic blowdown valve. The small pipe crossing the firebox into the base of the valve supplies steam and the large pipe running down from it carries away the scum. 'Improved rear sanding' is fitted. The lever controlling the rear steam sandng is in the centre, above the firehole door. It has two pipes coming from it and the leading sand handles have been cut off. The valve controlling the de-sanders was once situated behind the coal slacking pipe (lower right). The picture was taken by Michael Bentley, who as fireman rode on the engine from Buxton to Crewe, where it was going for scrap hauled by a class '5' 4-6-0. At Stockport the class '5' was turned, so as to run chimney-first but the 'D' continued tender-first. A pilot man took over on the class '5' and so its fireman also rode with Michael, who comments: 'Passing through Wilmslow, a thunderstorm befell us, and clad in overalls and slop jacket, the only place we could get out of the rain was in the firebox, where we duly went. So that was my last trip into the firebox of a 'Super D'.* J. M. Bentley

Plate 219: *'G1' class No. 9350 coupled to a Webb 2500-gallon tender about 1930.*

B. J. MIller collection

Plate 220: *Class 'G1' No. 9026 with a tender from an 'MM' 2-8-0 about 1930.*

A. G. Ellis collection

Plate 221: *The first of the 'G2' class No. 9395 with an eight-wheeled tender from a Lancashire & Yorkshire 0-8-0 at Bescot in 1931. On the right is a 'D' class.*

H. J. Stretton-Ward

Chapter Six
TENDERS - A SURVEY

Like all LNWR engines, the 0-8-0s when new were generally fitted with the latest type of tender standard at that time. So No. 2524 had the same 1800-gallon tender as *Greater Britain* with the deeper side frames to raise it to the same height as the footplate. This tender was soon given a 2000-gallon tank (the drawing is dated October 1893), and No. 2524, the 'A' class and the early 'B' class all received tenders of this type. To provide greater capacity, an enlarged version holding 2500 gallons of water was produced in 1902 and fitted to many new 'B' class built subsequently.

In photographs, Webb tenders can be distinguished by their deep wooden side frames, tool boxes at the front and flared coping round the top of the tank. In 1895 three coal rails began to be fitted along the coping and because the coping sloped slightly upwards towards the rear, the coal rails ran parallel to it and so were not horizontal. The 2000-gallon type, and all previous Webb types, had an uneven wheelbase, 6ft 6in plus 6ft, which is a distinguishing feature, but the 2500-gallon type had an even wheelbase, 6ft 6in plus 6ft 6in, and flat tie rods.

Whale's standard tender was basically the same as a Webb tender but with a steel frame and enlarged to carry 3000 gallons of water and 5 tons of coal. Although it appears in the official photographs of the first 'F' class and 'D' class, in practice most of these engines generally ran with Webb tenders. However, early in 1906 fourteen new Whale tenders were built for conversions from 'A' to 'D' class, and the following year twelve more were built. Nevertheless, this was still only enough for less than half of the class and throughout the Whale period most eight-coupled engines still ran with Webb tenders. When the new 'G' class were built in 1910, new Whale tenders were built for them.

In photographs Whale tenders can sometimes be confused with the 2500-gallon Webb type. Both have tool boxes and three coal rails. The Webb tender, however, has deep wooden side frames, which are inset only slightly beneath the tank, while in the Whale tender the tank overhangs the side frames to a much greater extent and, the most noticeable feature, the coal rails are horizontal.

All these tenders, both Webb and Whale, were 'coal well' types. That is, the fireman had to shovel the coal off the floor of the tender, where it lay between the sides of the U-shaped tank. When Bowen Cooke took over, he retained the Whale frame but produced a modernised tank, with a shovelling plate raised above footplate level and with sides that sloped inwards at the top so that the coal worked down into the coal space as it was used. He also did away with the tool boxes and instead incorporated lockers on either side at the front.

The absence of tool boxes is the distinguishing feature of all Cooke tenders. All those built on the Whale frame were essentially identical and differed only in the arrangement at the top of the tank: the first type had a single coal rail round the coping with a gap between the two; the second type had a second rail filling the gap; and the third type had a 'one-piece flared top' coping. All these Cooke tenders carried 3000 gallons of water and 5 tons of coal. The final type of Cooke tender was introduced in June 1916. It had increased coal capacity, 6 tons, and the frames were redesigned to give greater strength and rigidity, with 'square oval' openings and 'square end' with circular hole. These tenders had the same top as the third type.

During the Great War, as a general rule, most 'G1' and 'G2' class generally had Cooke tenders. Many other 0-8-0s still had Webb tenders but in 1917 eighty-five '17in Coal Engine' 0-6-0s were fitted with 2500-gallon tenders for use by the War Department and sent overseas. Many of these tenders must have come from eight-coupled engines, which then must have had other Webb tenders as replacements, including some 1800-gallon type. Forty-two of the tenders sent abroad were not returned and twenty more 3000-gallon tenders were built to replace them in 1919-20 but some eight-coupled engines probably still had 1800-gallon tenders at this time.

After the Grouping there was an ever greater tendency to fit any suitable 3000-gallon tender, Whale or Cooke, to a 'Super D' and photographs also exist showing an ROD tender on No. 9026. Unlike the LNWR passenger engines, which often had these tenders in the late 1920s and early 1930s, it seems that such tenders were rarely used on the 0-8-0s, possibly because they had no need of the increased water and coal capacity. Similarly, some 'Super Ds' were occasionally tried with tenders from Lancashire & Yorkshire Railway 0-8-0s but these experiments lasted only a short time and came to nothing.

In the 1930s and 1940s 'Super Ds' were commonly fitted with any type of Whale or Cooke tender and this situation continued right into the BR period, except that as the engines began to be withdrawn, so the older tenders were withdrawn too, with the result that in the final years only the last type of Cooke tender survived.

Some of these tenders originally had two other small variations to enable them to run with 'Claughtons', which were the only LNWR tender engines to have doors on the cab. Firstly, the floor was built up 9in with timber to match the higher floor of the engines. Secondly, the side sheet at the front of the tender was set further out, almost as an extension of the tank, and a stanchion type handrail was fitted on the end of it, instead of the normal handrail. The catch on the door of the engine then fitted into a slot inside the side sheet. Cooke tenders modified for 'Claughtons' consisted of one of the second type, nineteen of the third type and probably a hundred of the fourth type.

When the 'Claughtons' were withdrawn, the tenders were altered for use with other engines by lowering the floor to the normal height. Generally,the side sheets seem to have been left unchanged but there are exceptions. Photographs of 'Super Ds' with 'Claughton' tenders invariably show the final type, as is most likely, because they were the newest and most numerous, but it is quite possible that other types were also used on 'Super Ds' at times.

Another variation is believed to have occurred with the final type of Cooke tender in the late 1940s, though nothing about it appears in official records. On some of them, the water capacity was increased to 3500 gallons by making the angle of slope of the coal bunker steeper, reducing the coal capacity to 5½ tons. The vent pipes at

the front were then removed, presumably to allow more coal to be piled up at that point without blocking the pipes but increasing water capacity to 3500 gallons. At Abergavenny these tenders were coupled to 'G2s', as the GWR would not permit them into Merthyr. After 1950 when the Western Region took over, this rule was relaxed.

Cabs

The 0-8-0 cab was adequate in fine weather but, when running tender-first or shunting, the crew had no protection whatsoever and in bad weather were forced to rig a sheet from the cab roof to the front of the tender to obtain some sort of shelter. In 1915 cabs were introduced, known as 'tender cabs' or, especially by enginemen, as 'back cabs'. Originally, they are thought to have been fitted on 'Super Ds' banking 'Jellicoe Specials' in South Wales. This seems likely as the only known picture of one with an LNWR numberplate was

Plate 222: *The earliest known picture of a 'Super D' with a tender cab. 'G1' class No. 1891, converted from class 'B' in December 1920, at Tredegar shed with a Cooke tender of the second type complete with cab. The roof has the characteristic LNWR flare, matching that on the engine cab roof. There is a brace from the cab roof to the side of the tender as on all later cabs, though it does not show up well on the print, and a sheet is fitted to cover the gap between the two cab roofs.* J. P. Richards

Plate 223: *'Super D' No. 8933 at Crewe being hauled into the works for attention probably in the early 1940s. The LNWR chimney cap has come off and is lying round the base of the chimney, which perhaps shows why the cast Stanier chimney was introduced. The tender is the third Cooke type, fitted with a cab, and the rear sandbox filler pipe is in the cab side-sheet.*
J. M. Bentley collection

Plate 224: *No. 9146 at Chester soon after the Second World War. The tender is the third Cooke type, with a cab. The rear sandbox filler pipe is in the cab side-sheet.*

Plate 225: *No. 9006 in July 1947, with a Cooke tender of the first type with cab. Presumably, as it is summer, the crew have not fitted the sheet to fill the gap between the two cab roofs. The location is Shrewsbury, just south of Coleham shed, the Welshpool line coming in behind the engine.*
B. J. Miller collection

Plate 226: *'G1' No. 49151 in Crewe Works after overhaul on 26th February 1950 coupled to a Cooke tender of the final type with cab. Despite a full repaint it lacks a BR crest on the tender. The engine features in the detail pictures overleaf.*
Roger Carpenter collection

Plate 227: *General view of the tender of No. 49151 at Huddersfield in 1952. It is the final Cooke type introduced in 1916. Its tender cab is of the early type - with no steps or handrail at the rear, as were fitted later to allow the fireman easy access to the water filler. The style of the side-sheet at the front of the tender, with large bolts securing it, shows that the tender was originally built for a 'Claughton', but the stanchion type handrail of the 'Claughton' tender has now been replaced by one on the side.*

Peter Ward

Plate 228: *The tender cab photographed from an apparently precarious position on the coal! When coaled, the air vents often got blocked with coal as here and so drew coal dust into the tank as well as air. With these tender cabs fitted, to manoeuvre the fire-irons between their stowage position on the right and the firebox was a work of art. Often the windows were clipped up and the fire-irons were left with their handles protruding through the window frame, so that the fireman could reach them easily. They could only be used by swinging them out over the side of the engine. It needed considerable care to avoid lineside structures and oncoming trains, as well as burns from the hot irons to the fireman's person! Another problem for the fireman was reaching the water filler at the back of the tender. As is obvious here, he had to climb through the cab and up over the coal at the same time. Steps up the back of the tender were a later improvement and were much needed.*

Peter Ward

Plate 229 (right): *The front of the tender on the driver's side, showing the locker, the water-level pipe, the wheel operating the scoop and the water feed handle below it. The chain to secure the wheel and prevent the scoop dropping inadvertently is missing. Part of the edge of the tender side-sheet is bent inwards and has a slot for a door latch - only 'Claughton' tenders had the luxury of doors. Normally, 'Claughton' tenders had a stanchion-type handrail at the end of the side-sheet but the general view (plate 168) shows the handrail on the side, so this one has been altered for some reason.* Peter Ward

Plate 230 (below): *A Cooke tender of the final type, fitted with a cab for use on a 'Super D', in Crewe Works in May 1950. Originally, the gap between the cab roofs of engine and tender seems to have been covered simply with a sheet; but the later arrangement, seen here, had an extension piece which fitted under the roof of the engine. The tender also has the footsteps at the rear ('austerity' style, as used on the Ivatt class '2' engines) and the handrail, to allow the fireman to climb up to the water filler - no doubt, there are also steps up the back of the tender. At the front, the wheel on the left (facing forwards) operates the scoop, the one on the right the hand-brake. The handles controlling the water supply to the injectors can be seen just above the fall plate, one on either side. Generally, the right-hand locker was used for food, clothing and so on, and the left-hand one for oil and tools. The chain is only for use in the works.* Peter Ward

Plate 231: *Close-up view of No. 49348 at Buxton on 2nd September 1950, showing how the arrangement at the front of the tender cab fitted under the cab roof of the engine. The filler for the rear sandbox has been moved to the cab side-sheet, originally being in the floor under the fireman's seat.*
Peter Ward

Plate 232: *'G2' No. 49408 at Springs Branch, Wigan, on 29th May 1960. It has an original LNWR tender cab, with flared edge typical of LNWR cabs before the Grouping, but with all the post-Second World War improvements, the steps and handrail at the rear. Again, the rear sandbox filler is in the cab side-sheet.*
A. G. Ellis collection

taken at Tredegar, albeit as late as 1926. Another theory, however, is that it was due to a strike by Midland men at Buxton over tender-first working, which resulted in tender cabs being fitted to Midland engines. Whatever the reason, they were not numerous in LNWR or LMS days and only became more common after the Second World War.

Little is known about these early cabs. Photographs exist showing one of each of the first three Cooke types fitted with this type of cab but not one of the fourth type or a Whale tender. All these cabs are braced with a stay to the side of the tender inside the coping. Most if not all of the engines in LMS days have had the rear sandbox filler pipe moved to the cab side-sheet.

In 1946 an improved version of this cab was introduced, or rather, the cab was the same but certain improvements were made in association with it. On all LNWR tenders the fireman had to climb from the foot-plate over the coal to reach the water filler at the back of the tender. Often this had to be done when the tender was well filled with coal, as when the engine was about to move off shed to collect a train. On a Cooke tender, however, coal doors were fitted, because of the raised shovelling plate, and with a cab fitted on the tender front also, the fireman had two options, both undesirable: climb through the gap between the top of the coal doors and the cab or open the doors and spill coal on the footplate.

The solution was to enable him to climb up the back of the tender. A vertical handrail and footsteps, like those on Ivatt class '2' engines, were fitted to enable him to reach the bufferbeam, from where more footsteps up the rear of the tank gave access to the water filler. All tenders given these modifications seem to have been the final Cooke type, which seems likely, as they were the newest and most strongly built.

Plate 233: *One of the last surviving 'Super Ds', No. 48930 at Walsall about 1962; it is coupled to former 'Claughton' tender No. 1450 with cab, but the engine does not have the sandbox filler in the cab side-sheet. Probably, it was not one of those engines originally chosen to have a tender cab and has just acquired one that has become spare.* Roger Carpenter collection

Plate 234: *No. 49316 at Crewe South in the 1950s. One of the advantages of the back cab was that enabled more coal to be carried. But if the upper door burst open, coal would spill all over the footplate. The normal tender doors would not open as they hinged into the tender.*

J. Davenport

Plate 235: *A 'Super D' in its natural habitat, No. 49198 on hump-shunting duties in Norton Junction yards near Cannock on 6th June 1953. It seems to have just attached a brake van to the train in front. The main hump is behind the camera. In the right background is another hump, out of use.*
F. W. Shuttleworth

Chapter Seven

ALLOCATIONS AND WORK

When they were first introduced, the eight-coupled coal engines were naturally used on the hardest duties but as more and more became available, they came to be found all over the LNWR system, the hardest duties being performed by the latest classes. So by the early 1900s the type was to be found not only on main-line work from London to Carlisle, from Holyhead to Leeds, and from Crewe to Swansea and Abergavenny, but also on the lines and in the yards serving the industrial areas of the Midlands, Lancashire, Yorkshire and South Wales. Thanks to their wide route availability, they were prohibited only from such lines as the Cromford & High Peak, and from certain branches and sidings, usually because of sharp curves or weak underline bridges. These places, of course, were stipulated in the *Appendices* to the working timetables.

In addition, eight-coupled coal engines regularly worked at many places off the LNWR system proper. The company enjoyed extensive running powers over the lines of other companies and by this means gained access to the East Midlands and South Yorkshire, and particularly to the lucrative coal traffic originating in those areas. Thanks to its joint line with the Great Northern Railway, northwards from Market Harborough, it reached both Nottingham and Doncaster, where it had its own engine sheds. At one time it worked 16 coal trains a day south from Colwick Sidings, Nottingham, and 11 up from Doncaster over the Great Northern Railway main line as far as Newark (unfortunately, no photograph seems to have survived of an LNWR engine on the GNR main line with one of these trains). The company also reached both Sheffield and Burton-on-Trent by running powers, and again at both places had its own engine sheds. From the early 1900s at the latest, eight-coupled engines were regularly at work on all these lines.

The services on lines over which the company had running powers changed from time to time - for example, the number of coal trains from Doncaster was reduced to five by 1910 - and after the Grouping in particular, major changes took place. The sheds at Doncaster, Sheffield and Colwick (Nottingham) were all closed. On the other hand, as a result of the LNWR and Midland being in the same group, through working began between Toton and Willesden. LNWR 0-8-0s based at the latter shed are believed to have started through working late in 1923.

As a general rule, athough the services over the joint lines changed over time, the pattern of goods services established on the LNWR proper in the late 19th century remained unchanged throughout the LNWR, LMS and early BR periods and was only destroyed by the 'rationalisation' of the late 1960s. By that time the 'Super Ds' themselves had all been withdrawn.

The complexity of these services was considerable, as is illustrated by the details of the workings of eight-coupled engines at the various sheds which follow. Detailed allocations for various periods are to be found in *Appendix Six*.

Willesden and Watford

As the main-line goods shed for London, Willesden sent its 0-8-0s to virtually every point south of Crewe: Bletchley, Rugby, Bescot, Nuneaton, Stafford, Basford Hall and Northampton. Before the Grouping, its engines also worked to Colwick and Doncaster, and after it to Toton. In addition, it provided engines for the various cross-London workings to exchange freight with other companies, such as via Kensington to Clapham Junction and the southern companies, and over the North London lines to the Great Eastern Railway and to London docks.

In LNWR days, engines kept at sub-sheds seem to have been shown in official records as being allocated to the main shed, rather than separately to the sub-shed, even though the same engines usually stayed at the sub-shed for a long time and carried the appropriate shed code. So as Watford was a sub-shed of Willesden, Watford engines were shown in official records as being at Willesden but actually carried a '2W' shed plate. The same sort of arrangement continued in the early LMS period, the 0-8-0 workings from both sheds being shown as 'jointly allocated'.

In fact, by comparison with Willesden, Watford did not use many 0-8-0s but it had a few long-distance workings, including turns to Northampton. Its longest working was to Amington Sidings, near Tamworth. The up train brought coal to Watford, terminating in Watford North Sidings in the early morning, and the down working took the empties. One day in 1925, 'G1' No. 1568 was seen, with a '2W' shed plate, arriving at Watford on this working. In early LMS days, 'G2s' Nos. 9395-7 were at Watford with '2W' shed plates on the smokebox doors and regularly worked to Amington. When this turn ceased to be a Watford duty is not known, but Nuneaton engines worked to Watford in the 1950s, possibly on the Amington turn.

In the early 1950s Watford's top link, the Rugby link, worked both the Watford to Amington and the Bushey to Overseal turns usually as far as Bletchley, but certain Watford men continued to sign the route as far as Nuneaton and Coventry. The 12.55am Watford to Amington was made up of coal empties from local yards and St Albans gas works, the loading being 70 wagons. It was worked by Watford men with a Nuneaton engine which had arrived in Watford yard with the Amington - Watford coal train at about 3am. The engine did not go

Plate 236: *'G1' No. 9329 of shed '36', Carnforth, on the 1 in 173 gradient near Milnthorpe with a down goods in September 1933.*

H. Hall

straight to the shed but worked Target 79 - the shunt and trip turns in the London area were called 'Targets' and identified by numbers. Watford shed worked two Targets, T79, the Headstone Lane shunt, and T83, the Harrow shunt. On T79 the Nuneaton engine shunted at Headstone Lane, Kenton and North Wembley before running into Sudbury yard. It then ran back light to Watford shed, where it waited until it took out the 12.55am. All arrivals at Sudbury departed light engine, the hump being worked by a 350hp diesel shunter.

The only long-distance turn for a Watford engine in the early 1950s was the Bushey to Overseal, which ran as required. It took coal empties from Bushey yard, which supplied coal to Watford gas works by road, and was sometimes made up to 70 wagons at Watford.

Any other traffic for the north was taken by the 5.38am from Watford Yard to Hemel Hempstead, which was worked by Watford men with a Watford 'D'. At Hemel Hempstead they were relieved later in the morning by Bletchley men who worked the train forward to Northampton. The Watford men then relieved a southbound working, usually hauled by the previous day's northbound engine, shunted the yard and worked to Camden. This train mainly conveyed paper produced by Dickenson's at Apsley Mill and carried in containers. Engines which often worked this train were Nos 48915

and 49323. Later this turn was worked by a Watford engine going to Boxmoor only, shunting there and then going to Camden. In the mid 1950s it was worked by Ivatt class '2' No. 46431.

In the early 1950s, Watford New Yard was shunted by a 'D', which came off shed at 6am and shunted the yard throughout the day. Late in the evening it went to the Old Yard, where it relieved the 'D' which had been shunting there and which then went to the shed. The 'Ds' were replaced on these turns by LMS engines and later by 350hp diesel shunters. In the early 1950s Watford had three 'Super Ds', Nos. 48915, 49145 and 49323. They left Watford in August 1956 and were replaced by Derby '4Fs'.

Nuneaton

Before 1922 there were no 'Super Ds' at Nuneaton but in that year the enginemen pointed out that it was difficult for them to compete with other depots in timekeeping and coal consumption when working similar trains. They asked for 'Superheated Ds' to be allocated to the shed for the freight workings to London, and for the 4.35pm to Crewe and 1.5am return, which was then a '19in Goods' turn. Eventually, this was achieved and in 1945 33 of the class were at Nuneaton.

The turns to Willesden necessitated the men lodging

there as follow:

3.20am Nuneaton-Willesden (MO) book off 10.10am
2.55am Willesden-Nuneaton (TO) book on 1.35am
(At Willesden 15 hours 25 minutes)

2.30am Nuneaton-Willesden (MO) book off 6.55am
1.30am Camden-Nuneaton (TO) book on 12.30am
(At Willesden 17 hours 35 minutes)

3.25am Nuneaton/Hawkesbury Lane-Willesden (MO) book off 10.38am
12.50am Camden-Nuneaton (TO) book on 11.35pm
(At Willesden 12 hours 57 minutes; away from home 32 hours 15 minutes)

12.11am Nuneaton-Camden (MX) book off 5.45am
12.50am Camden-Nuneaton book on 11.35pm
(At Willesden 17 hours 50 minutes)

1.50am Nuneaton-Willesden (MX) book off 8.5am
1.10am Willesden-Nuneaton (MTX) book on 11.50pm
1.15am Willesden-Nuneaton (SUO) book on 11.55pm
(At Willesden 15 hours 45 minutes/15 hours 50 minutes)

4.50am Nuneaton-Willesden (MX) book off 8.32am
2.55am Willesden-Nuneaton (MTX) book on 1.35am
1.40am Willesden-Nuneaton (SUO) book on 12.30
(At Willesden 17 hours 3 minutes/15 hours 48 minutes)

Some men did not object to lodging but many disliked being away from home for such long periods, especially at times of illness in the family. In those days no one had telephones at home and the only convenience food was cheese on toast! Again, it was sometimes difficult to sleep in the lodge at Willesden because some young men living there were rowdy and noisy.

As well as lodging turns to Willesden, Nuneaton men also had a lodging turn to Oxford as follows:

8pm Nuneaton-Oxford arrive 4am; book on 7.30pm, engine prepared; 8pm Oxford-Bletchley, change; arrive Nuneaton 6am.

Lodging at Oxford was in a private house where admittance was prohibited until 9am. Consequently, the men spent the time in summer walking along the canal or, when it was raining, sitting in the van talking or playing cards. This lodge was run by a widow whose husband had been a railwayman. It was invariably cold and overcoats were normally kept on while sleeping!

Eventually, in the early 1940s lodging was discontinued. The following turns were then regularly rostered for 'Super Ds':

12.50am Nuneaton-Willesden (SO)
1.3am Nuneaton-Willesden (SX)

6.25am Nuneaton-Swanbourne (SX)
8.20am Nuneaton-Swanbourne (SO)

9.12am Nuneaton-Willesden (SX)

From about 1949 a 'Super D' was the power for the Abbey Street banker and remained so until the class left Nuneaton shed in the early 1960s. The only exception was when Ivatt class '4' 2-6-0s were used for a time on Target 86. In 1957-62 the roster was as follows:

T91 8.10am (MO) Nuneaton MPD to Abbey Street (book on 7am, reman 1.10pm) arrive back on shed 8.55pm.
Target 86 11.20pm (SX) Nuneaton Hawkestone Road (book on 10pm).
Target 91 book on 5.39am (MX), reman T86 (reman at 12.19) arrive back on shed 8.55pm.

'Super Ds' were provided on these workings only after being displaced from the mainline by Stanier '8Fs'. Before that, these turns had been performed by Webb 'Coal Engines' and 'Cauliflowers'. Complaints about the inadequacy of these engines resulted in Nuneaton receiving a batch of Ivatt '4' 2-6-0s, Nos. 43020-6, in 1949. In April 1945 complaints had been made about 'Super Ds' being unable to handle maximum loads on the Ansley Colliery branch because of priming (the quality of the water at Nuneaton was described by J. M. Dunn as being 'some of the worst on the system'). Engines with taper boilers were requested instead.

With experience enginemen learned little dodges that made the job easier. For example, there was a small rose wheel that could be unscrewed, disconnecting the steam supply to the brake and making things a little easier for the fireman on an engine that was not steaming well. It was of course prohibited, as it was dangerous, but it was done when conditions allowed. Occasionally a loco inspector would join the train to return on the engine. One Nuneaton driver, Jack Kiteley, had an arrangement with a signalman at Shackerstone that when an inspector was waiting, he would raise and lower the distant signal as a warning, giving him time to replace the wheel. It was said that drivers sometimes disconnected the brakes in this way near Sterling Metals on leaving Nuneaton and ran all the way to Willesden without re-connecting them.

Finally, Eddie Bray recalls:

'I used to work in the control office on the up side immediately above the refreshment rooms on Rugby station. My desk was next to the window for a while and I can recall controllers rushing in and taking all the window space up. One of them would say, "I've given the Nuneaton driver on the 1.3 Willesden the road up the 'old line'. I've told him I've put him in front of the Liverpool and to be smart about it." Then the deep nasal chuff-chuff-chuff-chuff approached hurriedly, the driver giving us a 'pop' on the whistle and a contented wave with an oily rag as he passed, and then 70 wagons of coal rattled by to pollute the London suburbs - no Beatles, no electric guitars, no motorways, no poll tax, no worries about pollution. Heaven!'

Crewe South

In the late 1930s Crewe South used its 'G2s' on workings to a very wide range of destinations: Bamfurlong (Wigan); Adswood (near Stockport); Leeds (Farnley Junction, Neville Hill and Copley Hill, though the engine was always brought back to Farnley, even though the train was left at the other two places); Hillhouse (Huddersfield); Edge Hill and Garston; Arpley (Warrington); Birkenhead and Mold Junction; Craven Arms (on the Swansea turn, and occasionally through to Llandovery); Coleham (Shrewsbury) and Hereford; Bushbury and Bescot; Rugby (or, if the train was late, Nuneaton); Northampton or Bletchley (on the Willesden turn; the engine worked through but the men were relieved, as they would have exceeded their time by too big a margin. Sometimes they changed footplates with Willesden men and at other times they returned to Crewe 'on the cushions').

Although this list refers particularly to the 1935-40 period, it would have been much the same in the early years after the Second World War, until the Stanier

'8Fs' finally displaced the 'Super Ds' from the hardest turns. What is more, it would have been much the same in about 1900 and before, as the pattern of traffic changed little once the Tranship Shed was opened at Crewe and was probably not much different for some years before that.

Buxton

Except for the 'A' class, the various eight-coupled classes were all allocated to Buxton at one time or another. In the 1920s, Buxton men worked them to Lees (Oldham), Mold Junction, Widnes, Warrington, Wigan and Edge Hill, mostly on lodging turns, as well as into the Manchester area on non-lodging turns. At that time the 0-8-0s were not allowed to work beyond Parsley Hay on the Ashbourne line, the through goods traffic being worked by '18in Tanks', but that restriction was lifted later and they then worked through to Uttoxeter. The 0-8-0s were also used on banking and shunting, though from 1911 Buxton had an allocation of 0-8-2 tanks specifically for those jobs.

In about 1950, a Buxton 'Super D' worked the 9.50am to Uttoxeter Pinfold Sidings every day except Sunday, stayed at Uttoxeter shed overnight and worked back to Buxton the following day. Buxton men did not work through to Uttoxeter but changed footplates with Uttoxeter men at Alsop-en-le-Dale. At Buxton this job was always known as 'the Burton', because originally and up to the Second World War, the train had gone through to Burton and had not terminated at Uttoxeter.

Before the Second World War, there was another turn from Buxton to Burton at 4pm. It was worked by Buxton men only as far as Parsley Hay, where they crossed footplates with Burton men who had shunted every siding and yard as necessary from Burton.

On another turn, the men booked on at 7.30am and went light engine with a 'D' to Rowsley, to work the 11.36am goods from Rowsley to Buxton. At Buxton the engine was re-manned and then went at 1.30pm, either light engine or with a goods, to Ashbourne. It always went tender-first, so that it was the right way round to work back, and so was a double-cabbed engine. On the return working it shunted all the stations and sidings as necessary.

At certain times of year, this job was done not by a 'D' but by a 'Crab', which worked the 9.30am London coach from Buxton to Millers Dale, before proceeding light engine to Rowsley.

Every day two 'Ds' were needed as 'bank' engines. They did all the shunting in the sidings and also banked trains to Bibbingtons and to Briggs as required. The engines on these turns were always double-cabbed. In winter another double-cabbed 'D' always had to be maintained for snowplough duty, for which it was coupled to a '4F' 0-6-0.

The 'Ds' were also used whenever necessary as substitutes for Stanier '8F' 2-8-0s on their diagrams, and so, for example, often went to such places as Warrington, Stockport and Longsight. One turn which was probably an '8F' diagram and on which a 'D' was used regularly was the 6.36pm goods to Rowsley. The engine was double-headed from Buxton by a '3F' 0-6-0, and on the return working, the 10.36pm goods from Rowsley to Buxton, the '3F' was used as a banker.

Huddersfield

The following notes are taken from the diaries of driver Ben Garner of Hillhouse shed, Huddersfield:

There are not many entries for 'C' class: No. 2553 in 1912 and No. 2552 in 1913; for 'E' class: No. 2056 in 1912, No. 1064 in 1914 and Nos. 1222/3 in 1913; and for 'F' class: No. 2553 in 1912-13, No. 352 in 1914, No. 906 in 1915, No. 899 in 1920 and No. 1273 in 1921-3 (sometimes used by Ben Garner to Mold Junction and Birkenhead).

21st January 1898. The first compound goods went to Farnley shed, No. 1817.

22nd January 1898. No. 1816 ran from Copley Hill to Crewe on goods.

18th August 1898. The first compound came to Hillhouse shed, No. 1832.

12th September 1900. The first use by Ben Garner of No. 1835, to Stockport.

1st March 1901. Moved to coal link. Local coal duties using No. 1877.

14th August 1901. Used No. 1875 to Longsight.

1902. Used Nos. 1875 and 1876 in the coal link.

December 1903. Moved to double trip link, which had turns to Bescot, Liverpool and Hull. Worked in this link but ran only to Hull from 24th August 1908 to August 1914.

1st March 1905. To Stockport on 7.10 goods with 'B' class No. 1122.

8th October 1905. 10.20pm goods to Stockport with 'B' class No. 1300.

1906. No. 1806 came to Farnley shed.

1911. Six trips to Hull with 'D' No. 1837, one trip with 'D' No. 1249 and two trips with No. 2566. These were the first trips to Hull using 0-8-0s.

16th July 1912. No. 2056 used to Hull for eighteen trips.

1912. 'C' class No. 2553 used to Hull for seventeen trips.

1913. 'G' class No. 1434 used to Hull.

11th July 1913. 'G1' No. 734 new, now Ben Garner's engine (No. 670 also came new to Hillhouse). Made 251 trips with No. 734 until the ending of the Hull job. Spent a few weeks learning the route west of Huddersfield with 'G' class No. 1464, used 141 times.

19th July 1915. Acquired 'G1' No. 931 which was used regularly until 5th October 1915.

During the period 1896-1917 Ben Garner had four days off work through illness. For 79 days he was suffering from minor injuries, such as broken fingers, a cut hand and so on, and he was late for work once, on 13th October 1906, when the 'knocker up' failed to call him! He ended his time after a long illness on 0-8-2 tank No. 2277 about 1924. This was used as bank engine (not 'banker') whose duties comprised double-heading a heavy train leaving Heaton Lodge or Hillhouse sidings up to Diggle Summit, then returning home light to work a local trip or the Hillhouse coal shunt. This was a 'light' duty for any driver who was suffering ill health. It was on this engine at Heaton Lodge that he suffered a stroke which eventually led to his demise.

In all, there were 15 'MMs' at Hillhouse, though not all at the same time, including Nos. 1820, 2052, 2849/61, 2812/27/62/3. The first to arrive was No. 2052, which when being placed on the shed was found to have the brake hard on. The attention of fitters was required before it was released, the problem being lack of lubrication. These engines arrived without any information being provided to the fitters on the maintenance of the Westinghouse pump.

One of the 912X series when used on the morning Hillhouse to Halifax and Bradford goods made a habit of letting its uncoupled wheels drop off the line in Wyke goods yard. For branch operation the engines were used on all local lines and seem to have been unrestricted to Birstall, Kirkburton, Meltham, Holmfirth and Clayton West, from where they worked heavy coal trains through to Bradley Wood Junction after the amalgamation with the LYR.

It was not uncommon for a 'Super D' to be used on a passenger train as a result of a failure or a shortage of engines. One was used in this way on the fairly frequent cheap Saturday evening excursions to Leeds Central via Low Moor (Huddersfield to Leeds 1s 3d return). The engines made light of this work. Anyone standing on Holbeck High Level platform when one set off from Leeds would witness a dramatic effect - the Transacord recording at Preston must have used this as a prototype!

The last 'Super Ds' at Hillhouse shed were Nos. 9381/9, which departed in March 1949, though the class continued to work into Huddersfield from other sheds until 1963.

Abergavenny

Abergavenny LMS locomotive depot had the shed code '4D' showing it was part of the Shrewsbury district, and its address was: 'LMS Motive Power Depot, Union Road, Abergavenny, Monmouthshire'. Brecon Road was the name of the station, top and bottom yards, control, and the engineer and signal departments. The shed only became Brecon Road in BR days. These details of the main-line workings from the shed are for the period 1939-52.

All trains started from Abergavenny Junction unless otherwise stated. Coleham and Harlescott are sidings at Salop, more commonly known as Shrewsbury.

Abbreviations
RR - runs as required
RL - crew relieved and train continuing to destination ('Stafford RL, Burton-on-Trent' means that the crew were relieved at Stafford but the engine and train continued to Burton-on-Trent.).

Monday
2.10am Stafford
3.40am Harlescott, RR Chester
5.40am Pontypool Road to Harlescott
8.15am Coleham
12.30pm Newport Dock Street
9.10pm Crewe RL, Liverpool
10.46pm Crewe RL, Leeds
11.30pm Harlescott, RR Crewe

Tuesday
12.10am Harlescott
2.10am Stafford RL, Burton-on-Trent
3.40am Harlescott
4.5am Newport Dock Street, RR
5.40am Pontypool Road to Harlescott
8.15am Coleham
12.30pm Newport Dock Street, RR
9.10pm Crewe RL, Carlisle
10.46pm Crewe RL, Leeds

11.30pm Harlescott, RR Chester

Wednesday
12.10am Harlescott
2.10am Stafford RL, Burton-on-Trent
3.40am Harlescott
4.5am Newport Dock Street, RR
5.40am Pontypool Road to Harlescott
8.15am Coleham
12.30pm Newport Dock Street, RR
9.10pm Crewe RL, Carlisle
10.46pm Crewe RL, Leeds
11.30pm Harlescott, RR Chester

Thursday
12.10am Crewe Bank
2.10am Stafford RL, Burton-on-Trent
3.40am Harlescott
4.5am Newport Dock Street, RR
5.40am Pontypool Road to Stafford
8.15am Coleham
9.10pm Crewe RL, Bamfurlong
10.46pm Crewe RL, Guide Bridge
11.30pm Harlescott

Friday
12.10am Crewe RL, Carlisle
2.10am Stafford RL, Northampton
3.40am Harlescott
4.5am Newport Dock Street, RR
5.40am Pontypool Road to Harlescott
8.15am Coleham
12.30pm Newport Dock Street
9.10pm Crewe RL, Preston
10.46pm Crewe RL, Leeds
11.30pm Harlescott

Saturday
12.10am Wellington
2.10am Stafford RL, Bushbury and Walsall
3.40am Harlescott
4.5am Newport Dock Street, RR
5.40am Pontypool Road to Harlescott
8.15am Coleham
11.30am Newport Dock Street
10.46pm Crewe RL, Leeds

By agreement with the GWR, there were four additional paths northward, including one to Bournville via Worcester and Droitwich, and one southward.

Abergavenny men lodged in railway hostels at Chester, Salop, Crewe and Stafford. The Stafford one was noisy as it was next door to W. G. Bagnall's locomotive works. They always had a fresh bed with clean sheets, which was quite different from the GWR idea of men having to look for lodgings and having to wait for a bed to come free.

The return workings were a mixture of freight, passenger, mails and parcels, and some of them were very complicated. For instance, a Stafford return working was a Burton-on-Trent to Swansea freight, which Abergavenny men worked as far as Coleham. Swansea men took over there and the Abergavenny men would re-man a freight from Crewe at the same spot and work it home. A return working from Basford Hall was a freight as far as Shrewsbury station 'back of the glass', then an express passenger to Hereford, where the men changed footplates with Salop men, who had brought a freight down, and worked it home to Abergavenny Junction. On Sunday mornings they worked the mails from Crewe, running non-stop from Shrewsbury to

Pontypool Road, and then ran back tender-first to Hereford, where they changed footplates with Salop men, who had brought a freight down, and worked the freight to Abergavenny.

All this required the trains to run to time and Abergavenny men have said that even in the war there was not much overtime. In fact, they did not want it, as it spoilt their mileage payments which they preferred. When the GWR took over in 1950, the whole system went to pot and there was much dissatisfaction due to loss of mileage pay.

In 1939 Abergavenny had the following allocation of engines for main-line work:

Class 5 2-6-0 'Crabs': 2772, 2785, 2815, 2885, 2920
Class '7F' 0-8-0 'G2A': 8899, 8932, 8934, 8944, 9243, 9247, 9280, 9306, 9388; Class '7F' 0-8-0 'G2': 9403

In 1947 the 'Crabs' were transferred away to Lancashire and replaced by twelve more 0-8-0s: 8921, 8951, 9046, 9064, 9113, 9121, 9161, 9168, 9174, 9226, 9276 and 9316. Two other 0-8-0s were transferred to Abergavenny shortly afterwards: 9409 and 9448. One last 0-8-0 came in 1952, 49341, which gave Abergavenny 25 'Super Ds', probably one of the largest allocations of the class on BR. These engines, of course, were shared with Tredegar, which needed about five to cover its work.

Plate 237: *An unidentified 'G1' rolls into Hednesford on Whit Monday 1935 with a train of GWR stock, believed to be carrying delgates to a Catholic Church convention..*
P. S. Kendrick

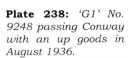

Plate 238: *'G1' No. 9248 passing Conway with an up goods in August 1936.*
H. Hall

Chapter Eight
WORKING WITH 'SUPER Ds'
by Harold Walkley

Double Home to Crewe

When I was a young fitter in the early days of nationalisation, I was always interested to see how locomotives were handled by different drivers in different situations. I was always asking questions of drivers and was on good terms with most of them. One day, one of them, Bill James, said, 'Get permission and come on a trip with us, say, to Crewe Saturday night and back on Sunday evening'.

I had a word with my shedmaster, Mr A. G. Williams, who advised me on the procedure for applying to the district locomotive superintendent. Within a few weeks permission was granted for both the outward and return journeys with the proviso that I submit a report on the trip to the DLS. I saw Bill to make the arrangements and he said he would never be able to live it down with the other drivers, but as I was giving lectures to the improvement classes run for footplate staff, I knew it was a joke. Some friends of mine at Crewe were contacted and agreed that I could stay with them, and needless to say, everyone thought I was crackers!

Fortunately, on the Saturday morning of the weekend of the planned trip I was booked to finish a week of nights and was not due to start again until the afternoon shift on the Monday. I reported to the afternoon running shift foreman at 10.10pm and showed him my pass. The driver and fireman were due on at 10.16pm. I checked the engine board to see which engine we had and it turned out to be No. M9388, built originally as a 'G1' in 1915 and converted to a 'G2A' in 1936.

I stow my overnight bag in the locker, put my flask on the faceplate and start checking the loco. She has already been prepared by the afternoon shift but the syphon trimmings need putting in, seven either side, and the mechanical lubricator needs a couple of turns by hand as well, to give her a start. Back on the footplate I check the tank glass, 42in long, which shows the full 3000 gallons, and light the two lamps. I put one showing white up on the chimney bracket and the other showing the red shade on the left-hand tender bracket. It is supposed to be on the centre one for a light engine but it will come off at the junction.

Bill James and fireman Fred Wall arrive with the words, 'Anxious, aren't you?' Both Bill and Fred are good mates of mine, in fact, and live near me. Bill checks the four-position brake valve and Fred tries both injectors. The four-position valve allows the reservoir side to be exhausted, if required, in an emergency. Fred looks at the fire. 'Nice and black', he says, 'and 150 on the clock.'

We are due off shed at 10.26pm and just before that time Brecon Road No. 2 box gives us the road to the junction. The two miles or so to the junction are covered in no time at all and the junction bobby turns us back into the south sidings on to our train. The guard hooks us on and gives us the tally, '32 equal to 38'. 'Not a bad load', says Bill. The full load to Crewe is 'equal to 43'. Under the LMS system, a 16-ton loaded wagon plus tare, 25 tons, was reckoned as 'equal to one class 1'. The Western Region class 1 was based on a 10-ton wagon plus tare.

I get the tail lamp and put it in the centre of the front bufferbeam, removing the red shade. This head code is an 'express freight' officially but to railwaymen is 'an up and downer'. The banker is already in position behind the train, Ivatt tank No. 1202, which had recently arrived in the area to replace the ageing Webb 'Coal Tanks'. It had worked the 8.30pm Merthyr to Abergavenny passenger, due in the junction at 10.5pm, put its coaches away and run to the bottom of the south sidings ready to assist us. So they had not hung around.

The junction bobby had given us the road, so Bill gives a single crow on the whistle and immediately the banker answers and starts pushing quietly. Bill had released the vacuum from the reservoir side, saying that you do not need brakes going up hill. He opens the regulator and she starts to move. We travel about twenty yards and Bill pulls her back one turn on the wheel. He leaves it there while we traverse the crossovers on to the main line. The pressure, which I thought a bit low at 155lb while standing on the train, starts to rise with the effect of the blast on the fire, and the water is just showing in the top of the glass. On asking about this, I am told it is good enginemanship not to stand blowing off but to raise pressure when under way. The banker whistles to say he is on the main line, so Bill opens the regulator more and brings the wheel back another turn, and we are now doing about 25mph.

Fred says, 'Now's the time to work your passage but keep it light with the shovel'. I put the right-hand injector on and set it to minimum with the ram handle. These are good trouble-free injectors designed by White and Webb many years ago. My first attempt at firing results in me hitting the firehole door with the shovel. I soon get it right though, one down each side, one in each back corner and one under the door. I find though that I am knocking my hand on the knob on the tender handbrake wheel so I have to watch that. The safety valves lift and Bill says that I am wasting coal and water - there is more in firing than meets the eye. I can hear the banker a long way back giving it all he can - he sounds like the Lickey banker - and Bill says he is working his fire down, probably because he is in for boiler-washing the next day.

Llanvihangel station looms up, the top of the bank. Bill blows up the vacuum brake as the banker gives us a toot to say, 'It's all yours now', and then Bill brings the wheel back another turn and eases the regulator a bit. I put the left-hand injector on now we are starting to go down, and the water level drops down in the glass momentarily. Pandy box gives us a set of greens and we sail through at about 40mph. I listen to the exhaust. It sounds just like a stutter. I shut off both injectors and put five shovelfuls round the box. Fred says to put the flap up. The ride is lovely and smooth. I thought it would be rougher than it is. Bill says, 'This is a lovely "D". We had her Tuesday and Thursday nights on this job.'

Going through Pontrilas, I fire over the flap again and put the right-hand injector on again. We are easing off now for Red Hill Junction, where we swing round to the right on to the line built by the LNWR in the 1860s, with the GWR having running powers over it. The GWR line proper bears left towards Barton. Bill drops the wheel forward one turn and opens her up. He tells me to give her a couple of shovelfuls but not to let her blow off in Hereford. We swing round the curve into Rotherwas Junction and up the rise over the river Wye bridge and as we approach the station, Fred shouts out, 'Through the platform'. I was told that it is usual to take the loop line behind the island platform but tonight it is through the platform for us.

I glance at the tank glass and see it is down to 30in. Bill says that there is plenty there. He nudges me and points out a 43XX class engine with a train for the north on the Barton loop line. He says that it is the Saltney goods and that if they had let him out in front of us, we would have had a bad run but we will not hold him up.

With the right-hand injector set to medium, I start firing in earnest to get a good fire for Dinmore tunnel and I am still knocking my hand on the tender wheel. We are really moving now with half regulator and three turns on the wheel, and apart from a slight occasional gland hiss up front M9388 is in good nick. We roar through Dinmore tunnel - it is deafening and I am glad when we are clear. I glance at my watch - midnight - and Bill says he thought we would have been through Leominster by now, but I think he is joking, because we certainly have not been hanging about.

I leave the injector on all the time now and every few minutes put five around the box. I am anxious about the water level, which is down to 24in, but Fred says that we are on a slight down gradient which puts the water to the rear of the tender. We have maintained 35-40mph from Hereford and the regulator and wheel have remained the same. Ludlow tunnel is coming up and Bill is easing off, as he says that there is a nasty kick along Ludlow platform, which is even worse on a passenger loco. I feel it - it is quite unpleasant - and I won-

der why the civil engineer does not do something about it.

We are clear now and Bill opens up to get some speed for Ludlow water troughs. If you are not going fast enough, you will not pick up enough water, and we do not want that. I operate the scoop wheel and watch the level rise in the glass. All the same, amateur that I am, I manage to have it overspill and get water splashing everywhere. Bill is disgusted with me!

I say to Bill that we have not seen an adverse signal yet and straightaway he starts whistling. 'You spoke too soon', he says. Onibury crossing distant is at caution, so Bill eases her off and speed drops to about 20mph. As we approach the home signal, it comes off, so Bill drops the wheel forward and opens her up. There is a steep rise on the other side of the crossing, so we want a run at it. I fire heavily here and put the right-hand injector on maximum. Half regulator and $1^{1}/_{2}$ turns on the wheel take us up the bank but the exhaust is pulling hard on the fire. As we level off, I put the left-hand injector on as well and fire hard again. I am a bit slow in shutting off the left-hand injector and have over-filled her and she starts to prime. So I have to open the cylinder cocks to clear the front end and I notice that there is a significant drop in power when the cocks are open. Bill tells me that on Monday to Friday nights they stop for examination at Craven Arms but on Saturday nights it is done at Salop.

Half regulator and $2^{1}/_{2}$ turns on the wheel roll us through Craven Arms and all the way to Church Stretton, where Bill eases off and we come to a stop at the Salop end of the station. Fred takes the coal pick and proceeds to pin down brakes for the descent to Salop. Normally the guard pins down the brakes but Bill had arranged with the guard that we would do it to save him the walk. I take the opportunity to make my notes up fully and I see that it is 1.20am. Fred comes back with the words, 'Fifteen down', meaning that the brakes are pinned down on fifteen wagons. The starter comes off, we give a short whistle and then ease forward on to the gradient. We look back and see the guard's lights, which show that he is still with us, so we are OK. I am watching the water level as the loco dips on the gradient. It comes down half way, then holds steady and Fred says, 'Good'.

Once we have the train completely on the gradient, the tender handbrake is screwed on lightly, leaving the power brake for any emergencies. The descent to Salop, although not steep by South Wales standards, takes about forty minutes. We pull up by Coleham sidings to lift the brakes and the shunter comes across to tell us that they are putting another six wagons on to us in the station. 'They will bank you to Harlescott crossing', he tells us. 'Thank you very much.' says Bill. 'You are putting on my good nature.'

I get the pricker down off the tender and loosen up the fire which had died down on the descent from Church Stretton, so that pressure is 170lb when we start towards the station. As we pass the junction with the Welshpool line, we can see our extra wagons and attendant loco, either a 'Cauliflower' or a '17in Coal'. We draw up in the centre road and stop under the water column. I drop the bag in and ponder why they call them 'bags'. Using the shovel, I throw the coal forward to fill the front of the tender. It is all Cannock hards and sharps, and it looks like slag, but it is good stuff. The Blaenavon coal we had used so far had been all right too, but there is one thing about a 'D' - they will steam on anything so long as they are fired correctly. My firing technique as an amateur seems to have been all right anyway.

The tank is full so I throw out the bag and Fred says to fill the firebox right up, which I do. We have not got the road yet, because we are still in front of running time. Two crows in the rear tell us that our banker is ready but I still have time for a bite and a drink - it is the last chance I shall get. A clank tells us that our signal is off. We give a crow on the whistle and the banker answers and then we are off. We start quietly as there is a sharp curve to the right here and speed is kept down. With 1/4 regulator and one turn on the wheel we keep moving at about 10mph and look back. When we see the lights of the van come into sight and the banker whistles to say that he is clear of the junction, Bill opens the regulator wide and winds the wheel back 2 1/2 turns and we leap forward as though we had to be in Crewe in twenty minutes. The exhaust of the banker tells us that it is a 'Cauliflower' and that he is giving us a good push.

I have the right-hand injector on now and I take a glance at the fire. It is one white seething mass. That is the hard coal. Fred says to put the flap up and fire over the top and just under the door. Apparently different types of coal require various techniques to get the best out of them. We are doing about 40mph when we pass Harlescott box. A shriek in the rear tells us that the banker has dropped off and immediately we feel a drag and our speed drops slightly. Bill eases the wheel forward half a turn but leaves the regulator open wide. I have got used to firing now and am not knocking my hands on the wheel any more. Fred puts the blower on as Bill starts easing off for a warning signal. According to Bill, there are automatic electric signals on this route and we are coming under the control of Whitchurch box. There is a down gradient as far as Nantwich and the bobby wants to see that all is well before he passes us on. We leave Whitchurch doing about 20mph but do not pin down any brakes. The Market Drayton line of the former GWR comes in on our right, shrouded in mists rising off the nearby canal. Passing Wistaston station we get splitter lights to route us into Gresty Lane sidings and we draw to a halt at 3.35am, 40 minutes early. The shunter hooks us off, as the guard comes up grumbling about having a cold van from Salop. They all go off to the South shed and the hostel, while I go to my friend's house where a bath awaits me and a few hours' sleep.

My conclusion from this run of 105 miles in 4hr 50min is that the engine was master of its load, even with my amateur firing. Coal burnt was about 38cwt (excluding preparation) and water used was about 2 1/2 tanks, say, 8000 gallons, but it could have been less. The brakes were excellent and the ride was reasonable, considering the short wheelbase and the absence of bogies. The footplate could be improved by more comfortable seats and sliding windows to the cab sides. The tender hand wheels would be better repositioned vertically with T-shaped handles having vertical hand-grips, and the handles for the front dampers and cylinder cocks would be better redesigned as vertical handles pivotting off a bracket on the floor. Both injectors were excellent and did all that was asked of them. The shovelling plate is perfect on these engines and the coal works down fairly well. The reversing wheel would be better with an indicator to show the driver the precise position of the gear. The load, equal to 38 class 1 as far as Salop and 46 class 1 on to Crewe, was well within the capacity of the engine and there is no reason why it should not be increased, within the limitations of the length of running loops and so forth.

At 7.20pm I arrived at Crewe South shed and showed my pass to the foreman on duty. He said that I was a little bit early and I had to wait for Bill and Fred, as I was not familiar with the layout of South shed. We had the same loco, No. M9388, and the shift foreman told Bill that they had used her to work a special to Edge Hill that morning. That was typical of Crewe, Bill said, to wear out somebody else's loco and save their own.

We make up the fire and Bill goes round with the oil can. I check the brake adjustment and see that it is all right. The coal is all Cannock hards, which Crewe men like - you can hold a candle to it and it will light. We fill the tank and at 8.35pm we are running to Basford Hall sidings. I look at all the lights and ask Bill how he can pick out the right ones. 'Easy', he says.

We arrive at our train, the 9pm Sundays only from Basford Hall sidings to Abergavenny Junction South Sidings, and find that it consists of only eight vehicles, all labelled for Newport Docks. They are all vacuum-fitted and Bill says that we will connect them up to the engine, although we run as a non-fitted freight. At 8.55pm we get our lights to lead us out on to the Shrewsbury line and we are soon doing about 45mph with the regulator just cracked open and the wheel on 3 1/2 turns. A train of this weight presents no problems. I only fire once to Salop and the right-hand injector is used only for short periods. Having the vacuum connected enables us to drop quickly into Salop where we are routed through the platform line instead of the usual 'back of the glass'. We are checked only momentarily by Foregate box and as the water is only down 3in in the glass, we are OK to Ludlow troughs. Pressure is kept steady at 165lb by keeping the firedoor open and the back damper half shut.

We are clear of Salop by 10pm, so it looks like an early arrival home. Bill had the regulator just cracked open and the wheel on three turns on the ascent of Stretton bank, the top of which we cleared at 10.30pm. I made certain that the water level did not drop by putting on the left-hand injector for a few minutes as we descended to Craven Arms. Speed was kept down until we were in sight of Ludlow troughs but then we put on a bit of a spurt to top the tank up and this time I got it right and earned a bit of praise from Bill. We had clear signals all the way to Hereford, which meant that firing was light and the water level easy to maintain. Then we were stopped by the bobby in Aylestone Hill box. He called Bill over for a word and when he came back he told us that a Worcester to Pontypool Road freight had broken down with superheater trouble at Red Hill Junction and we were requested, as the only available power in the area, to shift it. It appeared that as we were London Midland Region and the broken down train was Western Region, there was a conflict of managers. Anyway, we agreed to move the train as otherwise we would have been stuck in Hereford until it was moved by somebody else, Bill was issued with the appropriate written instructions by the bobby, and off we went, keeping a sharp look-out for the missing train. When we came up behind it, the guard hooked us on. We discussed with him what we should do and I was given the job of walking to the train engine and passing on the instructions. The Western driver grumbled about being helped by a 'blooming LMS man' but I stayed on the footplate of the GWR engine, a 43XX class.

The Western driver gave the necessary whistle and our loco answered and started pushing. We were turned into the loop at Tram Inn and I was most impressed by the GWR low whistle for warning purposes and to signal our loco to stop. Our loco reversed back out of the loop and then came up alongside on the main line. The Tram Inn bobby said that Newport control office had asked if we could tow the train home to Pontypool Road. 'Aye, anything to show those Western fellas up,' said Bill. He was making one of his jokes, of course. Leaving our train on the main line, we backed on to the 43XX, pulled it out and then backed it on to our short train. A bit more shunting saw us all coupled up and ready to go. With our vacuum pipes connected to the 43XX and our original train we set off. The higher vacuum of the 43XX was making our relief valve scream on the footplate and so I covered it with my coat to lessen the noise. Fred said, 'Get that fire going', but we took that train away without any trouble and it was an easy run to the top of Llanvihangel bank, where we stopped to pin down brakes even though we had fitted wagons on. The Western driver came on to our footplate and begrudgingly admitted that the 'Super D' was a better engine than he had thought, although he did not call it a 'Super D' but a 'Cockney', which was the first and only time I ever heard them called that.

The Abergavenny Junction distant was at caution and we were brought to a stand at the junction box. Abergavenny Junction loco depot had arranged relief for us and they were going to take the train on to Pontypool Road. Abergavenny LMS men had been working through Pontypool Road for many years and so there were no problems on route knowledge. We took over No. 7717, the Webb 'Coal Tank' that the relief crew had come up on, and we arrived at the shed at 1.40am.

I thoroughly enjoyed the double home trip and it gave me a real insight into the working conditions and problems that footplatemen are involved in. It was a pity that the LMS drawing office had not carried out the small improvements that were called for on the 'Super Ds'. Apart from the improvements to the footplate which I mentioned earlier, an alteration to the lubrication of the bottom slide bars and the small end bushes would have improved the class out of all recognition and at small cost.

Some time after the trip I learned that there was quite a row over our moving the train that had broken down. It was an inter-regional managerial argument and we were disgusted by it all. Our only concern had been to get the trains moving and to make a success of the industry.

Overloaded by Thirteen Wagons from Salop
as related by Fireman David Williams

In April 1950 we had come under the jurisdiction of the Western Region instead of the London Midland Region, and due to boundary changes and reallocation of locomotives, freight traffic was, to say the least, in a bit of a mess. Having worked the 8.15am freight from Abergavenny to Salop and taken rest, we had to work a train back the following day. Our train was the 5.35am freight from Coleham. Originally, Abergavenny men had worked the train only as far as Abergavenny Junction but now this was extended to Pontypool.

We booked on at 4.5am to get our engine ready. It was class '8F' 2-8-0 No. 8263, which was based in the Leeds area and looked rather run down. Probably it had not been to works for some time as it still had not got the '4' for its BR number.

The shift 'runner' (running shed foreman) told us that the train was a little bit over the load, 'So do your best, lads', and on arrival at Coleham Sidings, George Brimfield, our guard, said we were four over load, 'So the best of luck'. As we pulled out on to the main line and passed Baystone Hill box, the boiler pressure started to drop from 225lb and on looking at the fire we could see that there was no draw on it at all. Putting the blower on and giving the fire a good root up with the fire-iron had no effect and we gradually lost more pressure. We struggled on to Condover and whistled to the signalman to turn us into the loop. We made it with 80lb showing on the clock. Something was radically wrong and on looking inside the smokebox, we found that one of the main steam pipe joints was blowing very badly. That meant a total failure, and after the bobby had been informed of the situation, he routed us back to Salop for a fresh loco.

On arrival back at the shed, we found them rushing to get another loco ready. One had just arrived straight from the shops at Crewe after a general overhaul, 'Super D' No. 49029, one of Salop's long-time allocation of the class. Being only class '7F', it was not as powerful as the '8F', so problems were looming.

We left the shed and were soon back at Condover, dropping back on to the train. George said that we were now 13 over the load and we should put a couple off, but the bobby said that control knew about the overloading and hoped that we would do our best. My driver, Ernie Stephens (commonly known among the footplatemen at Abergavenny as 'Difer', rhyming with 'lifer'), said that he was prepared to have a go if they would get a good road for us. The bobby said that we would have to wait for a while as there were a couple of passengers and a fitted freight to go first but then we would be all right. Difer said to me, 'Whatever you do, don't let her blow off, and keep the water up', which was not the usual way a 'D' was worked.

When we got the road and Difer opened her up, 49029 dug her heels in and lifted that vast train out of the loop but Difer found that he could not notch her up at all because the loco wanted the lot to keep moving and that was how we made Stretton. I had the large injector on all the time and occasionally put the small one on as well and firing was pretty well continuous, which was something I had not had to do on a 'D' before. Our speed did not get much above 8mph and the noise from our exhaust was bringing people out of their houses to see where it was coming from. We were glad to see Stretton's signals and when we got to the box the bobby was holding a blackboard out with the words 'Clear to Ludlow'. With the gradient levelling out, we started to accelerate and Difer was able to notch up. I had a glance at the water level in the tank and saw that we had used more than half of our water in doing about ten miles. We topped up on Ludlow troughs and had no trouble to Hereford where we pulled up at Aylestone Hill signal box. They were going to hold us until they got a good road for us. The funny thing is that we always found the ex-GWR bobbies anxious to see that we were OK, knowing that we were always on long runs, whereas their own men only did short trips on the whole.

We set off from Hereford knowing that we were clear at least to Pontrilas but we actually did not get checked until we passed Abergavenny Junction, where Monmouth Road turned us into the running loop behind the down platform. We pulled up level with the signal box, which was manned by an ex-LMS man, one Eric Gwyther, who had been in more signal boxes than I had had cooked dinners. Eric said that he was holding us until we had a clear run into Pontypool Road, so I spent the time topping up the tank and throwing coal forward. I do not think we have ever used so much coal coming from Salop, and I expect the accountants will be looking at the figures and letters will be sent asking for an explanation.

Our signal comes off and Difer really lets 49029 rip and we are soon doing a rate of knots towards Penpergwm. There was no fear of breaking the speed limit over the river bridge and we hammered up the bank to Nantyderry. Our speed did not drop below 20mph and shortly we were routed into the goods lines at Pontypool Road station, where we were brought to a stand at the south box. A GWR 42XX was waiting to take our train off into a siding and the GWR driver played hell with Difer for bringing an overloaded train all that way without help. Difer knew that GWR men would not do what we had done so did not argue with him. We returned light engine to Brecon Road via Abergavenny Junction loop, ready turned to go back out on the main line, as Salop would be looking for their own loco. We arrived on shed and booked off at 3.55pm, giving us four hours overtime, which was not common on main line work and so was very welcome.

I have been told that in the old days it was an accepted thing to be overloaded, whether on passenger or freight. The old LNWR built rugged engines to do the work and was not worried about the expense of maintenance or coal consumption.

Cadbury's Excursion - Pontllanfraith to Bournville
August 1948

Every year except during the war, Cadbury's arranged excursion trains from various parts of the country to take trade's people to view their factory at Bournville and to enjoy their hospitality. It was, of course, a public relations exercise. One such train was arranged by the LMS at Abergavenny. It started at Pontllanfraith and picked up shopkeepers and their families at Blackwood, Tredegar, Brynmawr and Abergavenny Brecon Road stations. Depending on bookings, ten or twelve coaches would be brought down from Crewe and stabled on the long siding above the level crossing at Tredegar and parallel to the single line to Sirhowy.

On the appointed day Abergavenny would send two 'Super Ds' to work the train. They went up tender-first to work the empty stock to Tredegar Lower Junction and ran round the train there. The leading engine always carried a large headboard, proclaiming what the train was. On arriving at Brecon Road station, the two locos would leave the train in the platform and draw forward to No. 1 signal box where the rear loco would hook off, cross over and run down to No. 2 box, where it came up behind the train to bank it up to Llanvihangel. The leading loco would by now have dropped back on to the train and the men would top up the tank from the station column. A fresh set of men would take over the train loco for the run to Bournville. In 1948 the driver was George Lewis, who on the closure of the line drove the last train one Sunday in 1958. On arrival in Hereford they would pick up a Hereford LMS pilotman, as the former Midland men at Hereford had this route knowledge (the Midland had running powers from Worcester to reach their lines from Hereford to Brecon). On arrival at Bournville the loco would go to Bournville shed for servicing before the return journey.

The train usually left Blackwood around 9am and Brecon Road about 10am, arriving in Bournville in time for lunch. The GWR insisted that 'G2' class could not work over their lines, only 'G1' or 'G2A'.

Departure from Bournville was usually around 5pm and arrival at Abergavenny around 7.50pm. An assistant engine was attached there and a fresh set of men took over the train loco. The train arrived in Pontllanfraith around 9.20pm and then the two locos brought the train back to Abergavenny Junction, ready to go back to Crewe the same night.

In 1950 the Western Region took over responsibility for all Abergavenny's workings and stipulated that a passenger engine had to work the train forward from Abergavenny. So a 'Hall' class was to be sent down from Hereford tender-first with Hereford men. Our two locos were to stop at the splitting signals which were on the curve approaching the junction and on the steepest part, hook off and draw forward into the North sidings. The 'Hall' was to drop on to the train and take it from there.

On the day problems arose. The 'Hall' driver required a pilotman to see him on to the branch as he did not have the necessary route knowledge, so one of our drivers obliged. Then when the engine tried to start, it kept slipping, and the train began to move backwards and got dangerously close to the trap points by Ross Road bridge. Eventually, the 'Hall' driver gave up and asked for assistance. So one of the 'Ds' hooked on to the 'Hall' and assisted to Pandy (they did not want to risk getting stuck at Llanvihangel). They had, of course, by now lost their path but eventually arrived at Droitwich, where it was discovered that the 'Hall' had not been given clearance and was not allowed on to the Midland main line. What is more, the Hereford driver did not know the road and no pilotman had been requested. So a Midland '4F' that was in the vicinity was utilised to work the train to Bournville, where it arrived about two hours late.

Needless to say, after this fiasco no more trains were booked by Cadbury's from South Wales. The circular headboard inscribed 'Excursion to Cadbury's of Bournville' was kept in the stores and mysteriously disappeared one night just before the loco shed was due to be demolished. I was told later that it could be seen adorning the walls of a house in Worcester.

Night Shift Fitter,
Brecon Road Motive Power Depot, 1947-1952

The maintenance staff at Brecon Road shed consisted of eight fitters and eight fitters' mates, a boilersmith/tuber and a brickarcher/white-metaller. They were supervised by a leading-hand fitter who was assisted by a non-staff clerk. The fitters were split into two groups, four on shifts and four on regular days. The shift men carried out the running maintenance and the daily examinations. In the shed office there was always a 'runner', one working from 4pm to midnight, another from midnight to 8am and another from 8am to 4pm. We all worked closely together for our mutual benefit and to see that the depot ran smoothly.

In 1947 these men were responsible for the maintenance of 41 engines allocated to the shed as follows: Ivatt class '2' 2-6-2 tanks - 3; Webb class '2' 0-6-2 'Coal Tanks' - 18; class '7F' 'G2' and 'G2A' 0-8-0s - 12; class '5' Horwich 'Crab' 2-6-0s - 5; class '7F' Beames 0-8-4 tanks - 2; and Midland class '1P' 2-4-0 - 1.

On nights we had locos out at: 10.26pm, 11.10pm, 11.50pm, 1.50am, 3.20am and 5.5am; bankers for Monmouth Road to Llanvihangel at 4am (LMS men) and 6am (GWR men); and branch trains at 3.50am, 4.20am, 4.25am, 5.30am and 5.55am.

Arriving at the shed around 9.50pm, I find the afternoon shift man waiting to go home and to pass on any information he thinks necessary, usually to say that the first two locos out had been seen to. Picking up the loco roster sheet and any repair cards, I find my way to the workshop where my mate will have taken my tools out of the cupboard and, if he had any sense, will have put the kettle on for the first brew of the night.

My first job is to look round the shed to see where the locos are stabled and to see if any of them will need 'blocking' (new brake blocks). If the first one out needs blocks and I judge it will mean a late off, I get the runner to change the loco to another job and put another one in its place. I have a look around the ashpits and coaling plant to assess the loco position and then report to the runner to give him a chance to make adjustments to the roster.

The fires of ex-LNWR engines are cleaned out by lifting the firebars with special long tongs and dropping the clinker and ash into the ashpan. Standard LMS engines have their fires dropped by means of rocking grates and hopper ashpans, which means a quick turn-round of the loco. The GWR method of shovelling the fire out through the firehole door is a slow and unpleasant task, which means the locos are a long time being turned round.

There are normally about four engine cleaners on nights and by a long tradition at Abergavenny they work under the supervision of the night fitter, who being right on the spot can put them to assist a driver or fireman in preparation if things are running late, or to throw coal forward on a tender loco, to save it going under the coal stage, especially if it is only going to work on the branch. They might also be used to blow a loco down that is coming in for boiler washing and possibly start the cooling process. As we did not practice hot-water boiler-washing, the boilers had to be cooled down gradually to prevent shock stresses damaging the seams and stays. The cleaners preferred this to their normal work and were willing helpers. As for me, most of my work on nights would be adjusting brakes and carrying out statutory examinations.

If a pair of safety valves had been changed on the day shift, they had to be tested before the loco was released to traffic and a certificate signed to that effect. A special pressure gauge was fitted to the gauge frame drain cock and compared with the loco pressure gauge. Sometimes a driver will book a loco as blowing off 'light' and the special gauge will show that the loco gauge is faulty.

Occasionally, a big end on an 0-8-0 will develop a knock, usually after an extra long run when all the oil in the pot has gone. The big end then has to be dropped and the brasses re-metalled and machined. When this happens on nights, I get the loco put down the bottom end of the shed in the workshops, in the right position for stripping down, and put two cleaners to give it a wipe over. I then send another cleaner out to call the white-metaller (he loved overtime). It would take me about twenty minutes to drop the big end and I would take the two halves to the re-metalling hearth and turn the gas on to them and light the gas under the metal pot, so everything was ready for when the metaller came in. By the time the day shift came on the brasses would be cool and ready for machining and by midday the loco would be ready for work again.

On the LMS the control office had to be informed of all locos and the jobs they would be on, and if locos had to be changed round for some reason, an explanation had to be sent in writing. It always annoyed me that people sat in comfort in offices querying our methods in trying to run our part of the railway successfully. Thankfully, after nationalisation this stopped under the London Midland Region, but when we transferred to the Western Region in 1950, they had their own ideas that if a loco could not meet its scheduled job, that job was to be stopped and locos were not to be moved round. This did not go down too well at Brecon Road, with its long tradition of always running trains. However, we found that they did not know what we did not tell them, and that was how it was right up to the time the depot closed.

One of the stupid rules the Western forced on us was that if a loco had a hot box, we had to wait until they decided on a course of action. On one occasion they sent one of our 0-8-0s, No. 48932, to Ebbw Junction shed in Newport to have its hot box done. Ten days elapsed before she returned and when I spoke on the phone to the machinist who did the job he said that he hoped it would be the first and last he would have to do.

Of course, we knew that we could do the job quickly with our two wheel drops and made representations to the Western Region management over this delay. Eventually, they sent observers to Brecon Road to watch us do a hot box and I was the one selected by Sid James, our head fitter, to do the job. He told me to 'show the flag and not let us down'. We had the engine steam cleaned that night and positioned ready to start the next day. When the Western observers arrived, we started work and 1hr and 10min later I was knocking the axlebox off. I heard one of the visitors say, 'If I had not seen it myself, I would not have believed it'. I did not bother to tell them that I could not keep that pace up for long but we were trying to impress them and get work sent to the depot. Needless to say, the engine was back in traffic on the second day and the Western men could hardly believe their eyes.

After nationalisation when our five 'Crabs' were sent away to Lancashire, we had a lot of work to do at first with the twelve 0-8-0s which replaced them as they had been neglected. In particular, nearly every one of them had problems with the trailing sand gear and we usually found that years of small coal washed off the footplate and plenty of rust was the cause of the trouble. A good clean up and plenty of lubrication put everything right. In the end it was a great help to have the extra engines as Abergavenny had always been a bit tight on power. Then the ex-GWR depots at Hereford and Pontypool Road began sending us LMS locos for re-blocking, particularly on nights, and it was annoying to find that there was nothing wrong with the blocks. The problem was that the GWR blocks were parallel in form, while LMS blocks tapered from thin at the top to thick at the bottom, so the Western men thought ours were worn out.

From time to time we also had Western men from those sheds coming to borrow our locos. They did not take too kindly to our 'Super Ds' and occasionally I had the job of showing them the controls. Telling the firemen to keep a thin fire and the water in the top of the glass did not go down too well, but seeing one fireman a week or so later, I asked him how he got on. 'Magic', was his reply. He said it did not matter what his driver did, she still steamed and held her water level in the boiler. They had worked from Hereford to Stourbridge and from Ledbury where they had stopped to pick up a banker, the driver had flogged her all the way in full gear to Malvern and he got madder and madder when his efforts to burst her had failed.

Valve and Piston Examination on a 'Super D'

The various railway companies all worked out the best methods of repairing and maintaining their engines outside of the main works overhauls. There were two principles in deciding when to do such work, one based on time and the other based on mileage. For the 'Super D' 0-8-0s the LMS set the top limit at 36,000 miles and when an engine had achieved this mileage a No. 6 Examination was required. The limit was later increased to 48,000 miles after a modification was introduced in the design of the piston valves and better lubricating oil introduced.

At Abergavenny shed it fell to me as the youngest fitter to do most of the mileage examinations. The head fitter would tell me that on a certain day of the week I would have, say, 48932 to do. I would then go into the records office and look up the records of the sizes that were given when the loco came out of works last. These sizes were the cylinder diameter, piston valve diameter and the diameters of the crank pins. I would then check the availability of parts and make a list of any that were short for the stores clerk. He would make sure that everything was ordered and would notify me when the parts arrived. We always carried a spare set of side rod bushes ready metalled and I would machine these to size and stamp them for position.

When the day came for the examination, I would make sure that the loco came into the shed engine first. It had already been steam-cleaned and wiped dry to make it easier for us to work on. The steam-cleaning was better for the cleaners and was cheaper on cleaning materials as the cloths could be used over and over again.

When the engine was positioned near the end of the road with both side rods on bottom angles for ease of removal, work began. The side rods were removed and dragged to the power press where the old bushes were pressed out and the reconditioned ones pressed in. The rods were then returned to the loco and refitted. This ensures that the crank pins remain in the same position. If a loco is moved without the rods on, the odds are that the pins will be out of alignment and it will be difficult to refit the rods. So far the job has taken about two hours.

The next stage is to take off the front bufferbeam, support it on a trolley and push it out of the way. The front cylinder and steam-chest covers are then removed and placed on one side. Next the valves are disconnected and removed. They take a bit of getting out if the carbon has got cold, so we spray paraffin into the connecting tube and set it on fire. The heat softens the carbon and with a bit of luck the valve pops out.

The pistons are next to be removed. To do this we need the engine moved, which is why she is brought in engine leading - so we can hook another engine on to the tender and move her. One big end is set on bottom back angle, which puts the crosshead behind the leading axle. The safety cotter is removed and then the locking key is driven out. A thin steel disc is then fitted on

to the end of the piston rod and a steel wedge is jammed between it and the end of the connecting rod. A series of sharp blows with a 14lb hammer on the end of the wedge jars the piston out of the crosshead. The removal of the piston gland assembly allows the piston to be prised to the front of the cylinder ready for removal. Rope blocks hanging from the smokebox handrail support the piston as it is lowered to the floor. This is necessary as the pistons weigh about 3cwt each and are difficult to handle.

Back under the loco both valve gears are disconnected and removed. First the anchor link, then the stirrup links and then the valve link, which is lifted out of the weighbar shaft with the help of a rope slung over the side handrail and tied to it. The four slipper blocks are simply removed by pulling off their spindles. They have to be re-metalled.

Under the loco again, the gudgeon pins are next for attention. The main nut and safety clip are removed and a steel dolly is positioned between the main frame and the end of the gudgeon pin. The steel wedge that was used to start the pistons is used again here and is again struck with a 14lb hammer to jar the pin loose. The pin is withdrawn and the crosshead is prised forward out of the way.

Next the connecting rod to big end cotters are removed and for this again the 14lb hammer is used. The con rod is prised out of the big end strap and lowered to the floor. A spreader is fitted into the big end strap and the brasses removed. Then both con rods and big end brasses are lifted out of the pit for examination. The brasses go for re-metalling and the con rods to the press for the gudgeon pin bushes to be pressed out. Finally the two crossheads are taken down for re-metalling.

While the re-metalling is going on, the pistons are examined for flaws and to see if the rods are scored or bent. If they are scored, they are sent to Crewe for regrinding. If they are bent, we will straighten them with some special gear we have, although I have never seen it done. If all is well, the rings are removed and a special tool is used to clean the carbon from the grooves and the surrounding areas.

The valves are next to receive attention; they are clamped in a fly vice and the rings removed. We try not to break the rings as it is always useful to have a few spare ones of the right size, in case we break some of the new ones. There are six rings per head and four heads to a loco, so great care is needed. I make sure that my apprentice, Alex, has a go at all this work as it is the only way he will get experience, although some of the old hands do not like me entrusting this work to an apprentice.

Measuring the wear is next and for this we use fixed spile gauges and feelers. We take a gauge which is the same size as that which the engine left the works with and use feelers over the end to find the wear. I record this wear so that the head fitter can show it when he books the loco for shopping, and the works clerk can assess how much machining will be needed and the cost, when the loco goes into works.

The amount of wear in the cylinders, which are 20½in diameter, is not so important but the steam chests, which are nominally only 8in in diameter, are affected if the wear is much more than 10 thou out of round or out of parallel. The efficiency of the loco depends on a good fit between the valve rings and the walls of the steam chests to prevent steam passing to exhaust and being wasted.

After cleaning up the valve heads thoroughly, we start on the valve rings and place them in the steam chest. The gaps are checked and the rounded ends are also checked to see that they fit to the groove dowels correctly. When we are satisfied, we fit them to the heads. Care is needed in doing this, as it is easy to break one, which is why we keep a couple of the old rings just in case we are unlucky. The valves are then refitted into the steam chests and the covers refitted with new joints.

Next Alex will be machining new gudgeon pin bushes and will press them into the connecting rods, while I will be machining the big end brasses in the universal lathe. This lathe has many features not usually found on a lathe. This is necessary, as there is insufficient work for a large centre lathe on its own, and we are able to perform many feats with this lathe that are impossible on others.

After machining, I bed the brasses to the journals using marking yellow because the usual blue or red does not show up under a loco and when I am satisfied we refit the big ends to the cranks. The next job is to machine the crossheads and very careful setting up is required, as there are eight faces and you have to be sure to be on the same plane as the piston rod, otherwise you have trouble. I aim to get a working clearance of between .003in and .005in between the crossheads and the slide bars.

Back on the loco the crossheads are fitted into the slide bars and the connecting rods are lifted into posi-

tion and fitted to the big ends and crossheads. This gives a solid crosshead to fit the piston into. The gaps of the new piston rings are checked and then they are fitted, spacing the gaps evenly around the piston head.

Next the pistons are lifted into the cylinders and pushed in. Before entering them into the crossheads we make sure all the piston gland gear is on them. When we are satisfied, we drive the piston home with a baulk of timber. Fitting the locking keys and cotters completes the job.

The front cylinder covers are now fitted with new joints and then the bufferbeam is replaced. The four slipper blocks are rasped to a fit, because we cannot machine them due to their shape. They are then refitted to the weighbar shaft and lowered down. The valve gear is all connected up and the piston gland assemblies all replaced. We fill up all the oil pots and renew any trimmings that need it, and that completes the overhaul.

Next we move under the footplate, disconnecting all the pipes between engine and tender, and removing the securing bolt from the intermediate draw gear. We scotch up our loco and get another loco to give us a squeeze up to take the tension off the drawbar pin so that we can drive it out. It is a hefty piece of material and needs two hands to hold it. The assistant loco draws our tender out of the way and we check the intermediate buffer springs, renewing them if required as we do with the drawbar pin. When we are satisfied, we get another squeeze up, recouple the tender to the loco and reconnect all the pipes. All that remains to be done now is measure the tyre wear, record it on the loco's record card and sign it. The engine is now ready for traffic and we hope to get another 48,000 miles out of her.

We have spent about eight working days on this examination and overhaul, and the white-metaller has probably had a full day's work too. There is not enough work for him to do white-metalling full time, so he combines the job with brick-arching. As for apprentices, I feel that this type of work is excellent training and prepares them for entry into the main works.

Changing a Spring

Changing a spring on the leading and driving axles was quite an easy job and could be done in about twenty minutes. First the loco was jacked up and then a spring compressor was fitted to the spring which was to be replaced. This compressor was like a large hook with a tensioning bolt at the lower end. The compressor was fitted over the spring with the top of the hook resting on to the top leaf of the spring and the bolt fitted under the spring arm socket, where it was tightened up, pulling the top leaf of the spring down until the spring arm could be pulled clear. Then by slackening off the bolt and removing the compressor, the spring could be lifted out and the new one fitted.

To change a spring on the intermediate or trailing axles was a different job, because of the type of springs,

but in fact these springs were so robust that they very rarely needed to be changed anyway. Before the intermediate spring could be changed the wheels were removed and two hydraulic jacks, more or less fully extended, were put under the spring one at either end. Then the spring was just lifted off the pillar guides, the bolts taken out of the guides, the guides removed and the spring lowered by releasing the jacks slowly down until the spring could be manhandled. Putting a new spring in was simply the reverse of this procedure.

In theory the trailing spring being under the axle could be changed without removing the wheels by removing the horn stay bolts and the round hornstays, plus the brake pull rod, and jacking the loco up until the spring centre pivots came clear of the centre bearing. It was, of course, essential to place packing timber under the centre of the spring to support it while the hangers were disconnected. To disconnect them, a large pinchbar was placed through the spokes of the wheel and under the end of the spring to take the weight whilst the pivot pin was removed. The spring could then be lowered on to the packing and the opposite pin removed after the end of the spring has once again been supported in the same way with the pinchbar. Four very strong men would be needed to get the old spring off the packing and a new one on ready to replace it.

In practice, however, we never did it that way, as we never had enough strong men to work like that underneath the engine. It was safer and easier to remove the wheels with the spring still attached.

The LMS Automatic Blowdown Valve

All steam locomotives use enormous quantities of water and the quality of this water can vary from one water column to another and from one set of troughs to another. In some areas the water is very acidic, in others it is alkali; very rarely is it neutral. In addition, the water can be dirty, due to picking up foreign matter on its way to the tanks and in autumn there is the problem of falling leaves. All these things have an adverse effect on boilers and can cause all sorts of problems.

Regular boiler-washing is the accepted way of keeping boilers clean and was standard practice with all the main-line companies and industrial users. The Great Western Railway washed out their boilers at ten-day intervals, irrespective of the state of the water or the boiler or the pressure it worked at, and this policy caused the company to be short of locos from time to time and to have more engines than it would otherwise have needed.

The LMS adopted a system of draining off some of the boiler water as the loco was working and with it the impurities which were in suspension. The original idea was always believed at Abergavenny to have come from John Ramsbottom and to have been developed into a practical fitting by F. W. Webb. Whatever the truth of that, the system was that there was a small hole through the outer firebox wall into the water space and to this was bolted the blowdown valve. The valve had a brass body containing only two moving parts: a ball valve in the top half under boiler pressure and a steel piston about 2in in diameter in the bottom half. The piston was under the influence of boiler pressure either from the regulator or from one of the injectors.

When the regulator or injector steam valve was opened, steam would come under the piston. As it had a greater surface area than the ball valve, it moved upwards, lifting the ball valve off its seat, and so allowing dirty water to pass through and discharge on to the track. Several sizes of valve, with various sizes of orifice, could be fitted, giving a discharge capacity of from ½ gallon to 2 gallons per minute.

When either the regulator or injector steam valve was closed, the pressure under the piston would fall and the pressure on the ball valve would reseat it and cut off the flow of dirty water. One problem was that if the loco was working continually in an area where the water was clean, such as Abergavenny and Tredegar, the valve was discharging clean water on to the track.

'Old sweat' drivers always carried a hobnail in their pockets and if they could see that the water in the gauge glasses was clean they would slacken off the nut holding the operating pipe on to the blowdown valve, place the hobnail into the end and then refit the pipe. This prevented the valve from working and so saved water. At the end of their shift, they would remove the nail. This valve allowed LMS locos to work for 14 days between washouts, if the boilers were pressed to 200lb psi or more, and to 28 days if less. This was a great saving in locos.

After nationalisation we found that a few foreign drivers using our locos were flattening the operating pipe to stop the valve working. Probably they thought the valve wasted water but in fact it was a very small quantity compared to the total amount of water used in the boiler, especially in view of the money saved by reducing the frequency of washouts. Eventually an instruction was issued to all Western Region sheds, which were the only ones doing it, to refrain from the practice.

One area of the LMS where the system did not work was the London, Tilbury & Southend section. There foreign matter in the water did not float to the surface, as is normal, but settled in the bottom of the boiler and around the foundation ring of the firebox, so that at regular intervals tubes and stays had to be removed to enable the debris to be cleaned out. I was always surprised that the LMS did not give more attention to the water quality on this section, as it was costly to strip parts and boilers down at regular intervals and to have locos out of service for long periods. Probably, it was the accountants again proving that one and two make four.

Strange Things that Happen to Steam Locomotives

In 1949 one of our 'Super Ds' at Abergavenny gave us a problem which took a couple of weeks to sort out and a week's hard work to put right. No. 49316 had only been out of Crewe Works about two weeks following a general repair when drivers started reporting that the left-hand cylinder cocks were not clearing the water from the cylinders. On removing the cocks we found that they were blocked by a soft gooey substance. We stripped them down, cleaned them thoroughly and then refitted them on the loco.

Within two weeks the problem was back and this time the hole into the cylinders was blocked as well. The boss said to take the cover off and see what was happening. We found that the piston and the cover were covered with a thick layer of soft carbon. So we cleaned it all off and replaced the cover but within two weeks she was stopped again, the driver reporting that there was a knock coming from the cylinders.

We could not find any wear in the small or large ends, so we removed the front cylinder cover again and found that the carbon had built up again and was allowing the piston to strike the cylinder cover or rather the carbon deposited on it. So we were then told to take the piston out, which meant taking off the bufferbeam as well, and found that the rear of the piston and the back cover had the same thick layer of carbon as the front. The ports to the steam chest were coated as well, so the valve had to come out too, which took some doing as the carbon was taking up the clearance.

While one of our mates worked on decarbonising, we searched for the cause of the problem. We checked the mechanical lubricator to see if it was pumping too much oil into the cylinders but found it was set to minimum, so that was not the cause. We then took the brickwork out of the smokebox to check the oil pipes and to see if there was a crack in the cylinder casting but all was sound. We were now scratching our heads, wondering what to look for next, when the driver who had worked her last came into the workshop to see what we had found. He said that the loco had to be steamed downhill and would not run freely without putting steam on. Sid James, our foreman fitter, said that it sounded like anti-vacuum trouble and told us to check that next.

On 'Super Ds' the valve is on the side of the smokebox at platform level and is covered with a deflector plate held on by four nuts. It is shaped like a small saucer with a spindle through the centre working in guides in the cylinder casting and in the seat itself. On removing the plate, we could see that the disc valve was hard up against the seat and we found that we could not move it with a screw driver. When we removed the seat, the valve came out with it and it had to be driven out with a punch - it was that tight.

What apparently happened was that when the valve was fitted at Crewe, no one checked to see that it was free to move on its spindle and come off the seat to allow air to be drawn in when the loco was coasting with the regulator shut. As it was, ashes from the smokebox were drawn in instead, causing all the trouble.

Setting the disc valve in the lathe, I skimmed the spindles so that they were free to move in the guide, and the anti-vacuum valve was then refitted. Rebuilding the engine took another day and as a result of our efforts, there was no more trouble. This was a minor fault in one place that caused no end of trouble, was expensive to rectify and caused the loss of a loco for a week, all because someone in Crewe Works was lax and guilty of bad workmanship which went unchecked.

Main Points in Working on a 'G2' Class

(Copy of letter sent to the National Railway Museum when work started on restoring No. 9395)

These are the main things that are useful to know when working on a 'G2'. Before parting the loco from the tender, remove the large set bolt that is under the tender coupling where the spring box is. This is under tension when the tender is parted from the loco and difficult to remove. If you attempt to screw it out under tension, the threads might be stripped and the spring box fly out.

Parting the pistons from the crossheads is done by putting a steel disc into the recess at the end of the piston rod and using a long tapered wedge between it and the small end of the connecting rod and then striking with a 14lb hammer. This is, of course, after removing the locking cotter. The piston will not come out of the cylinder until the piston gland back bush is removed and to do this draw the piston out until it is resting on the front cover studs and then use a $^3/_4$in rod about 4ft long with the end flattened to drift the split gland out. The gudgeon pins are released by putting a dolly between the main frame and the end of the pin with a long wedge between and striking with a hammer.

To remove the brake cylinders, which have a rubber diaphragm inside sandwiched between two discs, it is best to remove a couple of the $^3/_8$in bolts and put a couple of $^3/_8$in long-threaded studs in their place (at least four). Then remove the remainder plus the pipes and using the long-threaded studs lower down. Warning: these items are very heavy.

The injectors can be removed from the firebox backplate by first disconnecting the feed pipe underneath and then removing the rectangular tab held by a $^3/_8$in nut that holds the injector to the firebox. On the footplate disconnect the steam pipe at its joint near the injector stop valve. Using a horseshoe spanner slacken off the large brass nut under the clack box. The injector is now ready to be lowered. We used to use a length of rope over the stop valve and tied to the ram spindle bracket. Tap up the ram handle and remove the small tapered key. Note which way the ram handle fits as this is important when refitting. Turn the ram wheel which is on top of the clack box and the injector will lower down into the pit - steady it by means of the rope and by someone underneath guiding it. On getting the injector to the workshop for stripping, it is best to mark the ram rod coupling and the spindles so it can be coupled up correctly. If it is coupled up incorrectly, the injector will not work as the water sleeve inside will be the wrong way round. When the injector is parted, the joint seal will be broken and will have to be resoldered later to prevent ingress of air.

The automatic blowdown valve is on the footplate near the gauge glasses. It has two moving parts, a ball valve in the top half, which is normally under boiler pressure, and a piston in the bottom half, which is influenced by pressure from the regulator being opened. This piston lifts the ball valve off its seat and allows dirty water to be discharged.

If the vacuum ejector is noisy, it is caused by the expansion gland behind the panelling on the right-hand side. Take the top cover plate off to expose the ejector. The gland is held by two fiin nuts and is only a compressed coil of asbestos rope.

The trailing sand gear is under the footblocks and if it is seized up all the floor items have to be removed to get at it. First take off the long steel plate that runs the full length across the back of the footplate and then the section that has square holes in it for small wooden blocks. Then the footblocks themselves can be removed to expose the sand valve rods and arms.

When the wheels are removed, the trailing axle has a cantilever spring across between the wheels supported by two links coupled to the axlebox keeps. The spring is under tension at all times and to take off the tension and to disconnect it from the axleboxes, put a longish lever or pinchbar through the spokes and under the end of the spring and bear down. This will allow the pin on one side to be driven out. Support the centre of the spring on wooden blocks and release the lever gently. The pin on the opposite side will come out easier. Refitting is by doing the same operation in reverse.

Where the trailing wheels fit into the loco, there are two steel plates spanning across between the horns, with means of adjusting the spring weights in the centre. These usually seize up shortly after leaving the works and we had to fit plates over the horseshoe-shaped spring bearing in the centre, if ever a trailing axle had to be machined following a hot box, and adjustments had to be made to keep the loco on an even keel. These two cross-bearing plates are secured by three studs either side and sometimes a stud breaks off. Then we had to hand-drill through the horn face with a very short drill and tap through.

The regulator valve is in the dome and to release it after taking the cover off remove the split pin and brass nut and then get an associate on the footplate to force the regulator handle to the closed position, while the spindle through the centre of the valve is struck with a copper hammer until it frees. The valve can then be lifted out of the body. We never machined the valve if it was pitted but set it up on a mandrel and filed round it until the old seating marks could just be seen. Lapping in to the seat was done by means of a handle that was

bolted to the valve by hook bolts. The handle had a hole in the centre so the valve spindle could stick through. All LNWR engines with this sort of valve were done like this. In the closed position the regulator handle top section had a little clearance in the quadrant to allow for varying thicknesses of valve.

Both before and after nationalisation I submitted suggestions regularly and had several accepted. Two were for the 'Super D' and in case they were never applied to No. 9395 I will outline them here.

The front cylinder covers were regularly blowing out on all the 'Ds' and so I suggested that the joint faces on the covers should be machined to allow the thick copper joint to sit in a recess. All the engines at Abergavenny were done before I moved away in 1952 but some locos may have escaped this modification.

The second suggestion concerned the lubrication of the gudgeon pin bushes. Originally the bushes only had a hole in the top and because oil could not get round the pin due to close tolerances wear rapidly took place and a knock resulted. I suggested that after machining the bore to size the bush be offset in the lathe with the oil hole slightly nearer to the centre line and an oil groove machined from the oil hole to the thrust faces. Cross grooves could be cut across the thrust faces by turning the cutting tool in the tool bar 90 degrees and using the saddle wheel. We experimented with this at Abergavenny and found that instead of having to renew the bushes about every two or three months they were lasting eight or nine months, and this was on regular main-line work to Crewe. The bushes on the 'G2' are, of course, thin-wall compared with the thick-wall bushes on the 'G1s' and 'G2As'. We used to machine out the centre of old thick-wall bushes from the latter and re-use them on the 'G2s'.

As the axles and the large and small ends on the 'G2s' were of larger diameter, they did not suffer with overheating as much as the 'G1s' and 'G2As', but there was a design fault in the axleboxes, which I suggest you attend to now, as it will extend the time the loco will be able to run before requiring further repairs. Except for the driving axleboxes, there is no means of lubricating the sliding horn faces and they get dry, with the resultant bad ride on the footplate and wear to the metal faces causing a knock. Perhaps oil pots and pipework can be fitted. If so, they will definitely pay for themselves.

The trailing axleboxes tend to be pulled away from the wheels by the action of the cantilever spring and as the sides of the axlebox horns are only faced with white-metal, this gets squashed out due to the pressure. As a result some of the tension on the spring comes off and the loco main frames settle on top of the axlebox resulting in a bad ride on the footplate. I suggested that the white-metal side strip be replaced with a steel strip secured with high-tensile countersunk bolts. This suggestion was turned down and I was told there had never been any problems in that area.

Another suggestion concerned the lubrication of the crossheads. The top bars have oil pots but there is no lubrication for the bottom bars, which causes the white-metal faces on the underside of the crossheads to wear rapidly, which in turn causes the piston glands to blow as there is very little clearance in the stuffing box for the cast-iron packing segments. My suggestion was for a system of oil pipes using bundy pipes and connections, as used on car brakes, with a small hole drilled up through to the sliding faces. I suggested that to save drilling the slide bar, which may have weakened it, a short piece of steel could be welded underneath and be drilled and tapped to take the connector. This was turned down by the authorities with the same comment as for the axleboxes.

Valve setting was done in the loco sheds without any specialist gear. What we did was this and it was very successful. We had a length of steel rod about $^3/_8$in thick. One end was flattened and bent at right angles for about 1in. With the valves out of the steam chests, we put this rod into the steam chest and the bent end was put into the front port and pushed tight up against the edge of the port nearest the centre. A straight edge was then put across the steam chest front and a line scribed on to the rod. The same was now done for the rear port, only this time the rod was pulled tight and again the scribing was done. On the valves the inside rings had been removed and the rod was placed so that the bent end fitted into the ring groove and the rod lay on top of the valve. Using an L square on the valve spindle we lined up on the scribing marks on the rod and scribed the valve rod, so we had two marks on the valve spindles. Replacing the rings and fitting the valves enabled us to move the loco and using a straight edge across the valve spindles enabled us to check the valve travel and to see that the leads were equal. Any adjustments had to be made by taking the valve rod down and

having it lengthened or shortened by the blacksmith. On Stanier's locos we could adjust the shims on the valve heads.

To find mid gear we would measure the reach rod where it travelled through the guide on the intermediate splasher. There was always a section of the rod that was oily where it rubbed through the guide. We would equalise the amount either side of the guide by slowly turning the reversing wheel. When we had got it centralised, we would make a cut mark across the guide and another one level with it on the reach rod. It seemed that this was a long-established procedure at Abergavenny, as I never found the marks on locos from other depots. The thread behind the reversing wheel was either left hand or right hand depending whether it was indirect or direct valve gear. This was to avoid confusion, so that the driver moved the reversing wheel in the same direction in both cases.

The weighbar shaft has eight small oil wells across the top to lubricate the slipper block rubbing surfaces, and the trimmings fitted in these wells by the works were always too tight and had tails that were too long, causing a restriction in oil flow and reducing the amount of oil that the wells could hold. The result was rapid wear of the whitemetal surfaces of the slipper blocks, which in turn caused the valves to lose some of the stroke, reducing the efficiency of the front end. I was appointed by my shedmaster to check any loco coming from overhaul at the works and put trimmings in with fewer strands and shorter tails, and this kept the wear rate down considerably.

Boiler washing under the LMS was done every three to five weeks but with the clean water we had in our area it was usually done every 30 days. The gauge glasses were changed every other washout.

Plate 239: *'G1' No. 2172 with an up loaded coal train, Nuneaton Target 17, at Shackerstone Junction, Nuneaton, on 15th August 1925.*
V. Forster collection

HAROLD SIGLEY - 'WESSIE' ENGINEMAN
by Michael Bentley

In the 1950s when I started on the footplate at Buxton, there was little if any classroom training for enginemen. Our training was 'on the job' and so everything depended on the drivers we had to work for. Most men were decent types and competent enough drivers. They remembered when they were new on the job and were willing to help new recruits. One or two were really horrible characters, who would not take the trouble to help anybody and could put a young man off for life, and one or two were just the opposite, really expert enginemen who would do everything to pass on their knowledge to a keen young man. Fortunately for me, I worked with one of the latter quite often when his regular mate was driving. His name was Harold Sigley.

Though he had started on the railway after the Grouping, he had been brought up entirely in the LNWR tradition and had spent virtually all his working life on LNWR engines. There were only LNWR types at Buxton until one or two Stanier '8Fs' appeared in the late 1930s and even then the 'Super Ds' still carried on until the 1960s. Like lots of old 'Wessie' men, he never carried a watch and though I often tried to catch him out, he always knew the time to a minute. He just used to cock an eye at the station clocks as we went by. Also like lots of old 'Wessie' men, he had 'coil spring knees', as he put it - his knees had lost their strength after a life-time of bouncing up and down on the footplates of LNWR engines with coil springs - and in general, being in his early sixties, he was far from being fit and well.

But while I was a strong healthy 18-year-old, who could jump about like a ballet dancer and shovel coal all day, Harold could still get better results than me with a 'Super D' because he fired 'with his head'. He could put the coal exactly where he wanted it, with little or no effort. What he lacked in strength or energy or youth, he more than made up with skill and know-how.

A typical job we used to have with a 'Super D' was the morning goods from Buxton to Uttoxeter Pinfold Sidings. One of the best engines we had on this turn was No. 9277 and another good one was No. 9446. Out of Buxton, Harold would drive and I would fire. When we got to Parsley Hay, he used to get down from the engine and go into the signal box to read the paper and have a cup of tea. He left me to do the shunting and prepare the train. Of course, that was only when he knew he could trust me. He was not being lazy but just knew that that was the best way for me to get to know how to handle the engine. 'You will learn', he used to say. When I had finished, I used to pull up to the box and have a cup of tea myself.

From Parsley Hay he would fire and I would drive, but he always kept an eye on what I was doing. His advice was always worth listening to, and if I did not listen, I got a good cussing. If he thought speed was rising too much and we would be unable to stop on the brakes, he would just say, 'Reverser'. Then I had to wind it back a bit to get things under control. At first I thought he was being over-cautious but I soon realised that I had

Plate 240 (opposite): *Driver Harold Sigley at the regulator of No. 49277 as it climbs from Hartington to Parsley Hay with a freight from Uttoxeter Pinfold Sidings to Buxton. Fireman J. M. Bentley is in the tender taking the photograph. The staff has been dropped over the handle of the leading sanders, the rod connecting it to the handle on the driver's side passes above the coffee plate. The lever for the trailing sanders is under the fireman's seat - the spindle going down to the sandbox can just be seen. On the side-sheet above is the boiler pressure gauge, by Budenberg of Broadheath, suppliers to the LNWR (the steam-heating gauge, when fitted, would have been beside it on the same wooden block); on the opposite side-sheet is the vacuum brake gauge. The handle for the blower (the 'jet') is on the right, just in front of the seat, which has been repositioned by the men, slightly away from the side-sheet, to allow those of 'larger proportions' to sit down more comfortably! Next to it is the vacuum brake ejector, with shiney top. To the left of this but slightly higher, on the corner of the firebox, is the automatic blow-down valve. The thick pipe leading down from the front of it carries away the dirty water to the ashpan. The pipe leading to it, across the firebox from the driver's side, brings steam from the smokebox, when the regulator is opened, to operate the valve. To the left of the staff is the ram wheel on the clack valve - there is a cloth on top of it. The handle lower down controls the water. The steam pipes for the injectors come down from the manifold above the firebox. Coming off the right-hand injector pipe is the slacking pipe, for spraying the coal with water to keep down the dust. Hidden by the lamp on the floor, are two handles: the top one is pushed in to open the front damper and pulled out to close it; the lower one is pulled out to open the drain cocks and pushed in to close them. In other words, they function the opposite way round, which sometimes caused confusion! Usually, the front damper was not used, otherwise the fire burnt away too quickly. The rear damper is fully open - the handle is to the left of the lamp under the seat. The tea can is hanging off the handle of the boiler water gauge - one handle opened both valves. The handle for the right-hand gauge is more clearly seen. Underneath this gauge is the steam valve operating the desanding gear - no engine at Buxton was known to have either desanding gear or rear sanders in working order in the 1950s or 1960s. The piece of timber on the left of the tender front is the brake stick, used by the fireman when pinning down brakes, very necessary on some sections of this line. The firedoor is the LMS type. Above it on the coffee plate is a bottle containing Driver Sigley's tea, many a footplateman's favourite beverage when at work. The engine is returning to Buxton having worked out to Uttoxeter the previous day. It was the practice to do the return trip without taking coal at Uttoxeter but there is still plenty in the tender, evidence of the economical working which this much-used veteran was still capable of. Driver Sigley has the regulator just slightly open and the reverser back about 1¼ turns, giving just the right blast to keep the fire lively and the boiler steaming perfectly.*

Michael Bentley

misjudged things. In fact, his judgement was always right. He knew exactly what the engine would do and what it would not do.

At Hartington he would go to the signal box again and come back when it was time to leave, and at Alsop-en-le-Dale we both went straight to the box - there was no work to be done there - to wait for the goods from Uttoxeter to arrive. The engine stopped with the two footplates opposite and we just swapped over.

As a rule, the hardest work on this job was on the return to Buxton. On one trip we were in trouble on the 1 in 60 climb from Alsop-en-le-Dale to Biggin Moor. Then I had to climb out on the footplate, use my hands to scoop sand out of the sandboxes on to the shovel, jump down on to the track and spread it on the rails. But normally on this bank he would fire and tell me how to drive - 'One and a half turns back', and so on. That was when I really saw his skill at firing. He might start with the pressure 40lb down and the box apparently full of dead ash - he did not stand with the blower roaring away, or with the huge fire necessary on a Stanier engine. In fact, he did not use the 'jet' at all but would use the blast of the engine to bring the fire round as we got under way. He would just put on four or five or six shovelfuls. 'Don't look at the pressure gauge,' he used to say. 'It's up and down 20 or 30lb. Just listen to the exhaust. When it rasps, pull it back a turn.' Then he would put on a bit more, exactly the right amount. It was precision little-and-often firing. The same kind of thing was done all over the North Western - 'Princes' going off Crewe North shed to take on an express would leave with the fire in the same state, because they could rely on the blast from the engine to raise pressure quickly as they got under way.

The full load from Parsley Hay up Hurdlow Bank was 26 wagons of mineral, 23 tons each, plus a van. Sometimes, however, when there were more loaded wagons than one full load, we would take as many as 30 mineral, to avoid leaving any behind and having to go back again to Parsley Hay for them. 'Aye, put 'em on', he would say. Then I would have to make up the fire properly before we started, perhaps running the pricker through it, as the steep gradient started too soon for us to get pressure up under way. We did not want to stop on the bank because then we would have to go back and split the train, and it might make us an hour or more late.

As we charged the bank, he would just keep banging the regulator open a bit more, until eventually it was fully open and the reverser was not far off full forward gear. I have never heard anything like it, before or since. It was broad daylight but I could see white sparks from the chimney shooting high up into the sky. Somehow, when the engine was being worked like that, any leaks of steam at the front end disappeared. All the time, Harold just looked straight ahead. He knew what the engine was doing without looking at the gauges. Only near the top, he might just cock an eye at the water.

His advice on handling a 'Super D' was: 'You are all right if you are not afraid of them. If you're afraid of them, you are done for, like a man who's afraid of his wife'. At Rowsley, when they had them on the shed, they feared and detested them, and when we went there, if there was a 'D' away from the shed up the yard by itself, we always knew it was our engine. What the 'Ds' needed was a good steam brake. They should have been fitted with the Midland steam brake after the

Plate 241: *A typical 'Super D' of the late BR period, No. 49281 at Ashbourne with the morning goods from Buxton to Uttoxeter on 7th April 1960. The leading milk tank has not come from Buxton but has been added during shunting at Ashbourne and will be worked to Uttoxeter.*

Dr G. Smith

Grouping. Then they would have given many engine-men more confidence in them. Even so they could do the job if handled properly - I never knew one to run past the signal at the end of the viaduct at Buxton, after coming down the 1 in 62 from Briggs with a heavy train - and they were certainly much more economical than modern engines.

One day Harold and I had a Stanier '8F' from Longsight. Starting with a full tender, I had to open the coal doors at Coombs on Whaley Bank only 22 miles from the start. A 'D' on the Uttoxeter job used to go there and back on the coal it had from Buxton - they were not coaled at Uttoxeter. The '8F' was heavy on coal and water, because it had only a 21-element super-heater, but being modern in style it was accepted. On another occasion we had a '9F'. The box could hold enough coal for half a dozen 'Super Ds' and the design was quite impractical for shunting, which all goods engines had to do. Winding the reverser back and forth needed too much effort for Harold at his age. 'I can't do with this', he said, and I had to do it for him.

Of course, the '8Fs' and '9Fs' were modern engines and were much faster than the old 'Ds'. They had out-side valve gear, which made maintenance and oiling much easier, they had good brakes, the '8F' in particular having a wonderful brake, and they were much more comfortable, with cabs that offered far more protection from the weather than the rather sparse affair sported by the 'D'. But they were 'everyman's engines'. Little if any skill was called for to work them, and all that was needed to fire them was just the strength to fill the box and keep it full.

By comparison, the 'Ds' were old-fashioned and seemed strange to people who were not familiar with them. But in the hands of men who knew how to handle them they were very effective machines, and on the basis of the work they did, and of their coal and water consumption, they were not really inferior to these more modern engines at all. Men like Harold Sigley, who had been brought up with them, were experts in handling them and in getting the best out of them, and in the 1950s they still did a lot of useful work very economically. They were a credit to those who had designed and built them in an earlier age, and to the traditions of Crewe.

Plate 242: *'G1 No. 9217 leaving Rowsley in 1934. It was sub-shedded there for a time up to 1935.* E. R. Morten

Plate 243: No. 7885 at Bescot on 17th March 1935, still with Cooke buffers, surprisingly, and Ramsbottom safety valves. The high viewpoint shows the gap between the bufferbeam and the cylinders. In the background, the yard is full of wagons, mostly coal empties, ample evidence of the work these engines were built for, and that there was plenty of it.

W. L. Good

Chapter Nine
EIGHT-COUPLED TANK ENGINES

The growth of goods traffic in the late 19th century and early 20th century led to many improvements in the facilities for handling it, of which the introduction of eight-coupled engines was only one. Among the others was the construction at strategic points on the system of 'hump' yards, in which the 'gravity principle', pioneered by the company in the 'Gridiron' at Edge Hill, was used to facilitate the sorting of wagons. Another development at this time was the introduction of the Tranship Shed at Crewe.

To work in these hump yards and in other yards where heavy trains were regularly dealt with, more powerful shunting engines were needed than the six-coupled types then available. Apart from small numbers of four-coupled tank engines, built for special jobs, the only engines built at Crewe specifically for shunting had been the 260 'Special Tanks' introduced by Ramsbottom in 1870, which were used as much for shunting passenger stock in stations as in goods yards. In addition, there were 45 '17in Coal Engines' converted from tender engines by the fitting of square saddle tanks in 1905-6. Nominally they were more powerful than the 'Special Tanks', but in practice there was virtually no difference in performance. The 'Coal Tanks' themselves were also regularly used on shunting, as well as on local goods and passenger work, but again were only as powerful as the 'Coal Saddle Tanks'. Shunting the larger yards could have been carried out by eight-coupled tender engines, and most certainly was, both before the introduction of eight-coupled tanks and after, but nevertheless there was a clear need for a more powerful tank engine designed specifically for the purpose.

The 0-8-2 Tanks

The new engine was produced under the instructions of C. J. Bowen Cooke, as chief mechanical engineer, and was worked out in the usual Crewe manner, being based on the 'new G' class 0-8-0 tender engine of 1910. In essence, it was a tank version of the 'G' class, with rear pony truck supporting the coal bunker and a few minor alterations to make it more suitable for shunting. To give a greater reserve of power for short periods of heavy working, the boiler pressure was increased to 170lb psi from the 160lb of the 'G' class, and the rear tube plate was recessed into the boiler to make a combustion chamber, the tubes being 13ft 4in long (as in the 'A' and 'B' class compounds) instead of 14ft in the 'G' class. The firebox heating surface and overall dimensions remained the same.

The production of this modified boiler for the 0-8-2 tanks has been questioned but is confirmed by the lower tube heating surface shown both on the weight diagram and in several official lists of dimensions of various engine classes, and also by a letter signed by W. A. Stanier in response to an enquiry. This states that the same boiler was used on the 0-8-2 tanks 'as on the 0-8-0 "D", "F" and "G" classes, with minor modifications, the most important being decreasing the distance between the tubeplates from 14ft to 13ft 4in, this accounting for the decreased heating surface, the barrel remaining the same in all cases, 14ft 6in'. Standard 'G' class boilers had the same overall dimensions and in later days were fitted when none of the special boilers were available. This is quite clear from the *Engine History Cards*, which record the number of the previous engine a boiler was fitted to. New round-top boilers

Plate 244: *Official view of 0-8-2 tank No. 289, the fourth to be built, taken in January 1912. Basically, it is a tank version of a 'New G' class 0-8-0.*
LNWR B147

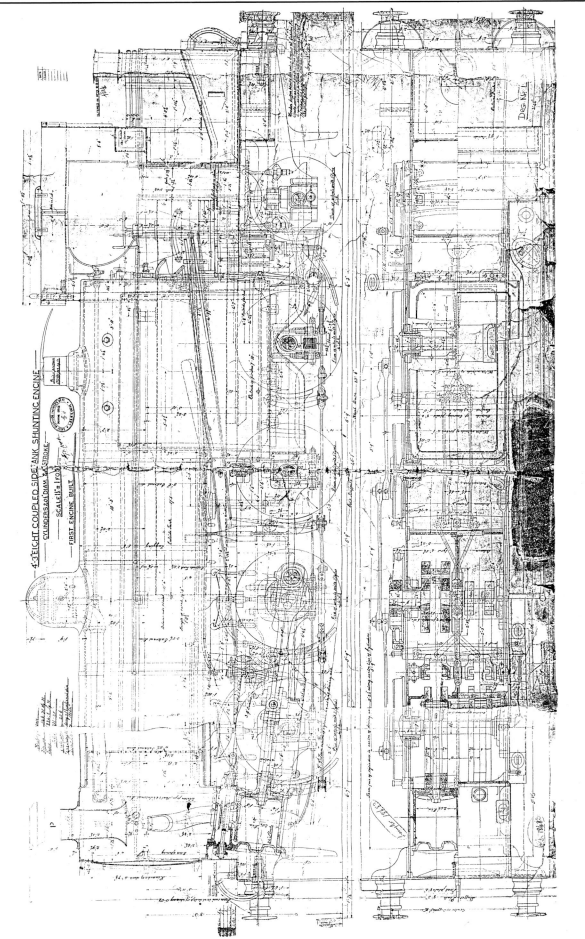

Figure 34: *General arrangement drawing of an 0-8-2 tank engine. It is dated 1911 but has been altered to show later details. For instance, Cooke buffers are not shown but the type fitted to the later batches. A note states: 'Wooden buffer blocks to be used on engines at Garston Docks'.*

Courtesy LNWR Society

Plate 245: *No 2277 in plain wartime black at Hillhouse shed, Huddersfield.*

P. F. Cooke

Plate 246: *No. 1548, with paintwork which has been touched up, so it has probably just had a wartime, or immediate post-war, overhaul. The buffers are the standard large Webb buffers with 18in rather than 13in heads, as used on 2-4-2 tanks for motor-train working; the original Cooke buffers seem to have soon proved unsatisfactory. Another change is the built-up water filler in the bunker; presumably, with the original arrangement, it was difficult to take water when the bunker was piled high with coal. Just visible on the frame near the lifeguard is the 1916 power classification code - (1).*

built as replacements were still being fitted, however, as late as 1931, though whether they were special 0-8-2 tank boilers or standard 'G' class boilers is uncertain.

The valve gear was also modified slightly to make starting easier, by lengthening the valve travel, and a lever reverser was fitted in the cab, much more suitable for a shunting engine than the screw reverser fitted to all Crewe engines since it was invented by Ramsbottom and introduced on his 'DX' class in 1858.

One other difference from the standard 'G' class was that although the engine itself had steam brakes, it was also fitted with vacuum brake for handling vacuum-fitted wagons or passenger stock. The first 0-8-0 tender engines to be built with vacuum-brake equipment was the 1914 batch of 'G1s'. Otherwise the engine had the standard 'G' class arrangements, such as three coupling rods, the centre one being fitted outside the other two, sandboxes on the two leading splashers, plus one either side under the cab, and three-link couplings.

Plate 247: *No 1185 appears to have also been through the works and had its paintwork touched up but as it has also had 'LNWR' painted out, the date must be after 1923. So it has probably not had a full repaint since being completed in late 1911.*

Plate 248: *LMS No. 7888 about 1925 in LMS livery and with a capuchon on the chimney.*

Ten 0-8-2 tanks were built in 1911-12, all fully lined and with 'LNWR' in 12in letters on the tank sides, and doubtless because of the enormous increase in traffic during the Great War, ten more were built in 1915 and ten more in 1916-17, making a total of thirty altogether. The two later batches were turned out in plain black but still with 'LNWR' on the tank sides.

In 1914 a scheme which may have been a development of an 0-8-2 tank was proposed for five 'steam crane shunting engines' capable of lifting 10 tons (the Webb saddle tanks lifted either 3 or 4 tons) 'to do the shunting at large sheds and being always in steam to attend minor derailments and so save time and the expense of calling out the breakdown gang'. Clearly, this came to nothing, as did an LMS proposal in 1930

to fit a booster to an 0-8-2 tank. Eventually, of course, the kind of work done by the 0-8-2 tanks was taken over by the diesel shunter, of which the LMS was a pioneer in the 1930s.

The 0-8-2 tanks were widely used on the LNWR system and were to be found at work in most of the larger yards. In 1913 *The Railway Magazine* reported that 'most' of them were working 'in the large sorting sidings at Crewe'. Allocations of the 1917 batch when new were as follows:

No.	Shed	No.	Shed
24	Crewe South, later Patricroft	2105	Bushbury
92	Crewe South	2294	Springs Branch
714	Crewe South, later Abergavenny	2341	Bescot
1291	Speke Junction	2348	Sutton Oak
1331	Bushbury	2391	Sutton Oak

Plate 249: *No. 7880 in Crewe Works yard on 14th April 1935. It has pop safety valves and as part of its repair seems to have acquired new wooden buffer pads.* L. Hanson

Plate 250: *Rear view of No. 7881 at Edge Hill in the late 1930s, now fitted with LMS buffers.* L. B. Lapper

Plate 251: *No. 7892 of shed '10A', Wigan Springs Branch, inside the erecting shop at Crewe on 14th June 1936, still with Ramsbottom valves.*

L. Hanson

Plate 252 (above): *An 0-8-2 tank at Buxton in 1933, probably No. 7896 or 7897 (the last digit is illegible).* R. G. Jarvis

Plate 253 (right): *No. 7898 at Buxton shed about 1936, with a new '9D' shed plate.*

Plate 254 (right): *No. 7899 in Crewe Works yard, still with front numberplate and Ramsbottom safety valves.*

After a time, however, certainly by 1928, they seem to have been moved away from Crewe South, presumably being replaced by 0-8-0 tender engines. Places where they worked for many years were Willesden, Springs Branch, Speke Junction and Patricroft, while Swansea, Bescot, Nuneaton, Huddersfield and Buxton were also regular users. They are also known to have been allocated at times to Stafford, Shrewsbury and Rugby. The Willesden engines were occasionally used in emergency to take over from the engine of an up express that had failed and as a result Nos. 1514 and 1515 both appeared at Euston at various times. On one occasion No. 1090 passed Watford on an up express, having probably hauled it from as far afield as Rugby.

In 1928 the LMS block allocation was as follows:

No.	Shed	No.	Shed
7870	Swansea	7887	Nuneaton
7871-4	Patricroft	7888	Huddersfield
7875-7	Speke Junction	7889-90	Shrewsbury
7878-82	Willesden	7891	Rugby
7883-4	Stafford	7892-5	Springs Branch
7885-6	Bescot	7896-9	Buxton

The engines were moved around slightly shortly afterwards but the sheds which had the class remained the same. In 1939 No. 7892 was at Abergavenny but soon afterwards it was moved to Patricroft or Springs Branch.

As regards annual mileages, No. 7877 ran 20,104 miles in 1933 and 20,957 in 1936 but ran only 7,113 in 1930, 1,456 in 1931 and 9,279 in 1932. The reason for such low mileages was that the engine was stored for much of the time. Presumably, this was due simply to lack of traffic as a result of the slump, many engines being stored at this time. It was allocated to Speke from March 1928 but went to Edge Hill in July 1932. From 1937 to 1950, however, it averaged well over 20,000 miles a year, the highest being 30,472 in 1946, in June

of which year it was transferred back to Speke. Even in 1950, when it was scrapped, it ran 17,081 miles. Its total mileage was 701,005. The figures for No. 47881 are not significantly different and its total mileage was closely similar, 692,706. No. 7884 avoided the low mileages of 1929-32, being transferred from Willesden to Speke in October 1929 and from there to Springs Branch in June 1930, but otherwise had generally similar figures. Its highest annual mileage was 30,531 in 1942 and its total when scrapped in 1951 was 732,425. No. 7885 at Bescot in 1930 ran only 580 miles, being out of service for 271 days (263 stored, 3 not required and 5 under repair on shed). Its total mileage was 553,433, while No. 7896 had a total mileage of 715,830.

Over the years no major alterations were made to the 0-8-2 tanks and very few minor ones. The most common external detail alteration concerned buffers. The first batch was built with long-taper Cooke buffers, which were then standard, but they must have proved unsuitable in some way. Possibly they were not robust enough to withstand the constant buffering up to and pushing of heavy loads or perhaps the heads were too small and led to buffer-locking on sharp curves in yards. At any event they were soon replaced by the standard large Webb buffers, with 18in instead of 13in heads, which were available from stock, as they were used on 2-4-2 tanks for motor-train working. The second and third batches seem to have had these buffers from new.

Engines used at Garston Docks had 'wooden buffer blocks' on the rear, according to the general arrangement drawing, simply large pieces of timber, or dumb buffers, as used on some 0-4-2 'Bissel' tanks. Exactly what the reason was is not known, but clearly, in a shunting engine, especially one used with heavy loads,

Plate 255: *A 'D tank', as LNWR enginemen called these engines, in final condition about 1950. Though it is difficult to be certain, it is probably No. 47877. It has LMS buffers, smokebox door handles instead of a wheel, and a cast Stanier chimney. The 'LMS' on the tank side and the BR number on the bunker seem to be in straw and in the block style used by Crewe in early BR days.*

buffers are subject to far more wear than in a normal engine. Dumb buffers are not only a cheap solution but can be made large enough to avoid all possibility of buffer-lock, so presumably the engines had to work over some sharp curves in the docks. In LMS days standard parallel-sided LMS buffers were used as replacements for the Webb type.

Other detail alterations were very few. All engines were built with plain-top chimneys but at least one is known to have had a chimney with a capuchon for a time, no doubt a replacement from a tender engine. In LMS days alterations were confined to standard LMS fittings, safety valves and lamp irons. Unlike the larger LNWR engines, both passenger and goods, no 0-8-2 tanks ever had the cab roof cut back to the LMS composite loading gauge, were ever superheated or fitted with Belpaire fireboxes. At some stage in LMS days the water filler in the bunker was raised in height, probably to allow water to be taken more easily when the bunker was well filled with coal, and also in later days some engines lost their vacuum brake equipment. No doubt it had fallen into disrepair on some engines as it was rarely if ever needed in certain yards and its removal was merely in recognition of this.

Minor technical 'improvements' were very similar to those applied to the 0-8-0 tender engines. In the period up to 1935 Midland type water gauges were fitted, as was desanding apparatus, and Ross pop safety valves replaced the Ramsbottom type, though it is possible that in one or two cases Ramsbottom valves later replaced pop valves once again. Ashblowers were removed, as were blow off cocks, and an improved method of fitting the internal main steam pipes in the smokebox was adopted. Lubricators were removed from the boiler faceplates and some engines had receptacles fitted for spare gauge glasses.

The first of the class to be scrapped, in October 1934, was LMS No. 7882, the first of the second batch, originally LNWR No. 58. Sixteen of the class were still in service at the outbreak of the Second World War and all survived to the end of it, but only ten were allotted BR numbers in 1948 and only four actually carried them. The last to be scrapped was BR No. 47877 in March 1953, outliving the last of the 0-8-4 tanks by just over a year.

The 0-8-4 Tanks

The final class of LNWR eight-coupled engine, and indeed the final LNWR class of any kind, was the 0-8-4 tank produced under H. P. M. Beames, which appeared some four months after the Grouping. In the usual manner, the engine was based on the latest 0-8-0 tender engine and so was essentially a 'G2' with a rear bunker, supported by a standard double radial truck, and with side tanks. It had the same arrangement of coupling rods, with the centre one pin-jointed to the outer ones, and the same arrangement of sandboxes. Some detail changes were that it had: vacuum brakes, operated by two 24in diaphragm-type vacuum cylinders, and a hand brake operating on the rear four coupled wheels only; steam-heating apparatus for working passenger trains; a chimney without a capuchon; anti-vacuum valves at the sides of the base of the smokebox; and wire mesh on the rear windows as protection when coaling. The buffers were the parallel ones of the type which replaced the original buffers on the 0-8-2 tanks, and the bufferbeam ends were shaped to provide clearance on curves in view of the additional throw-over compared to the tender engine.

In all major respects, however, the engine was a tank version of the 'G2'. Though it had a boiler pressure of 185lb psi instead of 175lb, it had the same frames, $1^{1}/_{8}$in thick instead of 1in, and the same enlarged axleboxes, slide bars and horn blocks. The gudgeon pins were about an inch more in diameter than the 'G1s' and 'G2As', the cross heads were deeper in section to allow for the larger pins, and the piston rods were of a larger diameter also. Of course, the reason for some of these changes was the need to provide for the extra weight of the water in the side tanks. All journals were lubricat-

Plate 256: *Official view of the first of the 0-8-4 tanks, No. 380, on 27th April 1923, showing the engine in full LNWR livery but with 'LMS' on the side tanks and with LMS lamp irons instead of LNWR sockets.*
LNWR E310

209

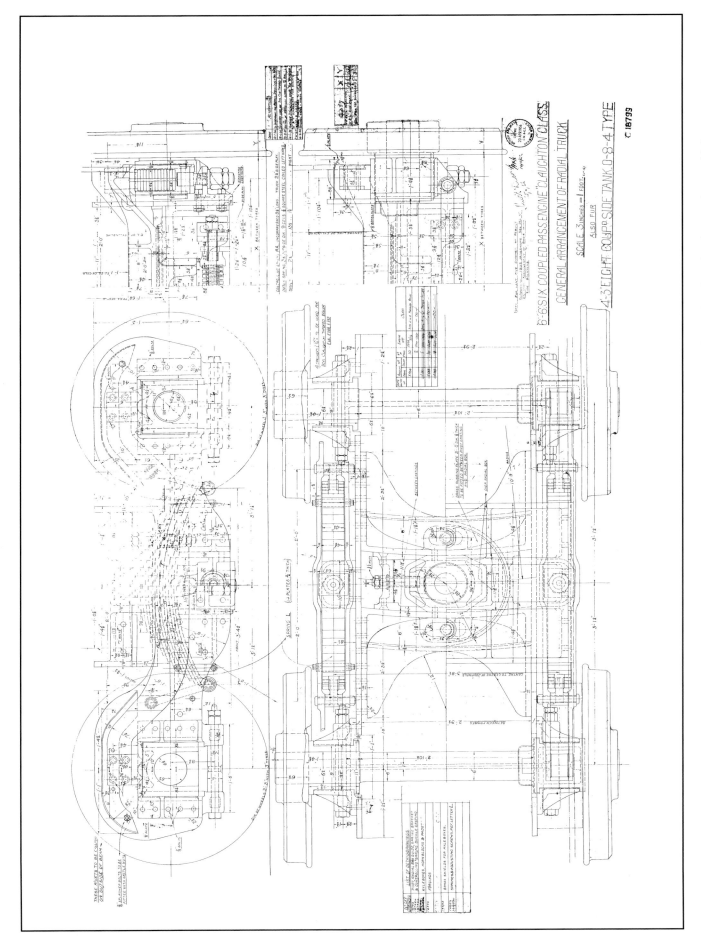

Figure 35: *Official drawing of the double radial truck used on both the 0-8-4 tanks and the 'Claughtons'. It is sometimes said that this truck had no central boss but, as J. P. Richards has pointed out, the works drawing shows clearly that this was not so. In fact it had as strong a boss as any bogie in Britain. No truck of this type was ever torn off in an accident.*

LNWR, courtesy R. Bell

Plate 257: *No. 739 at Crewe South about 1925. In the background are 'MM' 2-8-0s*

ed by a Silvertown mechanical lubricator on the left-hand side, just ahead of the sandbox on the driving axle, and the cylinders and steam chests by a Wakefield hydrostatic lubricator in the cab. The injectors were standard LNWR-type Webb injectors, 9mm on the right and 11mm on the left. Water feeds were brass hand wheels on the top of the tanks.

Whereas the 0-8-2 tanks were built purely for shunting, the 0-8-4 tanks were intended for short-distance haulage of heavy trains, as in the South Wales colliery area, where many of the class spent their lives. Coal and water capacity was 3½ tons and 2,030 gallons, compared with 2½ tons and 1,200 gallons in the 0-8-2 tanks. Working in colliery areas still involved considerable shunting, and so a type of reverser was fitted which allowed either a screw or lever to be used. The shape of this reverser precluded the fitting of a boiler

with Belpaire firebox and so the class always had the round-top variety. In fact, the reach rod was low down at the side of the firebox and it might have been possible to fit a Belpaire but the tanks took up a large area of the footplate, so that the driver would not have been able to look forward out of the cab. It was already difficult enough with the round-top boiler.

The first of the class, No. 380, was turned out in the standard LNWR lined livery but with 'LMS' on the tank sides instead of 'LNWR', and there was one other concession to the new company: LMS lamp irons were fitted in place of the usual LNWR sockets. Again, although the first engine had Webb safety valves, Ross pop safety valves were introduced very soon, possibly on the second of the class.

In all, three batches of ten engines were built and they were turned out at the time when the LMS was decid-

Plate 258: *No. 7955, one of the engines tried on the Manchester - Buxton line, arriving at Manchester London Road on six-wheeled passenger stock about 1925.*
W. H. Whitworth

Plate 259: *One of the same batch, No. 7956, also at Manchester London Road. It has pop safety valves and is in early LMS plain black goods engine livery. Those engines of this class which were painted in LMS maroon must have been a magnificent sight, even for die-hard LNWR enthusiasts, as they had full gold lining, even round the wheels. Unfortunately, it has not been possible to locate a good photograph of one.*

ing its new livery. Thus, the class appeared in four different schemes, as detailed in the table below, which uses Crewe motion numbers to identify the individual engines rather than listing the LNWR numbers:

Crewe MN	Livery Details
5722-9	LNWR lined black, LNWR numberplates, 'LMS' on tanks
5730-4	Plain black, LNWR numberplates, no lettering on tanks
5735-40	LMS 'crimson lake' with gold lining, LMS No. 7943-8
5741-51	LMS plain black, LMS No. 7949-59

The first seven engines to be built were allocated to Abergavenny on entering service, as were three of the following six also, but Nos. 739, 468 and 793 were sent first to shed '28', Tebay. Presumably, they were tried on banking up to Shap Summit but then were transferred, probably quite soon, to Abergavenny. The next eleven,

up to LMS No. 7955, also went new to Abergavenny, but whether the last six went there initially or directly to Edge Hill is uncertain.

Soon after the class arrived at Abergavenny, trials were held with one of them in the South Wales District. A load of 209 tons, consisting of 31 vehicles, 30 wagons and a 20-ton brake van, was started from rest on a ruling grade of 1 in 34 in bad weather, after the train had been 'brought up' (presumably by another engine). On 1 in 40 a load of 392 tons behind the engine, 59 empty wagons and a 20-ton brake van, was taken with ease, and several more wagons could have been added but for the fact that a greater length of train was inadmissible on the section of line. In passenger service on 1 in 34, a train of 14 vehicles, equivalent to 184 tons behind

Plate 260: *No. 7959 passing Chapel-en-le-Frith with an up special from Liverpool to either Buxton or quite possibly Ashbourne on 2nd August 1926. It was then allocated to Edge Hill, having been transferred away from Buxton earlier that year or late in 1925.*

J. M. Bentley collection

Plate 261: *No. 7942 about 1936. Except for now having desanding gear, it seems to be unaltered from its original condition.*
C. L. Hodgetts

Plate 262: *No. 7936 at Crewe in 1936.*

R. G. Jarvis

Plate 263: *No. 7932 at Tredegar probably in the early 1930s. The injector feed pipe is still in its original position. It was found that when the brake shoes wore, the hand brake arm would come up and foul the pipe causing fracture.*

the engine, was easily handled, the test not being extended to a greater load owing to the length of 14 vehicles being the maximum the platforms could accommodate. The report concluded that nineteen of the engines were at work in the Abergavenny District and were doing the work of thirty of the former side tanks (that is, 'Coal Tanks').

Some of the class were also sent to work between Manchester and Buxton, the idea being to have one class of engine which could work all traffic, both passenger and goods, as well as doing the shunting at Buxton. They were, of course, fine on goods trains and, no doubt, had better acceleration from the frequent stops when working uphill towards Buxton than either the 4-4-2 'Precursor Tanks', which had worked the line from the mid-1900s, or the 4-6-2 'Superheater Tanks', which had replaced them about 1921. But with their small wheels they were less suitable for passenger work and were certainly unsuitable for the express passenger trains. Eventually, a few years later, the Buxton services were taken over by Fowler 2-6-4 tanks.

Published accounts record the engines used on the Buxton line as being allocated to Longsight. In July 1925 two of the class, Nos. 7955 and 7956, are shown as being sent there, and according to the *Engine History Card*, No. 7932 was at Longsight on 1st January 1927 (when the card starts) but was transferred to Edge Hill the following day (in November of that year it went to Abergavenny). However, it seems more than likely that they were actually allocated to Buxton. At that time it was a sub-shed of Longsight under the LNWR shed organisation, so quite possibly Buxton engines were officially recorded as being at Longsight. The note-book of a Buxton fireman shows that at different dates in

December 1924 he worked Nos. 7952, 7958 and 7959 up to Buxton from Longsight 'light engine'. Certainly, it seems that wherever they were shedded officially, many of the class actually worked from Buxton. No. 7959 is shown as 'light engine' from Buxton to Longsight in January 1926, when it was probably on its way to Edge Hill. The 0-8-2 tanks, which had been moved away when the 0-8-4 tanks arrived, returned to Buxton in late 1925.

Otherwise, apart from these brief exceptions, the whole class was shared between two places, Edge Hill and South Wales for the whole of its life. In the 1928 LMS block allocations they were shedded as follows: Nos. 7930-7946 Abergavenny; 7947-7948 Swansea; 7949-7959 Edge Hill. These allocations remained basically in force for many years but some of the South Wales engines were moved around between Abergavenny, which always had the largest number, Swansea and Tredegar. They seem to have moved to Edge Hill in 1947-8, and to have been replaced by 'Super Ds' which had been specially modified for the purpose.

Having higher boiler pressure than the 'G2s' and greater adhesive weight, thanks to the side tanks, the 0-8-4s were powerful engines. They also had excellent brakes but were still not popular with the men because the footplate was cramped and uncomfortable. As the tanks protruded into the cab, the driver had to stand too near the fire, and as the firehole was low, the fireman had to bend low to shovel and then could easily hit his head on the handle of the rack-type firehole door. Wooden footblocks were fitted for the men to stand on but took up much of the floor space. These problems would not have existed if the tanks had been further forward and the footplating lowered.

When the 0-8-4 tanks first went to South Wales, they are reputed to have straightened the track in several places. This is hardly surprising in view of the fact that they were new, with a long rigid wheelbase, and had to negotiate sharp curves in sidings and engine sheds, which the previous Webb 0-6-2 'Coal Tanks' had long adapted to. The biggest fault with them, in fact, lay in the lubrication of the trailing driving axleboxes, which was by a flexible oil pipe from the mechanical lubricator. It was clipped to the main frame behind the wheel. When new, this arrangement caused no trouble but when side-play developed in the axlebox, the wheel eventually rubbed away the pipe, causing loss of oil and overheating. It would have been possible to overcome this fault easily by re-routing the pipe but nothing was done.

In *The Railway Magazine* for April 1953, J. M. Dunn gives a graphic account of these engines and the problems he encountered with them at Blaenavon, when they first arrived in South Wales. One problem he describes concerns the difficulty of working long passenger trains at short platforms, when the engine has to draw up into a tunnel so that the rear coaches can stand in the platform. Nevertheless, however serious the difficulty may be, when the driver cannot communicate with the platform staff to get the 'right-away'

because his cab is in a tunnel and shrouded in steam, it cannot reasonably be blamed on the design of the engine.

A more relevant problem was their propensity to straighten the track and to derail, especially the flangeless wheels on the intermediate axle coming off on sharp curves in the shed yard. According to Dunn, the flangeless wheels and their axleboxes simply moved sideways, even when left standing on curved track, and he issued instructions for the hand brakes to be screwed on tight. Derailments became so frequent that the enginemen learnt to ignore them, knowing that the offending wheels would soon re-rail themselves at the next set of points.

Although there seems no doubt that Dunn's problems were genuine, it remains something of a mystery as to how this could happen. There was no side play in these axleboxes at all (there was no need for it), the treads of the wheels were wide, $6^3/_8$in, and the coupling rods to the neighbouring wheels were only 5ft 9in long. Even if the axleboxes had been free to move sideways, it is hard to imagine how they could do so, as the coupling rods should have restrained them. So it seems unlikely that they would derail in any normal circumstances, and several drivers at Abergavenny, who were questioned about this in the early 1940s, could not recall an 0-8-4 tank ever derailing. Of course, all engines derail at

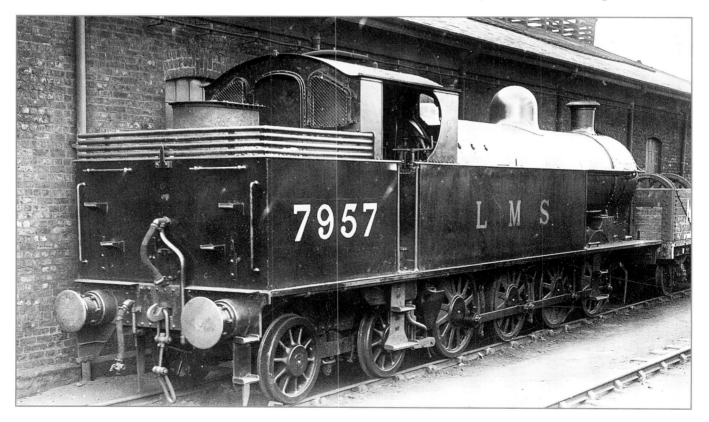

Plate 264: *Rear view of No. 7957 at Edge Hill shed on 14th April 1934. Just visible, but only just, is the carriage-heating relief valve, protruding above the front right-hand corner of the cab roof. This class and a few 'Super Ds' were fitted with these valves, but they are much more difficult to see in photographs than, for example, on 'Jumbos'.*

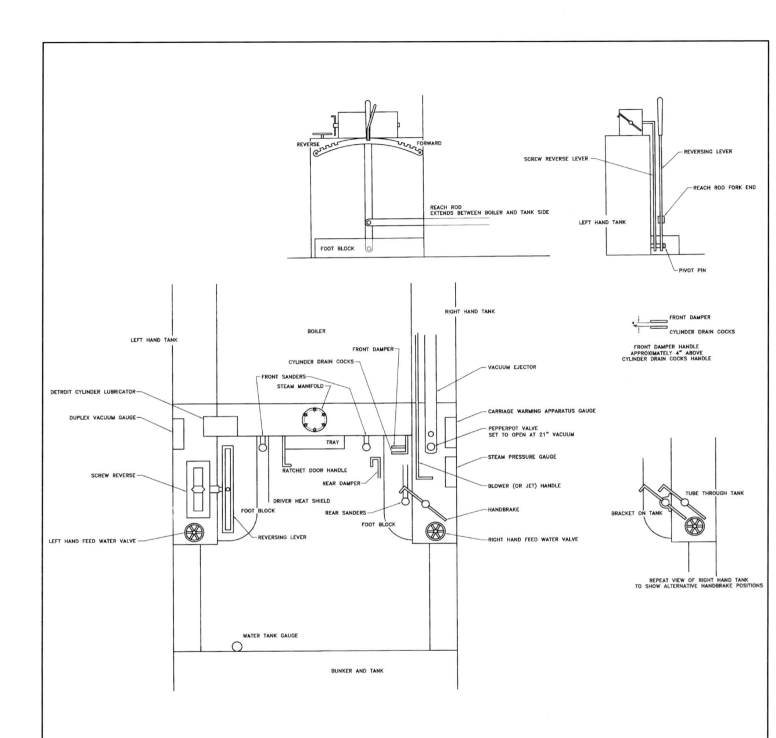

Figure 36: *Drawing, not to scale, showing footplate details of an 0-8-4 tank engine. A Detroit lubricator is shown, as an example. Originally the class had Wakefield hydrostatic cylinder lubricators in the cab, probably to the left of the position shown for the Detroit lubricator.* Drawing prepared by Andy Lowe from sketches by Harold Walkley

Plate 265: *No. 7954 from the rear at Buxton shed on 22nd August 1948, fitted with LMS buffers. The reversing lever can be seen in the cab, as can the lubricator, to the left of the driver's window.*
F. W. Shuttleworth

Plate 266: *No. 7954 at Buxton shed during the 'big freeze' of 1947. It had just been recovered from Briggs Sidings, where it had got stuck in deep snow drifts, while on snow plough duty, and been abandoned by its crew. Standing in front of the engine is the Buxton shed foreman, Joe Wilson. The usual practice at Buxton for clearing snow drifts was to use an 0-8-4 tank back to back with a '4F' 0-6-0 fitted with a small plough.*
E. R. Morten

times, but the flangeless driving wheels seem no more likely to cause this than any others. Nevertheless, though it may be difficult to explain how it happened, it seems certain that it did. Similar things are known to have occurred at times with the flangeless wheels of 'Super Ds' and of '9F' 2-10-0s.

In the early 1940s Abergavenny had ten 0-8-4 tanks: Nos. 7931-2, 7935-6, 7940, 7943-5, 7947 and 7956. They were used to service collieries in the area, on goods trains to Newport and Dowlais Central and on banking at Monmouth Road. They were also used to bank to Brynmawr, and then work to Blaina or Ebbw Vale, or to shunt at Brynmawr, Beaufort and Rassau Siding. Two of the Abergavenny engines were sub-shedded at Blaenavon (closed in 1944), where they serviced collieries in the area, the coal being worked to

Abergavenny.

Tredegar had four of the engines - Nos. 7933, 7937, 7939 and 7952 - and worked them very hard; they did not spend much time idle on shed. They serviced the collieries in the Sirhowy Valley, worked freight to Ystrad Mynach via Hengoed Viaduct and, after the war started, ran to Aber sidings, Caerphilly and Rogerstone yard. They also regularly worked passenger trains for miners, made up of wooden-seated four and six-wheeled carriages, between Nantybwch and Nine Mile Point colliery, with a banker from Tredegar to Nantybwch in the reverse direction. On Tuesdays they worked a special market train to Abergavenny, running non-stop from Sirhowy to Brecon Road in front of the 10am Merthyr-Abergavenny passenger and returning about 4.30pm. In the summer they worked excursion trains to Barry Island and in the football season to such places as Cardiff and Pontypridd. They also worked rugby specials for Murrayfield from Pentllanfraith as far as Abergavenny, where main-line engines would take them on.

Swansea Upper Bank, a former Midland shed, also had 0-8-4 tanks at that time, probably four. They were used for servicing the collieries in the Swansea valley area and brought the coal to sidings near St Thomas's station where it was handed over to the GWR. When the war started, they worked through over GWR metals. To reach Upper Bank they ran from Crewe via the Central Wales line to Swansea Victoria and then over the elevated line joining the east and west sides of Swansea docks.

In the Liverpool area the 0-8-4 tanks were used mostly on goods workings on the branches to the docks. They worked trains from the branches to the top of the 'Grid Iron' and then ran back for another trip. They also worked on local goods to Speke. But perhaps the main reason why they were sent to Edge Hill was to work the Bootle branch, both passenger and freight. Previously, the load limit for goods trains from Wapping was 31 wagons up the 1 in 63 from Atlantic Junction to Walton. These trains were usually hauled by a 'Cauliflower', '19in Goods' or 0-8-0, and were always banked, perhaps by a 'Coal Tank'. The 0-8-4 tanks could take the whole train single-handed with ease, and the intention was to double the load. But the

guards refused to take such heavy trains, as 31 wagons was the most a guard's van could hold on the banks. On passenger trains the 0-8-4 tanks were very quick in getting away from Lime Street up the cutting to Edge Hill. The 4pm to Bootle went up the bank parallel to the 4pm to Leeds and invariably the 0-8-4 tank won the race. They also worked passenger trains to Alexandra Dock and Canada Dock via Atlantic Junction, and in doing so provided plenty of excitement for enthusiasts. When they began to be withdrawn, their work on the Bootle branch was taken by 'Super Ds' specially modified for the purpose.

At Edge Hill the 0-8-4 tanks generally seem to have been well liked. The men said the firehole door was too low and that with the rack type door, the firemen were hitting their heads on the handle when firing. If both men were on the large side, the driver used to stand by the cab door out of the way, when the fireman was at work. When he had finished firing, he often used to sit on the end of the tank and stretch his legs across the opening to the cab, while running light to Alexandra or Canada docks to pick up another load for Edge Hill. Hot boxes were not uncommon but in general there were none of the complaints about the engines that were so often heard from South Wales. Why that should have been so is a minor mystery. There were plenty of steep gradients and hard work in the dock area and around the 'Grid Iron', but perhaps one factor was that the sharp curves in the docks were banned to main-line

Plate 267: *No. 7932 of '8A', Edge Hill, at Patricroft about 1946 with a Stanier chimney* B. J. Miller collection

Plate 268: *No. 7940 at Blaenavon in the 1930s. The lubricator in the cab is to the left of the driver's window, so is probably the Wakefield lubricator fitted originally, rather than the Detroit type which obscured his view. Part of the reverser can also be seen.*
J. M. Dunn, LNWR Society

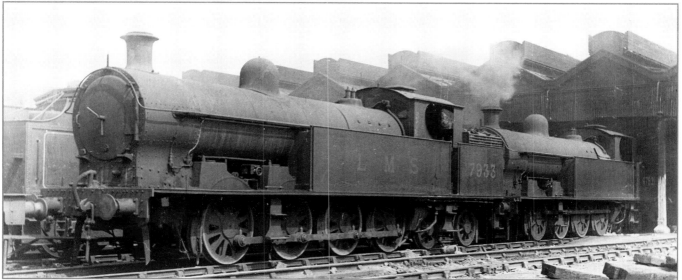

Plate 269 (above): *LMS No. 7933 and BR No. 47931 at Edge Hill shed on 14th May 1950, with LMS buffers, Stanier chimneys, smokebox door handles instead of wheels (presumably, in the case of 47931) and lubricators between the splashers to supply the axlebox journals.*
R. K. Blencowe collection

Plate 270 (right): *No. 47937 in Crewe Works probably after withdrawal in 1950. It seems to have been the only member of the class to have its number in the small standard BR numerals*
B. K. B. Green

engines, being worked by dock tanks of various kinds.

Allocations were not static but the following engines were at Edge Hill in 1938: 7943-4, 7946, 7948, 7950, 7953, 7955, 7957-9; in 1947: 7930, 7933, 7938-9, 7946, 7951, 7956, 7958-9; in 1948: 7930-3, 7937, 7939, 7951, 7956, 7958-9. At first, when Edge Hill engines were withdrawn, they were replaced by engines from South Wales but eventually 'Super Ds' took over.

All the 0-8-4 tanks went to Rugby Works for shopping. The South Wales engines reached Rugby via Shrewsbury, Wellington and Stafford. But occasionally they went via Crewe and the South shed often borrowed them when en route and sent them on a freight to Liverpool, so that the whole class could be seen there in time.

As regards distances run, No. 47931 had an annual mileage between 1927 and 1936 which varied between a low of 11,912 in 1930 and a high of 19,228 in 1936, but between 1937 and 1950 its average was over 20,000 miles, 25,409 being achieved in 1940 and 26,116 in 1942. It was allocated to Abergavenny from 1927 to September 1942, and to Swansea from then to February 1948, when it went to Edge Hill. Its total mileage when withdrawn was 522,542. No. 7933 ran 26,585 miles at Swansea in 1943 and 26,060 at Abergavenny in 1946. In all, it ran 510,987 miles. No. 7939 ran a total of 534,584 miles. In fact, it was difficult for engines in South Wales to run up large mileages, as their work was confined to either Abergavenny to Dowlais, about 18 miles, and Nantybwch to Newport via Tredegar, 22 miles. They were fully occupied doing two trips a day up the bank and also banking main line over the GWR tracks.

Changes in external appearance were few right up to withdrawal. LMS buffers began to be fitted, probably in the late 1930s, front numberplates were removed generally earlier than that, and anti-vacuum valves were removed from the sides of the base of the smokebox of some engines but remained in use on those at Abergavenny. Some engines can be seen in photographs running without carriage-heating hoses but that may well have been temporary, perhaps in summer, and the apparatus itself may well still have been fitted. However, the distinctive LNWR cab roof remained unaltered, unlike most of the tender engines, and the original chimneys were retained, as were the characteristic smokebox door wheels.

Many minor technical changes occurred, however, especially in the 1923-36 period, almost all of them being the same as those applied to the 'Super Ds'. Pop safety valves were fitted on the few that originally had Ramsbottom valves but in the early days at least, it is quite possible that *vice versa* Ramsbottom valves

replaced pop valves in some cases. The 8in piston valves originally had one broad ring per head but were later fitted with four narrow rings. Midland type water gauges and desanding apparatus were also fitted. Ashblowers and blow off cocks in the door plates were removed. The improved method of fitting the main steam pipes in the smokebox was adopted, and copper ejector steam pipes were used instead of steel, as were standard type coal unions and continuous blowdown apparatus. Crosshead vacuum pumps appear to have been retained in many cases and ejectors added (only No. 7931 has 'pump' crossed out on the *History Card*). One engine is recorded as having been provided with 'driver's seats', presumably improved seats for both members of the crew, and probably other engines were also so fitted.

The first engine to be withdrawn was No. 7947 in August 1944 and the rest of the class followed as their boilers required replacement. At first, when replacement boilers were fitted in the works, they had come from other 0-8-4 tanks and had been repaired, but after about 1930 boilers previously on 'Super Ds' were fitted. When it became uneconomic to repair round-top boilers, replacements were no longer available, as all spare boilers built since the 1920s had had Belpaire fireboxes. So withdrawal was inevitable. Just over half of the class, sixteen, had been withdrawn by nationalisation in 1948, and of the fourteen which became BR property only two survived long enough to receive BR numbers, 47931 and 47937. The latter was scrapped in October 1950 but the former survived for more than a year, being withdrawn in December 1951.

Finally, there is the question as to what the 0-8-4 tanks sounded like, whether they had the same uneven beat as a 'Super D' or, as they must have been designed from scratch, the weight of the side tanks being taken into account, an even beat. Jack Gahan of Liverpool recalls them as sounding like a 'Super D' but when working flat out up 1 in 63 or on the 'Grid Iron' the beat was almost even. So the question was also put to Harold Walkley, 'Can you recall ever hearing these Beames tanks in action?' His reply was as follows:

'I noticed the 0-8-4 tanks were permitted ten ICI 35-ton tank wagons unassisted into Abergavenny Junction whereas the 0-8-0s were restricted to nine. The way these trains were driven was like this. They would come down from Brynmawr with brakes pinned down (average grade 1 in 38 for 7½ miles) and stop at Llanfoist Cutting to lift the brakes. When ready, the driver gave a coded whistle to Brecon Road No. 2 box, and when the signalman had a clear road to the junction, he would pull off the distant signal by the train, and off they would set - full regulator, full gear, accelerating bunker first up the 1 in 60 through Brecon Road station, then the track eased to 1 in 90 where the driver would pull the lever back to the fourth notch. The noise was tremendous and each of the exhaust beats was even.'

Chapter Ten
THE 'MM' OR 'ROD' 2-8-0s

Plate 271: *An unidentified ROD, with number stencilled on the cabside, rolling through Colwyn Bay on a down freight about 1920. The train contains quite a few cattle wagons which are no doubt destined for Holyhead.* H. Gordon Tidey

During the Great War the demands made on the capacity of Crewe Works for military production were substantial, and locomotive maintenance, at a time when engines were being worked harder than ever before because of the enormous increase in traffic, fell seriously into arrears. At the end of the war, therefore, when large numbers of new Robinson 2-8-0s, which had been ordered by the government for war use, became surplus to requirements, the LNWR agreed to buy 30 of them. They were commonly referred to as 'ROD' 2-8-0s, having been chosen by the Railway Operating Division of the Royal Engineers as its standard freight engine. But on the LNWR they were officially described as class 'MM', as they had been ordered by, and probably acquired from, the Ministry of Munitions. Thus, LNWR enginemen commonly referred to them as 'Military Marys'.

The 30 2-8-0s were delivered in June-August 1919, many of them via Bushbury, and most if not all were new engines, having been completed after the war ended. In September 1919 a further 70 engines were obtained on loan and in December another 50, though delivery of the latter was not completed until January 1921. Finally, 31 more 'MMs' were obtained (21 from the Lancashire & Yorkshire Railway in May-June 1920; 6 from the South Eastern & Chatham Railway and 2 from the London & South Western Railway in June

1920; and 2 others in January 1921). All these engines remained on the LNWR until August 1921, when all except the original 30 were returned to the government and put into huge dumps at Gretna, Birkenhead and elsewhere.

The first 30 engines obtained by the LNWR were at first numbered in the capital list in the usual way. But for some reason their purchase was delayed, and further engines were obtained on loan. It was then decided that all the 'MMs' would be on loan, so the first 30 were renumbered 2800-29 and the remaining 151 became 2830-2980.

While these 181 engines were on loan, their numbers were painted on the cab sides. Their tenders were actually given LNWR tender numbers, which were carried on standard LNWR tender numberplates attached to the back of the tenders in the proper manner. The following tender numbers were noted:

Engine No.	Tender No.	Engine No.	Tender No.
2803	170	2823	1189
2805	247	2867	884
2817	351	2891	1883

Subsequently, the first 30 engines and tenders were bought by the LNWR, the order being covered by account E304 for the engines and T304 for the tenders, dated 28th June 1920. In November 1920 the 30 engines were given new numbers in the capital list,

Plate 272 (above): *After the Great War, Great Central-type 2-8-0s used by the Railway Operating Division returned from France and were stored at various places while the government tried to find buyers for them. Here, ROD No. 1722 stands at Tattenham Corner station..*

Courtesy Dr Adrian Collyns

Plate 273 (right): *The Caledonian Railway hired some of the surplus ROD 2-8-0s for a while but when it was decided not to buy them they were dumped in sidings at Gretna, where this picture of Nos 2135, 1834 and others was taken on 25th March 1926.* J. J. Cunningham

Plate 274: *LNWR 'MM' No. 2406 at Crewe South about 1920.* W. H. Whitworth

Plate 275: *LNWR 'MM' 2-8-0 No. 1336 at Bushbury on 26th August 1922.*

P. J. T. Reed

2800 becoming 1315, for example, and the 30 tenders were allotted the following tender numbers: 13, 36, 39, 44, 65, 78, 92, 140, 146, 158, 170, 173, 177, 187, 195, 216, 219, 227, 230, 247, 301, 310, 314, 330, 342, 343, 344, 351, 397 and 410. Then in August 1921 the other 151 engines and tenders were returned to the Government. The ROD engine numbers were restored and the LNWR tender numbers were removed. In the LMS renumbering the 30 'MMs' became 9616-45 but their tenders retained their LNWR numbers, as did LNWR tenders proper.

In 1927 a further 75 'MMs' were obtained very cheaply by the LMS, as by that time the Government Disposals Board was keen to sell them. The price was £25,000 or just under £340 per engine, and they were delivered to Crewe. The reason for the purchase was to obtain the tenders, as there was 'a considerable shortage of tenders on Divison A' at the time. Crewe Works was then being reorganised and it seems that the overhaul of tenders was particularly disrupted. It was decided to repair 20 of the engines and put them into service, and to do the same with the tenders of the remaining 55, the repairs and alterations to the tenders costing £400 each, more than the price of the engine and tender together. The 55 engines were dismantled and used to provide spares for the other 20 and the original 30. It was intended that 20 boilers from the 55 engines to be dismantled would be repaired by an outside contractor and be fitted with copper fireboxes in place of their steel boxes. These boilers were to be used as replacements when those on the 20 engines in service were worn out. Whether this plan was actually carried out, however, is not certain, but it seems unlikely

in view of the short life of the class as a whole. The tenders were used mainly on ex-LNWR passenger engines, 'Claughtons', 'Princes', 'Georges' and 'Precursors', but they also appeared on 0-8-0s. In the event, only 49 tenders were used, and very soon afterwards, certainly within a couple of years, the tender shortage seems to have given way to a surplus, as tenders were being withdrawn.

The additional 20 engines were numbered 9646-65. At first their tenders were given the same numbers as the engines they were attached to but after a few weeks they were renumbered 6271-89 and 6339, and the additional 49 tenders became 6290-6338. Details of these 20 engines and tenders are as follows:

'MM' Eng. No.	LMS Eng. No.	'MM' Ten. No.	First Ten. No.	New Ten. No.	Date in Traffic
1865	9649	1912	9649	6271	29.2.27
1891	9646	1934	9646	6272	30.9.27
1835	9647	1835	9647	6273	18.10.27
1938	9673	1938	9653	6274	19.10.27
1926	9652	1926	9652	6275	27.10.27
1851	9656	1851	9656	6276	11.11.27
1871	9650	1871		6277	22.11.27
1832	9654	1832		6278	16.12.27
1934	9657	1924		6279	27.2.28
1912	9655	1877		6280	23.3.28
1801	9662	1801		6281	29.3.28
1888	9663	1888		8282	29.3.28
1803	9659	1803		6283	4.4.28
1918	9664	1918		6284	4.4.28
1602	9661	1602		6285	14.4.28
1837	9648	1850		6286	23.4.28
1924	9651	1931		6287	25.4.28
1850	9658	1843		6288	27.4.28
1877	9660	1900		6289	22.5.28
1853	9665	1906		6339	19.7.28

Although it is sometimes stated that the 'MMs' were

Plate 276: *ROD No. 1645, which was built by Robert Stephenson in June 1919, at Crewe South shed probably later that year. It was given LNWR number 2858 but was returned to the government in August 1921.* Roger Carpenter collection

Plate 278 (right top): *LNWR 'MM' No. 2946, which was built by the Hyde Park Works of the North British Locomotive Company in May 1919. It was hired in December 1919 and returned to the government in August 1921. In 1927 it went to the LNER. The products of each works of the NBL differed slightly in their details.*

Plate 279 (right centre): *One of the RODs bought by the LMS, No. 9646 about 1925. The 'MMs' retained their Westinghouse air pumps, as both engine and tender were air-braked.*

Plate 280 (right bottom): *LMS No. 9616, previously ROD 1787 and LNWR 2400, was built by the Atlas Works of the North British Locomotive Company in 1919 and is seen here in the late 1920s. Somehow it has acquired an L&Y chimney.*

Plate 277: *LNWR No. 2966. The number is stencilled on the cabside below the crest of the Lancashire & Yorkshire Railway, on which the engine worked after return from Europe. It was built by the Queens Park Works of the North British Locomotive Company in December 1917.* W. H. Whitworth

Plate 281: *LMS No. 9633 at Crewe South in 1931. It was built by the Hyde Park Works of the NBL in 1919..*

Plate 282: *Another view of No. 9616 but after renumbering as 9455 in July 1931. It still has its L&Y chimney.*

not very popular with LNWR enginemen in general, there is in fact little information on this point. Certainly, they were regarded as very fine engines indeed by the LNWR men at Hillhouse without exception, a considerable compliment coming from a group of men not without prejudice. So it seems more than likely that they were similarly regarded throughout the LNWR. Moreover, they had an excellent reputation elsewhere, especially on their native Great Central Railway. On the other hand, so far as Crewe was concerned, they were non-standard engines, with boilers needing expensive repairs, and in the slump of the late 1920s and early 1930s there was probably no point in keeping them, as the LMS had more engines than it needed.

Another factor may have been that they were right-hand drive. LNWR engines were left-hand drive, so the sighting of signals would be more difficult, which would not make the engines popular. Indeed most of the French lines, such as the Nord and Est, which the 'MMs' were originally intended for, were also left-hand drive. The reason why right-hand drive was used on the 'MMs' seems to have been that the Great Central design was adopted in great haste, with a minimum of alteration, Gorton supplying the drawings from its originals. The only changes were the fitting of Westinghouse brakes for the train and the removal of scoops from the tender. No thought was given to such niceties as which

side of the cab the driver should be on.

At the Grouping the 'MMs' were classified '5' by the LMS but in 1928 the power classification scheme was revised and the 'MMs' now became class '7'. Because their axle load was too high for certain bridges, they were not allowed on the main line south of Stafford. In the 1928 block allocation they were distributed as follows:

9616-25	Llandudno Junction	9641-3	Shrewsbury
9626-34	Mold Junction	9644-7/9	Bangor
9635-40	Abergavenny	9650/2-4/6	Crewe South

This accounts for only 38 of the 50 engines but presumably the missing 12 were still being overhauled in Crewe Works. The 'MMs' were thus commonly to be found along the North Wales coast and the Welsh borders. Latterly they were concentrated at Mold Junction, from where again they worked along the North Wales coast, south to Crewe, and to Birkenhead, Liverpool, Manchester, Wigan and occasionally to Buxton. As they were withdrawn, they were replaced by 'Super Ds'.

The 'MMs' did not survive long on the LMS, partly no doubt because they were a non-standard class, the first being scrapped in February 1928. By July 1931 only 28 of the original 50 survived to be renumbered 9455-82, making way for new 'G3' 0-8-0s in the 96XX series; the last of the class, No. 9460, was scrapped just over two years later, in October 1933.

Plate 283: *LMS No. 9628 at Llandudno Junction on 8th August 1930.*

J. M. Bentley collection

APPENDICES
Appendix One - Mineral Traffic in Great Britain 1875-1912

Throughout the second half of the nineteenth century and right up to the First World War, mineral traffic was on a steadily rising trend, as a result of the growth in industrialisation and of the increased population it was able to support. The growth in this traffic is illustrated by the following table showing the annual tonnages of mineral traffic hauled by the leading companies serving England and Wales; by all companies in England and Wales, by the two leading Scottish companies; and by all companies in Scotland. 'Mineral' traffic includes not only coal, coke and patent fuel but also iron ore, limestone, building stone and so forth. One major haulier of mineral traffic, the Great Central Railway, is omitted from the table, since it was not in existence as one company for the whole period.

	1875	1876	1877	1878	1879	1880	1881	1882
GNR	2,747,005	2,696,781	2,923,679	3,002,950	3,540,091	3,688,101	4,090,647	4,252,328
GWR	12,351,445	14,211,822	14,698,310	14,577,788	15,148,279	16,216,106	16,525,242	18,128,811
LNWR	26,517,376	26,931,795	30,128,210	28,949,289	29,782,614	25,026,600	25,808,100	26,920,397
LYR	7,855,398	8,367,341	8,830,915	8,784,537	8,833,161	9,202,017	9,543,430	9,956,044
MR	11,507,972	11,203,034	11,219,941	11,841,745	12,941,026	13,379,493	14,206,971	14,221,300
NER	26,403,067	26,446,298	26,302,203	24,763,104	23,825,471	29,106,322	30,137,962	30,028,061
Eng/Wales	95,661,394	100,412,568	100,812,224	98,963,165	103,672,695	140,965,835	417,366,844	153,848,044
CR	9,815,331	10,108,534	10,678,916	9,922,754	10,043,505	10,744,489	11,569,822	11,353,992
NBR	7,179,665	7,369,848	7,290,299	7,123,483	7,743,796	8,206,932	9,158,914	9,743,516
Scotland	21,431,072	22,019,974	22,510,784	21,237,596	22,161,743	23,704,436	25,963,501	26,414,452

	1883	1884	1885	1886	1887	1888	1889	1890
GNR	4,736,270	4,875,795	4,963,626	5,248,843	5,597,927	5,689,250	6,004,488	5,978,793
GWR	18,904,015	18,504,224	17,959,018	17,340,416	17,784,502	18,762,152	19,653,714	19,607,565
LNWR	27,101,816	25,294,639	24,849,419	25,104,875	27,286,802	27,898,314	29,192,778	28,837,922
LYR	10,405,981	10,445,451	10,759,582	10,859,363	11,271,161	11,339,684	11,697,607	12,005,092
MR	15,431,513	14,846,106	15,155,182	14,986,537	15,450,385	16,191,574	17,687,542	18,346,253
NER	30,782,718	28,732,548	28,080,115	27,338,459	28,428,245	30,530,824	32,279,626	33,144,524
Eng/Wales	160,522,029	155,432,872	156,220,110	154,725,763	164,934,563	171,433,249	179,996,664	184,818,223
CR	11,986,864	11,784,489	11,411,667	11,051,784	11,473,550	12,241,678	12,981,200	12,650,501
NBR	10,297,839	10,009,187	10,080,254	10,112,940	10,377,810	11,181,080	11,710,852	11,280,067
Scotland	27,767,095	27,063,389	26,553,827	26,246,665	27,308,278	29,080,119	30,626,514	29,800,519

	1891	1892	1893	1894	1895	1896	1897	1898
GNR	6,213,342	6,383,424	5,288,856	7,204,168	7,164,339	7,366,598	7,877,567	8,483,067
GWR	20,149,609	20,773,460	19,882,713	22,659,001	22,567,363	24,313,613	25,519,952	22,815,391
LNWR	29,119,277	29,034,567	25,407,751	28,839,389	28,554,594	30,180,341	31,718,358	32,695,982
LYR	12,472,372	12,640,116	11,017,649	13,060,789	13,014,421	13,724,284	14,071,541	14,740,407
MR	19,198,699	19,226,878	15,192,935	18,912,917	18,898,790	19,755,553	20,522,994	21,700,623
NER	32,528,466	27,558,882	31,800,920	34,923,806	33,937,909	35,749,395	37,412,049	39,251,969
Eng/Wales	188,410,498	185,327,982	172,268,608	202,018,845	200,275,270	212,576,413	223,083,727	220,769,402
CR	13,508,575	14,691,096	14,825,147	13,337,770	17,567,190	18,623,885	19,876,741	21,410,787
NBR	12,358,448	13,074,160	13,104,427	11,807,225	14,145,328	15,158,796	15,904,530	16,873,293
Scotland	31,931,083	34,492,068	34,503,200	30,988,531	40,698,102	42,290,560	45,449,754	46,219,940

	1899	1900	1901	1902	1903	1904	1905	1906
GNR	9,033,318	9,452,467	9,129,584	9,681,403	13,651,596	13,589,742	13,543,738	14,657,677
GWR	28,345,054	30,076,786	29,338,894	32,780,539	34,181,544	35,144,760	35,004,911	39,215,928
LNWR	34,662,194	34,815,230	33,185,907	35,302,744	35,599,532	36,670,142	38,519,104	41,077,313
LYR	15,193,254	15,374,141	15,036,945	15,649,870	15,769,012	15,827,582	16,633,446	17,130,131
MR	22,823,238	23,908,879	22,656,221	23,801,976	32,509,770	31,943,494	33,376,744	36,876,222
NER	39,715,285	41,251,796	39,821,678	40,909,004	42,023,323	42,802,618	44,162,749	46,578,227
Eng/Wales	248,801,147	256,895,900	249,050,148	267,803,622	290,834,210	295,472,057	302,269,540	322,454,801
CR	21,444,564	22,274,954	21,954,579	22,989,997	23,084,470	23,168,910	23,772,626	24,898,850
NBR	17,565,004	18,382,418	18,143,268	19,803,579	20,017,590	20,958,899	21,942,895	22,823,790
Scotland	47,979,707	47,979,707	47,405,397	50,600,790	50,976,134	52,152,430	53,845,739	56,173,230

	1907	1908	1909	1910	1911	1912
GNR	16,242,446	15,899,163	15,540,782	16,307,010	16,557,754	16,702,654
GWR	41,610,812	42,484,783	43,981,815	44,700,004	44,927,244	44,302,418
LNWR	44,322,200	41,954,424	42,056,820	43,383,866	43,699,795	43,141,667
LYR	18,777,318	18,039,188	18,399,516	18,776,870	18,930,386	18,468,593
MR	40,518,789	38,033,415	39,410,363	41,351,036	41,780,500	40,978,344
NER	49,695,440	48,072,870	49,457,176	48,914,902	51,064,551	47,713,503
Eng/Wales	346,597,290	330,894,917	337,605,590	346,351,345	350,233,463	344,439,202
CR	25,033,212	23,186,226	22,614,627	21,737,730	21,700,902	20,590,593
NBR	23,246,384	22,179,570	23,009,468	24,406,330	24,991,466	23,923,852
Scotland	56,504,327	53,143,573	53,246,004	54,088,802	54,850,007	52,437,56

Appendix Two - Annual Production of Eight-coupled Coal Engines

No. 2524

Date	Number built	Total in Service
1892	1	1

Class 'A'

Date	Number built	Total in Service
1893	1	1
1894	4	5
1895	6	11
1896	20	31
1897	19	50
1898	31	81
1899	20	101
1900	10	111

Class 'B'

Date	Number built	Total in Service
1901	15	15
1902	65	80
1903	60	140
1904	30	170

Class 'G'

Date	Number built	Total in Service
1910	60	60

Class 'G1'

Date	Number built	Total in Service
1912	46	46
1913	24	70
1914	30	100
1915	0	100
1916	10	110
1917	10	120
1918	50	170

Class 'G2'

Date	Number built	Total in Service
1921	50	50
1922	10	60

0-8-2 Tank

Date	Number built	Total in Service
1911	3	3
1912	7	10
1913	0	10
1914	0	10
1915	10	20
1916	0	20
1917	10	30

0-8-4 Tank

Date	Number built	Total in Service
1923	29	29
1924	1	30

Appendix Three - Boilers built by the LMS

The following table gives details of new boilers built by the LMS for LNWR eight-coupled engines. The date given, up to order BS1.544, is the date when the order was placed and thereafter the date the boilers were built.

Abbreviations:

Sat - saturated
Sup - superheated
VF - Vuklcan Foundry
RT - round top
Belp - Belpaire

Date	Account No.	No.	Details
26.4.1923	S.469	10	Sat,'D'
26.4.1923	S.470	5	Sat,'C'and'C1'
26.4.1923	S.471	10	Sup,'G2',RT
26.4.1923	S.472	10	Sup,'G2',RT
23.1.1924	S.490	10	Sup,Belp
23.1.1924	S.491	10	Sup,Belp
23.1.1924	S.492	10	Sup,Belp
23.1.1924	S.493	10	Sup,Belp
23.1.1924	S.494	10	Sup,Belp
11.3.1924	S.495	50	Sup,Belp,exVulcanFoundry
31.3.1927	S1.539	5	Sat,'G',RT
31.3.1927	S1.540	10	Sat,'D',cancelled
31.3.1927	S1.544	60	Sup,'G1',Belp
6.1928	S5.22851	10	Sat,'G',RT
9.1928	S5.22854	10	Sup,'G2',Belp
10.1928	S40.29267	5	Sup,'G2',Belp
10.1928	S40.29268	5	Sup,'G2',Belp
10.1928	S40.29270	5	Sup,'G2',Belp
8.1930	S40.97115	5	Sat,'G',RT

Date	Account No.	No.	Details
6.1931	S40.97116	5	Sat,'D',RT
4.1931	S40.97121	5	'G1/G2',Belp
1.1932	S40.19826	5	'G1/G2',Belp
2.1932	S40.19827	5	'G1/G2',Belp
9-10.1932	S40.75833	5	'G1/G2',Belp
2-3.1933	S40.93708	25	'G1/G2',Belp
8-11.1933	S40.7099	25	'G1/G2',Belp
1-3.1934	S40.17740	25	'G1/G2',Belp
5-7.1934	S40.21822	25	'G1/G2',Belp
9.1934	BS1.1	15	'G1/G2',Belp
11.34-3.35	BS1.2	20	'G1/G2',Belp
8.35-7.36	BS1.10	29	'G1/G2',Belp
9.36-4.37	BS1.19	21	'G1/G2',Belp
9.1937	BS1.22	25	'G1/G2',Belp
8.1938	BS1.26	13	'G1/G2',Belp
10.1938	BS1.27	15	'G1/G2',Belp
12.38-8.39	BS1.28	15	'G1/G2',Belp
4-5.1940	BS1.41	12	'G1/G2',Belp
12.41-1.42	BS1.45	10	'G1/G2',Belp
6.1943	BS1.55	7	'G1/G2',Belp
11.1943	BS1.58	10	'G1/G2',Belp
9.1944	BS1.61	10	'G1/G2',Belp

In the 1945 programme 30 boilers ordered under No.BS1.64 were not built and 10 more ordered later under BS1.71 were deferred and later cancelled. Thus, the last LNWR boilers were built in 1944, making a total of 597 boilers built by the LMS for LNWR eight-coupled engines.

Appendix Four - Classification of Engines 1915

During the First World War an enormous increase in goods traffic took place, causing all the railway companies serious difficulties. As a result, the LNWR put into effect a number of measures to improve its goods operations. A control system was introduced and, perhaps as part of it, a classification system for goods engines came into use in late 1915 or early 1916. (A classification system had been introduced for passenger engines in 1913, when the tonnage system had been adopted.)

Engines were grouped according to haulage capacity and allocated to one of six power classes, the most powerful being numbered 1 and the least 6. The number was painted on the frames of the engine over the life guard (see Plate 97). Maximum loads were laid down for each power class over the various sections of line, and were published in the *Appendix* for the guidance of operating staff. They were to be applied only in normal conditions and good weather. In bad weather they were to be reduced by consultation between drivers and traffic staff. In determining these loads, factors such as gradient, braking capacity, length of loops and so forth were all presumably taken into account.

General maximum loads, including brake van, were laid down as follows: class 5 engines 525 tons of mineral and 400 tons of goods; class 4 engines 600 tons of mineral and 500 tons of goods; and class 1 engines 825 tons of mineral and 600 tons of goods. These loads were laid down 'for main line and branches except as specified below'. There then followed some 30 pages covering virtually the whole system.

For instance, over certain sections of line the load for mineral traffic was varied as follows:

675 tons between Stafford and Tring.
825 tons between Tring and Willesden.
250 tons on the West London line.
420 tons between Nottingham and Northampton.
160 tons between Harborne and Rotton Park Road.

On some lines there was a limit on the maximum number of wagons that could be taken on one train and in some cases this even varied with the time of day and the day of the week. For example, on Saturday nights and Sundays empty wagon trains with large engines and 20-ton brake vans between Camden and Stafford could be made up to 79 wagons (otherwise the load was 70 wagons). From time to time, of course, in subsequent issues of both the *Appendix* and working timetables, loads were altered for certain lines and for certain classes.

The list of engine classes in each power group as set out in the April 1916 *Appendix* is reproduced below and has some interesting as well as puzzling features. Firstly, there is the phrase '20½in D or superheater goods'. The '20½in D' class presumably refers to what is more strictly described as the 'G' class, since the 'D' class proper had 18½in cylinders, and shows the widespread use of the term 'D' class. It was only a small step to extend this term to 'Superheated D' class, referring to the 'G1' class., leading to the term 'Super D'. Presumably again, the description '19½in large boiler' refers to class 'D', though the latter had 18½in cyls, '19½in small boiler' refers to class 'C' and '18½in' to class 'C1'. In the April 1916 *Appendix*, the Whale 0-8-2 tanks, '4ft 3in 8 wheel coupled shunting engine', were added to class 1.

Classification Engine		*Maximum Loads*
1*	20½in D or superheater goods	The Appendix maximum for the 4-cylinder compound 8-wheels coupled coal engine to apply.
2	4-cylinder - large boiler 19½in - large boiler 4-cylinder - small boiler 19½in - small boiler	
	* With the 20½in class, the Appendix maximum loading over some sections of the line has been increased and must continue to be worked to.	
3	19 inch cylinder 18½in cylinder 'Experiment' passenger 'Prince of Wales' class 6-wheels coupled superheater tank 6-wheels coupled non-superheater tank	Five wagons less than the Appendix maximum laid down for the 4-cylinder compound 8-wheels coupled coal engine.
4	18 inch cylinder - goods 18 inch side tank Small coal '1400' class 'Precursor' superheater 'Precursor' non-superheater 4-wheels coupled Precursor tank 'George the Fifth' class 'Queen Mary' class 4 feet 3 inches side tank coal 4 feet 3 inches special tank 4 feet 3 inches saddle tank	The appendix maximum load for 18 inch cylinder - or coal engine - to apply.
5	'DX' 'Jubilee' 'Benbow' 'Renown' 17 inch cylinder goods (converted 18 inch)	The appendix maximum for 'DX' engine to apply.
6	6 feet 6 inches 4-wheels coupled 6 feet 4-wheels coupled 5 feet 6 inches side tank	Five wagons less than the appendix maximum load for 'DX' engine to apply.

Class	1892	1893	1894	1895	1896	1897	1898	1899	1900	1901	1902	1903	1904	1905	1906	1907	1908	1909	1910	1911
2524	1	1	1	1	1	1	1	1	1	1	1	1	1	1						
'A'		1	5	11	31	50	81	101	111	111	111	111	110	98	86	61	38	23	11	3
'B'										20	80	140	166	162	144	136	127	121	109	108
'C'													1	13	15	15	15	15	15	15
'C1'																		11	23	31
'D'													4	8	11	36	59	63	63	63
'E'															22	23	24	24	24	24
'F'															3	9	12	12	12	12
'G'															1	2	7	13	85	86
'G1'																				
'G2'																				
'G2A'																				
0-8-2T																				3
0-8-4T																				
'MM'																				

Class	1912	1913	1914	1915	1916	1917	1918	1919	1920	1921	1922	1923	1924	1925	1926	1927	1928	1929	1930	1931
'A'																				
'B'	108	107	106	104	103	99	94	88	86	71	57	35	21	16	12	6	6	6	1	1
'C'	15	15	15	15	15	15	15	15	15	15	15	15	15	14	11	6				
'C1'	34	34	34	34	34	34	34	34	34	34	34	34	34	34	34	29	25	24	8	8
'D'	63	63	63	63	63	63	63	63	63	63	63	62	61	57	51	45	28	25	14	12
'E'	24	24	24	24	24	24	21	20	18	13	12	8	6	6	6	5				
'F'	12	12	12	12	12	12	12	12	12	9	6	3	3	2	2	1				
'G'	85	86	87	89	90	91	91	91	89	89	89	87	82	76	73	55	46	40	34	27
'G1'	47	71	101	101	111	126	182	189	195	218	235	267	289	306	322	349	385	384	401	410
'G2'													60	60	60	60	60	60	60	60
'G2A'																				
0-8-2T	20	20	20	20	20	20	30	30	30	30	30	29	30	30	30	30	30	30	30	30
0-8-4T	30	30	30	30	30	30	30	30	30	30	30	30	30	30	30	38	49	38	32	15
'MM'	1															60				

Class	1932	1933	1934	1935	1936	1937	1938	1939	1940	1941	1942	1943	1944	1945	1946	1947	1948	1949	1950	1951
'A'																				
'B'																				
'C'																				
'C1'	1																			
'D'	9	6	2	2	2															
'E'																				
'F'																				
'G'	21	16	10	7	3															
'G1'	419	427	437	435	439	444	412	332	249	217	202	192	179	172	152	123	85	48	25	14
'G2'	60	60	60	60	60	60	60	60	60	60	60	60	60	60	60	60	60	60	60	60
'G2A'						5	37	117	200	232	248	257	270	277	297	319	319	271	240	220
0-8-2T	30	30	26	21	19	18	18	16	16	16	16	16	16	15	11	9	5	5	3	1
0-8-4T	30	30	30	30	30	30	30	30	30	30	30	30	28	26	16	14	7	4	1	
'MM'	1																			

Class	1952	1953	1954	1955	1956	1957	1958	1959	1960	1961	1962	1963	1964
'G1'	5	2	1										
'G2'	60	60	60	60	60	60	60	41	41	26	6	3	
'G2A'	214	214	211	211	206	166	153	96	91	62	3	3	
0-8-2T	1												
0-8-4T													

Appendix Six - Allocations

The following list shows the allocations of eight-coupled coal engines at various dates. Those for 1912 and 1917 are complete but those for 1913 are for a few sheds only. Those for 1928 are the LMS block allocations, which were issued in January and February 1928. Sheds are listed roughly in LNWR order but shed codes are not given, as they were changed at different times, especially in the BR period.

Willesden

1912

'G1'	674, 1384, 1697, 1698, 1783, 1791, 2018, 2104, 2254, 2337, 2345, 2385, 2393
'G'	1122, 1507, 1577, 1637, 1727, 1735
'D'	2539
'C'	2550
0-8-2 Tank	1592

October 1917

'G1'	43, 326, 633, 734, 1128, 1192, 1343, 1655, 1746, 1783, 1791, 2018, 2195, 2284, 2337, 2378, 2380, 2393, 2421
'C1'	1849, 2549
'B'	1241
0-8-2 Tank	736, 1514, 1515, 1592

1928

'G2'	9395-9417 (jointly with Watford)
'G1'	9159-73
'G'	9072, 9077-8
'C'	8960
0-8-2 Tank	7878-82

1933

'G2'	9395-9401, 9407-12, 9416-7
'G1'	9020, 9072, 9077-8, 9110, 9128, 9146, 9161-9, 9180, 9356, 9373, 9380
'G'	9105, 9127, 9129, 9143
'C1'	8969, 8973, 8976, 8978, 8991
0-8-2 Tank	7836

1945

'G2'	9448, 9453-4
'G2A'	8943, 8953, 9003, 9021, 9041, 9062, 9139, 9163-4, 9300, 9393 'G1' 9012, 9128, 9196, 9272, 9277, 9297, 9334

1950

'G2'	49413
'G2A'	49070, 49078, 49122, 49164, 49277, 49344

Watford

1928

'G2'	9395-9417 (jointly with Willesden)
'C'	8957-9

1945

'G2A'	8964, 9145, 9262, 9323

1950

'G2'	48915, 49145, 49157, 49323, 49375, 49393

Bletchley

1912

'G'	1619
'D'	1813, 1842
'C'	1840, 1858, 1861, 2531, 2555

October 1917

'G'	1775
'C1'	1838, 1869, 2529, 2544, 2550, 2554
'E'	1017
'B'	826, 1035, 1110, 1226

1928

'G1'	8915, 8917-8, 9057, 9060, 9064-6
'D'	9059, 9061-3

1933

'G2'	9403-6, 9413, 9431
'G1'	8915, 8917-8, 9043, 9049, 9053, 9158-9, 9190, 9364

1945

'G2'	9403, 9406, 9409, 9416, 9427
'G2A'	8925, 8952, 9005, 9007, 9064, 9127
'G1'	8894, 8913, 8931, 8935, 9056, 9076, 9100, 9138, 9173, 9175, 9179, 9193, 9201, 9208, 9213, 9332, 9350

1950

'G2'	49406, 49417, 49427, 49443, 49448
'G2A'	48951-3, 48964, 49005, 49007, 49014, 49049, 49061, 49070 49088, 49144, 49154-5, 49173, 49287-9, 49292

1959

'G2'	49403, 49443, 49450
'G2A'	48898, 48951, 48953, 49061, 49093, 49094, 49287, 49289, 49310

Nuneaton

1912

'G1'	1162, 2001, 2015
'D'	1805, 1814, 2541, 2549
'C'	1849, 1867
'E'	1017, 1064, 1883
'B'	1041, 1242, 1547
0-8-2 Tank	1494

October 1917

'G1'	1778, 2033, 2091, 2258
'G'	1190, 1619, 2014
'D'	1810, 1814, 1815, 1823, 1900
'E'	18, 437, 1065
'B'	1043, 1047
0-8-2 Tank	1090

1928

'G2'	9418-29
'G1'	8926-7, 8929, 9226-8, 9343-52
0-8-2 Tank	7887

1933

'G2'	9432-8
'G1'	9112, 9300, 9342-6, 9348-52
0-8-2 Tank	7878

1945

'G2'	9400, 9412, 9428-30, 9432, 9434, 9437-9
'G2A'	8954, 9068, 9080, 9082, 9114, 9150, 9181, 9264, 9268, 9276, 9318, 9342, 9345, 9351-2, 9366
'G1'	8911, 8962, 9167, 9190-1, 9346

1950

'G2'	49396-7, 49414, 49418, 49424, 49429, 49432, 49434-6, 49451, 49453
'G2A'	48927, 49068, 49181, 49186, 49304, 49318, 49339, 49350, 49368, 49385

1959

'G2'	49414-5, 49425, 49430-2, 49440-1
'G2A'	48927, 49002, 49112, 49120, 49142, 49144, 49181, 49270, 49293, 49314, 49342, 49350

Northampton

1912

'G'	1286, 2661
'D'	1868, 2537

October 1917
'G1'   2289
'D'   1806, 1831, 1851

1928
'G1'   9331-42

1933
'G2'   9402, 9414-5, 9418, 9422, 9426, 9439, 9443-5, 9454
'G1'   9181, 9333-41, 9353-4

1945
'G2'   9395, 9401-2, 9414, 9426, 9440, 9444
'G2A'   8896, 8914, 8936, 9042, 9104, 9153, 9157-8, 9169,
            9203, 9205, 9249, 9270, 9271, 9291, 9321
'G1'   8929, 9103, 9324, 9391

1950
'G2A'   48914, 48936, 49153, 49203, 49270-1, 49321, 49357,
            49366

1959
'G2A'   49105

Bescot
1912
'G1'   2119, 2284
'G'   1411
'D'   1807, 2540
'C'   1852, 1859
'E'   2563
'B'   815, 1040

31st May 1913
'G1'   2119, 2284
'G'   2662
'D'   1853, 2540
'C'   1807
'C1'   1801, 1852
'E'   2563
'B'   1040, 1088

October 1917
'G'   1507, 1639, 1660, 2661
'D'   1825, 1832, 1833, 1835, 2546
'F'   2114
'E'   1042
'B'   134, 1242, 1285, 1555, 1890, 2080, 2567, 2571
0-8-2 Tank 58, 2341

1928
'G2'   9451-4
'G1'   9174-81
'G'   9102, 9105, 9127-30, 9134, 9136
'D'   9009-10, 9012, 9017-8, 9020, 9023-5, 9028, 9032-3,
            9035-42, 9045, 9047, 9056, 9058
0-8-2 Tank 7885-6

1933
'G2'   9423-5, 9428
'G1'   8892, 8912, 9012, 9015-6, 9023, 9025, 9028, 9032,
            9035-7, 9041-2, 9045, 9047, 9061, 9063, 9089, 9108,
            9173-4, 9176, 9179, 9201, 9372, 9374-5
'G'   9102
'D'   9017, 9038-40, 9056, 9062
0-8-2 Tank 7885-6

1945
'G2'   9425, 9431
'G2A'   8909, 9006, 9022, 9025, 9039, 9078, 9083-4, 9089,
            9096-7, 9106, 9177, 9180, 9211, 9245, 9265, 9294,
            9301, 9308, 9313, 9328, 9335, 9361, 9372
'G1'   8917, 9063, 9081, 9131, 9142, 9160, 9165, 9189, 9195,
            9202, 9259, 9274, 9279, 9282, 9286, 9354, 9367, 9371,
            9374
1950
'G2A'   48905, 48907, 48917, 48950, 49009, 49022, 49025,

            49045, 49063, 49077, 49081, 49089, 49093, 49096,
            49099, 49106, 49114, 49142, 49180, 49189, 49202,
            49216, 49223, 49245-6, 49265-6, 49282, 49308, 49313,
            49327-8, 49354, 49361, 49367
'G1'   49071, 49334, 49359, 49371

1959
'G2A'   48930, 48964, 49021, 49045, 49063, 49077, 49099,
            49106, 49114, 49125, 49216, 49246, 49275, 49278,
            49308, 49313, 49327, 49328, 49343, 49361, 49373,
            49387

Netherfield and Colwick
1912
'G1'   1633, 1655, 1696
'G'   898, 1380, 1424, 1634, 1895, 2656, 2660
'B'   904, 1237, 1882

October 1917
'G1'   1426, 1633, 2117, 2162, 2225
'G'   1385, 1403, 1497, 1648, 1699
'D'   1277

1928
'G2'   9443-50
'G1'   9370-5

1933
'G2'   9446-53

Rugby
1912
'G1'   1329, 1426, 1568, 1790
'G'   1035, 1229, 1403, 1540, 1591, 1609, 1699, 1774, 1775,
            2659
'D'   2538
'C'   1826, 2535, 2545
'E'   352, 1236, 1886
0-8-2 Tank 1185

October 1917
'G1'   93, 138, 328, 669, 670, 1314, 1384, 1696, 1698, 2034,
            2245, 2254, 2349, 2374, 2385, 2452, 2653
'G'   1687, 1690, 1788, 2566
'D'   1830
'B'   1274
0-8-2 Tank 1494

1928
'G2'   9418-29
'G1'   9260-79
0-8-2 Tank 7891

1933
'G2'   9427, 9429-30
'G1'   8920-2, 8924-6, 8943, 9083, 9260-70, 9272-3

1945
'G2'   9397-9, 9404, 9408, 9410, 9415, 9418,
'G2A'   8895, 9004, 9034, 9061, 9137, 9319, 9336, 9344, 9368
'G1'   8892, 8901, 8915, 8934, 9013, 9049, 9107, 9133, 9152,
            9162, 9229, 9337
1950
'G2'   9398, 49408, 49411, 49413, 49415-6, 49423, 49431,
            49433, 49447, 49452
'G2A'   49392

1959
'G2'   49442
'G2A'   49245, 49266, 49377

Coventry
1928
'D'   9052-5
1945
'G2A'   9278
'G1'   8926, 9135, 9200, 9253, 9340

1950
'G2'   49405, 49441-2, 49444, 49446
'G2A'   49330

Market Harborough
1959
'G2'   49444, 49447

Peterborough
1912
'D'   1860

October 1917
'D'   1817, 2524
'C1'   2531

Warwick
1912
'G'   1503
'D'   1823
'B'   1894

October 1917
'G'   1411, 1539
'D'   1878

1928
'G1'   8920-2, 8924, 8925

1945
'G2A'   8897, 8910, 8922, 8924, 9384

1950
'G2'   49430

Walsall
October 1917
'C1'   1852

1928
'G'   9080-1, 9083-4, 9086, 9088-91

1933
'G1'   9024, 9081, 9084, 9088, 9134
'G'   9068, 9080, 9090

1945
'G2A'   9048, 9174, 9266, 9325
'G1'   8902, 9015, 9040, 9222, 9232, 9248, 9283, 9364

1950
'G2'   49401
'G2A'   49031, 49048, 49066, 49258, 49300, 49322, 49373,
              49388
'G1'   49171, 49193, 49208, 49213, 49222, 49326, 49364

Aston
1912
'C'   1835

2nd July 1913
'C'   1805

October 1917
'D'   1867

1928
'G1'   9198-9201
1933
'G1'   9054, 9199, 9200, 9302

1945
'G2'   9423
'G2A'   9036, 9099, 9327
'G1'   9017, 9050, 9309, 9359, 9362

1950
'G1'   49017, 49140, 49261, 49370

Monument Lane
1912
'C'   2534

2nd July 1913
'B'   916

Burton
October 1917
'C1'   1826, 1859, 2543

Bushbury
1912
'D'   1838
'B'   916

31st May 1913
'D'   1838

October 1917
'B'   2565

1928
'G1'   9202-8

1933
'G1'   9202, 9204-6, 9228, 9233
1945
'G2A'   9110
'G1'   9011, 9204, 9206, 9233, 9236, 9295, 9356

1950
'G2A'   48940, 49037, 49044, 49167, 49196, 49240
"G1'   48902, 49162, 49204, 49346

1959
'G2'   49411, 49452
'G2A'   48950, 49037, 49044, 49240

Stafford
1912
'G1'   2349
'D'   1873

October 1917
'G1'   1127, 1790

1928
'G1'   9011, 9019, 9021, 9022
0-8-2 Tank   7883-4
1933
'G1'   9019, 9021-2, 9239

1945
'G2A'   8940, 9031, 9113
'G1'   9091, 9098, 9144, 9194, 9320

1950
'G2'   49410
'G2A'   48922, 49047, 49115, 49158, 49229

1959
'G2'   49410, 49446
'G2A'   48943, 49081, 49115, 49126, 49198, 49357

Crewe South
1912
'G1'   1505, 2653
'G'   1401, 1900, 2032
'D'   1802, 1812, 1818, 1819, 1839, 1854, 1863, 1864, 2525,
              2537
'C'   2533
'F'   2570
'B'   410, 1066, 1272, 1285, 1881, 2118, 2564
0-8-2 Tank   289

October 1917
'G1'   62, 107, 767, 942, 982, 1528, 1697, 2015, 2119, 2156,
            2201, 2224, 2237, 2246, 2336
'G'   2657, 2662
'D'   1803, 1808, 1864, 1882, 2537
'B'   41, 405, 1040, 1055, 1224, 1233, 2561
0-8-2 Tank 92, 714, 1124

1928
'MM'   9650, 9652-4, 9656
'G1'   9229-52
'D'   9048-51

1933
'G1'   9203, 9231-2, 9234-7, 9241-3, 9245-7, 9249-50, 9274-6,
            9278

1945
'G2'   9396, 9445
'G2A'   9027, 9146, 9198, 9209, 9296, 9357
'G1'   8906, 9210, 9230, 9241, 9263, 9349

1950
'G2'   49407
'G2A'   49210, 49230, 49319

1959
'G2'   49407, 49417, 49454
'G2A'   48922, 49048, 49158, 49229

Longsight

1912
'G'   1228, 1647, 1660
'B'   842, 2060, 2272

October 1917
'G'   1370, 1647, 2659
'D'   509, 898, 1840, 1858
'C1'   1855, 2535, 2555
'B'   815

1928
'G1'   9280-7

1933
'G1'   9283-7

1945
'G2A'   9002, 9010, 9226, 9238, 9284, 9298, 9343, 9363
'G1'   9108, 9156, 9171, 9183, 9187, 9285, 9380

1950
'G2'   49428, 49439

1959
'G2A'   49428, 49439

Buxton

1912
'G'   1385, 1606
'D'   1879
'B'   1094, 2080

October 1917
'G'   508, 1280, 1380, 1634
1928
'G1'   9209-25
0-8-2 Tank 7896-9

1933
'G1'   9212-27
0-8-2 Tank 7896-9
1945
'G2A'   9009, 9093, 9132, 9212, 9214, 9216, 9220, 9224, 9240,
            9315-6, 9331, 9347, 9376, 9386
'G1'   9059, 9140, 9166, 9221, 9225, 9326
0-8-4 Tank 7936, 7954

1950
'G2'   49450, 49454
'G2A'   49057, 49132, 49214, 49347-8, 49387

1959
'G2'   49395, 49400, 49423
'G2A'   48932, 49210, 49281, 49348, 49391

Lees

1912
'G'   1299, 1556, 2014
'D'   1865
10th July 1913
'G'   1354, 2569

October 1917
'D'   1271, 1820, 1887
'B'   1066, 1281

1928
'G1'   9288-92

1933
'G1'   9288-92, 9297

Stockport

1912
'G'   1492, 1775, 1788, 1794, 2251
'D'   1827, 1832, 1877, 2544
'F'   1036
'B'   1039

October 1917
'G'   1582, 1664, 2552
'D'   503, 1804, 1843, 1868, 1891
0-8-2 Tank 1163

1928
'G1'   9182-7
'G'   9092, 9095-8

1933
'G1'   8939, 9092, 9095, 9182-7, 9279, 9369-70
1945
'G2A'   9044, 9111, 9184-6
'G1'   9043, 9054, 9092, 9227, 9305, 9369-70

1950
'G2A'   49002, 49010, 49108, 49281
'G1'   49098, 49156, 49187

1959
'G2'   49418, 49453
'G2A'   49010, 49191

Farnley and Wortley

1912
'G'   1274
'D'   1803, 1822, 1836, 1848, 1856, 1866, 1871, 1878, 2528,
            2530, 2532
'C'   1862
'E'   437
'B'   1047
October 1917
'G1'   108, 131, 170, 175, 176, 203, 329, 885, 965, 1142, 1181,
            1214, 1485, 1500, 2200, 2301
'G'   1401, 1556
'D'   1854, 1857, 1865, 1876, 1893, 2526
'B'   2118

1928
'G1'   8962, 8964, 8966, 9376-94, 9600, 9604, 9607, 9609,
            9610, 9612, 9613
'C'   8961, 8963

1933
'G1'   8933-5, 8964, 8966, 9013, 9018, 9052, 9055, 9106,

9123, 9297, 9377-9, 9381-3, 9385-7, 9389-94

1945
‘G2A’   9055, 9217, 9223, 9288-90, 9292, 9377, 9379, 9381-2,
9389
9390, 9392, 9394

Birkenhead

1912
‘D’   1828
‘C’   1829, 1850

26th October 1913
‘D’   2553
‘C1’   1809, 1829

1928
‘G1’   9194-7

1933
‘G1’   9194-7, 9376

1945
‘G2A’   9244, 9246, 9256, 9258, 9281
‘G1’   9267

Chester

October 1917
‘G’   1629, 1637

1933
‘G1’   9175, 9376

Huddersfield

1912
‘G’   1789, 2566
‘D’   1820, 1834, 1837, 1845, 1874, 2553
‘E’   1585, 2056
‘B’   1226, 1249, 1288, 2038, 2575

2nd November 1913
‘G1’   670, 734
‘G’   1280, 1464, 1789, 2575
‘D’   1815, 1816, 1822, 1831, 1833
‘F’   906, 2573
‘B’   1224, 1436, 1899, 2575

October 1917
‘G1’   931
‘G’   1464, 1700, 2656
‘D’   1813, 1818, 1822, 1853, 2527
‘B’   813
0-8-2 Tank   1665

1928
‘G1’   9006-8, 9121-2, 9124-5, 9188-93
‘G’   9120, 9123, 9126
‘D’   9002-5
0-8-2 Tank   7888

1945
‘G2A’   9018, 9087, 9121-3, 9126, 9329,   9360, 9387

Bangor

1912
‘D’   1872
‘C’   1847, 1869, 2542
‘B’   2571

October 1917
‘F’   1369
‘B’   640, 1543

1928
‘MM’   9644-7, 9649

Holyhead

1923
‘G1’   1894, 2169

Carnarvon

October 1917
‘D’   1844

Warrington

1912
‘E’   2558
‘B’   1243, 1310, 1404, 1896, 2559

October 1917
‘G1’   351, 545, 2390
‘G’   2030
‘D’   2536, 2539
‘E’   905
‘B’   916, 1243, 1279, 1300

1928
‘G1’   9293-9303
‘D’   9013-6

1933
‘G1’   9137, 9171-2, 9293, 9295-6, 9298-9, 9301

1945
‘G2’   9411
‘G2A’   9008, 9085, 9101, 9168,
‘G1’   9075, 9136, 9178

1950
‘G2A’   49008, 49119, 49149, 49247

Peasley Cross (Sutton Oak)

1912
‘E’   1222
‘B’   1051, 1318, 2556, 2557
0-8-2 Tank   1163

October 1917
‘B’   1094, 1237, 1240, 1272, 1892
0-8-2 Tank   2348, 2391

1928
‘G’   9113-4, 9117-9

1933
‘G1’   9008, 9014, 9109, 9113, 9117, 9303
‘G’   9069, 9118

1945
‘G2A’   9312, 9317
‘G1’   8918, 9102, 9303

1950
‘G2A’   49205, 49262, 49312, 49377, 49389

1959
‘G2’   49448
‘G2A’   49262, 49288, 49304

Springs Branch

1912
‘G’   1070, 1462, 1539, 1570, 1578, 1582, 1600, 1664, 1687,
1690, 2030
‘D’   2548
‘C’   1817, 1844, 2546
‘B’   1240, 1241
10th October 1913
‘G’   898, 1385, 1403, 1690, 1700
‘D’   1836, 1838, 1868
‘C’   2549
‘C1’   1817, 1844, 1869, 2542

'F'	899
'B'	640, 918, 1370, 1896, 1898, 2024, 2567

October 1917
'G'	2569, 2654
'D'	818, 1122, 1816, 1836, 1850, 1895, 2532
'F'	647
'B'	1044, 1088, 1231, 1287, 1436
0-8-2 Tank	2277, 2294

1928
'G1'	9131-3, 9135, 9137, 9142, 9144, 9149, 9151, 9153-8
'G'	9138-41, 9143, 9145-8, 9150, 9152
0-8-2 Tank	7892-5

1933
'G1'	8908-9, 8911, 9002, 9096-8, 9131, 9139-40, 9142, 9149, 9152-7, 9178, 9281-2, 9365
'G'	9120, 9136, 9138, 9147-8, 9150
'D'	9048
0-8-2 Tank	7884, 7892-5

1945
'G2'	9422, 9424
'G2A'	8905, 8930, 8951, 9014, 9023-4, 9026, 9029, 9119, 9124-5, 9134, 9141, 9148-9, 9161, 9172, 9176, 9192, 9197, 9207, 9299, 9310-1
'G1'	9030, 9053, 9090, 9118, 9129, 9159, 9197, 9257

1950
'G2'	49402
'G2A'	48895, 48930, 49018, 49023, 49024, 49034, 49050, 49082, 49090, 49129, 49160, 49228, 49264, 49268, 49306, 49310, 49311, 49331, 49341, 49352, 49378, 49381, 49394
'G1'	49030, 49092
0-8-2 Tank	47877, 47881, 47884, 47896

1959
'G2'	49401-2, 49408, 49422, 49436, 49438
'G2A'	48895, 48905, 48915, 49007, 49009, 49018, 49020, 49023, 49025, 49049, 49079, 49129, 49139, 49150, 49154, 49155, 49160, 49203, 49228, 49267, 49268, 49311, 49321, 49352, 49378, 49381

Edge Hill
1912
'D'	1846
'E'	2114
'B'	134, 1110, 1300, 1555, 2369, 2496, 2562, 2567

26th October 1913
'G'	1411, 1449, 2654
'D'	1824, 1846, 1863, 2536
'F'	2114
'E'	1885
'B'	826, 1094, 1242, 1282, 1555, 2565

October 1917
'G1'	20, 48, 72, 99, 795, 1729, 2288, 2379
'G'	1353
'D'	1276, 1848, 1870, 1872, 1873
'E'	2558
'B'	1039, 1061, 1070, 2575
1928
'G1'	9353-64
0-8-4 Tank	7949-59

1933
'G1'	9115, 9135, 9193, 9280, 9355, 9357-9, 9361-3
0-8-2 Tank	7865, 7877, 7880, 7887, 7889, 7890-1
0-8-4 Tank	7943, 7949-55, 7957-9

1945
'G2'	9449
'G2A'	8898, 8908, 8927, 8933, 8966, 9016, 9130, 9155, 9237, 9239, 9242, 9287, 9333, 9355, 9385

0-8-2 Tank	7870, 7877, 7887
0-8-4 Tank	7930, 7934, 7938, 7943, 7946, 7949-51, 7953, 7957-9

1950
'G2'	49399, 49404, 49412, 49419, 49437, 49445, 49449
'G2A'	48898, 48932, 48933, 48943, 49126, 49137, 49224, 49239, 49301, 49355
0-8-4 Tank	47931, 47937, 47939

1959
'G2'	49399, 49404-5, 49412, 49416, 49419, 49427, 49429, 49434-5, 49437, 49445
'G2A'	49082, 49116, 49132, 49137, 49173, 49200, 49224, 49355, 49366, 49375, 49392, 49394

Preston
1912
'E'	1884
'B'	405, 918, 1282, 1432

October 1917
'G1'	1167
'B'	1404, 1448

1928
'G1'	9306-13

1933
'G2'	9419-21
'G1'	9306-13, 9366
1945
'G2'	9417, 9419-21, 9442, 9451
'G2A'	9219, 9348
'G1'	9231, 9250

1950
'G2A'	49104, 49134, 49141, 49150, 49191, 49200, 49267, 49382, 49390

1959
'G2'	49396
'G2A'	49104, 49141, 49196, 49382

Carnforth
1912
'G'	2655
'D'	1876
'E'	18, 1065, 1247
'B'	644, 1043, 1892, 2565

October 1917
'D'	1866
'F'	899
'B'	859, 918, 1041, 1225, 2056

1928
'G1'	9314-22, 9366-7

1933
'G1'	9151, 9314-22, 9327-30

1945
'G2A'	9109, 9117, 9154,
'G1'	9151, 9188, 9269, 9314, 9338
1950
'G2'	49438
'G2A'	49109, 49112, 49130
'G1'	49151, 49241

Tebay
1912
'D'	1808, 1825, 1830, 1870, 1880
'E'	1888
'B'	1248, 1289, 2387

October 1917
'D'	2547

'F'   1036
'E'   2169
'B'   1547

1928
'G1'   9323-30

1933
'G1'   9323-5

1945
'G2A'   9088, 9252, 9339

Oxenholme
1912
'B'   1224, 1276

October 1917
'B'   1230, 1284

Carlisle
October 1917
'G1'   1217, 2058

1928
'G1'   9255-9

1933
'G1'   9033, 9085

Salop (Shrewsbury)
1912
'G'   1322
'D'   1815, 1821, 1824, 2527, 2529, 2547
'C'   1841, 2534
'B'   640, 1230, 2561

October 1917
'D'   1819, 1827, 1880, 2540, 2548
'C1'   1861

1928
'MM'   9641-3
'G1'   8907-14, 9026-7, 9029-31, 9034, 9044, 9046
0-8-2 Tank   7889-90

1933
'G1'   8910, 8913-4, 8940, 9026, 9027, 9029-31, 9034, 9044,
             9046, 9058, 9141, 9144, 9145, 9198, 9238, 9332

1945
'G2'   9407, 9413
'G2A'   8945, 9019, 9028, 9035, 9037, 9046, 9069, 9116, 9143,
             9234, 9275, 9373, 9375

1950
'G2'   49440
'G2A'   48901, 48945, 49138, 49276

1959
'G2A'   49243

Abergavenny
1912
'G'   1245, 1639
'D'   1831

October 1917
'G1'   2094
'D'   1839

1928
'MM'   9635-40
'G1'   8930-4, 9615
0-8-4 Tank   7930-46

1933
'G1'   8899, 8929-34, 9011, 9229, 9230

0-8-4 Tank   7930-42, 7944-6, 7956

1945
'G2A'   8899, 8932, 8944, 9051, 9243, 9247, 9280, 9306, 9341,
             9388
0-8-4 Tank   7933, 7935, 7940, 7944-5

1950
'G2'   49403, 49409, 49422
'G2A'   48899, 48921, 49006, 49028, 49046, 49051, 49064,
             49113, 49121, 49146, 49161, 49168, 49174, 49226,
             49243, 49316, 49345

Tredegar
October 1917
'G1'   631

1945
0-8-4 Tank   7932, 7937, 7939

1950
'G2'   49409
'G2A'   49064

Blaenavon
October 1917
0-8-2 Tank   289, 482, 2013

Swansea
1912
'G'   1190
'D'   2526
October 1917
0-8-2 Tank   563

1928
'G1'   8943-5, 8948, 8950-4, 9304-5, 9365
0-8-2 Tank   7870
0-8-4 Tank   7947-8

1933
'G1'   8944-5, 8948, 8950-4, 9133, 9304-5
0-8-2 Tank   7870, 7881
0-8-4 Tank   7947-8

1945
'G2A'   8893, 8948, 9033, 9260, 9358
0-8-4 Tank   7931, 7941, 7948, 7956

1950
'G2A'   48893, 49033, 49035, 49148, 49177, 49260, 49358,
             49376

Patricroft
1912
'F'   1273
'E'   1223, 1586
'B'   1448

14th April 1913
'E'   1586
'B'   813, 1284, 1448
October 1917
'D'   1849, 1899
0-8-2 Tank   24

1928
'G1'   8901-6, 9253-4
0-8-2 Tank   7871-4

1933
'G1'   8901-7, 9103, 9130, 9252-5, 9331
0-8-2 Tank   7871, 7873-4
1945
'G2'   9405
'G2A'   8903, 8912, 8920, 8941, 9085, 9273, 9304, 9330
'G1'   9199, 9254, 9255, 9353

1950
'G2'   49400, 49421, 49426
'G2A'   48920, 48926, 49027, 49087, 49094, 49178, 49199, 49209, 49234, 49254, 49335, 49340, 49386

1959
'G2'   49421, 49426
'G2A'   48926, 49027, 49034, 49087, 49119, 49147, 49149, 49199, 49209, 49234, 49249, 49323, 49335, 49340, 49386

Plodder Lane
1912
'B'   41, 500, 859, 1044, 1091, 1278, 1279, 1283, 2057, 2568
October 1917
'D'   1856
'B'   842, 2060, 2272

1933
'G1'   9086
'D'   9009,

1945
'G2A'   9147, 9378

1950
'G2A'   49205, 49262, 49312, 49377, 49389

Speke Junction
1912
'D'   1843
'F'   647, 1369
'E'   1042
'B'   1055, 1308, 1370, 1890, 2024
0-8-2 Tank 1548, 1659, 1663, 1665

October 1917
'G'   1591
'D'   1877
'F'   1247, 2573
'B'   410, 644, 904, 2496
0-8-2 Tank 1185, 1291, 1659, 1663, 2105

1928
'G1'   9082, 9085, 9087, 9093-4, 9099, 9100-1, 9103-4, 9015-6, 9368
'G'   9106-12
0-8-2 Tank 7875-7

1933
'G1'   9057, 9059, 9064-6, 9091, 9093-4, 9099, 9101, 9104, 9107, 9111, 9189, 9371
0-8-2 Tank 7872, 7875-6, 7879, 7882-3

1945
'G2'   9447
'G2A'   8942, 9057, 9065-6, 9070, 9086, 9094, 9293, 9365
'G1'   8904, 9032, 9060, 9215, 9218, 9302
0-8-2 Tank 7875, 7881, 7886, 7891, 7897-8
1950
'G2'   49395, 49420
'G2A   48942, 48944, 49074, 49105, 49120, 49125, 49143, 49172, 49212, 49218, 49219, 49244, 49249, 49253, 49293, 49302

1959
'G2'   49397-8, 49406, 49420, 49424, 49433, 49451
'G2A'   48942, 48944, 49008, 49134, 49143, 49153, 49306

Widnes
1912
'B'   641, 1233, 1353, 2560

26th October 1913
'D'   1843
'F'   647, 1038, 1247
'E'   1884
'B'   843, 1055, 1249, 1308, 1890

October 1917
'B'   1898, 2057

1928
'G1'   9067, 9071, 9073-6, 9079, 9369
'G'   9068-70
1933
'G1'   9060, 9067, 9071, 9073-6, 9079, 9082, 9116, 9170

1945
'G2A'   9020, 9073-4, 9079, 9170,
'G1'   8907, 8939, 9038, 9058, 9067, 9071, 9307

1950
'G2A'   49020, 49073, 49079, 49116, 49343

Mold Junction
1912
'E'   1889
'B'   1231, 1277, 1436, 1543

1928
'MM'   9626-34
'G1'   8935-6, 8939-42

1933
'MM'   9460, 9462
'G1'   8936, 8941-2, 9051, 9100, 9132, 9256-9, 9294
'G'   9070

1945
'G2A'   8950, 9047, 9072, 9077, 9105, 9112, 9115, 9120, 9228, 9235, 9322
'G1'   9052, 9182, 9251, 9261, 9383

1950
'G2A'   49278

Llandudno Junction
1912
'E'   2574

October 1917
'E'   1885
'B'   1897

1928
'MM'   9616-25

1933
'G1'   9160, 9240, 9248, 9277, 9367-8

Stoke on Trent
1933
'G1'   9010, 9326, 9347, 9384, 9388

Newton Heath
1933
'G1'   8962, 9191-2, 9271

Wellingborough
1945
'G2'   9438, 9443

Appendix Seven - Engine History Lists

The columns in the following lists show:

No.	the engine number in the LNWR capital list.
Plate date	the building date as stamped on the regulator quadrant or shown on the engine number plate.
Date to stock	the date when the engine went into stock as shown in the company's official records.
Motion No.	the Crewe Works motion number.
Rebuilt to	details of any rebuilding to other classes with dates.
LMS No.	the LMS number and date of renumbering.
LG	the date of alteration to suit the LMS composite loading gauge.
BF	the date of first fitting with a Belpaire firebox.
VB	the date of fitting with vacuum brakes.
IBP	the date of fitting with 'improved brake power'.
BR No.	the British Railways number and the date of renumbering.
Wdn	the date of withdrawal from stock.
Scrap	the date when breaking up was completed, as shown in works records or the date when the engine was sold for scrap.

Numbers allotted but never carried are shown in brackets. Dates are calendar dates except for those prefixed 'p', which are LMS four-weekly period dates. The dates of alteration to suit the LMS loading gauge and the date of fitting of Belpaire fireboxes are incomplete (many engines had round-top boilers replaced by Belpaire boilers, replaced by round-top boilers, and so on, so that full details, even if available, would be extremely lengthy) but the dates of fitting of vacuum brakes and of improved brake power are complete. All engines were scrapped at Crewe Works, except those marked with a suffix as follows:

(1)	sold to J. Cashmore, Great Bridge
(2)	sold to Central Wagon Company, Ince, Wigan
(3)	sold to Maden & McKee, Stanley, Liverpool
(4)	sold to G. H. Campbell, Airdrie
(5)	sold to T. W. Ward, Killamarsh
(6)	sold to W. & F. Smith, Ecclesfield East
(7)	sold to R. S. Hayes, Bridgend
(8)	sold to A. Loom, Spondon, Derby
(9)	scrapped at Horwich Works
(10)	scrapped at Rugby Works

No. 2524

No.	Plate date	Date to stock	Motion No	Rebuilt to Class Date		LMS No.	Date	LG	BF	VB	IBP	BR No.	Date	Wdn	Scrap
2524	10.92	10.92	3364	D	12.06										
				G	18.25	9011	6.27	1.33	1.33	1.33	1.33	49011	11.48	12.49	6.1.50 (3)

Class 'A'

No.	Plate date	Date to stock	Motion No	Rebuilt to Class Date		LMS No.	Date	LG	BF	VB	IBP	BR No.	Date	Wdn	Scrap
50	9.93	9.93	3471	D	7.06										
	2525		7.94	G1	3.24	9008	11.27	.38	12.32	12.32					
				G2A	8.43							49008	4.48	12.62	22.2.63
2526	11.94	11.94	3546	D	3.08	9043	2.28	12.35							
				G1	2.28							49043	5.48	9.49	30.9.49
2527	11.94	11.94	3547	D	7.08	9051	7.27								
				G1	p5.30	5.30	5.30								
				G2A	8.39							49051	12.51	2.57	8.3.57
2528	11.94	11.94	3548	D	7.07	9027	12.26		10.28	12.26	12.26				
				G1	12.26										
				G2A	p12.40							49027	4.50	11.59	24.1159

No.	Plate date	Date to stock	Motion No	Class	Date	LMS No.	Date	LG	BF	VB	IBP	BR No.	Date	Wdn	Scrap
2529	11.94	11.94	3549	C	3.05										
				G1	1.25	8954	9.27		1.25	1.25	1.25				
				G2A	p12.40				.34			(48954)		6.49	12.8.49
2530	2.95	2.95	3550	D	5.08	9049	9.27								
				G1	p3.30			11.32		3.30	3.30				
				G2A	p9.46							49049	7.51	11.62	20.2.63
2531	2.95	2.95	3551	C1	12.09	8978	6.26							11.32	1.12.32
2532	2.95	2.95	3552	D	8.07										
				G1	2.26	9029	10.27			2.26	2.26				
				G2A	12.39							49029	8.48	5.30	26.2.50
2533	2.95	2.95	3553	C1	1.10	8979								9.29	3.10.29
2534	2.95	2.95	3554	C1	8.12	(9000)								10.27	2.12.27
2535	2.95	2.95	3555	C1	5.10	8986	7.27							12.30	12.8.32
2536	8.96	8.96	3661	D	4.07										
				G1	1.28	9033	1.28	2.31		1.28	1.28				
				G2A	p2.40							49033	12.49	12.57	3.1.58
2537	8.96	8.96	3662	D	4.07										
				G1	6.25	9019	6.27		6.25	6.25	6.25				
				G2A	p5.40							(49019)		6.49	1.7.49
2538	8.96	8.96	3663	C	9.05										
				G1	6.27	8962	6.27			6.27	6.27	(48962)		12.48	11.1.49
2539	8.96	8.96	3664	D	9.07										
				G1	12.27	9031	12.27		.29	12.27	12.27				
				G2A	p3.43							(49031)		5.51	15.6.51
2540	8.96	8.96	3665	D	4.07										
				G1	2.28	9020	2.28			2.28	2.28				
				G2A	p8.38							49020	4.51	10.61	26.6.62 (3)
2541	8.96	8.96	3666	C	11.04	8953	10.23								
				G1	12.26					12.26	12.26				
				G2A	p12.39							48953	11.48	10.61	22.10.62
2542	8.96	8.96	3667	C1	8.10	8990	6.27							12.30	8.1.31
2543	8.96	8.96	3668	C1	2.10	8981	11.27							6.30	18.6.30
2544	8.96	8.96	3669	D	2.08	9040	12.27	6.37							
				G1	10.37					10.37		(49040)		4.49	6.5.49
2545	8.96	8.96	3670	C1	1.10	8980	6.27							p3.30	2.4.30
2546	9.96	9.96	3671	C1	4.09	8969	10.27							12.32	17.2.33
2547	9.96	9.96	3673	D	12.06										
				G1	2.28	9012	2.28		2.28	2.28	2.28	(49012)		12.48	31.12.48
2548	9.96	9.96	3673	D	5.06										
				G1	2.28	9004	2.28	7.30	2.28	2.28	2.28				
				G2A	3.41							(49004)		6.49	25.6.49
2549	12.96	12.96	3674	C	9.05	8963	7.27							12.30	21.1.31
2550	12.96	12.96	3675	C1	11.09	8976	11.27							p12.32	5.12.32
2551	12.96	12.96	3676	D	10.07										
				G1	5.25	9034	10.27		5.25	5.25	5.25				
				G2A	p8.40							49034	5.51	9.62	16.10.62
2552	12.96	12.96	3677	D	7.08	9052	5.27								
				G1	p2.30				.34	2.30	2.30	(49052)		4.49	6.5.49
2553	12.96	12.96	3678	C	7.05	8958	5.27							12.30	21.1.31

No.	Plate date	Date to stock	Motion No	Rebuilt to Class Date	LMS No.	Date	LG	BF	VB	IBP	BR No.	Date	Wdn	Scrap
2554	12.96	12.96	3679	C1 6.11	8997	9.26							12.30	18.12.30
2555	12.96	12.96	3680	C1 7.11	8998	8.26							p5.32	19.5.32
1801	10.97	10.97	3806	C1 12.09	8977	8.27							12.30	21.1.31
1802	10.97	10.97	3807	D 3.07 G1 p1.28 G2A p10.39	9016	1.28	7.31	.35	1.28	1.28	(49016)		3.49	18.3.49
1803	10.97	10.97	3808	C 3.06	(8967)								10.27	3.12.27
1804	10.97	10.97	3809	D 3.07 G1 10.34	9017	10.27			10.34	10.34	49017	6.48	6.52	4.7.52
1805	10.97	10.97	3810	C 8.05	8959	6.26							12.30	19.1.31
1806	10.97	10.97	3811	C1 5.10	(8984)								p3.28	19.3.28
1807	10.97	10.97	3812	C 9.05	8961	8.23							p4.32	22.4.32
1808	10.97	10.97	3813	D 5.08 G1 p6.33 G2A p7.39	9047	2.28	6.33	6.33	6.33	6.33	49047	11.51	1.58	17.1..58
1809	10.97	10.97	3814	C1 7.09	(8971)								10.27	18.10.27
1810	10.97	10.97	3815	C 4.05	(8955)								10.27	24.11.27
1811	10.97	10.97	3816	C1 1.11	8991	11.27							P12.32	21.11.32
1812	10.97	10.97	3817	D 2.07 G1 5.31 G2A p9.38	9014 29014	8.28 .34	7.31	5.31	5.31	4.35	49014	8.48	5.51	15.6.51
1813	11.97	10.97	3818	D 11.08 G1 6.27	9060	6.27			6.27	6.27	(49060)		5.49	22.7.49
1814	11.97	11.97	3819	C 8.05	8960	6.27							12.30	16.1.31
1815	11.97	11.97	3820	D 4.08 G1 1.27 G2A p10.39	9044	1.27		.35	1.27	1.27	49044	3.51	10.59	6.11.59
1816	11.97	11.97	3821	D 4.08 G1 p10.30 G2A p5.39	9045	11.27		10.30	11.34	11.34	49045	5.49	12.62	11.3.63
1817	12.97	12.97	3822											
1818	12.97	12.97	3823	D 1.07 G1 4.30	9013	11.27			10.39	10.39	(49013)		5.48	20.5.48
1819	12.97	12.97	3824	D 10.08 G1 2.28	9058	1.28		2.28	2.28	2.28	(49058)		p3.50	18.3.50
1820	1.98	1.98	3825	D 7.08 G1 p10.32 G2A 6.47	9050	4.28	10.32	10.32	10.32	10.32	(49050)		10.50	14.10.50
1821	4.98	4.98	3826	D 3.09 G1 8.26 G2A p1.39	9064	8.26			8.26	8.26	49064	8.50	6.60	17.6.60
1822	4.98	4.98	3827	D 6.06 G1 1.28 G2A 4.41	9005	1.28	11.30	1.28	1.28	1.28	49005	2.51	8.57	20.9.57
1823	4.98	4.98	3828	C 12.05	(8965)								10.27	30.11.27
1824	4.98	4.98	3829	D 11.07 G1 10.30 G2A p11.40	9035	12.27		.38	10.30	10.30	49035	8.49	1.57	8.2.57

No.	Plate date	Date to stock	Motion No	Rebuilt to Class	Date	LMS No.	Date	LG	BF	VB	IBP	BR No.	Date	Wdn	Scrap
1825	4.98	4.98	3830	D	8.08	9053	6.27								
				G1	4.29					4.29	4.29	(49053)		5.50	19.5.50
1826	4.98	4.98	3831	C1	4.11	8995	7.27							11.30	11.11.30
1827	5.98	5.98	3832	D	3.07										
				G1	1.28	9018	1.28			1.28	1.28				
				G2A	p2.41							49018	10.49	9.59	9.10.59
1828	5.98	5.98	3833	C	7.05	8957	9.28							12.30	14.1.31
1829	5.98	5.98	3834	C1	8.10	8988	8.26							12.30	15.7.32
1830	5.98	5.98	3835	D	3.08	9041	9.28								
				G1	9.29			9.29	9.29	9.29	9.29				
				G2A	1.44							49041	1.48	8.50	16.9.50
1831	7.98	7.98	3836	D	2.08	9039	11.27			7.31	7.31				
				G1	p12.34				.36						
				G2A	p3.40							(49039)		1.50	13.1.50
1832	7.98	7.98	3837	D	1.08	9038	2.28			1.32	1.32				
				G1	p9.34							(49038)		p4.48	13.5.48
1833	7.98	7.98	3838	D	10.06	9009	6.28								
				G1	7.37				7.37	7.37	7.37				
				G2A	5.40							49009	1.51	11.59	7.12.59
1834	7.98	7.98	3839	D	8.07	9028	12.27								
				G1	8.30					8.30	8.30				
				G2A	p12.39							49028	10.48	p3.56	30.4.56
1835	7.98	7.98	3840	C1	8.12	9001	4.26							p7.28	25.7.28
1836	7.98	7.98	3841	D	2.09	9061	7.27								
				G1	8.30					8.30	8.30				
				G2A	p5.40							49061	3.52	10.62	22.11.62
1837	7.98	7.98	3842	D	9.08	9055	3.28								
				G1	3.30					3.30	3.30				
				G2A	7.40							(49055)		4.49	22.4.49
1838	8.98	8.98	3843	D	10.07	9032	10.26								
				G1	8.28			6.30		8.28	8.28	49032	5.48	6.50	9.6.50
1839	8.98	8.98	3844	D	10.06	9010	12.27								
				G1	11.31			2.32	11.31	1.31	11.31				
				G2A	11.39							49010	9.52	6.59	5.12.59 (1)
1840	8.98	8.98	3845	C1	11.09	8975	6.26							12.30	5.8.32
1841	10.98	10.98	3846	C1	4.10	8983	9.26							12.30	5.8.32
1842	10.98	10.98	3847	C	1.06										
				G1	8.26	8966	8.26			8.26	8.26				
				G2A	p12.44							48966	8.48	2.50	25.2.50
1843	10.98	10.98	3848	D	5.08	9048	10.27								
				G1	8.33					8.33	8.33				
				G2A	12.39							49048	1.50	11.59	19.11.59
1844	10.98	10.98	3849	C1	5.10	8985	1.27							11.30	3.12.50
1845	10.98	10.98	3850	D	4.06	9003	10.27								
				G1	9.32			9.32	9.32	9.32	9.32				
				G2A	p2.40							(49003)		3.49	25.3.49
1846	10.98	10.98	3851	D	10.08										
				G1	1.28	9059	1.28			1.28	1.28	49059	8.48	2.50	18.2.50
1847	10.98	10.98	3852	C1	3.10	8982	9.28							p3.30	4.4.30
1848	10.98	10.98	3853	D	6.07										
				G1	7.26	9022	7.26	11.32	1.32	7.26	7.26				
				G2A	p6.39							49022	11.49	4.51	4.5.51

No.	Plate date	Date to stock	Motion No	Rebuilt to Class	Date	LMS No.	Date	LG	BF	VB	IBP	BR No.	Date	Wdn	Scrap
1849	10.98	10.98	3854	C1	6.10	(8987)								p2.28	27.2.28
1850	11.98	11.98	3855	C1	6.09	(8970)								10.27	10.27 (10)
1851	2.99	2.99	3888	C1	1.11	8992	4.27							p11.32	8.11.32
1852	2.99	2.99	3889	C1	2.11	8993	10.26							p11.32	25.10.32
1853	2.99	2.99	3890	D G1 G2A	11.07 2.28 p6.40	9036	2.28		2.28	2.28		(49036)		p11.49	9.12.49
1854	2.99	2.99	3891	D G1 G2A	6.07 2.28 p2.42	9023	2.28		2.28	2.28	2.28	49023	5.51	10.61	2.1.62 (2)
1855	2.99	2.99	3892	C G1 G2A	10.05 6.26 p7.40	8964	6.26			6.26	6.26	48964	11.49	4.62	25.5.62
1856	2.99	2.99	3893	D G1 G2A	7.07 4.25 p9.38	9026	10.27		4.25	4.25	4.25	(49026)		9.49	18.11.49
1857	2.99	2.99	3894	D G1 G2A	3.08 5.29 p4.40	9042	1.27		.37	5.29	5.29	(49042)		4.49	29.4.49
1858	2.99	2.99	3895	C1	5.11	(8996)								10.27	10.27 (10)
1859	2.99	2.99	3896	C1	3.11	8994	7.27							8.30	5.9.30
1860	2.99	2.99	3897	C	6.05	(8956)								10.27	15.11.27
1861	5.99	5.99	3898	C1	8.09	8972	8.28							2.30	26.3.30
1862	5.99	5.99	3899	C1	3.09	(8968)								11.27	8.11.27
1863	5.99	5.99	3900	D G1 G2A	7.06 11.27 p5.44	9006	11.27		.35	11.27	11.27	49006	5.48	5.51	1.6.51
1864	5.99	5.99	3901	D G1 G2A	6.09 p3.30 p9.46	9063	12.27		12.34	12.34	10.39	49063	2.51	8.59	4.9.59
1865	5.99	5.99	3902	D G1 G2A	2.09 9.34 7.42	9062	11.27		9.34	9.34	9.34	49062	4.49	5.51	1.6.51
1866	5.99	5.99	3903	D G1 G2A	3.06 12.32 p12.39	9002	10.23	12.32	12.32	9.29	12.342	49002	3.50	9.62	5.10.62
1867	5.99	5.99	3904	C1	8.09	8973	8.28							5.33	26.5.33
1868	5.99	5.99	3905	D G1	9.08 12.33	9056	9.28		12.33	12.33		(49056)		8.48	28.9.48
1869	5.99	5.99	3906	C1	8.10	8989	6.26							11.28	23.11.28
1870	5.99	5.99	3907	D G1 G2A	9.08 7.23 p5.40	9057	10.23			9.31	9.31	49057	5.48	5.57	7.6.57
1871	4.00	5.00	4025	D G1	9.07 6.26	9030	6.126			6.26	6.26	49030	1.50	6.51	27.7.51
1872	5.00	5.00	4026	D G1	2.07 7.30	9015	9.27			7.30	7.30	(49015)		5.49	25.6.49
1873	5.00	5.00	4027	D G1 G2A	7.06 3.26 p2.40	9007	2.28		2.28	3.26	3.26	49007	4.51	10.61	2.1.62 (2)

No.	Plate date	Date to stock	Motion No	Rebuilt to Class	Date	LMS No.	Date	LG	BF	VB	IBP	BR No.	Date	Wdn	Scrap
1874	5.00	5.00	4028	D	8.08	9054	7.26								
				G1	2.28				2.28	2.28	2.28	(49054)		4.49	27.5.49
1875	5.00	5.00	4029	C1	9.09	8974	1.26							1.30	13.2.30
1876	5.00	5.00	4030	D	5.07										
				G1	1.27	9021	11.27			11.27	11.27				
				G2A	7.39							49021	8.51	10.61	5.12.61 (1)
1877	5.00	5.00	4031	D	4.08										
				G1	12.27	9046	12.27	12.32		12.27	12.27				
				G2A	p6.40							49046	6.48	3.57	23.3.57
1878	5.00	5.00	4032	D	6.07										
				G1	2.28	9024	2.28			2.28	2.28				
				G2A	3.41							49024	11.49	2.57	27.3.57
1879	5.00	5.00	4033	D	6.07										
				G1	5.28	9025	5.28			5.28	5.28				
				G2A	p11.42							49025	1.50	9.62	4.10.62
1880	11.00	11.00	4034	D	12.07										
				G1	1.28	9037	1.28		1.28	1.28	1.28				
				G2A	p7.40							49037	9.49	12.62	3.4.63

Built in 5.00 with an experimental boiler having two cylindrical chambers one above the other but put into stock in 11.00 with a standard boiler.

Class 'B'

No.	Plate date	Date to stock	Motion No	Rebuilt to Class	Date	LMS No.	Date	LG	BF	VB	IBP	BR No.	Date	Wdn	Scrap
1881	8.01	9.01	4155			8900	12.26							p7.28	26.9.28
1882	9.01	9.01	4156	G1	2.20	9344	9.27	10.29	.36	6.34	6.34				
				G2A	p10.39							49344	7.51	11.62	27.2.63
1883	9.01	9.01	4157	E	11.04										
				G1	9.18	9319	9.27			3.33	3.33				
				G2A	p3.42							(49319)		10.50	14.10.50
1884	9.01	9.01	4158	E	12.04										
				G1	8.17	9266	11.26			5.35	5.35				
				G2A	p8.41							49266	6.48	11.59	28.5.60
1885	9.01	9.01	4159	E	1.05										
				G1	8.17	9267	8.23	5.30		10.36	10.36				
				G2A	p11.46							49267	5.48	11.62	5.2.63
1886	9.01	9.01	4160	E	8.04										
				G1	1.23	9390	1.27	6.29		10.24	10.24				
				G2A	p2.40							49390	8.48	12.57	17.1.58
1887	9.01	10.01	4161	G	8.14	9148	2.27								
				G1	1.36					1.36	1.36				
				G2A	p6.41							49148	6.48	7.57	9.8.57
1888	9.01	10.01	4162	E	12.04										
				G1	1.24	9600	11.25								
						8892	7.30			8.32	8.32	(48892)		p1.49	18.2.49
1889	9.01	10.01	4163	E	8.06										
				G1	6.20	9345	12.27	7.31		12.28	12.28				
				G2A	p3.42							49345	10.50	1.58	15.2.58
1890	9.01	10.01	4164	G1	3.24	8901	11.26			10.36					
				G2A	1.47							48901	9.48	5.52	13.6.52
1891	12.01	12.01	4185	G	11.07										
				G1	12.20	9348	8.27	6.30		5.30	5.30				
				G2A	p6.40							49348	12.48	11.59	28.4.61
1892	12.01	12.01	4186	G1	5.25	8902	1.28		5.25	5.25	5.25	48902	12.49	2.53	6.3.51

No.	Plate date	Date to stock	Motion No	Rebuilt to Class	Date	LMS No.	Date	LG	BF	VB	IBP	BR No.	Date	Wdn	Scrap
1893	12.01	12.01	4187	G G1 G2A G1	3.10 10.27 p9.38 p1.43	9085	10.27			10.27	10.27	49085	1.49	8.50	18.8.50
1894	12.01	12.01	4188	G1 G2A	1.23 p11.45	9391	8.27		8.27	5.30	5.30	49391	6.48	1.62	9.2.62
1895	12.01	12.01	4189	G G1 G2A	5.08 1.25 p10.38	9066	11.26		1.25	1.25	1.25	49066	6.49	p11.57	22.11.57
1896	12.01	12.01	4190	G1	5.22	9380	8.27			9.32	9.32			11.47	31.12.47
1897	12.01	1.02	4191	G1 G2A	12.21	9370	10.26		.35	6.32	6.32	49370	6.48	6.51	3.8.51
1898	12.01	1.02	4192	G1 G2A	10.22 p9.47	9385	9.26			9.26	9.26	49385	12.52	12.57	17.1.58
1899	12.01	1.02	4193	G1 G2A	6.22 p11.40	9382	5.27		.33	5.27	5.27	49382	4.48	9.62	11.3.63 (4)
1900	12.01	1.02	4194	G G1 G2A	11.06 6.24 p8.39	9065	2.28		2.28	6.24	6.24	49065	6.48	3.50	14.4.50
813	3.02	4.02	4235	G1 G2A	2.23 p11.38	8903	4.27			4.27	4.27	(48903)		9.49	4.10.49
815	4.02	4.02	4236	G1 G2A	2.22 10.40	9375	12.26			8.24	8.24	49375	4.50	12.62	15.1.65 (5)
823	4.02	4.02	4237	G1	5.23	8904	3.28			8.38		(48904)		10.49	14.10.49
826	4.02	4.02	4238	G1 G2A	1.27 12.38	8905	1.27	.32	11.26	1.27	1.27	48905	4.48	6.59	5.12.59 (1)
843	4.02	4.02	4239	G1	10.23	8906	1.26			8.37		(48906)		3.49	18.3.49
859	4.02	4.02	4240	G1 G2A	5.19 p2.41	9336	8.28		.31	1.32	1.32			7.47	9.9.47
898	4.02	4.02	4241	G G1 G2A	6.11 p3.32 p5.41	9146	5.27			5.27	5.27	49146	7.50	2.58	28.2.58
899	4.02	4.02	4242	F G1 G2A	5.07 6.23 p6.40	9610 8896	4.28 7.30			2.32	2.32	(48896)		1.50	28.1.50
904	4.02	4.02	4243	G1 G2A	5.19 1.48	9337	8.28			1.45	1.45	(49337)		7.49	5.8.49
905	4.02	4.02	4244	E	11.05	9601	11.26							p7.28	20.9.28
18	5.02	6.02	4245	E	11.05	(9602)								p4.28	3.5.28
352	5.02	6.02	4246	F	1.07	(9611)								12.27	3.1.28
405	5.02	6.02	4247	G1 G2A	2.26 p7.46	8907	10.27			2.26	2.26	48907	8.48	9.57	1.11.57
2074	5.02	6.02	4248	G1	8.23	8908	10.23			8.40		48908	5.48	9.50	9.9.50
2114	5.02	6.02	4249	F G1 G2A	7.08 10.22 p5.39	9386	5.27	2.31		5.27	5.27	49386	1.49	11.59	11.12.59
2342	5.02	6.02	4250	G1 G2A	3.23 p1.40	8909	5.28	5.28		10.32	10.32	(48909)		2.49	25.2.49

No.	Plate date	Date to stock	Motion No	Rebuilt Class	Rebuilt Date	LMS No.	Date	LG	BF	VB	IBP	BR No.	Date	Wdn	Scrap
2369	5.02	6.02	4251	G1	5.23	8910	7.28			9.34		(48910)		1.48	18.8.48
2496	5.02	6.02	4252	G1	4.23	8911	9.28			3.41	3.41	(48911)		12.49	6.1.50
842	5.02	7.02	4253	G1	6.19	9338	12.26			11.34	11.34	(49338)		4.49	3.6.49
906	5.02	7.02	4254	F	12.07										
				G1	5.23	9612	7.28								
						8897	7.30			1.34	1.34				
				G2A	p8.44							(48897)		10.49	11.11.49
2556	7.02	8.02	4255	G1	5.23	8912	4.27	10.29	.35	10.35	10.35	(48912)		8.48	10.9.48
2557	8.02	8.02	4256	G1	8.24	8913	8.26		.37	8.24	8.24	(48913)		8.48	10.9.48
2558	8.02	8.02	4257	E	3.06	9603	1.28							12.28	9.1.29
2559	8.02	8.02	4258	G1	1.24	8914	11.27	.32	.32	11.25	11.25				
				G2A	10.39							48914	9.48	7.57	9.8.57
2560	8.02	8.02	4259	G1	4.23	8915	10.27	12.29	.37	8.32	8.32				
				G2A	4.46							48915	2.50	10.61	2.1.62
2561	8.02	8.02	4260			8916	9.28							p11.28	31.10.28
2562	8.02	8.02	4261	G	6.17	9152	2.28								
				G1	p3.30				3.30	3.30	10.36	(49152)		p10.48	12.10.48
2563	8.02	8.02	4262	E	6.08										
				G1	11.24	9604	2.27		11.24	11.24	11.24				
				G2A	p12.41	8893	7.30					48893	12.49	10.54	22.10.54
2564	8.02	8.02	4263	G1	4.24	8917	11.26			12.37	12.37				
				G2A	p3.46							48917	8.48	11.57	6.12.57
2565	8.02	9.02	4264			8919	5.27							12.28	19.2.29
1017	9.02	9.02	4265	E	1.06	(9605)								10.27	8.11.27
2251	9.02	9.02	4266	G	6.08										
				G1	11.27	9067	11.27	4.30	11.27	11.27	11.27	(49067)		12.49	23.12.49
1035	9.02	9.02	4267	G	9.10										
				G1	9.23	9133	9.27		9.27	10.34		(49133)		2.50	25.2.50
1036	9.02	9.02	4268	F	4.07										
				G1	10.21	9365	2.28			6.32	6.32				
				G2A	p3.39				.39			(49365)		7.49	5.8.49
1038	9.02	9.02	4269	E	12.05										
				F	4.07										
				G1	1.27	9349	2.28	7.31		3.31	3.31	(49349)		12.48	11.1.49
1039	9.02	9.02	4270	G1	10.25	8918	8.28	7.31		10.25	10.25	(48918)		3.49	6.5.49
1040	9.02	10.02	4271	G1	3.23	8920	12.26	10.28		12.26	12.26				
				G2A	p10.38							48920	10.48	5.51	18.5.51
1041	10.02	10.02	4272	G1	3.21	9355	6.27		12.24	12.24	12.24				
				G2A	p11.39							49355	6.49	11.59	28.4.60
1042	10.02	10.02	4273	E	6.06	9606	10.27							12.28	11.1.29
1043	10.02	10.02	4274	G1	6.18	9304	4.28		3.28						
				G2A	8.38					8.38	8.38	49304	10.51	12.59	30.12.59
2566	10.02	10.02	4275	G	11.10										
				G1	3.25	9153	9.27	.32	3.25	3.25	3.25				
				G2A	p11.40							49153	8.48	11.59	21.4.61
2567	10.02	10.02	4276	G1	5.24	8921	11.26	11.28	.31	1.32	1.32				
				G2A	p3.40							48921	9.52	4.58	16.5.58
2568	10.02	10.02	4277	G1	12.19	9342	12.27		12.27	2.31	2.31				
				G2A	010.35							49342	9.48	10.61	10.9.62 (1)

No.	Plate date	Date to stock	Motion No	Rebuilt to Class	Date	LMS No.	Date	LG	BF	VB	IBP	BR No.	Date	Wdn	Scrap
2569	10.02	10.02	4278	G	9.09										
				G1	3.32	9072	3.27			3.32	3.32				
				G2A	7.40							49072	1.49	2.49	4.3.49
2570	10.02	10.02	4279	F	8.06										
				G1	10.21	9367	10.27		12.35	11.35	3.40				
				G2A	1.46							49367	11.49	p11.37	29.11.57
1044	11.02	11.02	4280	G1	2.22	9376	9.27		.32	7.32	7.32				
				G2A	p5.40							49376	1.50	3.58	21.3.58
1047	11.02	11.02	4281	G1	12.22	9387	6.27	6.30	.35	6.35	2.38				
				G2A	p1.40							49387	8.49	11.59	5.5.60
1051	11.02	11.02	4282	G1	9.26	8922	9.26	1.29	.35	9.26	9.26				
				G2A	p9.45							48922	4.48	5.59	20.6.56
1055	11.02	11.02	4283	G1	3.22	9377	2.26			2.26	2.26				
				G2A	6.40							49377	1.51	10.62	18.4.63
1061	11.02	11.02	4284			(8923)								10.27	8.12.27
1064	11.02	12.02	4295	E	5.06										
				G1	2.23	9607	5.27	11.29		11.29	11.29				
						8894	7.30		.34			(48894)		2.49	18.2.49
1065	11.02	12.02	4296	E	10.06										
				G1	9.19	9340	2.26	2.32							
				G2A	p1.47							49340	4.49	8.59	17.8.59
1066	12.02	12.02	4297	G1	12.17	9272	5.27			5.27	5.27	(49272)		2.48	18.3.48
1070	12.02	12.02	4298	G	8.10	9120	9.27								
				G1	8.33				.33	8.33	8.33				
				G2A	p9.38							49120	9.51	9.59	25.9.59
1088	12.02	12.02	4299	G1	2.23	8924	9.26		.32	3.32	3.32	(48924)		12.48	31.12.48
1091	12.02	12.02	4300	G1	5.24	8925	2.28			5.30	5.30				
				G2A	12.39							48925	7.48	9.49	4.11.49
1094	12.02	12.02	4301	G1	10.18	9324	8.28			8.28	8.28	49324	4.48	3.50	18.3.50
1190	12.02	12.02	4302	G	2.10										
				G1	1.25	9076	9.27		1.25	1.25	1.25	(49076)		5.50	26.2.63
1222	12.02	12.02	4303	E	5.06	9608	8.27							12.28	10.1.29
1223	12.02	12.02	4304	E	2.06										
				G1	11.21	9368	10.26		.34	4.29	4.29				
				G2A	p9.38							49368	1.50	3.59	5.12.59 (6)
1224	1.03	1.03	4305	G1	1.21	9350	11.27		11.27	8.35	8.35				
				G2A	p3.46							49350	5.49	12.62	20.2.63
1225	1.03	1.03	4306	G1	2.26	8926	6.28		.35	2.26	2.26				
				G2A	p9.45							48926	1.52	8.59	4.9.59
1226	1.03	1.03	4307	G1	2.26	8927	1.28		1.28	3.26	3.26				
				G2A	9.47							48927	1.50	11.61	15.12.61
1227	1.03	1.03	4308	E	6.08										
				G1	8.21	9363	3.28		3.28	6.31	6.31				
				G2A	p5.40							(49363)		3.49	25.3.49
1228	1.03	1.03	4309	G	10.10										
				G1	6.23	9142	12.26	.33		7.29	7.29				
				G2A	p9.45							49142	3.50	12.62	8.3.63
1229	1.03	1.03	4310	G	5.09	9070	6.28								
				G1	12.37				12.37	12.37	12.37				
				G2A	12.40							49070	2.51	11.62	8.3.63
1230	1.03	1.03	4311	G1	3.22	9378	4.27	2.32		4.27	4.27				
				G2A	p9.38							49378	10.48	11.59	1.4.60

No.	Plate date	Date to stock	Motion No	Rebuilt to Class	Date	LMS No.	Date	LG	BF	VB	IBP	BR No.	Date	Wdn	Scrap
1231	1.03	1.03	4312	G	12.13	9147	7.28			8.25	8.25			9.62	5.10.62
				G1	p3.36										
				G2A	12.39							49147	5.49		
1233	1.03	1.03	4313			(8928)								12.27	4.1.28
1236	1.03	2.03	4314	E	2.06										
				G1	2.21	9351	7.28								
				G2A	p11.42							49351	6.48	11.49	18.11.49
1237	3.03	4.03	4315	G1	8.23	89290	10.23			6.30	6.30	48929	6.48	7.50	11.8.50
1240	4.03	4.03	4316	G1	5.21	9358	2.28			3.32	3.32				
				G2A	p2.40							49358	3.50	3.58	3.5.58
1241	4.03	4.03	4317	G1	9.20	9346	7.27		7.27	10.34	5.43	49346	5.50	5.52	30.5.52
1242	4.03	4.03	4318	G1	12.22	9388	12.27		.33	4.33	4.33				
				G2A	p2.40							(49388)		3.51	20.3.51
1243	4.03	4.03	4319	G	2.15	9150	2.27	11.29		11.29					
				G1	p8.34										
				G2A	p6.39				.39			49150	8.48	11.59	7.2.61
1245	4.03	4.03	4320	G	10.09										
				G1	4.27	9073	4.27	11.29		4.27	4.27				
				G2A	12.39							49073	6.48	1.58	27.1.58
1247	4.03	4.03	4321	F	8.06										
				G1	9.23	9613	10.23								
				G2A	p3.42	8898	7.30			12.37	12.37	48898	10.49	6.62	30.8.62
1248	4.03	4.03	4322	G1	3.23	8930	8.28	11.28		1.26	1.26				
				G2A	p3.43							48930	5.48	12.62	24.1.63
1249	4.03	4.03	4323	G1	10.25	8931	3.28	7.29		10.25	10.25	(48931)		6.49	25.6.49
1271	4.03	4.03	4324	G	11.10	9145	2.28								
				G1	11.31					11.31	11.31				
				G2A	p4.44							49145	6.48	1.58	17.1.58
1272	5.03	5.03	4325	G1	3.24	8932	8.27	4.30		6.35	9.39				
				G2A	p11.40							48932	9.48	10.61	22.11.61
1273	5.03	5.03	4326	F	5.06	9614	6.28							12.28	11.1.29
1404	5.03	5.03	4327	G1	11.23	8933	10.27		10.27	6.30	6.30				
				G2A	p4.40							(48933)		12.50	22.12.50
2024	5.03	5.03	4328	G1	8.23	8934	10.23		.35	10.30	10.30				
				G2A	p12.45							(48934)		3.50	18.3.50
1274	5.03	6.03	4329	G	9.09										
				G1	11.27	9071	11.27	2.30		11.27	11.27	49071	8.48	1.51	19.1.51
2571	5.03	5.03	4330	G1	4.25	8935	9.27		4.25	4.25	4.25	(48935)		2.49	4.3.49
2572	5.03	5.03	4331	G1	3.24	8936	11.26			4.34	4.34				
				G2A	p1.40							(48936)		4.51	4.5.51
2573	5.03	5.03	4332	F	8.08										
				G1	1.22	9373	10.25			1.31	1.31				
				G2A	p2.44							49373	10.48	12.62	23.1.63
2574	5.03	5.03	4333	E	10.06										
				G1	1.20	9343	8.27			10.34	10.34				
				G2A	p6.41							49343	6.48	10.61	5.12.61 (1)
2575	5.03	5.03	4334	G1	1.23	9394	10.26		8.24	8.24					
				G2A	4.40							49394	8.50	10.62	19.4.63
41	6.03	7.03	4345	G1	8.21	9362	8.27		.33	7.37	7.37	(49362)		7.48	24.11.48
2080	6.03	7.03	4346	G1	2.24	8940	7.27	12.29		4.34	4.34				
				G2A	p1.40							48940	3.50	5.57	31.5.57

No.	Plate date	Date to stock	Motion No	Rebuilt to Class	Date	LMS No.	Date	LG	BF	VB	IBP	BR No.	Date	Wdn	Scrap
1276	6.03	7.03	4347	G1 G2A	1.23 p2.41	9389	6.27	2.29	.35	10.30	10.30	49389	6.48	8.54	10.9.54
1277	6.03	7.03	4348	G G1 G2A	1.15 1.27 p12.39	9149	11.27			11.27	11.27	49149	9.48	11.59	28.3.61
1278	6.03	7.03	4349	G1 G2A	6.22 p9.38	9381	6.27	.29		11.29	11.29	49381	4.49	11.62	11.4.63
1279	7.03	7.03	4350	G1 G2A	2.21 p3.40	9352	5.27		6.35	1.39		49352	5.48	9.62	22.11.62
1280	7.03	7.03	4351	G G1	5.10 5.24	9100	6.27			11.36	11.36	(49100)		5.50	26.5.50
1281	7.03	7.03	4352			8937	10.26							p7.28	18.7.28
1282	7.03	7.03	4353			8938	5.27							12.28	19.2.29
1283	7.03	7.03	4354	G1	3.24	8939	12.26			1.35	5.40	(48939)		1.48	3.12.48
2118	9.03	9.03	4355	G1 G2A	4.18 p6.41	9292	9.27		9.27	4.25	4.25	(49292)		3.51	22.3.51
1284	9.03	9.03	4356	G1 G2A	10.23 p11.39	8941	8.27		8.27	9.29	9.29	48941	6.48	5.50	26.5.50
1285	9.03	9.03	4357	G1 G2A	8.19 p5.41	9339	5.27	10.29		6.34	6.34	49339	9.48	12.54	14.1.55
1286	9.03	9.03	4358	G G1 G2A	11.08 10.20 p12.40	9347	3.27		10.24	10.24		(49347)		1.51	2.2.51
1287	9.03	9.03	4359`	G1 G2A	9.25 p6.40	8942 28942 8942	12.27 31.3.34 14.4.34		.34	9.25	9.25	48942	9.48	10.61	2.1.62 (2)
1288	9.03	9.03	4360	G1 G2A	4.23 p12.39	8943	6.28			5.31	5.31	48943	2.50	9.59	12.10.59
1289	9.03	9.03	4361	G1 G2A	6.21 p9.38	9361	8.23			10.25	10.25	49361	9.49	12.64	22.2.65 (1)
1308	9.03	10.03	4362	G1 G2A	2.24 p7.40	8944	11.26	6.28		3.31	3.31	48944	7.48	9.57	1.11.57
1310	10.03	10.03	4363	G1 G2A	11.24 p2.40	8945	4.27		11.24	11.24	1.24	48945	5.48	3.59	4.12.59 (7)
1318	10.03	10.03	4364	G1 G2A	10.21 p12.35	9366	2.28		.33	12.35	12.35	49366	11.49	10.59	23.10.59
134	10.03	10.03	4366	Exploded at Buxton 11.11.21; cut up No. 3626											3.22
500	10.03	10.03	4367	G1 G2A	6.17 p10.38	9265	7.27		2.25	2.25	2.25	(49265)		3.52	25.4.52
916	10.03	10.03	4368	G1 G2A	3.21 p8.46	9354	7.28	7.31		4.31	4.31	49354	11.49	3.56	20.4.56
1547	10.03	10.03	4369			(8946)								6.28	20.6.28
2272	10.03	10.03	4370	G1 G2A	5.21 p4.40	9360	1.26	9.32	9.27	12.25	12.25	(49360)		5.49	17.6.49
1299	10.03	11.03	4371	G G1 G2A	10.09 3.26 p1.39	9074	4.27		3.25	3.25	3.25	49074	3.49	12.50	22.12.50
1401	10.03	11.03	4372	G G1	1.090 12.27	9075	12.27			12.27	12.27	49075	6.48	1.50	4.2.50

No.	Plate date	Date to stock	Motion No	Rebuilt to Class	Date	LMS No.	Date	LG	BF	VB	IBP	BR No.	Date	Wdn	Scrap
1448	11.03	11.03	4373	G1	12.17	9273	8.27			6.29	6.29				
				G2A	p12.39										
				G1	12.41							(49273)		2.48	12.8.48
2038	11.03	11.03	4374	G1	4.21	9356	6.26	5.28		6.26	6.26				
				G2A	p3.40							(49356)		4.50	28.4.50
2208	11.03	11.03	4375	G1	8.21	9364	9.26	11.28	.35	7.31	7.31	(49364)		12.50	15.12.50
640	1.04	1.04	4385	G1	7.22	9383	3.27		9.24	9.24	9.24	(49383)		5.48	1.6.48
1300	1.04	1.04	4386	G1	3.22	9379	3.27		10.24	10.24	10.24				
				G2A	8.40							49379	6.48	10.49	11.11.49
1370	1.04	1.04	4387			(8947)								10.27	16.11.27
1449	1.04	1.04	4388	G	8.10										
				G1	11.27	9122	11.27	10.29	.33	11.27	11.27				
				G2A	p12.39							49122	9.48	11.62	7.2.63
1586	1.04	1.04	4389	E	7.06										
				G1	7.21	9353	3.27			5.32	5.32	(49353)		12.49	30.12.49
508	2.04	2.04	4390	G	4.10	9090	3.27			9.29					
				G1	3.36						3.36				
				G2A	p11.39							49090	12.48	12.50	22.12.50
641	2.04	2.04	4391	G	11.16										
				G1	3.27	9151	3.27	7.33		3.27	3.27	49151	2.50	8.52	15.8.52

Altered to 'G1' in 3.27 but officially classified as such only in 5.28, when fitted with slide valves. It received a new boiler and cylinders in 3.40.

No.	Plate date	Date to stock	Motion No	Rebuilt to Class	Date	LMS No.	Date	LG	BF	VB	IBP	BR No.	Date	Wdn	Scrap
918	2.04	2.04	4392	G1	5.27	8948	5.27	1.30	.34	5.27	5.27				
				G2A	4.40							(48948)		7.48	26.8.49
1555	2.04	2.04	4393			(8949)								11.27	1.12.27
2036	2.04	2.04	4394	G1	12.19	9341	5.26	10.28	.38	5.26	5.26				
				G2A	9.41							49341	1.50	3.57	10.5.57
410	4.04	4.04	4395	G1	11.18	9331	8.27	12.29		9.34	9.34				
				G2A	9.42							49331	11.49	10.50	3.11.50
509	5.04	5.04	4396	G	11.08	9069	3.27			6.29	6.29				
				G1	p11.33										
				G2A	p8.39							49069	8.48	6.50	24.6.50
647	5.04	5.04	4397	E	2.07										
				F	10.08										
				G1	2.25	9615	6.27		2.25	2.25	2.25				
				G2A	p5.41	8899	7.30					48899	8.49	3.56	30.4.56
1110	5.04	5.04	4398	G1	12.21	9369	2.26		.33						
				G2A	10.46							(49369)		4.50	12.2.50
1122	5.04	5.04	4399	G	5.10	9099	3.26								
				G1	10.27				.36	10.27	10.27				
				G2A	p2.41							49099	9.49	7.62	30.8.62
503	5.04	5.04	4400	G	10.08	9068	1.28			7.31	7.31				
				G1	p2.35				2.35						
				G2A	p2.43							49068	2.52	1.57	4.2.57
818	5.04	5.04	4401	G	9.10										
				G1	1.24	9132	8.27			3.33	3.33				
				G2A	1.40							49132	11.51	4.59	24.7.59
1585	5.04	5.04	4402	E	10.06										
				G1	4.23	9609	9.27	5.30		4.30	4.30				
				G2A	3.44	8895	7.30					48895	11.48	12.64	4.5.65 (1)
2056	5.04	5.04	4403	E	1.07										
				G1	5.21	9359	5.27			8.31	8.31	49359	4.51	2.52	27.2.52
2387	5.04	5.04	4404	G1	4.21	9357	6.27		.38	4.35	4.35				
				G2A	p9.42							49357	5.48	10.61	12.7.63 (1)

No.	Plate date	Date to stock	Motion No	Rebuilt to Class	Date	LMS No.	Date	LG	BF	VB	IBP	BR No.	Date	Wdn	Scrap
437	7.04	7.04	4405	E	8.06									12.47	22.1.48
				G1	2.22	9374	4.27		.34	4.27	4.27				
644	7.04	7.04	4406	G1	1.24	8950	9.28			4.33	4.33			12.61	1.2.62
				G2A	p9.41							48950	5.48		
1353	7.04	7.04	4407	G1	12.18	9335	6.27			4.29	4.29			9.62	11.3.63 (4)
				G2A	p1.43							49335	7.50		
1369	7.04	7.04	4408	F	12.07										
				G1	1.22	9372	3.28		3.28	7.24	7.24				
				G2A	p10.38										
				G1	p6.40										
				G2A	p3.47							(49372)		4.49	3.6.49
1432	7.04	7.04	4409	G1	7.22	9384	8.27			9.34		(49384)		12.48	7.1.49
1436	8.04	8.04	4410	G1	10.23	8951	9.27			6.29	6.29			8.57	1.11.57
				G2A	p2.39							48951	6.52		
1543	8.04	8.04	4411	G1	2.24	8952	3.24	10.28		4.26	4.26			4.57	31.5.57
				G2A	p9.38							48952	11.48		
2057	8.04	8.04	4412	G1	12.21	9371	2.27			2.27	2.27	49371	8.49	1.52	15.2.52
2060	8.04	8.04	4413	G1	1.23	9392	10.26		.34	11.24	11.24			10.61	19.5.62 (3)
				G2A	11.38							49392	12.48		
2169	8.04	8.04	4414	E	9.06										
				G1	1.23	9393	4.27	2.32		10.24	10.24			6.57	6.7.57
				G2A	p1.44							49393	9.48		

Plate 284: *Nowadays it is easily forgotten that the LNWR enjoyed extensive mineral traffic in the East Midlands, where the Midland, Great Northern and Great Central Railways had every right to regard it as an interloper. Things changed after the Grouping but here, on 2nd September 1915, 'G' class No. 1411 waits at Pinxton with a brake van. F. Gillford, courtesy J. M. Bentley*

Class 'G'

No.	Plate date	Date to stock	Motion No	LMS No.	LMS Date	Rebuilt to Class	Rebuilt to Date	LG	BF	VB	IBP	BR No.	Date	Wdn	Scrap
2653	1.10	2.10	4890	9154	11.27	G1	1.12		12.27	12.27	12.27				
						G2A	p10.44					49154	7.48	11.62	5.12.63
2654	1.10	2.10	4891	9077	8.27	G1	11.32		12.31	5.37	5.37				
						G2A	p6.40					49077	8.50	10.61	5.12.61 (1)
2655	1.10	2.10	4892	9078	2.28	G1	11.32	11.32	11.32	11.32	11.32				
						G2A	p6.39					49078	6.49	12.62	28.10.64 (8)
2656	2.10	2.10	4893	9079	9.28	G1	2.26			2.26	2.26				
		for a few days only:- 29079 28.3.34				G2A	p12.39					49079	9.48	11.62	18.1.63
2657	2.10	2.10	4894	9080	10.26	G1	4.34		4.34	4.34	4.34				
						G2A	p11.39					(49080)		2.50	4.2.50
2658	2.10	2.10	4895	9081	9.27	G1	5.30	5.30		5.30	5.30				
						G2A	p3.46					49081	1.50	11.62	23.1.63
2659	2.10	3.10	4896	9086	5.28	G1	6.30		6.30	6.30	6.30				
						G2A	p7.40					(49086)		4.49	13.5.49
2660	2.10	3.10	4897	9087	10.23	G1	11.27			11.27	11.27				
						G2A	8.39					49087	1.50	9.62	6.11.62
2661	2.10	3.10	4898	9088	9.28	G1	8.33			1.26	1.26				
						G2A	p7.39					49088	12.48	11.57	6.12.57
2662	2.10	3.10	4899	9089	2.27	G1	12.29			12.29	12.29				
						G2A	9.38								
						G1	p6.40					49089	1.50	4.54	14.5.54
1354	3.10	3.10	4900	9082	8.28	G1	8.25		8.25	8.25	8.25				
						G2A	12.39					49082	4.48	10.60	3.11.60
1380	3.10	3.10	4901	9083	5.28	G1	5.28	11.31		5.28	5.28				
						G2A	9.38								
						G1	p4.40					(49083)		1.50	20.1.50
1411	3.10	3.10	4902	9084	1.27	G1	3.28		3.28	3.28	3.28				
						G2A	p10.38					(49084)		9.49	4.11.49
1456	3.10	4.10	4903	9092	5.27	G1	6.29		.33	6.29	6.29	49092	6.48	9.52	3.10.52
1497	3.10	4.10	4904	9093	10.27	G1	10.27		10.27	10.27	10.27				
						G2A	p9.39					49093	8.48	11.62	20.3.63
1556	3.10	4.10	4905	9094	1.28	G1	1.28		.36	4.25	4.25				
						G2A	6.39					49094	9.48	11.62	20.3.63
1582	3.10	4.10	4906	9095	1.28	G1	2.30	12.32		2.30	2.30	(49095)		6.48	30.7.48
1591	3.10	4.10	4907	9096	2.28	G1	11.31	10.31	10.31	10.31	10.31				
						G2A	8.40					49096	5.48	4.52	23.5.52
1619	4.10	4.10	4908	9097	8.27	G1	6.33	6.33	6.33	9.29	9.29	(49097)		p3.50	11.3.50
1629	4.10	4.10	4909	9098	1.26	G1	1.34		1.34	1.34		49098	3.50	5.51	18.5.51
1322	4.10	4.10	4910	9091	6.26	G1	p5.28			3.26	3.26	(49091)		9.49	30.9.49
1464	4.10	5.10	4911	9101	4.27	G1	4.27			4.27	4.27				
						G2A	p8.38					49101	7.49	9.50	6.10.50
1511	4.10	5.10	4912	9102	9.26	G1	1.34			1.34	1.34	(49102)		6.49	19.8.49
1570	4.10	5.10	4913	9103	4.27	G1	4.27		.31	4.27	4.27	(49103)		6.48	22.7.48
1578	4.10	5.10	4914	9104	9.26	G1	5.24			3.34	3.34				
						G2A	5.40					49104	11.48	11.62	18.10.63
1600	5.10	5.10	4915	9105	3.28	G1	10.35			2.30	2.30				
						G2A	12.39					49105	8.48	11.59	10.6.60

No.	Plate date	Date to stock	Motion No	LMS No.	LMS Date	Rebuilt to Class	Rebuilt to Date	LG	BF	VB	IBP	BR No.	Date	Wdn	Scrap
1647	5.10	5.10	4916	9106	12.27	G1 G2A	2.30 p5.42			2.30	2.30	49106	9.49	12.62	15.3.63
1664	5.10	5.10	4917	9107	6.27	G1	10.29	10.29		8.44	8.44	49107	6.48	4.50	12.5.50
1687	5.10	5.10	4918	9108	5.28	G1 G2A	11.31 p11.47		11.31	11.31	11.31	49108	11.52	11.57	6.12.57
1699	5.10	5.10	4919	9109	6.26	G1 G2A	11.29 p12.39	11.29	11.29	11.29	11.29	49109	5.50	3.59	5.12.59 (1)
1503	5.10	6.10	4920	9110	6.28	G1 G2A	8.32 11.39	8.32	8.32	8.32	8.32	(49110)		3.49	1.4.49
1540	5.10	6.10	4921	9111	1.28	G1 11.39	1.28			1.28	1.28	(49111)		3.49	8.4.49
1609	6.10	6.10	4922	9112	1.28	G1 G2A	1.28 10.42			1.28	1.28	49112	9.50	11.59	16.2.61
1634	6.10	6.10	4923	9113	8.27	G1 G2A	4.33 p10.39		4.33	4.33	4.33	49113	7.48	1.59	5.12.59 (1)
1637	6.10	6.10	4924	9114	8.28	G1 G2A	8.28 12.38		12.38			49114	4.51	11.62	28.2.63
1639	6.10	6.10	4925	9115	7.28	G1 G2A	11.24 p1.39		11.24	11.24	11.24	49115	9.48	11.59	12.2.60
1660	6.10	6.10	4926	9116	11.27	G1 G2A	11.27 12.38	10.29		11.27	11.27	49116	11.52	11.59	29.4.60
1789	6.10	6.10	4927	9117	8.26	G1 G2A	12.32 p3.43	12.32	12.32	12.32	12.32	49117	9.50	3.59	5.12.59 (1)
2030	6.10	6.10	4928	9118	11.27	G1	p12.34		12.34	11.27	11.27	(49118)		12.47	8.1.48
2032	6.10	6.10	4929	9119	7.27	G1 G2A	11.32 p12.40	11.32	11.32	11.32	11.32	49119	6.48	10.61	5.12.61 (2)
1385	7.10	8.10	4930	9121	2.28	G1 G2A	7.25 p11.39		7.25	7.25	2.32	49121	8.48	9.58	21.10.58
1492	7.10	8.10	4931	9123	7.28	G1 G2A	12.30 p1.40		12.30	6.25	6.25	(49123)		6.49	1.7.49
1507	7.10	8.10	4932	9124	12.27	G1 G2A G1	12.27 p9.38 p4.43	11.31	.35	12.27	12.27	(49124)		1.50	28.1.50
1539	8.10	8.10	4933	9125	6.27	G1 G2A	6.27 p8.44			6.27	6.27	49125	2.50	9.62	25.10.62
1577	8.10	8.10	4934	9126	6.27	G1 G2A	12.29 7.39	10.29		6.27	6.27	49126	11.48	9.62	25.10.62
1606	8.10	8.10	4935	9127	5.28	G1 G2A	9.36 p7.41		9.36	1.31	1.31	(49127)		3.50	3.3.50
1648	8.10	8.10	4936	9128	6.26	G1	3.31	7.31	7.31	6.26	6.26	(49128)		11.48	9.12.48
1690	8.10	8.10	4937	9129	3.28	G1 G2A	12.35 p6.47		12.35	5.25	5.25	49129	7.52	11.62	21.2.63
1774	8.10	8.10	4938	9130	5.28	G1 G2A	3.31 5.39	7.31	3.31	3.31	3.31	49130	10.49	11.62	28.2.63
1776	8.10	8.10	4939	9131	12.26	G1	12.26		12.26	12.26	12.26	(49131)		7.48	18.11.48
1403	8.10	9.10	4940	9134	7.26	G1 G2A	12.37 7.41		12.37	7.31	7.31	49134	5.49	3.62	13.4.62
1424	8.10	9.10	4941	9135	11.27	G1	11.27		.39	11.27	11.27	(49135)		11.49	25.11.49
1462	9.10	9.10	4942	9136	10.25	G1	1.37		1.37	9.25	9.25	(49136)		8.48	17.9.48

No.	Plate date	Date to stock	Motion No	LMS No.	LMS Date	Rebuilt to Class	Rebuilt to Date	LG	BF	VB	IBP	BR No.	Date	Wdn	Scrap
1700	9.10	9.10	4943	9137	10.27	G1	10.27			10.27	10.27				
						G2A	p8.42					49137	12.48	10.61	26.6.62
1727	9.10	9.10	4944	9138	2.28	G1	p11.34			10.34	7.40	49138	3.50	p2.52	29.2.52
1735	9.10	9.10	4945	9139	9.28	G1	p9.28			6.33	6.33				
						G2A	p10.38					49139	12.49	9.62	16.10.62
1794	9.10	9.10	4946	9141	9.26	G1	2.30			2.30	2.30				
						G2A	p3.41					49141	8.49	7.62	27.9.62
1775	9.10	9.10	4947	9140	2.28	G1	p10.28		10.33	10.33	10.33	49140	11.50	9.55	4.11.55
1788	9.10	10.10	4948	9143	9.26	G1	p10.31		10.31	9.31	9.31				
						G2A	p1.41					49143	5.48	10.59	4.11.59
2014	9.10	10.10	4949	9144	10.27	G1	3.26	1.30		3.26	3.26				
						G2A	1.47					49144	5.50	11.62	22.2.63

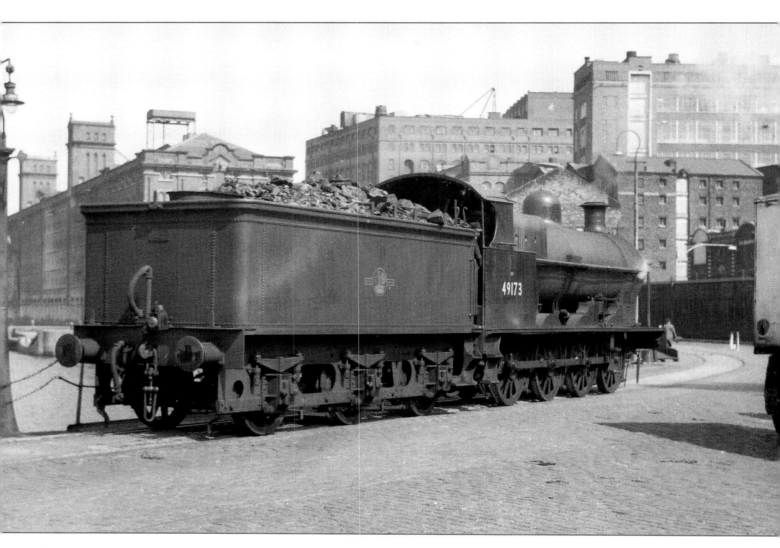

Plate 285: *Super D No. 49173 at Princes Dock, Liverpool on 2nd May 1959.*

J. A. Peden

Class 'G1'

No.	Plate date	Date to stock	Motion No	LMS No.	LMS Date	LG	BF	VB	IBP	Rebuilt to Class	Rebuilt to Date	BR No.	Date	Wdn	Scrap
1329	2.12	2.12	5050	9155	3.27		9.24	9.24	9.24	G2A	p11.39	49155	2.51	5.62	15.8.62
1384	2.12	3.12	5051	9156	1.28							49156	8.49	2.51	9.2.51
1426	2.12	3.12	5052	9157	7.27	11.30		7.27	7.27	G2A	p8.39	49157	12.48	1.59	5.12.59 (1)
1633	2.12	3.12	5053	9158	4.27	8.29	.36	3.34	3.34	G2A	p1.39	49158	4.48	10.61	29.5.62
1697	2.12	3.12	5054	9159	6.27		.24					(49159)	5.49	11.6.49	
1778	3.12	3.12	5055	9160	9.26			6.31	10.40	G2A	p9.47	49160	5.50	11.59	1.7.60 (2)
1791	3.12	3.12	5056	9161	10.27		10.27	4.32	4.32	G2A	11.39	49161	8.49	4.57	10.5.57
2001	3.12	3.12	5057	9162			8.27	8.27	8.35			49162	10.50	p5.53	29.5.53
2015	3.12	3.12	5058	9163	5.26		9.27	9.24	9.24	G2A	p1.41	49163	6.48	12.51	14.12.51
2034	3.12	3.12	5059	9164	6.28		.33			G2A	p5.44	49164	12.48	10.61	2.1.62 (2)
1568	3.12	4.12	5060	9165	3.28			9.36	9.36			(49165)		9.48	13.10.48
1655	4.12	4.12	5061	9166	10.27	7.31		1.32	1.32			(49166)		3.49	14.4.49
1696	4.12	4.12	5062	9167	6.28				2.29	G2A	12.45	49167	3.50	12.57	24.1.58
1698	4.12	4.12	5063	9168	6.26	11.30	.31	1.32	1.32	G2A	p9.39	49168	12.48	1.58	7.2.58
1783	4.12	4.12	5064	9169	12.27			8.32	8.32	G2A	p12.39	(49169)		12.49	9.12.49
1790	4.12	5.12	5065	9172	7.27	7.31	.35	3.31	3.31	G2A	p10.38	49172	6.49	8.57	6.9.57
2018	4.12	5.12	5066	9173	4.27		.24	11.24	11.24	G2A	p3.47	49173	4.49	7.64	11.64 (1)
2104	5.12	5.12	5067	9174	9.26	9.32		7.24	7.24	G2A	p12.39	49174	9.48	1.58	15.2.58
2119	5.12	5.12	5068	9175	7.27		8.27	11.34						1.48	22.2.48
2284	5.12	5.12	5069	9176	8.27	9.29		9.29	3.36	G2A	p11.41	(49176)		1.50	20.1.50
1162	5.12	5.12	5070	9170	8.26		.34	6.32	6.32	G2A	p3.41	(49170)		6.49	12.8.49
1505	5.12	5.12	5071	9171	2.28		3.25	10.31	10.31			(49171)		2.52	28.3.52
2254	5.12	6.12	5072	9177	9.26		.32	1.29	1.29	G2A	p5.40	49177	6.48	2.59	26.6.59
2337	6.12	6.12	5073	9178	9.26	3.29		11.31	11.31	G2A	p12.46	49178	10.48	5.51	4.5.51
2345	6.12	6.12	5074	9179	3.27	12.32		8.36				(49179)	12.48	10.2.49	
2349	6.12	6.12	5075	9180	7.27		3.28	7.27	7.27	G2A	p12.38	49180	12.48	3.59	5.12.59 (1)
2385	6.12	6.12	5076	9181	5.27	9.29		9.38	9.38	G2A	4.40	49181	6.49	4.59	5.12.59 (6)
2393	6.12	6.12	5077	9182	7.26			9.24	9.24					12.47	10.12.48
674	7.12	7.12	5078	9183	1.27	7.29	.29	1.27	1.27			(49183)		p6.50	16.6.50
1746	7.12	9.12	5079	9184	6.28	11.32		11.32	11.32	G2A	12.39	(49184)		p1.49	18.1.49
										G1	12.43				
955	10.12	11.12	5097	9185	12.27			9.31	9.31	G2A	4.39	(49185)		4.49	14.4.49
1108	10.12	11.12	5098	9186	4.27		11.24	11.24	11.24	G2A	2.41	49186	9.49	9.57	15.11.57
2162	10.12	11.12	5099	9187	8.27	7.31	.36	6.31	6.31			49187	12.50	2.52	14.3.52
2225	10.12	11.12	5100	9188	1.26		.35	7.30	7.30	G2A	p3.47	49188	8.48	9.49	23.9.49
2281	10.12	11.12	5101	9189	8.23	12.32		12.34	12.34	G2A	p4.46	49189	10.49	1.57	4.2.57
2289	11.12	11.12	5102	9190	11.28	12.28		12.31	12.31			(49190)		2.50	10.2.50

No.	Plate date	Date to stock	Motion No	LMS No.	LMS Date	LG	BF	VB	IBP	Rebuilt to Class	Rebuilt to Date	BR No.	Date	Wdn	Scrap
2301	11.12	11.12	5103	9191	11.28		.35	2.30	2.30	G2A	p11.45	49191	7.48	10.61	2.1.62 (2)
2374	11.12	11.12	5104	9192	6.27		.35	9.24	9.24	G2A	p6.39	(49192)		11.49	18.11.49
2380	11.12	12.12	5105	9198	2.28	.29		9.33	9.33	G2A	p8.42	49198	12.50	11.59	19.2.60
2405	11.12	12.12	5106	9199	3.27	.32		7.42		G2A	p6.47	49199	8.50	9.62	1.11.62
328	11.12	12.12	5107	9193	11.27		11.27	2.44	2.44			(49193)		p11.51	16.11.51
631	12.12	12.12	5108	9194	1.27	8.29	.36	8.24	8.24			(49194)		10.49	11.11.49
1529	12.12	12.12	5109	9195	10.23	11.29		11.29	11.29			(49195)		3.49	1.4.49
2091	12.12	12.12	5110	9196	2.28		2.28	6.38		G2A	p8.47	49196	2.50	10.61	28.6.62
2286	12.12	12.12	5111	9197	12.27		12.27	1.41				(49197)		5.48	26.11.48
2421	12.12	12.12	5112	9200	9.27		10.24	10.24	10.24	G2A	2.47	49200	6.48	4.59	2.7.59
326	1.13	1.13	5113	9201	9.27				11.43			(49201)		6.48	22.7.48
633	1.13	1.13	5114	9202	2.27		.35	8.38	8.38	G2A	p4.46	49202	6.48	10.57	15.11.57
1192	1.13	1.13	5115	9203	2.27	12.28		3.32	3.32	G2A	p9.40	49203	5.51	11.59	3.6.60
2245	1.13	2.13	5116	9204	8.26			8.24	8.24			49204	11.49	4.51	13.4.51
107	6.13	6.13	5147	9205	5.26			5.26	5.26	G2A	12.41	(49205)		4.51	27.4.51
93	7.13	7.13	5148	9206	3.27	12.32		3.27	3.27					12.47	16.1.48
138	7.13	7.13	5149	9207	6.28		.34	9.24	9.24	G2A	p11.39	(49207)		7.49	19.8.49
670	7.13	8.13	5150	9208	2.27		10.24	10.24	10.24			(49208)		2.51	9.2.51
734	7.13	8.13	5151	9209	6.26			3.29	3.29	G2A	p11.40	49209	8.48	10.61	5.12.61 (2)
767	7.13	8.13	5152	9210	8.27		11.24	11.24	11.24	G2A	p12.46	49210	8.50	10.61	24.11.61
1127	7.13	8.13	5153	9211	8.26	2.30	.34	12.43	12.43	G2A G1	12.43 p10.48	(49211)		9.49	4.11.49
1128	8.13	8.13	5154	9212	4.26			10.33	10.33	G2A	p12.40	49212	11.49	3.56	1.6.56
2201	8.13	8.13	5155	9213	6.26			6.26	6.26			(49213)		9.51	28.9.51
2378	8.13	8.13	5156	9214	6.26			6.26	6.26	G2A	7.41	49214	6.48	8.57	13.9.57
43	8.13	9.13	5157	9215	4.28									12.47	2.1.48
669	8.13	9.13	5158	9216	1.27			8.24	8.24	G2A	p5.40	49216	6.48	11.62	7.6.63
1314	8.13	9.13	5159	9217	6.26	2.29		6.26	6.26	G2A	p8.39	(49217)		2.49	4.3.49
1343	9.13	9.13	5160	9218	2.27		.31	7.24	7.24	G2A	1.47	(49218)		3.51	9.3.51
2117	9.13	9.13	5161	9219	7.27			12.38	12.38	G2A	p10.44	49219	7.48	9.50	29.9.50
2195	9.13	9.13	5162	9220	9.27	2.31	9.27	9.32	9.32	G2A	p7.42	49220	5.48	2.50	10.2.50
2246	9.13	9.13	5163	9221	10.26			8.24	8.24			(49221)		9.49	30.9.49
2258	9.13	9.13	5164	9222	4.28	2.29		9.36	9.36			49222	6.49	9.51	5.10.51
2390	9.13	10.13	5165	9223	3.28	5.33	.38	3.28	3.28	G2A	10.40	49223	6.48	4.57	18.4.57
2452	10.13	10.13	5166	9224	11.27			6.32	6.32	G2A	p12.40	49224	1.49	11.62	5.4.63
20	3.14	3.14	5197	9225	9.26	7.31		3.14	9.26			(49225)		3.48	24.3.48
131	3.14	3.14	5198	9226	11.26		.37	3.14	6.24	G2A	12.41	49226	6.49	3.59	5.12.59 (1)
795	3.14	3.14	5199	9227	5.28	1.29		3.14	3.34	G2A	p5.46	(49227)		2.49	18.12.49

No.	Plate date	Date to stock	Motion No	LMS No.	LMS Date	LG	BF	VB	IBP	Rebuilt to Class	Rebuilt to Date	BR No.	Date	Wdn	Scrap
1486	3.14	4.14	5200	9231	10.27	7.31		4.14	4.35			(49231)		2.48	30.4.48
1500	4.14	4.14	5201	9232	7.27		.34	4.14	6.24			49232	4.48	6.50	24.6.50
329	4.14	4.14	5202	9228	2.27	6.29	.25	4.14	6.29	G2A	p6.39	49228	10.48	4.59	5.12.59 (6)
1181	4.14	4.14	5203	9229	10.25		8.27	4.14		G2A	10.47	49229	6.48	11.60	8.12.60
1214	4.14	4.14	5204	9230	12.27		.25	4.14		G2A	p12.47	49230	9.48	11.57	3.1.58
2033	4.14	4.14	5205	9233	12.27		12.27	4.14	12.25			(49223)	5.48	25.6.48	
2200	4.14	4.14	5206	9234	7.27	8.32	.32	4.14	1.30	G2A	p1.40	49234	2.50	6.60	25.8.60
108	5.14	5.14	5207	9235	8.27		.32	5.14	1.29	G2A	p11.39	49235	8.48	2.50	18.2.50
175	5.14	5.14	5208	9236	3.28		.35	5.14	3.26			(49236)		3.48	18.3.48
1142	5.14	5.14	5209	9239	5.28	1.30	.33	5.14	2.26	G2A	p3.42	49239	6.51	9.57	1.11.57
2336	5.14	5.14	5210	9241	9.27		.25	5.14	3.25			49241	6.48	9.52	3.10.52
2379	5.14	5.14	5211	9242	9.26			5.14	7.24	G2A	p2.41	(49242)		5.49	25.6.49
351	5.14	5.14	5212	9237	3.27		10.24	5.14	10.24	G2A	p1.39	(49237)		12.49	13.1.50
965	6.14	5.14	5213	9238	8.26			5.14	5.24	G2A	p7.39	(49238)		8.49	19.8.49
1485	6.14	5.14	5214	9240	9.27		.25	5.14	4.29	G2A	p11.40	49240	2.50	9.62	8.11.62
2058	6.14	6.14	5215	9243	7.28	9.32		6.14	10.25	G2A	p11.39	49243	8.50	3.61	23.3.61
2237	6.14	6.14	5216	9245	3.27	10.29		6.14	1.39	G2A	p10.40	49245	11.49	12.59	18.12.59
2156	6.14	6.14	5217	9244	5.28	6.29	12.32	6.14	12.32	G2A	p9.41	49244	5.50	4.52	2.5.52
48	7.14	7.14	5218	9246	9.27	9.29		7.14	9.29	G2A	12.39	49246	9.51	1.62	15.2.62
62	7.14	7.14	5219	9247	3.27	12.28		7.14		G2A	9.38	49247	5.48	11.57	3.1.58
72	7.14	7.14	5220	9248	10.26			7.14				(49248)		5.49	27.5.49
99	7.14	7.14	5221	9249	9.25		3.28	7.14	8.25	G2A	4.40	49249	4.50	12.59	17.12.59
176	7.14	7.14	5222	9250	6.27		.34	7.14	9.25			(49250)		4.48	6.5.48
203	7.14	7.14	5223	9251	9.27		9.27	7.14	1.33					1.48	24.2.48
931	8.14	7.14	5224	9252	7.27		8.24	7.14	8.24	G2A	9.40	49252	8.48	11.59	30.1.61
2094	8.14	7.14	5225	9253	8.27	9.29		7.14	9.25	G2A	p6.47	49253	9.50	3.52	9.5.52
2224	8.14	7.14	5226	9254	5.27			7.14	6.24	G2A	10.47	49254	10.51	4.57	3.5.57
170	5.16	5.16	5327	9255	8.26		.24	5.16				(49255)		3.50	31.3.50
545	5.16	5.16	5328	9256	6.27		.25	5.16	11.32	G2A	11.38	(49256)		5.49	11.6.49
885	5.16	5.16	5329	9257	9.27		.25	5.16	7.29	G2A	p1.46	49257	1.49	11.50	10.11.50
942	5.16	5.16	5330	9258	2.28	9.29		5.16	11.33	G2A	6.41	(49258)		3.51	16.3.51
982	5.16	5.16	5331	9259	4.27		.37	5.16	7.29			(49259)		3.49	8.4.49
1167	5.16	5.16	5332	9260	2.26			5.16	9.30	G2A	p10.38	49260	5.49	4.58	3.5.58
1217	5.16	5.16	5333	9261	3.28	2.31	.25	5.16	3.28			49261	11.48	3.51	16.3.51
1528	6.16	6.16	5334	9262	5.28			6.16	4.28	G2A	p2.39	49262	5.48	12.62	10.4.63 (1)
1729	6.16	6.16	5335	9263	4.27		12.24	6.16	12.24			(49263)		3.49	29.4.49
2288	6.16	6.16	5336	9264	11.26			6.16	6.24	G2A	p8.40	49264	9.48	1.51	19.1.51

No.	Plate date	Date to stock	Motion No	LMS No.	Date	LG	BF	VB	IBP	Rebuilt to Class	Rebuilt to Date	BR No.	Date	Wdn	Scrap
112	10.17	12.17	5397	9269	9.26	2.29		12.17	9.24			(49269)		9.49	7.10.49
2088	10.17	12.17	5398	9274	12.25	12.17(49274)		4.48	4.5.48						
2256	10.17	12.17	5399	9275	7.27			12.17	5.35	G2A	11.39	49275	5.53	10.61	5.12.61 (1)
2290	11.17	12.17	5400	9276	5.27	11.30		12.17	11.30	G2A	p12.35	49276	11.48	12.58	20.6.59
2296	11.17	12.17	5401	9277	2.27		.37	12.17		G2A	p8.47	49277	2.53	2.62	16.2.62
94	11.17	12.17	5402	9268	4.28	10.48		12.17	11.39	G2A	7.40	49268	4.49	11.59	1.7.60 (2)
360	11.17	12.17	5403	9270	6.27		9.24	12.17	9.24	G2A	10.35	49270	7.52	11.59	19.1.60
851	11.17	12.17	5404	9271	3.27			12.17	11.24	G2A	2.40	49271	10.48	11.57	8.11.57
2274	11.17	1.18	5405	9278	3.26		11.24	1.18	11.24	G2A	p9.40	49278	5.48	10.59	13.11.59
2423	12.17	1.18	5406	9279	7.27		8.28	1.18	5.30			49279	9.48	2.50	18.2.50
83	1.18	2.18	5277	9280	6.27		.37	2.18	6.37	G2A	p3.40	49280	6.48	9.49	7.10.49
720	1.18	2.18	5278	9281	6.27		12.38	2.18	6.24	G2A	p12.38	49281	10.48	12.62	5.4.63
750	1.18	2.18	5279	9282	12.26		.36	2.18	9.24	G2A	p10.47	49282	7.49	1.51	2.2.51
943	1.18	2.18	5280	9283	8.26			2.18	8.26			(49283)		6.49	12.8.49
1121	1.18	2.18	5281	9284	2.26			2.18	3.27	G2A	p10.40	(49284)		3.50	18.3.50
1313	2.18	3.18	5282	9285	10.26		.24	3.18	9.24			(49285)		8.49	19.8.49
2082	2.18	3.18	5283	9286	6.27			3.18				(49286)		4.48	11.5.48
2167	2.18	3.18	5284	9287	8.27		10.24	3.18	10.24	G2A	p9.44	49287	5.49	11.62	15.3.63
2172	2.18	3.18	5285	9288	10.26			3.18	5.29	G2A	11.39	49288	6.48	10.61	17.7.62 (3)
2412	3.18	3.18	5286	9289	1.28		.25	3.18	3.32	G2A	p8.39	49289	3.49	11.59	7.4.60
1129	3.18	4.18	5287	9290	2.26		11.24	4.18	11.24	G2A	p1.40	(49290)		3.49	11.3.49
1614	3.18	4.18	5288	9291	3.26			4.18	5.28	G2A	p4.43	49291	5.48	5.50	2.6.50
2150	3.18	4.18	5289	9293	8.27			4.18	11.25	G2A	p1.40	49293	12.48	11.6	5.4.63
2250	3.18	4.18	5290	9294	1.26			4.18	4.32	G2A	p2.40	(49294)		12.49	6.1.50
2297	4.18	4.18	5291	9295	1.27		10.24	4.18	10.24			(49295)		8.48	24.11.48
2343	4.18	4.18	5292	9296	6.27	7.31	.25	4.18	9.32	G2A	6.39	49296	4.49	5.51	22.6.51
2376	4.18	5.18	5293	9299	5.27		12.24	5.18	12.24	G2A	p5.43	49299	6.48	7.49	12.8.49
2410	4.18	5.18	5294	9300	6.26		.25	5.18	9.28	G2A	3.42	49300	2.50	11.51	30.11.51
2422	4.18	5.18	5295	9301	9.26	.32		5.18	7.28	G2A	6.39	49301	5.49	3.59	30.3.59
2441	5.18	5.18	5296	9302	4.28	4.30	.25	5.18	4.28	G2A	p12.46	(49302)		12.51	4.1.52
230	5.18	5.18	5407	9297	7.27			5.18	1.26			(49297)		4.49	6.5.49
264	5.18	5.18	5408	9298	3.26	8.29		5.18	2.26	G2A	p10.39	49298	11.48	12.49	20.1.50
880	5.18	6.18	5409	9303	3.28		3.28	6.18	3.28			(49303)		11.48	21.12.48
1071	5.18	6.18	5410	9305	3.28		3.28	6.18	9.32			(49305)		4.49	22.4.49
1657	6.18	6.18	5411	9306	5.2		.33	6.18	5.26	G2A	p8.40	49306	9.48	11.59	20.10.60
1693	6.18	6.18	5412	9307	5.27			6.18	3.36	G2A	p1.46	49307	4.48	9.50	6.10.50
2066	6.18	6.18	5413	9308	12.26			6.18	1.30	G2A	p1.43	49308	10.48	4.59	5.12.59 (6)

259

No.	Plate date	Date to stock	Motion No	LMS No.	LMS Date	LG	BF	VB	IBP	Rebuilt to Class	Rebuilt to Date	BR No.	Date	Wdn	Scrap
2199	6.18	6.18	5414	9309	6.28		11.24	6.18	11.24			(49309)		7.48	26.8.48
2235	7.18	7.18	5415	9310	8.25			7.18	5.34	G2A	10.40	49310	6.48	10.61	9.11.62
2253	7.18	7.18	5416	9311	10.27	9.32		7.18	9.32	G2A	p1.41	49311	3.50	10.59	30.10.59
757	7.18	8.18	5417	9312	10.27			8.18	5.36	G2A	3.40	(49312)		4.51	27.4.51
829	7.18	8.18	5418	9313	7.28			8.18	9.24	G2A	p12.39	49313	5.48	12.61	26.1.62
894	7.18	8.18	5419	9314.	9.26		.37	8.18	3.33	G2A	p1.47	49314	8.48	11.62	19.4.63
1107	8.18	8.18	5420	9315	8.27			8.18	10.31	G2A	p8.39	49315	8.4	6.59	7.8.59
1435	8.18	8.18	5421	9316	1.28	10.32	.34	8.18	5.24	G2A	p10.39	49316	11.48	1.57	8.2.57
1495	8.18	8.18	5422	9317	2.27		.33	8.18	6.37	G2A	4.40	(49317)		3.50	6.4.50
1785	9.18	9.18	5423	9318	6.28			9.18	6.34	G2A	p6.40	49318	3.50	11.57	6.12.57
2054	9.18	9.18	5424	9320	1.26		.33	9.18				(49320)		12.49	9.12.49
2160	9.18	9.18	5425	9321	8.28	11.32	12.35	9.18	10.30	G2A	p11.35	49321	1.49	6.60	25.8.60
2236	9.18	9.18	5426	9322	10.23	3.30		9.18	9.33	G2A	p1.39	49322	2.50	3.56	11.5.56
172	10.18	10.18	5427	9323	4.28		.33	10.18	3.37	G2A	p4.41	49323	9.48	9.62	15.11.62
1306	10.18	10.18	5428	9326	3.27	1.29		10.18	1.26			49326	2.51	7.53	8.8.53
1487	10.18	10.18	5429	9327	7.28	9.29	.37	10.18	5.34	G2A	p3.40	49327	8.49	11.59	1.4.60
1793	10.18	10.18	5430	9328	1.27			10.18	1.27	G2A	p4.44	49328	8.49	11.62	18.1.63
2287	10.18	10.18	5431	9329	6.27		.33	10.18	1.37	G2A	p1.40	(49329)		3.49	1.4.49
1261	11.18	10.18	5432	9325	8.26	5.30		10.18	6.28	G2A	p7.43	49325	6.48	11.49	18.11.49
279	11.18	11.18	5433	9330	8.26			11.18	8.28	G2A	p1.40	49330	12.52	3.59	5.12.59 (6)
1158	11.18	11.18	5434	9332	2.26		.34	11.18	6.29			49332	9.48	7.50	4.8.50
1359	11.18	11.18	5435	9333	3.28			11.18	4.29	G2A	7.40	49333	12.48	5.50	2.6.50
2497	11.18	12.18	5436	9334	12.27			11.18	10.30			(49334)		9.50	22.9.50

Plate 286: *Beames 0-8-4 tank No. 7956 leaving Manchester London Road with an express to Buxton.*

D. J. Patrick collection

Class 'G2'

No.	Plate date	Date to stock	Motion No	LMS No.	LMS Date	LG	BF	VB	IBP	BR No.	Date	Wdn	Scrap
485	6.21	8.21	5662	9395	7.28			8.21		49395	9.50	5.11.59	Preserved
742	7.21	8.21	5663	9396	4.27			8.21	4.27	49396	9.50	11.59	6.10.60
253	7.21	10.21	5664	9401	9.27	6.30		10.21	5.30	494015	.48	10.61	12.12.61
434	7.21	10.21	5665	9402	10.27		9.25	10.21	10.25	49402	6.49	11.62	10.4.63
1154	7.21	10.21	5666	9403	3.26			10.21	3.26	49403	10.48	6.62	30.8.62
215	7.21	10.21	5667	9397	11.27		11.27	10.21	1.26	49397	11.48	11.59	3.11.60
216	7.21	10.21	5668	9398	8.27			10.21	2.35	49398	10.49	11.59	26.10.60
220	7.21	10.21	5669	9399	6.27	12.32		10.21		49399	5.50	10.61	19.5.62 (3)
221	8.21	10.21	5670	9400	6.28		.35	10.21	10.31	494006	.48	11.59	2.8.60
223	8.21	11.21	5671	9404	4.27			11.21	3.31	49404	3.49	4.62	1.6.62
367	8.21	11.21	5672	9405	2.27	5.30		11.21	11.24	49405	4.50	10.61	19.5.62 (3)
369	8.21	11.21	5673	9406	12.26			11.21	10.24	49406	12.50	6.63	4.10.63
373	8.21	11.21	5674	9407	9.27			11.21	10.30	49407	8.48	12.64	22.2.65 (1)
407	8.21	12.21	5675	9410	2.28	8.30		12.21	1.26	49410	6.48	11.59	18.3.60
411	8.21	12.21	5676	9411	8.27	8.30		12.21	8.35	49411	10.48	10.61	5.12.61 (1)
417	8.21	12.21	5677	9412	11.27			12.21	10.24	49412	9.48	10.61	17.7.62 (3)
429	8.21	12.21	5678	9413	8.26		.35	12.21	8.24	49413	8.49	10.61	1.11.62
1530	8.21	12.21	5679	9414	12.26			12.21	7.24	49414	11.49	10.61	1.6.62
396	9.21	12.21	5680	9409	10.26			12.21	6.24	49409	8.50	6.59	5.12.59 (1)
382	9.21	12.21	5681	9408	5.26	7.31		12.21	8.24	49408	9.48	11.62	25.10.63
567	9.21	2.22	5682	9415	7.26	11.28	.35	2.22	6.24	49415	2.50	11.62	11.6.63
568	9.21	2.22	5683	9416	10.27	3.30		2.22	3.35	49416	12.48	9.62	7.9.62
569	9.21	2.22	5684	9417	9.27		.37	2.22	1.30	49417	7.53	11.59	4.2.60
570	9.21	2.22	5685	9418	8.26	10.28		2.22		49418	7.50	11.59	18.3.60
571	9.21	2.22	5686	9419	1.28			2.22	2.31	49419	1.49	11.59	7.4.60
572	10.21	3.22	5687	9420	7.27		12.24	3.22	12.24	49420	5.50	11.59	26.10.60
573	10.21	3.22	5688	9421	8.27			3.22	6.30	49421	6.50	10.61	4.7.62 (2)
574	10.21	3.22	5689	9422	8.27		10.24	3.22	10.24	49422	8.49	9.61	12.10.61
575	10.21	3.22	5690	9423	12.27			3.22		49423	6.49	11.61	10.11.61
576	10.21	3.22	5691	9424	4.27		.25	3.22	4.27	49424	10.48	11.592	5.11.60
134	10.21	4.22	5692	9425	8.27		9.24	4.22		49425	10.48	9.62	11.3.63 (1)
869	10.21	4.22	5693	9426	7.27		12.32	4.22	10.24	49426	6.48	9.62	11.3.63 (4)
2047	10.21	4.22	5694	9427	9.27			4.22	7.30	49427	3.49	11.59	28.6.60
2050	10.21	4.22	5695	9428	11.26		.24	4.22		49428	5.49	12.62	17.8.63 (9)
2171	10.21	5.22	5696	9429	11.27			5.22	2.35	49429	10.48	11.59	13.5.60
2226	10.21	5.22	5697	9430	3.27			5.22	6.40	49430	4.48	12.64	22.2.65

No.	Plate date	Date to stock	Motion No	LMS No.	LMS Date	LG	BF	VB	IBP	BR No.	Date	Wdn	Scrap
2255	11.21	5.22	5698	9431	5.27			5.22	5.39	49431	5.48	11.62	27.2.63
2367	11.21	5.22	5699	9432	6.28			5.22	5.24	49432	9.49	11.62	3.4.63
2371	11.21	5.22	5700	9433	3.27			5.22	3.27	49433	11.51	10.61	17.11.61
2372	11.21	6.22	5701	9438	8.27		8.27	6.22	2.30	49438	4.48	11.62	10.4.63
344	11.21	6.22	5702	9434	11.27		10.27	6.22	3.30	49434	9.48	10.62	11.3.63 (1)
872	11.21	6.22	5703	9435	7.27	1.33	.25	6.22	9.34	49435	4.48	11.59	13.8.60
2182	11.21	6.22	5704	9437	6.27		.34	6.22	6.34	49437	1.52	9.62	7.9.62
895	12.21	6.22	5705	9436	12.26	10.28		6.22	2.30	49436	12.48	5.59	26.6.59
994	12.21	7.22	5706	9440	2.28		2.28	7.22	5.36	49440	4.50	3.62	6.4.62
361	2.21	7.22	5707	9439	4.26			7.22	4.26	49439	3.49	12.62	28.5.63
2381	12.21	7.22	5708	9441	9.27	8.29	.33	7.22	4.25	49441	12.51	10.61	27.9.62
2383	12.21	8.22	5709	9443	10.26		.25	8.22		49443	4.50	10.61	9.11.62
2386	12.21	8.22	5710	9444	8.27		.35	8.22	8.25	49444	5.51	10.61	19.5.62 (3)
2399	12.21	8.22	5711	9445	2.27			8.22	12.24	49445	4.50	11.59	9.11.60
758	1.22	8.22	5712	9442	3.26	1.29		8.22	2.26	49442	6.48	11.59	16.2.61
1012	1.22	9.22	5713	9446	6.25		12.24	9.22	12.24	49446	9.48	4.64	7.64 (1)
2414	1.22	9.22	5714	9447	12.26	11.28	.35	9.22	11.28	49447	1.49	11.62	19.4.63
2429	1.22	9.22	5715	9448	11.26			9.22	5.28	49448	12.49	6.63	9.8.63
2517	1.22	9.22	5716	9449	7.27	7.31	8.29	9.22	7.24	49449	4.50	12.62	17.8.63 (9)
231	1.22	10.22	5717	9451	5.27	1.30		10.22	6.31	49451	6.48	11.62	10.4.63
308	1.22	10.22	5718	9452	10.26			10.22	10.26	49452	10.48	12.62	4.6.64 (1)
403	1.22	10.22	5719	9453	1.28		.33	10.27	4.36	49453	8.48	10.61	15.12.61
2178	1.22	10.22	5720	9454	8.25		9.27	10.22	6.31	49454	11.48	6.63	16.8.63
13	1.22	10.22	5721	9450	1.28	.32	.34	10.22		49450	2.51	11.59	22.4.60

Plate 287: *LMS No. 27943 in Crewe Works after withdrawal in 1947.*

0-8-2 Tank

No.	Plate date	Date to stock	Motion No	LMS No.	LMS Date	BR No.	BR Date	Wdn	Scrap
1185	12.11	12.11	5040	7870	5.28			12.45	4.4.46
1665	12.11	12.11	5041	7872	6.26			10.36	30.10.36
1790	12.11	12.11	5042						
1548	.12			7871	7.28			5.35	18.6.35
289	1.12	1.12	5043	7873	8.28			1.35	30.1.35
1163	1.12	1.12	5044	7874	2.26			6.35	1.8.35
1494	1.12	1.12	5045	7875	10.26	(47875)		8.48	17.9.48
1592	1.12	1.12	5046	7876	4.28			7.47	12.9.47
1659	1.12	1.12	5047	7877	2.28	47877	5.48	2.53	6.3.53
1663	1.12	1.12	5048	7878	11.26			6.47	12.12.47
2013	2.12	1.12	5049	7879	9.27			12.36	9.3.37
58	8.15	9.15	5247	7882	12.27			10.34	24.10.34
482	8.15	9.15	5248	7880	6.27			3.37	19.3.37
563	8.15	9.15	5249	7881	2.28	47881	9.48	7.51	3.8.51
736	8.15	9.15	5250	7883	9.25			p3.35	1.10.35
1090	9.15	9.15	5251	7884	9.25	47884	10.48	6.51	29.6.51
1124	9.15	9.15	5252	7885	7.26	(47885)		3.50	24.3.50
1414	9.15	9.15	5253	7886	5.28	(47886)		3.46	16.5.46
1514	9.15	9.15	5254	7887	11.27	(47887)		8.48	17.9.48
1515	9.15	9.15	5255	7888	8.26	(47888)		12.48	17.12.48
2277	9.15	9.15	5256	7889	4.28			10.34	1.11.34
241	2.16	1.17	5357	7890	9.26			6.39	2.8.41
92	12.16	1.17	5358	7891	8.27			6.46	31.7.46
714	1.17	1.17	5359	7892	8.25	(47892)		2.48	4.6.48
1291	1.17	1.17	5360	7893	8.28			10.34	1.11.34
1331	1.17	1.17	5361	7894	2.28			8.39	4.12.40
2105	1.17	1.17	5362	7895	10.25			10.34	2.11.34
2294	1.17	1.17	5363	7896	6.28	47896	6.48	p11.50	10.11.50
234	12.17	1.17	5364	7897	4.28			6.46	9.8.46
2348	2.17	2.17	5365	7898	6.27			1.46	11.2.46
2391	2.17	2.17	5366	7899	1.28			p8.35	10.10.35

0-8-4 Tank

No.	Plate date	Date to stock	Motion No	LMS No.	LMS Date	BR No.	BR Date	Wdn	Scrap
380	2.23	3.23	5722	7930	6.28	(47930)		8.48	29.9.48
78	22.23	4.23	5723	7931	12.27	47931	11.48	12.5	14.1.52
1189	2.23	4.23	5724	7932	6.28	(47932)		9.49	14.10.49
1677	2.23	5.23	5725	7933	2.28	(47933)		6.50	16.6.50
1976	3.23	5.23	5726	7934	8.28			p5.46	4.1.47
256	3.23	5.23	5727	7935	2.28			9.46	20.12.46
731	4.23	5.23	5728	7936	4.28	(47936)		6.49	29.7.49
739	4.23	5.23	5729	7937	3.28	47937	2.49	10.50	20.10.50
1908	4.23	6.23	5730	7938	8.28	(47938)		2.48	4.6.48
1956	4.23	6.23	5731	7939	8.26	(47939)		12.50	8.12.50
468	6.23	7.23	5732	7940	8.28			p1.46	13.4.46
792	6.23	7.23	5733	7941	7.26			12.46	9.1.47
793	6.23	7.23	5734	7942	6.26			11.43	30.12.44
(1904)	6.23	8.23	5735	7943	8.23	27943	(1)	2.47	13.8.47
(609)	6.23	8.23	5736	7944	8.23			11.47	18.12.47
	8.23	8.23	5737	7945	8.23			9.46	12.11.46
	8.23	8.23	5738	7946	8.23			12.46	9.4.48
	8.23	8.23	5739	7947	8.23			8.44	2.11.44
	9.23	9.23	5740	7948	9.23	(47948)		7.48	25.8.48
	9.23	9.23	5741	7949	9.23			10.46	26.11.46
	10.23	10.23	5742	7950	10.23			6.46	10.10.46
	10.23	10.23	5743	7951	10.23	(47951)		1.49	10.2.49
	10.23	10.23	5744	7952	10.23			p8.45	12.45
	10.23	10.23	5745	7953	10.23			p5.45	6.8.45
	10.23	11.23	5746	7954	10.23	(47954)		10.48	27.10.48
	10.23	10.23	5747	7955	10.23			8.46	31.12.46
	11.23	11.23	5748	7956	11.23	(47956)		11.48	10.12.48
	11.23	11.23	5749	7957	11.23	27957	(2)	1.46	24.1.46
	11.23	11.23	5750	7958	11.23	(47958)		12.48	24.12.48
	1.24	1.24	5751	7959	1.24	(47959)		6.48	3.8.48

(1)   Numbered 27943 on 24.2.45 and was so numbered on withdrawal.

(2)   Renumbered 27957 in error for a short time in April 1934.

The 'MM' or 'ROD' 2-8-0s

LNWR Numbers 6-8.19	9.19	1920	Builder	No.	Date	ROD No.	LMS Numbers No.	Date	No.	Date	Wdn	Scrapped
56	2800	1315	NBQ	22117	.19	2022	9619	8.28	9458	7.30	10.31	9.12.31
635	2801	1317	RS	3750	.19	1642	9620	8.28			12.29	21.1.30
1620	2802	1336	RS	3749	.19	1633	9621	8.28	9459	7.31		13.11.31
686	2803	1337	NBQ	22116	.19	2021	9622	1.28			12.30	5.1.31
812	2804	1347	NBQ	22118	.19	2023	9623	8.28			5.31	26.5.31
969	2805	1348	NBA	22233	.19	2143	9635	8.28	9467	9.31	3.32	22.3.32
67	2806	2039	NBH	22127	.19	2033	9624	8.28			10.29	6.11.29
1321	2807	2041	NBH	22129	.19	2035	9625	12.27			12.30	21.1.31
1341	2808	2048	NBH	22128	.19	2034	(9626)				p.2.28	2.28 (9)
1355	2809	2071	NBH	22130	.19	2036	9627	9.28	9460	9.31	p10.33	17.10.33
1408	2810	2079	NBH	22131	.19	2037	9628	9.28	(9461)		p7.31	3.7.31
1422	2811	2093	NBH	22132	.19	2038	9629	3.28	9462	9.31	p12.32	25.11.32
1478	2812	2099	NBH	22133	.19	2039	9630	9.28	(9463)		p7.31	1.7.31
1535	2813	2100	NBQ	22178	.19	2088	9631	9.28	9464	9.31	p11.32	15.11.32
1542	2814	2102	NBQ	22179	.19	2089	9632	8.28	9465	9.31	p2.32	8.3.32
1549	2815	2103	NBH	22180	.19	2090	9636	3.28	(9468)		p7.31	7.8.31
1557	2816	2108	NBH	22181	.19	2091	9637	8.28	(9469)		p7.31	24.7.31
1694	2817	2109	NBH	22182	.19	2092	9638	9.28	(9470)		p8.31	8.31
1726	2818	2389	NBQ	22183	.19	2093	9639	8.28			p10.29	21.12.29
1741	2819	2394	NBA	22228	.19	2138	9640	8.28	9471	9.31	p4.32	7.4.32
1747	2820	2400	NBA	22080	.19	1787	9616	8.28	9455	7.30	p8.32	2.9.32
2035	2821	2402	NBH	22135	.19	2041	9633	1.28	(9466)		p7.31	30.10.31
2083	2822	2404	NBH	22136	.19	2042	9641	12.27	9472	9.31	p12.31	2.12.31
2231	2823	2406	NBA	22082	.19	1789	9618	12.27	9457	7.30	p1.32	1.6.32
2268	2824	2407	NBA	22081	.19	1788	9617	3.28	9456	7.30	.32	26.1.32
12	2825	2413	NBH	22134	.19	2040	9634	1.28			1.30	22.2.30
85	2826	2439	NBA	22229	.19	2139	9642	4.28	9473	9.31	p1.32	9.2.32
98	2827	2444	NBA	22230	.19	2140	9643	9.28	9474	9.31	.2.32	1.3.32
103	2828	2447	NBA	22231	.19	2141	9644	9.28	9475	9.31	p1.32	2.2.32
201	2829	2451	NBA	22232	.19	2142	9645	9.28	9476	9.31	p3.32	14.3.32
	2940		NBH	21868	.18	1891	9646	p10.27	p13.29			
	2930		NBQ	21802	.17	1835	9647	p11.27	9477			p8.31
	2932		NBQ	21804	.17	1837	9648	p5.28	9478			p9.31
	2934		NBH	21842	.18	1865	9649	p10.27	9479			p12.31
	2936		NBH	21848	.18	1871	9650	p12.27				p11.29
			NBQ	21901	.18	1924	9651	p5.28				p13.29

LNWR Numbers 6-8.19	9.19	1920	Builder	No.	Date	ROD No.	LMS Numbers No.	Date	No.	Date	Wdn Scrapped
		2886	NBQ	21903	.18	1926	9652	p11.27	9480		p10.31
		2866	NBQ	21915	.18	1938	9653	p11.27			p13.30
		2929	NBQ	21799	.17	1832	9654	p13.27	9481		p2.32
		2862	NBQ	21889	.18	1912	9655	p3.28	9482		p11.31
		2969	NBH	21828	.18	1851	9656	p12.27			p13.29
		2860	NBQ	21911	.18	1934	9657	p3.28			p13.29
		2895	NBH	21827	.18	1850	9658	p5.28			p12.29
		2950	NBQ	21770	.17	1803	9659	p4.28			p12.29
		2937	NBH	21854	.18	1877	9660	p6.28			p11.31
			Kitson	5184	.18	1602	9661	p4.28			p12.31
		2918	NBQ	21768	.17	1801	9662	p4.28			p2.32
		2938	NBH	21865	.18	1888	9663	p4.28			p13.30
		2873	NBQ	21895	.18	1918	9664	p4.28			p13.30
		2890	NBH	21830	.18	1853	9665	p8.28			p13.29

Abbreviations:

NBA	North British Atlas Works
NBH	North British Hyde Park Works
NBQ	North British Queens Park Works
RS	Robert Stephenson

Plate 287: 'ROD' No. 9646 in the late 1920s, possibly not long before withdrawal.

INDEX

Plate 288: *"Super D' No. 49081, a long-time Stafford engine, accelerates round the curve past Stockton Lane south of Stafford with the morning pick-up goods from Stafford to Nuneaton, 8th August 1960. It has probably just stopped at the Vacuum Salt factory and is now heading for Milford.*

Dr G. Smith